POSITIONS

First published 1888
This edition published by Lector House in 2024

ISBN: 978-93-6138-349-6

Lector House LLP
Registered Office: H. No. 96, Block C, Tomar Colony,
Burari, Delhi – 110084, India
info@lectorhouse.com
www.lectorhouse.com

POSITIONS

RICHARD MULCASTER,
ROBERT HEBERT QUICK

2024

LECTOR HOUSE LLP

POSITIONS

BY

RICHARD MULCASTER,

First Headmaster of Merchant Taylors' School (A.D. 1561-1586);

WITH AN APPENDIX,
CONTAINING SOME ACCOUNT OF
HIS LIFE AND WRITINGS,
BY
ROBERT HEBERT QUICK,

Author of "*Essays on Educational Reformers*";
First University Lecturer at Cambridge on the History of Education (A.D. 1879).

POSITIONS

WHEREIN THOSE

PRIMITIVE CIRCUMSTANCES

BE EXAMINED, WHICH ARE

NECESSARIE FOR THE TRAINING

up of Children, either for skill in their
booke, or health in their bodie.

WRITTEN by RICHARD MULCASTER, master of the schoole erected in London anno. 1561, in the parish of Sainct Laurence Povvntneie, by the vvorshipfull companie of the merchaunt tailers of the said citie.

TO THE MOST VERTVOVS LADIE, HIS MOST DEARE, AND soueraine princesse, Elizabeth by the grace of God Queene of England, Fraunce, and Ireland, defendresseof the faith &c.

MY booke by the very argument, most excellent princesse, pretendeth a common good, bycause it concerneth the generall traine and bringing vp of youth, both to enrich their minds with learning, and to enable their bodies with health: and it craues the fauour of some speciall countenaunce farre aboue the common, or else it can not possiblie procure free passage. For what a simple credit is myne, to perswade so great a matter? or what force is there in common patronage, to commaunde conceites? I am therefore driuen vpon these so violent considerations, to presume so farre, as to present it, being my first trauell, that euer durst venture vpon the print, vnto your maiesties most sacred handes. For in neede of countenaunce, where best abilitie is most assurance, and knowne vertue the fairest warrant, who is more sufficient then your excellencie is, either for cunning to commend, or for credit to commaunde? And what reason is there more likely to procure the fauour of your maiesties most gracious countenaunce, either to commende the worke, or to commaunde it waie, then the honest pretence of a generall good, wherein you cannot be deceiued? For of your accustomed care you will circumspectlie consider, and by your singular iudgement, you can skillfully discerne, whether there be any appearance, that my booke shall performe so great a good, as it pretendeth to do, before you either praise it, or procure it passage. In deede it is an argument which craueth consideration, bycause it is the leader to a further consequence: and all your maiesties time is so busily employed, about many and maine affaires of your estate, as I may seeme verie iniurious to the common weale, besides some wrong offered to your owne person, to desire your Maiestie at this time to reade any part therof, much lesse the whole, the booke it selfe being very long, and your Maiesties leasure being very litle.

And yet if it maye please your most excellent Maiestie of some extraordinarie grace towardes a most obsequious subiect in way of encoraging his both toilsome and troublesome labour, to take but some taste of any one title, of smallest encumbraunce, by the very inscription, the paw of a Lion may bewraie the hole body in me by the prouerbe, in your highnesse by the propertie, as who can best iudge, what the Lion is. For the rest, which neither your Maiesties time can tarie on, neither my boldnesse dare desire that you should: other mens report, which shall haue time to read, and will lend an officious countrieman some parte of their leysure, will proue a referendarie, and certifie your highnesse how they finde me appointed. I haue entitled the booke POSITIONS, bycause entending to go on further, for the auauncement of learning I thought it good at the first to put downe certaine groundes very needefull for my purpose, for that they be the common circunstances, that belong to teaching and are to be resolued on, eare we begin to teach. Wherin I craue consent of my countrey, to ioyne with me in conceit, if my reasons proue likely, that therby I may direct my whole currant in the rest, a great deale the better. Now if it maye stand with your Maiesties most gracious good will to bestow vpon me the fauourable smile of your good liking, to countenance me in this course, which as it pretendeth the publike commoditie, so it threateneth me with extreme paines, all my paine will proue pleasant vnto me, and that good which shall come thereby to the common weale shall be most iustly ascribed to your Maiesties especial goodnesse, which encoraged my labour, and commended it to my countrey. Which both encoragement to my selfe, and commendacion to my countrey, I do nothing doubt but to obtaine at your Maiesties most gracious handes, whether of your good nature, which hath alwaye furthered honest attemptes: or of your Princely conceit, which is thoroughly bent to the bettering of your state, considering my trauell doth tend that way. For the very ende of my whole labour (if my small power can attaine to that, which a great good will towards this my cuntrey hath deepely conceiued) is to helpe to bring the generall teaching in your Maiesties dominions, to some one good and profitable vniformitie which now in the middest of great varietie doth either hinder much, or profit litle, or at the least nothing so much, as it were like to do, if it were reduced to one certaine fourme. The effecting wherof pretendeth great honour to your Maiesties person, besides the profit, which your whole realme is to reape therby. That noble Prince king HENRY the eight, your Maiesties most renowned father vouchesafed to bring all Grammers into one fourme, the multitude therof being some impediment to schoole learning in his happie time, and thereby both purchased himselfe great honour, and procured his subiectes a marueilous ease. Now if it shall please your Maiestie by that Royall example which otherwise you so rarely exceede, to further not onely the helping of that booke to a refining: but also the reducing of all other schoole bookes to some better choice: and all manner of teaching, to some redier fourme: can so great a good but sound to your Maiesties most endlesse renowne, whose least part gaue such cause of honour, to that famous King, your Maiesties father? By these few wordes your highnesse conceiueth my full meaning I am well assured, neither do I doubt, but that as you are well able to discerne it, so you will very depelie consider it, and see this so great a common good thoroughly set on foote. I know your Maiesties pacience to be exceeding great in verie petie arguments, if not I should haue bene afraid, to haue troubled you with so many wordes, and yet least tediousnesse do soure euen a sweete and sound matter, I will be no bolder. God blesse your Maiestie, and send you a long, and an healthfull life, to his greatest glorie, and your Maiesties most lasting honour.

Your Maiesties most humble and
obedient subiect
Richard Mulcaster.

AVTHOR IPSE AD *librum suum.*

INSITA naturæ nostræ sitis illa iuuandi
Ignauum vitæ desidis odit iter.
Parca cibi, saturata fame, deuota labori,
Prodiga nocturni luminis vrget opus.
Quod, simul ac lucis patiens fore viderit, edit
Inde licet multo plena timore gemat.
Pœnitet emissam per mille pericula prolem,
Quæ poterat patriæ tuta latere domi.
Iudiciumq́ timens alieni pallida iuris
Omine spem lædit deteriore suam.
Sed sine sole nequit viui, prodire necesse est,
Curaq́ quod peperit publica, iura vocant.
Fortunæ credenda salus, quam prouida virtus
Quam patris æterni dextera magna regit.
Sic sua Neptuno committit vela furenti
Spem solam in medijs docta phaselus aquis.
Sic mihi spes maior, cui res cum gente Deorum,
Quæ certo dubijs numine rebus adest.
Perge igitur, sortiq́ tuæ te crede, parentis
Tessera parue liber prima future tui.
Et quia, quà perges, hominum liberrima de te
Iudicia in medijs experiere vijs,
Quidnam quisq́ notet, quidnam desideret in te,
Quo possim in reliquis cautior esse, refer.
Interea veniam supplex vtrique precare,
Nam meus error erat, qui tuus error erit.
Qui neutrius erit, cum, quis sit, sensero, quippe
Nullum in correcto crimine crimen erit.
Ergo tuæ partes, quæ sint errata, referre:
Emendare, mei cura laboris erit.
Namq́ rei nouitas nulli tentata priorum
Hac ipsa, qua tu progrediere, via,

Vtriq́ errores multos, lapsusq́; minatur,
Quos cum resciero, num superesse sinam?
Cui tam chara mei lectoris amica voluntas,
Vt deleta illi displicitura velim.

R. M.

CONTENTS

CHAPTER 6.

CHAPTER 7.

CHAPTER 8.

CHAPTER 9.

CHAPTER 10.

CHAPTER 11.

CHAPTER 12.

CHAPTER 13.

CHAPTER 14.

CHAPTER 15.

CHAPTER 16.

CHAPTER 17.

CHAPTER 18.

CHAPTER 19.

CHAPTER 20.

CHAPTER 21.

CHAPTER 22.

CHAPTER 23.

CHAPTER 24.

CHAPTER 36.

CHAPTER 37.

CHAPTER 38.

CHAPTER 39.

CHAPTER 40.

CHAPTER 41.

CHAPTER 42.

CHAPTER 43.

CHAPTER 44.

CHAPTER 45.

ANALYTICAL CONTENTS

Page

CHAPTER I.

CHAPTER 2.

CHAPTER 3.

CHAPTER 4.

CHAPTER 5.

CHAPTER 6.

CHAPTER 7.

CHAPTER 8.

CHAPTER 9.

CHAPTER 10.

CHAPTER 11.

CHAPTER 12.

CHAPTER 13.

CHAPTER 14.

CHAPTER 15.

CHAPTER 16.

CHAPTER 17.

CHAPTER 18.

CHAPTER 19.

CHAPTER 20.

CHAPTER 21.

CHAPTER 22.

CHAPTER 23.

CHAPTER 24.

CHAPTER 25.

CHAPTER 26.

CHAPTER 27.

CHAPTER 28.

CHAPTER 29.

CHAPTER 30.

CHAPTER 31.

CHAPTER 32.

CHAPTER 33.

CHAPTER 34.

CHAPTER 35.

CHAPTER 36.

CHAPTER 37.

CHAPTER 38.

CHAPTER 39.

CHAPTER 40.

CHAPTER 41.

CHAPTER 42.

CHAPTER 43.

CHAPTER 44.

CHAPTER 45.

POSITIONS CONCERNING THE TRAINING UP OF CHILDREN.

CHAPTER I.

The Entrie to the Positions, conteining the occasion of this present discourse, and the causes why it was penned in English.

WHOSOEVER shall consider with any iudgement the maner of training vp children, which we vse generally within this Realme cannot but wish, that the thing were bettered, as I my selfe do: though I do not thinke it good here to displaie the particular defectes, bycause I am in hope to see them healed, without any so sharp a rehersall, ("for the error being once graunted and well knowen straight way craueth helpe without aggrauation, and that way in helping must needes be most gracious, which the partie helped confesseth least greiuouse.") If I should discouer all those inconueniences, wherby parentes and maisters, teachers and learners, do but enterchaunge displeasures, if I should rip vp those difficulties, wherby the traine it selfe, and bringing vp of children is maruellously empeached, I might reuiue great gaules, and euen therby worse remedie the greifes. And though I remedied them yet the partie pacient might beare in minde, how churlishly he was cured, and though he payed well for the healing, yet be ill apayd for the handling. Wherefore in helping thinges, that be amisse I do take that to be the aduisedest way, which saueth the man, and sowreth not the meane. If without quoting the quarrelles, I set down that right, wherunto I am led, vpon reasonable grounds, that it is both the best, and most within compasse, the wrong by comparison is furthwith bewraied, and the chek giuen without anie chiding.

The occasion of this discourse.

I haue taught in publike without interrupting my course, now two and twentie yeares, and haue alwaie had a very great charge vnder my hand, which how I haue discharged, they can best iudge of me, which will iudge without me. During which time both by that, which I haue seene in teaching so long, and by that which I haue tryed, in training vp so many, I do well perceiue, vpon such lettes, as both my selfe am subiect vnto, and other teachers no lesse then I, that neither I haue don so much as I might, neither any of them so much as they could. Which lettes me thinke I haue both learned, what they be, and withall conceiued the meane, how to get them remoued. Wherby both I and all other maie do much more good, then either I or anie other heretofore haue don. Wherin as I meane to deale for the common good, so must I appeal to the common curtesie, that my good will maie be well thought of, though my good hope do not hit right. For I do but that, which is set free to all, to vtter in publike a priuate conceit, and to claime kindnes of all, for good will ment vnto all: as I my selfe am ready both freindly and fauorably, to esteme of others, who shall enterprise the like, requiring euery one, which shall vse my trauell, either as a reader, to peruse, or as a reaper to profit, that he will think well of me, which may cause him allow: or if he do not, that yet he will be sorie for me, that so good a meaning had so meane an issue.

Why it is penned in English.

I do write in my naturall English toungue, bycause though I make the learned my iudges, which vnderstand Latin, yet I meane good to the vnlearned, which vnderstand but English. And better it is for the learned to forbeare Latin, which they neede not then for the vnlearned to haue it, which they know not. By the English both shall see, what I say, by Latin but the one, which were some wrong, where both haue great interest, and the vnlearned the greater, bycause the vnlearned haue not any but only such English helpes, the learned can fetch theirs from the same fountaines, whence I fetch mine. My meaning is principally to helpe mine owne countrie, whose language will helpe me, to be vnderstood of them, whom I would perswade: to get some thankes of them, for my good will to do well: to purchace pardon of them, if my good will do not well. The parentes and freindes with whom I haue to deale, be mostwhat no latinistes: and if they were, yet we vnderstand that tongue best, whervnto we are first borne, as our first impression is alwaie in English, before we do deliuer it in Latin. And in perswading a knowen good by an vnknowen waie, are we not to cal vnto vs, all the helpes that we can, to be thoroughly vnderstood? He that vnderstands no Latin can vnderstand English, and he that vnderstands Latin very well, can vnderstand English farre better, if he will confesse the trueth, though he thinke he haue the habite and can Latin it exceading well. When mine argument shall require Latin, as it will eare long, I will not then spare it, in the degree, that I haue it, but till it do, I will serue my countrie that waie, which I do surely thinke will proue most intelligible vnto her. For though the argument, which is dedicate to learning, and must therfore of force vse the termes of learning: which be mysteries to the multitude, maie seeme to offer some darkness and difficultie in that point: yet it is to be construed, that the thing it selfe must be presented in her owne colours, which the learned can discry, at the first blush, as of their acquaintance, who must be spoken to in their owne kinde: as the vnlearned must be content to enquire, bycause we straine our termes to haue them intitled. And yet, in all my drift, for all my faire promise, I dare warrant my countrie no more, then probabilitie doth me, which if it deceiue me, yet I haue it to leane vnto, and perhaps of such pith, as might easely haue beguiled a wiser man then me. But till I proue beguiled, I will dwell in hope, that I am not, to deliuer my minde with the better courage, and therby to shew that I thinke my selfe right. For the greatest enemy, that can be to any wel meaning conceit is, to mistrust his own power, and to dispaire of his good speede where happy fortune makes euident shew.

CHAPTER 2.

Wherfore these Positions serve, what they be, and how necessarie it was to begin at them.

MY purpose is to helpe the hole trade of teaching, euen from the very first foundation: that is, not only the Grammarian, and what shall follow afterward, but also the Elementarie, which is the verie infantes train, from his first entrie, vntill he be thought fit to passe thence to the Grammar schoole. My labour then beginning so low, am I not to follow the president of such writers, as in the like argumentes, haue vsed the like methode? The maner of proceding which the best learned authors do vse, in those argumentes, which both for the matter be of most credit, and for the maner of best accompt, kepeth alwaie such a currant, as they at the first laie downe certaine groundes, wherin both they and their readers, whether scholers onely, or iudges alone, do resolutely agree. Which consent enureth to this effect, that they maie therby either directly passe thorough to their ende without empeachment: or else if any difficulty do arise in the way, they may easely compound it, by retiring themselues to those primitiue groundes. The Mathematicall, which is counted the best maister of sound methode, of whome all other sciences do borrow their order, and way in teaching well, eare he passe to any either probleme or theoreme, setts downe certaine definitions, certaine demaundes, certaine naturall and necessarie confessions, which being agreed on, betwen him and his learner, he proceedeth on to the greatest conclusions in his hole profession, as those which be acquainted with *Euclide* and his friendes, do verie wel know. Wil the naturall philosopher medle with his maine subject, before he haue handled his first principles, matter, forme, priuation, motion, time, place, infinitie, vacuitie, and such other, whervnto *Aristotle* hath dedicated eight whole bookes? What shall I neede to take more paines in rehersall of any other writer, whether Lawyer, Physician, or any else, which entreateth of his peculiar argument learnedly, to prooue that I am first to plant by positions, seeing the verie diuine himselfe, marcheth on of this foote and groundeth his religion vpon principles of beleefe? I professe my selfe to be a scholer, wherby I do know this methode, which the learned do kepe, and I deale with an argument, which must needes at the first be verie nicely entertained, till proofe giue it credit, what countenaunce soeuer hope maie seeme to lend it, in the meane while. I maie therefore seeme to deale against mine owne knowledge, if I do not fortifie myselfe with such helpes, as vpon probable reason, maie first purchace their owne standing, and being themselues staid in place of liking maie helpe vp all the reste.

I am specially to further two degrees in learning, first the Elementarie which stretcheth from the time that the child is to be set to do any thing, till he be remoued to his Grammar: then the Grammarian, while the child doth continew, in the schoole of language, and learned tounges, till he be remoued for his ripenes, to some Vniuersitie: which two pointes be both of great moment.

For the Elementarie: Bycause sufficiency in the child, before he passe thence, helpes the hole course of the after studie, and insufficiencie skipping from thence to soone, makes a very weake sequele. For as sufficient time there, without to much hast, to post from thence to timely, draweth on the residew of the schoole degrees, in their best beseeming time, and in the ende sendeth abroade sufficient men for the seruice of their countrie: so to hedlong hast scouring thence to swiftly at the first, (for all that it seemeth so petie a thing,) in perpetuall infirmity of matter, procureth also to much childishnes in yeares to be then in place, when iudgement with skill, and ripenes with gray-haires should carie the contenaunce. And is not this pointe then to be well proyned, where hast is such a foe, and ripenes such a freind? Where pushing forward at the first before maturitie bid on, will still force that, which followeth till at the last it marre all?

For the Grammarian: As it is a thing not vnseemely for me to deale in, being my selfe a teacher, so is it verie profitable for my countrie to heare of, which in great varietie of teaching doth seeme to call for some vniforme waie. And to haue her youth well directed in the tounges, which are the waies to wisdome, the lodges of learning, the harbours of humanitie, the deliuerers of diuinitie, the treasuries of all store, to furnish out all knowledge in the cunning, and all iudgement in the wise, can it be but well taken, if it be well perfourmed? or can it but deserue some freindly excuse, yea though good will want good successe? If occasion fitly offered by the waie, cause me attempt any further thing then either of these two, though I may seeme to be beside my schoole, yet my trust is that I shal not seeme to be beside my selfe.

Now then dealing with these matters which appertaine to men, and must be allowed of men, if they deserue allowance, or wil be reiected by them if they seeme not to be sound, whether haue I neede to procede with consent or no? For what if some shall thinke their penny good siluer, and will not admit mine offer? neither receiue teaching at the hand of so meane a controwler? what if some other graunt, that there is some thing amisse in deede, but that my deuise is no meane to amend it? what if disdaine do worke me discredit, and why should he take vpon him? A petie companion, I confesse, but till some better do deale, why may not my petinesse fullwell take place? And if the ware which I do bring, proue marchandable, why may I not make shew, and offer it to sale? Such instances and obiections wilbe offered, with whom seeing I am like to encounter, why ought I not at the first to resolue those, which will relent at the voice of reason? and so entreat the other, which make more deintie, to be drawen on, as my deutie being discharged towardes the thing, by argumentes, towardes them, by curtesie, if there be any strayning afterwardes themselues may be in fault?

But bycause I must applie my positions to some one ground, I haue chosen the Elementarie, and him rather then the Grammarian: for that the Elementarie is the verie lowest and first to be dealt with, and the circunstances being well applyed vnto him, may with very small ado, be transported afterward to the Grammarian or anie other else. And vnder the title of the particular circunstance, (though it seeme peculiarly to appertaine to the Elementarie, by waie of mine example, which I do applie vnto him primitiuely) yet I do trauell commonly with the generall considerations in all persons which use the same circunstance, in anie degree of learning, as the places themselues hereafter will declare. Which I do both to ende these positiue arguments at once, and to make the precept also somewhat more pleasant to the reader, hauing the entertainement of some forreine, but no vnfit discourse.

The positions.

The positions therefore which I do meane, be these and such other. At what time the child is to be set to schoole. What he is to learne when he is at schoole. Whether all be to be set to schoole. Whether exercise be to be vsed as a principle in trayning. Whether young maidens be to be set to learne. How to traine vp young gentlemen. How to procure some vniformitie in teaching. Of curtesie and correction. Of priuate and publike education. Of choise of wittes, of places, of times, of teachers, of schoole orders. Of restrayning to many bookish people, and many other like argumentes, which the nature of such discourses useth to hale in by the waie. Wherin I require my countreymens consent, to thinke as I do, and will do mine endeauour to procure it, as I can, before I deale with the particular præceptes, and schooling of children. Which while I do, as I follow the præsident of the best writers, for the methode, which I chuse, so for the matter it selfe I will vse no other argument, then both nature and reason, custome and experience, and plaine shew of euident profit shall recommend to my countrie without either manifest appearaunce, or secrete suspicion of a fantasticall deuise: considering it were an argument of verie small witte knowing fantasticallnes to disgrace the man, and impossibilitie to displace the meane: in so necessarie a thing as I pretend this to be, to entermingle either fantasticall matter, for all men to laugh at, or impossible meane, for as many to muse at. If earnest desier to haue some thing bettered, do cause me wishe the amendement, I hope that will not be accounted fantasticall, vnless it be to such, as do thinke themselues in health when they are deadly sicke, and feeling no paine, bycause of extreme weaknes, do hold their freindes halfe foolish, which wishe them to thinke vpon alteration of life.

CHAPTER 3.

Of what force circunstance is in matters of action, and how warily authorities be to be vsed, where the contemplatiue reason receiues the check of the actiue circunstance, if they be not well applyed. Of the alleadging of authors.

SOME well meaning man, when he will perswade his countrie to this or that thing, either by penne or speache, if he find any good writers authoritie, which fauoureth his opinion, he presumeth streight waie therby both his owne perswasion to be sufficiently armed, and his countries execution to be strongly warranted. Which his assuraunce is sometime chekt by wisdome, sometime by experience: By wisdome, which forseeth, that the circunstance of the countrie will not admit that, which he would perswade: by experience, which giuing way at the first to some probability, is in the end borne back by vnfitting circunstance. So that in those cases, where authorities perswade, and circunstances controwle, such as vse writers for their credit, must feare circunstance for her chek. Bycause the misse in circunstance makes the authour no authour, where his reason is altered, and the alledger no alledger, where discretion wanteth. Seeing therefore my selfe deale with these two pointes of authoritie and circunstance, both to confirme mine owne opinion the surer, and to confute the contrarie sounder, where difference in opinion shall offer to assaile me, I thought it good in the verie entrie to say somwhat of both, considering their agreement doth promise successe, and their disagreement doth threaten defeat.

I do see many very toward wittes, of reasonable good reading, and of excellent good vtterance, both forreine abroad, and freindes at home marueilously ouershoot themselues by ouerruling the circunstance, and ouerstraining authoritie. For vpon some affiaunce in their owne wittes, that they see all circunstances, and some small assurance, that the authours which they reade, do soothe all that they say: they will push out in publike certaine resolute opinions, before either their wittes be settled, or their reading ripe: which is then to be thought wisely ripe, when after the benefit of many yeares, after much reading of the most and best writers, after sound digesting of that which they haue red, and applying it all to some certaine ende: time hath fined their iudgement, and by precise obseruing and comparing, both what others haue said, and what themselues haue seene, hath made them maister the circunstance. Which mastering of the circunstance, is the only rule, that wisemen liue by, the only meane, that wisedome is come by, the only ods between folie and witte. The marking wherof is of so great a force, as by it eche countrie discoueureth the travellour, when he seeketh to enforce his forreine conclusions, and clingeth to that countryman, which hath bettered her still, by biding still at home. It discrieth the young student, which is rauished with the obiect, eare he can discern it, and honoreth the wise learned, whose vnderstanding is so staied, as he may be a leader. The consideration of circunstance is so strong in all attemptes, where man is the subiect, as it maketh of all nothing, and of nothing all. The skill to iudge of it is so lingring, and so late, bycause man is the gatherer, and so long eare he learne it, as it seemes to be reserued, till he be almost spent. It is not enough to rule the world, to alleadge authorities, but to raunge authorities, which be not aboue the world, by the rule of the world, is the wisemans line.

I am to deale with training, must I entreat my countrey to be content with this, bycause such a one commendes it? or to force her to that, bycause such a state likes it? The shew of right deceiues us, and the likenes of vnlike things doth lead vs, where it listeth. Differences and ods discouer errors, similitude and likenes lead euen wise men awrie. The great philosopher *Aristotle*[1] in fining of reason, maketh the abilities to discerne these two pointes, where thinges like be vnlike, and where the vnlike be like, two of his principall instrumentes to trie out the trueth. Which skill to discern so narrowly, as it is not in all, so where it is, there is great discretion, there will nothing be brought from authoritie to practise, but that circunstance will praise, and yet hardly winne. For though circunstance in our countrie and others do seeme verie like, nay rather almost one, yet if our countrie do admit, where any ods appeareth, though it offer the relenting, when it comes to proufe, she auentureth her selfe, and we which perswade. haue great cause to thanke her, that she will harken vnto vs, as she also will thanke vs, if she praise at the parting. Wherfore seeing the ground is so slipperie to deale by authoritie, and therfore to approue it, bycause such a one sayth it till iudgement haue subsigned, and circunstance sealed, I thought it good, as I said before, to speake somwhat therof, that I may therby stay my selfe the better, marching by them, and thorough them: and also remoue some scrupulouse opinion, that I vse them not strangely, when I vse them so, as they wishe themselues to be vsed.

But for the better vnderstanding, with what warynes authoritie is to be vsed, may it please you to consider, that there be two sortes of authours wherwith we deale in our studie: wherof the one regardeth the matter only, and by ineuitable argument enforceth the conclusion. In this kinde be the Mathematicall sciences, and all such naturall philosophie, as proceedeth by necessitie of a demonstrable subiect. The other ioyneth the circunstance with the matter, as Morall, and politike Philosophie, as the Professions, as Poetes, as histories do, when they enforce not the necessitie of their conclusion, by necessitie of the matter, though by the fourme of their argument, which concludeth of force, in matters of least force. The argumentes of those Artes and Professions, which be in this second kinde, do depende vpon apparence in probable coniecture, and be creatures to circunstance, wherin as man is the mainest subiecte, so the respectes had to man haue the raine in their hand.

Hence commeth it that lawes in seuerall landes do differ so much, that Phisicke in seuerall subiectes is so seuerall in cure, that Diuinitie in ceremonies admitteth

[1] 1. Topic. de 4. instrumentis Dial.

change, where the circunstance is obserued, and yet the truth not tainted.

Hence it cometh that in diuersitie of states, there be diuersities of staie, whereby men gouerne, bycause circunstance commaundeth. Whervnto, he that affirmes, must still haue an eye, bycause it sheweth, what is seemely and conuenient, not in great states alone, but also in the meanest thinges of all: bycause it moderateth both what soeuer men do: and in what soeuer respect they do. In the first kinde of authours and authorities, the truth of the matter maintaines it selfe, without he said or he did: bycause it is true by nature, which staied it, not by authour which said it. And being so setled, it ministreth of it selfe no matter to debate, or at the least verie little. For in pointes of necessitie, naturally inferred, the difference of opinion is no proufe at all, that the matter is debatable, but it is a sufficient argument of an insufficient writer, if he penne his opinion, or of an vngrounded learner, if his error be in speeche, which harpeth still about some outward accident, and neuer perceth the inward substance. So that in such conclusions there is but one currant, what forceth the matter, and not what sayeth the man: what commandes the immutable truth, and not what commendes the changeable circunstance. All the controuersie is in the second kinde, where circunstance is prescription, wherin the writers credite oftimes authoriseth the thing, and the truth of the thing doth make the man an authour: wherin vnles he take verie good heede, which is the alleadger, he may do his writer exceeding great iniurie, by bringing him to the barre, and forcing that vpon him, which he neuer dreamed on, and harme himselfe to, who mistaking his ground, misplaceth his building, and hazardeth his credit.

Hence commeth it, that so many fantasticall deuises do trouble the world, while euerie man being desirous to breede somwhat worthy of commendacion either for shew of learning, or for shield of opinion, bringeth in the poore writers, and enioyneth them speach, where in deed they be mute: and if they could speake, they would aske the alledger why he did so abuse them. A generall and a verie hard case in these our dayes, when the most erronious opinions be fathered vpon the most honest writers, which meant nothing lesse, then that which is threpte vpon them. In matter of Pollicy this man wrote thus, and was verie well thought of, an other in some schoole pointes gaue his censure in this sorte, and became of account. Transport the circunstance the allowance is misliked, the alleadger laughed at: and yet the worthinesse of the writer not empayred at all, when he is rightly weyed, bycause he was forced: In this kinde of argument wherin I presently deale, it is no proufe, bycause *Plato* praiseth it, bycause *Aristotle* alloweth it, bycause *Cicero* commendes it, bycause *Quintilian* is acquainted with it, or any other else, in any argument else, that therfore it is for vs to vse. What if our countrey honour it in them, and yet for all that may not vse it her selfe, bycause circunstance is her check? Nay what if the writers authoritie be alledged without consideration of their owne circunstance? who then offereth his countrey the greatest wrong? is it not he which wringeth the writer, and wreasteth his meaning? And yet such alledgers there be, which passe it ouer smoothly, till they be espyed, where then their owne weaknes appeareth, the writers worthinesse is euident, and his wrong reuenged, by discouering the wreaster. Wherfore he that will deale with writers so, as to deriue their conclusions to the vse of his countrey, must be verie well aduised, and diligently marke, that their meaning, and his applying be both of one ground, and also how much of their opinion his countrey will admit, which, as she will not be forced by idle supposalles, so pronounceth she him to be but a fleeter, who so euer shall offer to force her that waye. If the matter be well pikt, and properly applyed, she embraceth it forthwith, and giues it the growing. Whether I shall perfourme so much my selfe, as I require in others, I dare not warrant, but I will do my best, to vse my authour well, and to obserue the circunstance, and not once to profer any thing to my countrey, which shall not haue all those foundations, that I promised before, so much as I can, *Nature* to lead it, *reason* to back it, *custome* to commend it, *experience* to allow it, and *profit* to preferre it.

For alledging of Authours.

But here by the waye, I must aduertise my reader thus much, that I thinke a student ought rather to inuest himselfe in the habite of his writer, then to stand much vpon his title, and authoritie, in proofe or disproofe, seeing who knoweth not, that all our studies be generally detters to the first deuise, and fairest deliuerie? Therfore to auoide length therby, I will neither vse authoritie, nor example, seeing matter is the maine, and not the mans name, sauing onely where one mans deposition vpholdes or ouerthrowes: and the ground of the example is so excellent in that kinde, as it were to much vnkindenesse, not to let the person be knowen, where the fact is so famous. I will reste vpon reason the best, where I finde it, the next where that failes, and coniecture is probable, to proue such thinges, as reason must paterne. If the triall be in proofe, and experience must guide it, I will binde vpon proofe, and let triall be the tuche.

For with the alledging of authours, either to shew, what I haue read or to tuche common concordes, where any thing is to much, and nothing is enough, I meane not at all to buisie my selfe. Bycause we heape but vp witnesses, which be nothing needeful, in such cases, as be nothing doubtfull, when we vse many gaie names all agreeing in one, and none saying but so: wheras the naturall vse of testimonies is, to proue where doubt is, not to cloye, where all is cleare. In such cases for want of sound iudgement, a catalogue of names, and a multitude of sentences, which say but that is soothed, and no man denyes, are forced to the stage, to seeme to arme the alleadger, which fighteth without foe, and flyeth without feare.

In pointes of learning, which be wonne from quarrell, or resolute groundes, which be without quarrell, and neede no assurer, I referre my dealing to the iudgement of those, which can trace me, where I tread and shall finde my truth, without the authours name, whom they will confesse to be well alleadged, when I saye, as he sayeth, and proue as he proueth, either by habite got by reading, or by likenesse in iudgement, though I neuer red.

If controuersie arise, and be worth the recounting the matter shall not sleepe: if it hange of the man, and without him be lame, the man shall not slyp: but otherwise, no. Those that be learned know that witnesses, and wise mens names be verie good ware, where the question is, whether such a thing be done, and they be said to know it, and that *Rhetorick* takes testimonies for a principall proofe, and very neare the harte, as *Logick* placeth them in the utmost of her argumentes, being themselues of small pith, though their stuffe be worth praise, and both bind and loose, where reason beares the swaie, and probabilitie is to purpose. I do honour good writers but without superstition, nothing addicte to titles. But for so much as *Reason* doth honour them, they must be content to staie without them selues, and vse all meanes to preferre her to presence, as their ladie and mistresse, whose authoritie and credit procures them admission, when they come from her. It is not so, bycause a writer said so, but bycause the truth is so, and he said the truth, the truth giues him title, and that is it, which must passe, strong enough of it selfe, and oftimes weakened in the hearers opinion, though not in it selfe, by naming the writer: which commonly proues so when the hearer is wedded vnto names, and sworn to authoritie, not so much eying the thing which is vttered, as the persons title by whom it is vttered. If truth did depend vpon the person, she would oftimes be brought into a miserable plighte, and looke rufully vpon it, being constrained to serue fancie, and to alter vpon will, wheras she is still one, and should be bent vnto, neither will her selfe bend, howsoeuer opinatiue people do perswade them selues.

This the learned and wise know, whose curtesie I craue as I wish them well: for whose helpe and health, I vndertooke this paine, whose wisedom I appeal to, if either, diffidence do wrangle, or ignoraunce do quarrel. As for the vnlearned, I must needes ouertreat them, not to stand with me in pointes, where they cannot iudge themselues, if not for mine owne, yet for their sakes, which beleue me them-selues, and will giue their word for me. In such pointes, as be intelligible to both, I must praie them both to waie me well, and euer to haue before them, that my will wisheth well, howsoeuer I perfourme, wherin will deserues well, and weaknes prayeth excuse.

CHAPTER 4.

What time weere best for the child to begin to learne. What matters some of the best writers handle, eare they determine this question. Of lettes and libertie whervnto the parentes are subiect in setting their children to schoole. Of the difference of wittes and bodies in children. That exercise must be ioyned with the booke, as the schooling of the bodie.

The first question that of any necessitie commeth in place, seemeth to be at what yeares children be to be put to schoole: for neither would they be differed to long for leasing of their time, nor hastened on to soone, for hindering of their health. The rule therfore must be giuen according to the strength of their bodies, and the quicknes of their wittes ioyntly.

The auncient antecedents.

Such of the auncient writers, both Greek and Latin, as either picture vs out the platfourmes of the best framed common weales: or do lend vs the looking on of some such a paragon as in some particular kinde, they deuise to be peerelesse, before they call it in question, when their youth shall begin to learne, they do fetch the ground of their traine exceeding farre of. As, what regard is to be had to the infante, while he is yet vnder his nurse. Where they moile themselues sore, with the maners and conditions of the nurse, with the fines or rudenes of her speeche: with the comelynes of her person and fauour of her face. And in controuersie about milkes, sometime they preferre the mother, if her health, her complexion, her kinde of life, will best fit for her owne: sometime they yeeld: but with great choice to the forreine nurse: if any iust circunstance do discharge the mother, whom nature vnletted seemes to charge most. Againe they examine what companie is to be choosen for him, when he doth begin first to crepe abroad, wherby that good may begin betimes, which must continew longe, and is greatly furthered by choice of companie, that pikked and choice play fellowes may succede after a fine and well fitted nursery. Againe, they debate in good sadnes, what an exquisite traine is to be deuised for him, when he is to go to schoole, either priuate, or publike, though they still preferre the publike as most beseeming him, which must liue among many and neuer be recluse. And such other considerations they fall into, which do well beseeme the bringing vp of such a one, as they did but wishe for: and we may not hope for: but by no meanes can be applyed to our youth, and our education, wherin we wishe for no more, then we hope for to haue. Nay they go further, as whether may not wishers? and appoint the parentes of this so perfect a child, to be so wise and so well learned, as is in verie deede most consonant with their platte, but to farre surmonting the modele of my positions. Wherfore leauing those meanes, which they do but deuise, to bring vp those people, which they do but patterne, I meane to proceede from such principles, as our parentes do build on, and as our children do rise by, to that mediocritie, which furnisheth out this world, and not to that excellencie, which is fashioned for an other. And yet the pretence of these so fine pictures, by pointing out so absolute a president, is, to let vs behold thereby, both wherin the best consisteth: what colours it is best knowen by: what a state it keepeth: and also by what ready meane, we may best approache neare it, bycause dispaire to obtaine the verie best it selfe, discourageth all hope. For that missinge any one of these so fined circunstances, as our frailtie will faile either in all, or in most, then we marre the whole moulde. Howbeit we are much bounde to the excellent wittes of those diuine writers, who by their singular knowledge, approaching neare to the truest, and best, could most truly, and best discern, what constitution they were of: and being of a good ciuill inclination, thought it their parte, to communicate that with their posteritie, which they from so nighe, had so narrowly decifred, as auailable to others, for this onely cause, if there ensewed no more of it, that in despaire of hitting the highest, yet by seeing where it lodged, with verie great praise, they might draw neare vnto it. For as it is but for paragons to mount quite aboue all, so is it worthy praise to rest in some degree, which declareth a pearcher, though abilitie restraine will, that it cannot aspire whervnto it would.

But to returne from this so exquisite, to our ordinarie traine, I perswade my selfe, that all my countreymen wishe themselues as wise, and as well learned, as those absolute parentes are surmised to be, though they be content with so much of both, or rather with so litle, as God doth allot them: and that they will haue their children nursed as well as they can, without question where, or quarrelling by whom: so as they may haue that well brought vp by nurture, which they loue so well, bequeathed them by nature. And that till the infant can gouerne himselfe, they will seeke to saue it from all such perilles, as may seeme to harme it any kinde of way, or by companie or by occasion: and that with such warinesse, as ordinarie circunspection may, or can worke, in considerate and careful parentes. And finally that for his well schooling, they that cannot, will wish it, they that can, will haue it, with small charge if they may, if they may not with some coste, and very carefully commend the silly poore boy at his first entry, to his maisters charge, not omitting euen how much his mother makes of him, if she come not her selfe and do her owne commendacions. So that for these antecedents, as they in precisenes do passe vs, so we in possibility go farre beyond them. For our hope is at ankar, and rides in assuraunce, their wishe wandereth still, not like to win the rode. These and such like circunstances they handle formally as in an absolute picture, I tuche but by the waye, as being quite of an other perswasion, nothing giuen to the vnpossible, where possibilitie must take place, though the vnpossible *Idea*, offer great force to fancie. Wherfore I will now take my leaue of them, and retourne to my question, when children be to be set to learning. A thing in reason very worthy to be wayed, and in perfourmaunce, very like to proue good, both for health of the bodie, and helpe of the minde, and so much the rather to be well entreated, by cause it is the very first principle, which enterteneth our traine. My countrey parentes then, being so naturall to their children, both for care before schoole, and for choice in schooling, I will commend to their charge, all that which is to be considered in their first infancie, and tendrest spring, before they be thought fit, to be set to learning, which they will diligently looke to, I am very well assured. Bycause euery thing drawes liking, while it is pretie and young, and specially our owne which hath nature to sollicite, and needeth no exhorting, to haue it well cherished, where there is no daunger, but in to much dalying, neither yet any feare, but in to fond cokkering.

Lettes.

But in very good earnest, when shall our boye be set to schoole? In all considerations, wherin vpon the resolution, something must be executed, and done, this thing is necessarily to be first enquired, whether all, or most, or any of all the circunstances, which be incident to the execution, be in, or without the parties power, which is to execute, so as he may either proceede at his owne libertie, if nothing withstand him, or may not proceede, if he be thwarted by circunstance. For otherwise the liberty to passe on, or the restraint, to staie, being not agreed vpon, he that directs by rule may be chekt by arrest. And where he biddes on thus, circunstance maye replie, Ifayth sir no. Wherfore I leaue those parentes to their owne discretion, in whom will seekes libertie, to do as she would, and circunstance commandes her, to do as she may. The parent would haue his child begin to learne at such a time: circunstance sayes, no. He would haue him learne with such a man: some cause contrarieth. In such a place, in such a sorte: his power is to poore, to compasse that he coueteth. Be not all these lettes, and what so euer is so laid, to stop will of his will, where neither counsell can giue precept, nor the parent can execute, being so strongly ouercharged? It is euen like, as if one should saye, the freeman and the bond, be not both in one case. Preceptes be for freemen, which maie do as ye bid them, but circunstance bindes, and wilbe obeyed. Wherfore I must once for all, warne those parentes, which may not do as they would, vpon these same lettes which I haue recited, or any other like, that they take their oportunitie, when so euer it is offered, bycause occasion is verie bald behinde, and seldome comes the better. And seeing circunstance is their bridle, when they feele the raine loose, course it on a maine, and take the benefit of time, the oportunitie of place, the commoditie of the teacher, the equitie of the maner, and what so euer condition else, wherin the freedom of circunstance doth seeme to befreind them. For sauing with such a note as this is, I cannot direct them, which can giue no counsell, but where *necessitie* is in ward and *libertie* keepes the keyes.

Libertie.

But if the parent want nothing necessary, for his childes bringing vp, neither a place, both conuenient for receit, and commodious for distaunce, wherin to haue him taught: nor a teacher, sufficient for cunning, and considerate, for either curtesie, or correction, who can traine him vp well: nor fit companions, as so fit a place, and so good a maister may picke out of choice, which will throng vnto him: And if the child also himselfe, haue a witte apte to conceiue, what shalbe put vnto him: and a body able to beare the trauell, which belonges vnto learning: me thinke it were then best, that he began to be doing, when he maie well perceiue, without trauelling his braine, thorough the hardnes of the thing, and neede not be toiled to the wearines of his bodie, thorough the wise handling of his aduised maister. For being in the schoole, he may do somwhat very well, though not very much, wheras roming about, he might hap to do ill, and that very much.

Variety of wittes.

At what yeares I cannot say, bycause ripenes in children, is not tyed to one time, no more then all corne is ripe for one reaping, though mostwhat about one. Some be hastinges and will on, some be hardinges, and drawe backe: some be willing when their parentes will: some but willing, when they will them selues, as either will to do well, vpon cherishing wisely, or pleasure to play still, vpon cokkering fondly, hath possessed their mindes.

But he that deserueth to be a parent, must dispose himselfe to be also a iudge, in all these cases: and who is so ill freinded, as he hath not one, with whom to conferre, to learne by aduise, the towardnes and time of his young sonnes schooling, if he be not able to looke into it himselfe? They that limitte the beginning to learne by some certaine yeares, haue an eye to that knowledge, which it were pitie were loste, say they, and may easely be gayned in those young yeares. I agree with them, that it were great pitie, to lease anything, that neede not be loste, without great negligence, and may be well gotten, with very small diligence, not endammaging the child. But more pitie it were, for so petie a gaine, to forgoe a greater, to winne an houre in the morning, and lease the whole daie after: as those people most commonly do, which starte out of their beds to early, before they be well awaked: or knowe what it is a clocke: and be drousie when they are vp, for want of their sleepe.

If the childe haue a weake bodie, though neuer so strong a witte, let him grow on the longer, till the strength of his bodie, do aunswere to his witte. For experience hath taught me, and calleth reason to record, that a sharp young witte hastened on to wounder at, for the quiknesse of his edge, hath therby most commonly bene hastened to his graue, thorough the weaknesse of body: to the greife of the freindes, whose delite is cut of, and some wite of their witte, for ouerhasting their child: Nay, what if it hath pleased God to lend him longer life? he neuer sinketh deepe, but fleeteth still aboue, with some quicknesse of conceit, continuing that wonder, which he wanne in his childhood: neuer burdened with much to ballase his head: but still aunswering at reboundes, the fairest crop of so hasty an haruest. Sometime his witte will grow worse, the wonder will vanishe, the bodie will proue feeble, and soone after perishe.

But now if he liue, with all these infirmities, of decaying witte, decreasing wonder, puling bodie, he liues with small comfort, in such a world of weaknesse, which vsually commeth of to much moisture, the corrupter of such carcasses, the most vile, and violent massacrer, of the most, and best studentes, generally for want of trauell, sauing onely to their braine, which the more it is occupyed, the sorer it stilleth, and the sorer it stilleth, the sooner it killeth, the moe the more pitie. Wherfore I could wishe the wittier child, the lesse vpon the spurre, and either the longer kept from learning, for turning his edge, as a to sharpe knife: or the sklenderer kept at it, for feare of surfait, in one hungring to haue it. Yet must not this quickling be suffered to do nothing at all, for feare he grow reasty, if that nothing be dumpishe, and heauie: or passe beyond reclaime, if it be dissolute, and wanton.

The meane conceiuer, in some strength of bodie, is the best continuer, and as he serues all places best, in his height of learning, so in all respectes, ye may venture on his schooling, when it shall please you, with but ordinarie regard.

A dull witte in a strong body, if ye like to haue it learne, as by learning ye finde it: so till some degree, it may well learne, for necessarie seruice in the rest of his life: and may be hastened on boldly. For the bodie can beare labour, it is so well boaned, and the witte will not cloye, it so hardly receiueth. The sharpenesse of witte, the maister will sound by memorie, and number: the strength of the bodie, the mother will marke, by complaint, and cause.

A weake witte and as weake a bodie, is much to be moaned, for the great infirmity, and can hardly be helpt, bycause nature is to weake: and therefore it must be thought on, as in a case of despaire, againe against hope: if any thing be goten, a greife to the freindes, which cannot amend it: small ioye to him selfe, which cannot auoide it.

A strong witte, in as strong a bodie, is worthy the wishing, of the parentes to bring foorth, of the teacher to bring vp. For as it is a thing of it selfe not ordinarie, so where it lighteth, it giues vs the gaze, and bides all beginninges, but that which is to soone, bycause God hath prouided that strength in nature, wherby he entendes no exception in nurture, for that which is in nature. Such spirites there be, and such bodies they haue, if they will, and may so keepe them, with orderly regard, which is extreme hard vnto them. For that oftimes they will not do so, but distemper their bodies with disordinate doinges, when pleasures haue possessed them, and rashenesse is their ruler. Oftimes they maie not, thorough varietie and weight of important affaires, which commaundeth them too farre in some kinde of calling. But where so euer they light, or what so euer waye they take, they shewe what they be, and alwaye proue either the verie best, or the most beastly. For there can scantly be any meane in those constitutions, which are so notably framed, and so rarely endued. And therefore those parentes which haue such children must take great heede of them, as the tippes of euill, if they chuse that waye, or the toppes of good, if they minde that is best. For the middle and most moderate wittes, which commonly supplie eche corner in eche countrey, and serue most assaies, some ordinary meane will serue to order them: but where extraordinarie pointes begin to appeare, there common order is not commonly enough.

This is my opinion concerning the time, when the child shall begin to learne: which I do restraine to the strength of witte and hardnes of body: the one for to receiue learning, the other not to refuse labour: and therfore I conclude thus that the parent himselfe ought in reason to be more then halfe a iudge of the entrie to schooling, as being best acquainted with the particular circunstance of his owne child. Yet I do not allow him to be an absolute iudge, without some counsell, vnlesse he be a very rare father, and well able to be both a rule to himselfe, and a paterne to others. Bycause mostwhere men be most blinded: where they should see best, I meane in their owne: such a tyrant is affection, when she hath wonne the field, vnder the conducte of nature, and so imperious is nature, when she is disposed to make affection her deputie.

Exercises.

But now for so much as in setting our child to schoole, we consider the strength of his bodie, no lesse then we do the quicknesse of his witte, it should seeme that our traine ought to be double, and to be applyed to both the partes, that the body may as well be preserued in his best, as the minde instructed in that, which is his best, that the one may still be able to aunswere the other well, in all their common executions. As for the training vp of the minde, the waye is well beaten, bycause it is generally entreated on in euery booke, and beareth the honour and title of learning.

But for the bettering of the body, is there not any meane to maintaine it in health, and cheifly in the student, whose trade treads it downe? Yes surely, A very naturall and a heathful course there is to be kept in exercise, wherby all the naturall functions of the body be excellently furthered, and the body made fit for all his best functions. And therfore parentes and maisters ought to take such a waie, euen from the beginning, as the childes diet, neither stuffe the bodye, nor choke the conceit, which it lightly doeth, when it is to much crammed. That his garmentes which oftimes burden the bodie with weight, sometimes weaken it with warmth, neither faint it with heat, nor freese it with cold. That the exercise of the body still accompanie and assist the exercise of the minde, to make a dry, strong, hard, and therfore a long lasting body: and by the fauour therof to haue an actiue, sharp, wise and therwith all a well learned soule. If long life be the childes blessing for honoring his parentes, why should not the parentes then, which looke for that honour, all that in them lyeth, forsee in youth that their children may haue some hope of that benefit, to ensue in their age, which cannot take effect, vnlesse the thing be begon in their youth? Which if it be not by times looked vnto, they afterwardes become vncapable of long life, and so not to enioye the reward of their honour, for any thing that their parentes helpe to it, though God will be true, and perfourme that he promiseth, how so euer men hault in doing of their duetie. And yet tempting is pernicious, where the meane to hit right, is laid so manifest: and the childes honour to his parentes beginnes at obedience in his infancie, which they ought to reward, with good qualities for honour, and may worke them like waxe, bycause they do obey. This negligence of the parentes for not doing that, which in power they might, and in duetie they ought, giues contempt in the children some colour of iustice, to make their requitall with dishonour in their age, were it not that the Christian religion doth forbid reuenge: which in presidentes of prophanisme we finde allowed, where both curtesie to such parentes, as failed in education of their children is countercharged by lawe: and dissolute parentes by entreating ill, are well entertained of their neglected children: the vnfortunate children much moaned for their chaunce, that they came to so ill an ende: and the vndiscrete parentes more rated for their charge, which they looked so ill to, wherby themselues did seeme to haue forced such an ende.

The minde wilbe stirring, bycause it stirres the body, and some good meane will make it to furnish very well, so the choice be well made, wherin: the order well laid, wherby: and both well kept, wherwith: it shalbe thought best trained. The body which lodgeth a restlesse minde by his owne reste is betrayed to the common murtherers of a multitude of scholers, which be vnholesome and superfluous humors, needelesse and noysom excrementes, ill to feele within, good to send abroad.

Neither is it enough to saye, that children wilbe stirring alwaie of themselues, and that therefore they neede not any so great a care, for exercising their bodies. For if by causing them learne so and sitting still in schooles, we did not force them from their ingenerate heat, and naturall stirring, to an vnnaturall stilnesse, then their owne stirring without restraint, might seeme to serue their tourne, without more adoe. But stilnesse more then ordinarie, must haue stirring more then ordinarie: and the still breding of ill humours, which stuffe vp the body for want of stirring, must be so handled, as it want no stilling to send them away. Wherfore as stilnesse hath her direction by order in schooles, so must stirring be directed by well appointed exercise. And as quiet sitting helpes ill humors to breede, and burden the bodie: so must much stirring make a waie to discharge the one, and to disburden the other. Both which helpes, as I most earnestly require at the parent, and maisters hand: so I meane my selfe to handle them both, to the helping of both.

In the meane while, for the entring time thus much. The witte must be first wayed, how it can conceiue, and then the bodie considered, how it can beare labour: and the consorte of their strength aduisedly maintained. They haue both their peculiar functions, which by mediocrities are cherished, by extremities perished, hast doing most harme, euen to the most, and lingring not but some, sometimes to the best. And yet haste is most harmefull, where so euer, it setts foote, as we that teache alwaie finde, and they that learne, sometimes feele. For the poore children when they perceiue their owne weaknesse, whereof most commonly they maye thanke haste, they both faint, and feare, and very hardly get forward: and we that teach do meet with to much toile, when poore young babes be committed to our charge, before they be ripe. Whom if we beat we do the children wrong in those tender yeares to plant any hatred, when loue should take roote, and learning grow by liking.

And yet oftimes seueritie is to fowre, while the maister beateth the parentes folly, and the childes infirmitie, with his owne furie. All which extremities some litle discretion would easely remoue, by conference before, to forecast what would follow, and by following good counsell, when it is giuen before. Which will then proue so, when the parent will do nothing in placing or displacing of his childe, without former aduise, and communicating with the maister: and the maister likewise without respecting his owne gaine, will plainely and simply shew the parent or freind, what vpon good consideration he thinketh to be best. Wherein there wilbe no error if the parent be wise, and the maister be honest.

CHAPTER 5.

What thinges they be, wherin children are to be trained, eare they passe to the Grammar. That parentes, and maisters ought to examine the naturall abilities in their children, wherby they become either fit, or vnfit, to this, or that kinde of life. The three naturall powers in children, Witte to conceiue by, Memorie to retaine by, Discretion to discerne by. That the training vp to good manners, and nurture, doth not belong to the teacher alone, though most to him, next after the parent, whose charge that is most, bycause his commaundement is greatest, ouer his owne child, and beyond appeale. Of Reading, Writing, Drawing, Musick by voice, and instrument: and that they be the principall principles, to traine vp the minde in. A generall aunswere to all obiections, which arise against any, or all of these.

NOW that I haue shewed mine opinion concerning the time, when it were best to set the child to schoole, the next two questions seeme to be, what he shall learne and howe he shalbe exercised, when he is at schoole. For seeing he is compound of a soule and a bodie: the soule to conceiue and comprehend, what is best for itselfe, and the bodie to: The bodie to waite, and attend the commaundement and necessities of the soule: he must be so trained, as neither for qualifying of the minde, nor for enabling of the bodie, there be any such defecte, as iust blame therfore may be laide vpon them, which in nature be most willing, and in reason thought most skilfull, to preuente such defaultes. For there be both in the body, and the soule of man certaine ingenerate abilities, which the wisedom of parentes, and reason of teachers, perceiuing in their infancie, and by good direction auancing them further, during those young yeares, cause them proue in their ripenesse very good and profitable, both to the parties which haue them, and to their countries, which vse them. Which naturall abilities, if they be not perceiued, by whom they should: do condemne all such, either of ignorance, if they could not iudge, or of negligence, if they would not seeke, what were in children, by nature emplanted, for nurture to enlarge. And if they be perceiued, and either missorted in place, or ill applyed in choice, as in difference of iudgementes, there be many thinges practised, which were better vnproued, to the losse of good time, and let of better stuffe, they do bewray that such teachers, and trainers, be they parentes, be they maisters, either haue no sound skill, if it come of infirmitie, or but raw heades, if it spring of fansie. If they know the inclination, and do not further it rightely, it is impietie to the youth, more then sacrilege to the state, which by their fault be not suffered to enioy those excellent benefits, which the most munificent God, by his no niggardishe nature, prouided for them both. If they found them, and followed them, but not so fully, as they were to receiue: if for want wherwith, it deserues pardon, if for want of will, exceeding blame: and cryeth for correction of the state by them hindred, and small thankes of the parties, no more furthered.

Wherfore as good parentes, and maisters ought to finde out, by those naturall principles, whervnto the younglings may best be framed, so ought they to follow it, vntil it be complete, and not to staie, without cause beyond staie, before it come to ripenesse, which ripenesse, while they be in learning, must be measured by their ablenes to receiue that, which must follow their forebuilding: but when they are thought sufficiently well learned, and to meddle with the state, then their ripenesse is to be measured, by vse to themselues, and seruice to their countrey, in peace, as best and most naturall, in warre, as worse, and most vnnatural, and yet the ordinarie ende of a disordered peace. For when the thinges, which be learned do cleaue so fast in memorie, as neither discontinuaunce can deface them, nor forgetfulnesse abolishe them: then is abilitie vpon ascent, and when ascent is in the highest, and the countrey commaundes seruice, then studie must be left, and the countrey must be serued.

Seeing therfore in appointing the matter, wherin this traine must be employed, there is regard to be had first to the soule, as in nature more absolute, and in value more precious: and then to the bodie, as the instrument and meane, wherby the soule sheweth what is best to be done in necessity of fine force, in choice of best shew: I will remitte the bodie to his owne roome, which is peculiarly in exercises, sauing where I cannot meane the soule, without mention of the bodie, and in this place I wil entreat of the soule alone, how it must be qualified. And yet meane I not to make any anatomie, or resolution of the soule his partes and properties, a discourse, not belonging to this so low a purpose, but onely to pick out some natural inclinations in the soule, which as they seeme to craue helpe of education, and nurture, so by education, and nurture, they do proue very profitable, both in priuate and publicke. To the which effect, in the litle young soules, first we finde, a capacity to perceiue that which is taught them, and to imitate the foregoer. That witte to learne, as it is led, and to follow as it is foregone, would be well applyed, by proprietie in matter, first offered them to learne: by considerate ascent in order, encreasing by degrees: by wary handling of them, to draw them onward with courage. We finde also in them, as a quickenes to take, so a fastnesse to retaine: therfore their memorie would streight waye be furnished, with the verie best, seeing it is a treasurie: exercised with the most, seeing it is of receite: neuer suffered to be idle, seeing it spoiles so soone. For in defaulte of the better, the worse will take chaire, and bid it selfe welcome: and if idlenesse enter, it will exclude all ernest, and call in her kinsfolkes, toyes and triffles, easie for remembraunce, heauy for repentaunce.

We finde in them further an ability to discern, what is good, and what is ill, which ought foorthwith to be made acquainted with the best, by obedience and order, and dissauded from the worse, by misliking and frowne. These three thinges, witte to take, memorie to keepe, discretion to discern, and moe if ye seeke, though but braunches to these, which I chuse for my purpose, shall ye finde pearing out of the litle young soules: when you may see what is in them, and not they them-selues. Whose abilitie to encrease in time, and infirmitie to crawle at that time is commended to them, which first begot them, or best can frame them. Now these naturall towardnesses being once espied, in what degree they rise, bycause there is ods in children by nature, as in parentes by purchase, they must be followed with diligence, encreased by order, encouraged by comfort, till they come to their proofe. Which proofe trauell in time will perfourme, hast knittes vp to soone, and vnperfit, slownesse to late, and to weake.

The rule of discretion.

But for the best waie of their good speede, that witte maie conceiue and learne well, memorie retaine and hold fast, discretion chuse and discerne best, the cheife and chariest point is, so to plie them all, as they may proceede voluntarily, and not with violence, that will may be a good boye, ready to do well, and lothe to do ill, neuer fearing the rod, which he will not deserue. For wheresoeuer will in effecting, doth ioyne with abilitie to conceiue, and memorie to retaine, there industrie will finde frute, yea in the frowne of fortune. By discretion to cause them take to that, which is best, and to forsake that, which is worst, in common dealinges is common to all men, that haue interest in children, parentes by nature, maisters by charge, neighbours of curtesie, all men of all humanitie: whom either priuate care by cus-tome, or publike cure by commaundement of magistrate and lawe, doth compell in conscience to helpe their well doing, and to fray them from ill, wheresoeuer they meete them, or when so euer they see them do that, which is naught. And therfore that duetie to helpe them in this kinde for their manners, is incident to maisters but among others, though somwhat more then some others, as to whom it is most seemely, bycause of their authoritie, and most proper, bycause of their charge, whom knowledge best enfourmeth to embrew them with the best: and power best assisteth, to cause them embrace the best: euen perforce at the first, till acquaintaunce in time breede liking of it selfe.

But this mannering of them is not for teachers alone, because they communi-cate therin, as I haue said already, both with naturall parentes, to whom that point appertaineth nearest, as of most authoritie with them, and with all honest persons, which seing a child doing euill, are bid in conscience, to terrifie and check him as the quality of the childes offence, and the circunstance of their owne person doth seeme best to require.

Wherfore reseruing for the teacher so much as is for his office, to enstruct the child what is best for him in matter of manners, and to see to it, so much as in him lyeth: to set good orders in his gouvernment, to see them alwaye well, and one waye still executed and perfourmed, I referre the rest to those, whom either any vertuous consideration of them selues, or any particular duetie, enioyned by lawe, doth charge with the rest, either by priuate discipline at home, or by publike ordinaunce abroade, to see youth well brought vp that waye: to learne to discern that which is well from ill, good from bad, religious from prophane, honest from dishonest, commendable from blame worthy, seemely from vnseemely, that they may honour God, serue their countrey, comfort their freindes, and aide one an other, as good countreymen are bound to do. But how to handle their conceit in taking, and their memorie, in holding, bycause that appertaineth to teachers wholly: (for all that the parentes and freindes, wilbe medlers somtime, to further their young impes:) I will deale in that, and shew wherin children ought to be trained, till they be found fit for Grammer: wherin neuerthelesse, both the matters, which they learne: and the manners, which they are made to, serue for ground to vertue, and encrease of discretion.

As I might verie well be esteemed inconsiderate, if I should force any farre fet diuises into these my principles, which neither my countrey knew, nor her custome cared for, so dealing but with those, and resting content with those, which my countrey hath seuered to her priuate vse, and her custome is acquainted with of long continuaunce, I maye hope for consent, where my countrey commendeth, and looke for successe, where custome leades my hand, and feare no note of noueltie, where nothing is but auncient.

Reading.

Amongst these my countreys most familiar principles, *reading* offereth herselfe first in the entrie, chosen vpon good ground continued vpon great proofe, enrowled among the best, and the verie formost of the best, by her owne effectes, as verie many so verie profitable. For whether you marke the nature of the thing, while it is in getting, or the goodnesse therof when it is gotten, it must needs be the first, and the most frutefull principle, in training of the minde. For the letter is the first and simplest impression in the trade of teaching, and nothing before it. The knitting and iointing wherof groweth on verie infinitely, as it appeareth most plainely by daily spelling, and continuall reading, till partely by vse, and partely by argument, the child get the habit, and cunning to read well, which being once gotten, what a cluster of commodities doth it bring with all? what so euer any other, for either profit or pleasure, of force or freewill, hath published to the world, by penne or printe, for any ende, or to any vse, it is by reading all made to serue vs: in religion to loue and feare God, in law to obey and please men: in skill to entertaine knowledge, in will to expell ignorance, to do all in all, as hauing by it all helpes to do all thinges well. Wherfore I make *reading,* my first and fairest principle of all other, as being simply the first in substaunce, and leaning to none, but leading all other, and growing after so great, as it raungeth ouer all, being somwhat without other, other nothing without it: and a thing of such moment, as it is vainely begon, if it be not soundly goten, and being once sound it selfe: it deliuereth the next maister from manifest toile, and the childe himselfe from maruellous trouble, from feare where he failes not, from staggering, where he stops not, with comfort where he knowes, with courage, where he dare, a securitie to the parent, a safty to eche partie. I wishe the childe to haue his reading thus perfect, and ready, in both the English and the Latin tongue verie long before he dreame of his Grammar.

The reading of English first.

Of the which two, at whether it were better to begin, by some accident of late it did seeme somwhat doubtful: but by nature of the tongues, the verdit is giuen vp. For while our religion was restrained to the Latin, it was either the onely, or the onelyest principle in learning, to learne to read Latin: as most appropriate to that effect, which the Church then esteemed on most.

But now that we are returned home to our English abce, as most naturall to our soile, and most propter to our faith, the restraint being repealed, and we restored to libertie, we are to be directed by nature, and propertie, to read that first, which we speake first, and to care for that most, which we euer vse most: bycause we neede it most: and to begin our first learning there, where we haue most helpes, to learne it best, by familiaritie of our ordinarie language, by vnderstanding all usuall argumentes, by continuall company of our owne countreymen, all about vs speaking English and none vttering any wordes but those, which we our selues are well acquainted with, both in our learning and living.

There be two speciall, whether ye will call them rules, or notes, to be obserued in teaching, wherof the first is: That thinges be so taught, as that which goeth before, may induce that, which followeth by naturall consequence of the thing it selfe, not by erronious missorting of the deceiued chuser, who like vnto an vnskilfull hoste oftimes misplaceth euen the best of his guestes, by not knowing their degrees.

The second is, that those thinges be put vnto children, which being confessed to be most necessarie, and most proper to be learned in those yeares, haue lest sense, to their feeling, and most labour, without fainting. For can any growne man so moile him selfe, without to much cumber, with either the principles of Grammer, or cunning without booke, as a child will, the ones memorie being empty, the other being distracte with diuersitie of thoughtes? *Reason* directes yeares, and *roate* rules in youth, *reason* calls in sense and feeling of paine, *roate* runnes on apase and mindeth nothing else but either play in the ende, or a litle praise for a great deale of paines. Now praise neuer wearies, nor paine euer but wearies, and play pleaseth children with any, yea the greatest iniquitie of circunstance, whether the weather lowre, or the maister frowne, so he will giue them leaue to go. Though the Latin tongue be already discharged of all superfluities, exempt from custome, to chaunge it, and laid vp for knowledge, to cherish it: and of long time hath bene smoothed both to the eye, and to the eare: yet in course of teaching it doth not naturally draw on the English, which yet remaineth in her lees vnrackt and not fined, though it grow on verie faire. Our spelling is harder, our pronouncing harsher, our syllabe hath commonly as many letters, as the whole Latin word hath. So that both consequence, and hardnesse preferre the English. Euen here must memorie begin her first traine, and store her selfe with such stuffe, as shall laie the best foundation to religion and obedience, which beginning in these yeares, will crepe on very strongly and no lesse soundly: so that the child cannot but proue very good in age, which was so consideratly entred in his youth. What the thinges shall be, wherin both reading must trauell, and memorie must make choice, I will shew in mine Elementarie wherin the whole education before Grammer shalbe comprised.

Writing.

Next to reading followeth *writing*, in some reasonable distance after, bycause it requireth some strength of the hand, which is not so soone staied nor so stiffe to write, as the tongue is stirring and redy to read. And though writing in order of traine do succede reading, yet in nature and time it must needes be elder. For the penne or some other penlike instrument did carue and counterfeat the letter or some letterlike deuise first rawly and rudely, neither all at once: then finely and fully, when all was at once: and therby did let the eye beholde that in charact, which the voice deliuered to the eare in sounde, which being so set downe to vtter the power and knitting of the articulate voice, and afterward obserued to expresse them in deede, caused writing be much vsed as interpreter to the minde, and reading be embrased as expounder to the penne, and expressing that in force, which the penne set downe in fourme. Wherby it must needes follow, that raw and rude charactes, were the primitiue writing, which being expressed what they did signifie brought forth reading: and that experience vpon triall of their vertues made so much of them both, as she recommended them to profit, to haue them appointed for principles in the training vp of youth. So that reading being but the expresser of the written charactes must needes acknowledge and confesse her puniship to writing, of whom she tooke both her being and her beginning.

To limite any one cause how writing began, or to runne ouer the inuentours of thinges to finde out who deuised it first, were to gesse at some vncertaine, though probable coniecture, without any assuraunce, to build on, as the thing it selfe is of small importaunce, for any to tarie on. It is more then likely, wherof so euer the first charact came, that necessitie caught hold of it, to serue her owne tourne, and so enlarged it still, till it came to that perfection which we see it now in. I will neither paint out reading with such ornamentes, as it needes not, neither praise writing with such argumentes, as it craues not. For it is praise enough to a good thing to be confessed good, and what so euer is said more, is doubtfully to ground that, which is determinatly graunted, and to seeke for defence when the forte is surrendred. After that reading was reduced into forme, and brought to her best, she fined her foundresse, and is therfore aboue all praise, bycause she makes the eye, the paragon sense, by benefit of that obiect. And writing it selfe hath profited so much, since it hath bene perfited, as it now proues the proppe to remembraunce, the executour of most affaires, the deliuerer of secretes, the messager of meaninges, the enheritance of posteritie, whereby they receiue whatsoeuer is left them, in lawe to liue by, in letters to learne, in euidence to enioye. To come by this thing so much commended, so, as it may bring foorth all her effectes redily, and roundly, these notes must be kept.

That the maister learne himselfe and teach his scholer a faire letter and a fast, for plainesse and speede: That the matter of his example be pithie, and proper, to enrich the memorie with profitable prouision: and that the learning to write be not left of, vntil it be verie perfit: bycause writing being ones perfectly goten doth make a wonderful riddance in the rest of our learning. For the master may be bould to charge his child with writing of his geare, when he findes him able, to dispatch that with ease, what so euer is enioyned him. Neither shall that child euer complaine of difficultie after, which can read and write perfectly before. For first he hath purchased those two excellent faire winges, which will cause him towre vp to the top of all learning, as *Plato* in the like case of knowledge, termeth *Arithmetick* and *Geometrie*[2] his two wings wherwith to flie vp to heauen, from whence he doth fetch the true direction of his imprisoned ignorant. Secondly he hath declared eare he came to that cunning, that his wit would serue him, to proceede on further, as his winges will helpe him, to flie on faster. For in deede during the time, of writing and reading, his witte will bewraie it selfe, whether it may venture further vpon greater learning, or were best to stay at some smaller skil, vpon defect in nature. But if the child can not do that redily, which he hath rather looked on, then learned, before he remoue from his Elementarie, while his maister conceiues quickly, and he perceiues slowly, there is verie much matter offered vnto passion, wheron to worke. Which commonly brusteth out into much beating, to the dulling of the childe, and discouraging of the maister: and bycause of the to timely onset, to litle is done in to long a time, and the schoole is made a torture, which as it bringes forth delite in the ende, when learning is helde fast, so should it passe on verie pleasantly by the waye, while it is in learning: And generally this I do thinke of perfiting, and making vp, as children go on: (seing the argument it selfe doth draw my penne so forcibly forward,) that it must needes be most perfectly good. For what if oportunitie either to go any further at all, or at least to go so on, as their freindes did set them in, be suddenly cut of, either by losse of freindes, or lacke in freindes, or some other misfortune? were it not good that they had so much perfectly, as they are practised in? which being vnperfectly had, will either stand them in very small steede, or in none at all. To write and read wel which may be iointly gotten is a prety stocke for a poore boye to begin the world with all.

Writing the English hand first.

The same reasons which moued me to haue the child read English before Latin, do moue me also, to wishe him to write English before Latin, as a thing of more hardnesse, and redier in vse to aunswere all occasions. Thus farre I do thinke that all my countreymen will ioyne with me, and allow their children the vse, of their letter and penne. For those that can write and read may not gainsaie, least I aske of them why they learned themselues? If they that cannot, do mislike that they haue not, I will aske of them, why they wishe so oft for them?

Drawing.

Some controuersie before the thing be consideratly thought on, but none after, may arise about this next, which is to draw with penne or pencill, a cosen germain to faire writing, and of the selfe same charge. For penne and penknife, incke and paper, compasse and ruler, a deske and a dustboxe will set them both vp, and in these young yeares, while the finger is flexible, and the hand fit for frame, it will be fashioned easely. And commonly they that haue any naturall towardnesse to write well, haue aknacke of drawing to, and declare some euident conceit in nature bending that waye. And as iudgement by vnderstanding is a rule to the minde to discern what is honest, seemly, and sutable in matters of the minde, and such

[2] 7. De Rep.

argumentes as fall within compasse of generall reason exempt from sense: so this qualitie by drawing with penne or pencill, is an assured rule for the sense to iudge by, of the proportion and seemelines of all aspectable thinges. As he that knoweth best, how to kepe that himselfe, which is comely in fashion, can also best iudge, when comelinesse of fashion is kept by any other. And why is it not good to haue euery parte of the body: and euery power of the soule to be fined to his best? And seing that must be looked vnto long afore, which must serue vs best alwaye after, why ought we not to ground that thoroughly in youth, which must requite vs againe with grace in our age? If I or any else should seeme to contemne that principle, which brought forth *Apelles*, and that so knowen a crew of excellent painters, so many in number, so marueilous in cunning, so many statuaries, so many architectes: nay whose vse all modelling, all mathematikes, all manuaries do finde and confesse to be to so notorious and so needefull: both I and that any else might well be supposed to see very litle, not seing the use of that, which is laboured for sight, and most delitefull to see. Neither is the deuise mine, as if it were, repentance hath repulse. For what so euer I do allow in others, which for the deuise do deserue wel, I deserued not ill, in mine opinion, if I were my selfe the first deuiser therof. That great philosopher *Aristotle* in the eight booke and third chapter of his Politikes, and not there onely, as not he alone, ioyneth writing and reading, which he compriseth vnder this worde, γϱαμματικὴ, with drawing by penne or pencill, which I translate his γϱαφικὴ, both the two of one parentage and petigree, as thinges peculiarly chosen to bring vp youth, both for quantitie in profit, and for qualitie in vse. There he sayeth, that as writing and reading do minister much helpe to trafficque, to householdrie, to learning, and all publicke dealinges: so drawing by penne or pencill, is verie requisite to make a man able to iudge, what that is which he byeth of artificers and craftes men, for substaunce, forme, and fashion, durable and handsome or no: and such other necessarie seruices, besides the delitefull and pleasant.

For the setting of colours I do not much stand in, howbeit if any dexterity that waye do draw the child on, it is an honest mans liuing and I dare not condemne that famous fellowship: which is so renowned for handling the pencill. A large field is here offered to praise the praiseworthy, and to paint them out well, which painted all thinges so well, as the world still wondereth at the hearing of their workes. But the praise of painting is no part of my purpose at this time, but the appointing of it among the training principles, being so aunciently allowed, so necessarie in so many thinges, so great a ground to so gallant a misterie, as that profession is, wherof *Apelles* was: and last of all, so neare a cosen to the fairest writing, whose cradlefellow it is.

Musicke

Musicke maketh vp the summe, and is deuided into two partes, the voice and the instrument, wherof the voice resembleth reading: as yealding that to the eare, which it seeth with the eye: and the instrument writing, by counterfeting the voice, both the two in this age best to be begon, while both the voice and the iointe be pliable to the traine. The voice craueth lesse cost to execute her part, being content with so much onely, as writing, and drawing did prouide for their furniture, when they began their houshold. The instrumente seemeth to be more costly, and claimes both more care in keping, and more charge in compassing. For the pleasauntnesse of *Musick* there is no man that doth doubt, bycause it seemeth in some degree to be a medicine from heauen, against our sorowes vpon earth. Some men thinke it to be too too sweete, and that it may be either quite forborne, or not so much followed. For mine owne parte I dare not dispraise it, which hath so great defendours, and deserueth so well, and I must needes allow it, which place it among those, that I do esteeme the cheife principles, for training vp of youth, not of mine owne head alone, but by the aduise of all antiquitie, all learned philosophie, all skilfull training, which make *Musick* still one of the principles, when they handle the question, what thinges be best, to bring youth first vp in. If I had sought occasion of raunging discours which I still auoide, but where the opening of some point, doth lighten the thing, and may delite the reader, whom flatte and stearne setting downe, by waye of *aphorisme*, would soone weary, (though many not of the meanest would allow of that kinde exceeding well:) I might haue found out many digressions long agoe, or if I had taken holde of that which hath bene offered, I haue mette with many such, since I began first to write: but of all, in all sortes I do finde any, wherin speeche might so spreede all the sailes, which she hath, and the penne might vse, all the pencilling, which she can: as in painting out the praise and ornamentes of *Musick*. The matter is so ample, the ground so large, the reasons so many, which sound to her renowne: the thing it selfe so auncient, and so honorable, so generall, and so priuate, so in Churches, and so without, so in all ages, and in all places, both highely preferred, and richely rewarded: the princesse of delites, and the delite of princes: such a pacifier in passion, such a maistres to the minde, so excellent in so many, so esteemed by so many, as euen multitude makes me wonder, and with all to staie my hand, for feare that I shall not easely get thence, if I enter once in. I will not therfore digresse: bycause there is better stuffe in place, and more fit for my purpose, then the praise of *Musick* is. The Philosophers, and Physicians, do allow the straining, and recoyling of the voice in children, yea though they crie, and baule, beside their singing, and showting: by the waie of exercise to stretche, and kepe open the hollow passages, and inward pipes of the tender bulke, whereby *Musick* will proue a double principle both for the soule, by the name of learning, and for the body, by the waye of exercise, as hereafter shall appeare.

But for the whole matter of *Musick*, this shalbe enough for me to say at this time, that our countrey doth allow it: that it is verie comfortable to the wearyed minde: a preparatiue to perswasion: that he must needes haue a head out of proportion, which cannot perceiue: or doth not delite in the proportions of number, which speake him so faire: that it is best learned in childehood, when it can do least harme, and may best be had: that if the constitution of man both for bodie and soule, had not some naturall, and nighe affinitie with the concordances of *Musick*, the force of the one, would not so soone stirre vp, the cosen motion in the other. It is wonderfull that is writen, and strange that we see, what is wrought therby in nature of *Physick*, for the remedying of some desperate diseases.

Miscontentment.

Aunswere.

And yet there groweth some miscontentment with it, though it be neuer so good, and that not only in personages of whom I make small account, but in some verie good, honest, and well disposed natures, though to stearnly bent, which neuerthelesse, for al their stearnnes, wil resigne ouer their sentence, and alter their opinion, sometimes of themselues vpon deeper meditation, what the thing in it selfe is, sometime by inducement, when they fal in with other which are better resolued: but most cheifly then, when *Musick* it selfe considerately applyed, hath for a while obtained the fauorable vse of their listning eares. The science it selfe hath naturally a verie forcible strength to trie and to tuche the inclination of the minde, to this or that affection, thorough the propertie of number, wheron it consisteth, which made the *Pythagorian,* and not him alone to plat the soule out so much vpon number. It is also very pleasant for the harmonie and concent, wherby the hearer discouers his disposition, and lettes pleasure playe vpon the bitte, and dalye with the bridle, as delite will not be drowned, nor driuen to hidebare. For which cause *Musick* moueth great misliking to some men that waye, as to great a prouoker to vaine delites, still laying baite, to draw on pleasure: still opening the minde, to the entrie of lightnesse. And in matters of religion also, to some it seemes offensiue, bycause it carieth awaye the eare, with the sweetnesse of the melodie, and bewitcheth the minde with a *Syrenes* sounde, pulling it from that delite, wherin of duetie it ought to dwell, vnto harmonicall fantasies, and withdrawing it, from the best meditations, and most vertuous thoughtes to forreine conceites, and wandring deuises. For one aunswere to all, if abuse of a thing, which may be well vsed, and had her first being to be well vsed, be a sufficient condemnation to the thing that is abused, let glotonie forbid meat, distempering drinke, pride apparell, heresie religion, adulterie mariage, and why not, what not? Nay which of all our principles shall stand, if the persons blame, shal blemish the thing? We read foolish bookes, wherat to laugh, nay wherin we learne that, which we might and ought forbeare: we write strange thinges, to serue our owne fansie, if we sway but a litle to any lewde folly: we paint and draw pictures, not to be set in Churches, but such as priuate houses hide with curtaines, not to saue the colours, but to couer their owners, whose lightnesse is discouered, by such lasciuious obiectes. Shall reading therfore be reft from religion? shall priuate, and publike affaires, lease the benefit of writing? shall sense forgoe his forsight, and the beautifier of his obiect? Change thou thy direction, the thinges will follow thee more swifte to the good, then the other to the bad, being capable of both, as thinges of vse be, and yet bending to the better. Mans faulte makes the thing seeme filthie. Applie thou it to the best, the choice is before thee. It is the ill in thee, which seemeth to corrupte the good in the thing, which good, though it be defaced by thy ill, yet shineth it so cleare, as it bewraieth the naturall beautie, euen thorough the cloude of thy greatest disgracing. *Musick* will not harme thee, if thy behauiour be good, and thy conceit honest, it will not miscary thee, if thy eares can carie it, and sorte it as it should be. Appoint thou it well, it will serue thee to good purpose: if either thy manners be naught, or thy iudgement corrupt, it is not *Musick* alone which thou doest abuse, neither cannest thou auoide that blame, which is in thy person, by casting it on *Musick,* which thou hast abused and not she thee. And why should those people, which can vse it rightly, forgoe their owne good, or haue it with embasing to pleasure some peuishe, which will not yet be pleased? or seeke to heale sores, which will festure still, and neuer skinne, though ye plaster them daily, to your owne displeasure. But am I not to tedious? This therfore shall suffise now, that children are to be trained vp in the Elementarie schoole, for the helping forward of the abilities of the minde, in these fower things, as commaunded vs by choice and commended by custome. *Reading,* to receiue that which is bequeathed vs by other, and to serue our memorie with that which is best for vs. *Writing* to do the like thereby for others, which other haue done for vs, by writing those thinges which we daily vse: but most of al to do most for our selues: *Drawing* to be a directour to sense, a delite to sight, and an ornament to his obiectes. *Musick* by the instrument, besides the skill which must still encrease, in forme of exercise to get the vse of our small ioyntes, before they be knitte, to haue them the nimbler, and to put Musicianes in minde, that they be no brawlers, least by some swash of a sword, they chaunce to lease a iointe, an irrecouerable iewell vnaduisedly cast away. *Musick* by the voice, besides her cunning also, by the waye of *Phisick,* to sprede the voice instrumentes within the bodie, while they be yet but young. As both the kindes of *Musick* for much profit, and more pleasure, which is not voide of profit in her continuing kinde. All foure for such vses as be infinite in number, as they know best, which haue most knowledge and the parentes must learne, to lead their children to them: and the children must beleue, to winne their parentes choice, which may be in all, if they themselues liste, if they liste not, in no more then they like, their restraining conceite neither bridling, nor abbridging any other mans entent, which seeketh after more. And though all young ones be not thus farre trained, yet we may perceiue, that all these be vsed, in particular proofes, and not to be refused in generall trade, where all turnes be serued, by setting foor[t]h of all thinges that be generally in vse, though not generally used. Thus much of these thinges at this time, which I do meane by Gods grace to handle in their owne Elementarie, as precisely and yet, as properly, as euer I can.

CHAPTER 6.

Of exercises and training the body. How necessarie a thing exercise is. What health is, and how it is maintained: what sicknesse is, how it commeth, and how it is preuented. What a parte exercise playeth in the maintenaunce of health. Of the student and his health. That all exercises though they stirre some one part most, yet helpe the whole bodie.

THE soule and bodie being coparteners in good and ill, in sweete and sowre, in mirth and mourning, and hauing generally a common sympathie, and a mutuall feeling in all passions: how can they be, or rather why should they be seuered in traine? the one made stronge, and well qualified, the other left feeble, and a praye to infirmitie? will ye haue the minde to obtaine those thinges, which be most proper vnto her, and most profitable vnto you, when they be obtained? Then must ye also haue a speciall care, that the bodie be well appointed, for feare it shrink, while ye be either in course to get them, or in case to vse them. For as the powers of the soule come to no proofe, or to verie small, if they be not fostered by their naturall traine, but wither and dye, like corne not reaped, but suffered to rotte by negligence of the owner, or by contention in chalenge: euen so, nay much more, the bodie being of it selfe lumpishe and earthy, must needes either dye in drowsinesse, or liue in loosenesse, if it be not stirred and trained diligently to the best. And though the soule, as the fountaine of life, and the quickner of the body, may and will beare it out for some while, thorough valiauntnesse of courage: yet weaknesse will not be alwayes dissembled, but in the ende will and must bewraie her owne want, euen then perauenture, when it were most pittie. Many notable personages for stomacke and courage, many excellent men for learning and skill, in most and best professions haue then left their liues, thorough the plaine weaknesse, of their contemned bodies, when they put their countries in most apparent and gladsome hope of rare and excellent effectes, the one of valiantnesse and manhood, the other of knowledge and skill. Seing therfore there is a good in them both, which by diligent endeuour may be auaunced to that, for which it was ordained, and by negligent ouersight, doeth either decaye quite, or proues not so well, as otherwayes it might, I maye not slightly passe ouer the bodies good, being both so neare, and so necessarie a neighbour unto the soule: considering I haue bestowed so much paines already, and must bestow much more, in the seruice of the soule: nay rather considering I deale with the bodie but once, and that onely here, wheras I entreat of the soule, and the furniture therof in what so euer I shall medle with, in my whole course hereafter. If common sense did not teach vs the necessitie of this point, and extreme feeblenes did not force men to confesse, how great feates they could do, and how actiue they would proue, if their weake limmes and failing ioyntes, would aunswere the lusty courage, and braue swinge of their fierie and fresh spirites: I would take paines to perswade them by argumentes, both of proofe in experience, and of reason in nature, that as it is easie, so it were needefull to helpe the body by some traine, not left at random to libertie, but brought in to forme of ordinarie discipline, generally in all men, bycause all men neede helpe, for necessarie health, and ready execution of their naturall actions: but particularly for those men, whose life is in leasure, whose braynes be most busied, and their wittes most wearied, in which kinde studentes be no one small part, but the greatest of all, which so vse their mindes as if they cared not for their bodies, and yet so neede their bodies, as without the strength and soundnesse wherof, they be good for nothing, but to moane themselues, and to make other maruell, why they take no more heede, how to do that long, which they do so well, being a thing within compasse of their owne care, and knowledge. For who is so grosse, as he will denie that exercise doth good, and that so great, as is without comparison, seing olde *Asclepiades* is by *Galene* confuted, and stawled for an asse: as *Erasitratus* also his dissembling friend? or who is so sore tied either to studie, or to stocks, as he cannot stirre himselfe if he will, or ought not if he may? But the matter being confessed, euen by the most idle, and vnweildy to be healthfull and good, I shall neede no more reason, to procure assent, and allowaunce for exercise. My whole trauell therfore must be to finde out, and set foorth, what shalbe requisite to the perfourmaunce of this point, concerning the traine and exercising of the body, that it may proue healthy, and liue long: and be ready to assist, all the actions of the minde.

Wherin therfore consisteth the health of the bodie, and how is it to be maintained vntill such time, as nature shall dismantle, and pull it downe her selfe? To aunswere this question, and withall to declare, how great an officer to health exercise is: I will first shew, wherin health doth consiste, and how diseases do come: then how health is maintained, and disease auoided: Last of all how great a parte is appointed for exercise to plaie in the perfourmaunce therof, bycause I saye, and not I alone, but *Galen* also that great Physician, neither *Galen*[3] onely, though sufficient alone, but all that euer liued, and were cheife of that liuerie, that who so can applie the minde well with learning, and the bodie with exercise, shall make both a wise minde, and a healthfull bodie in their best kinde. Wherfore seing I haue set downe wherin the traine of the minde doth consist, so much as the Elementarie course doth admit, and must perfourme, and so farre as these my Positions require at this time, whose profession is not to tary, though it tuche them: I wil now handle that other part of exercise, wherwith the bodie is either to be kept in health, or to be helpt to health: and that not onely in the Elementarie, to whom this treatise should seeme to aunswere, but also in the generall student during his whole life: which must alwaye rule himselfe by those circunstances, which direct the application of exercise, according to time, age, &c. and shalbe handled herafter.

[3] 1. De sani. tuen.

What is health and sicknesse.

There be in the bodie of man, the force of foure elementes, fire and aire, water and earth, and the pith of their primitiue, and principall qualities, heat and couldnesse, moysture and drynesse, which the Physicians call the similarie partes, of the similitude and likenesse that they haue, not the one to the other, but the partes of eche to their owne whole, bycause euerie least part, or degree of these great ones, beare the name of the whole, as euerie part or parcell of fier, is called fier, no lesse then the whole fier, of water, water, of aier, aier, of earth, earth, and euerie degree of heat, is heat, of cold, is cold, of moysture, is moysture, of drynesse, is drynesse, though greater and smaller, lesse and more, be epithetes vnto them, as either their quantitie, or qualitie doth sprede or close.

There be also in the same bodie certaine instrumentall partes, compounded and consisting in substance of the similarie, which the bodie doth vse in the executing of the naturall functions, and workinges therof. Now when these similarie partes be so tempered, and disposed, as no one doth excede any other in proportion to ouerrule, but all be as one in consent to preserue: and the instrumentall partes also be so correspondent one to an other, in composition and greatnesse, in number and measure, as nature thorough the temperature of the first, may absolutely vse the perfectnesse of the last, to execute and perfourme without let or stoppe, what appertaineth to the maintenaunce of her selfe: it is called health, and the contrarie, disease, both in the whole bodie, and in euery part therof. In the whole bodie by distemperature of the whole, in some part, by composition, out of place, and disioynted, by greatnes, being to bigge or to small: by measure, being misshapen and fashionles: by number, being to many and needlesse: or to few, and failing. This health whether it be in the middle degre, wherin all executions be complete without any sensible let: and no infirmitie appeareth, that the bodie feeles with any plaine offence: Or if it be in the perfectest degree, which is so seldom, as neuer any saw, bycause of great frailty, and brittlenesse in our nature: it neuer continueth in one estate, but altereth still, and runnes to ruyne, without both speedy and daily, nay without hourely reparation.

The causes which alter, and chaunge it so, be somtime from within the bodie, and were borne with it: sometime from without, and yet not without daunger. From within, the verie propertie and pithe of our originall substance, and matter whence we grew, altereth vs first, which as it beginneth, and groweth in moysture, so it endeth, and stayeth in drynesse, and in the ende decayeth the bodie with to much drynesse, which extreame though naturall withering, we call olde age, which though it come by course, and commaundement of nature, yet beareth it the name, and title of disease, bycause it decayeth the bodie, and deliuereth it to death. From within also, the continuall rebating, and falling awaye of somwhat from the bodie, occasioneth much chaunge, nay that is most cause of greatest chaunge, and killeth incontinent by meere defect, if it be not supplyed.

To these two causes of inward alteration, there aunswere two other forreine causes, both vnholesome, and perillous, the aire, which enuironneth vs, and violence, which is offered vs. The former of the two, decaing our health with to much heat, cold, drynesse, and moysture of it selfe: or by noysomnesse of the soile, and corruption in circunstance. The second, by strong hand brusing, or breaking, wounding or wiping awaie, of some one part of the bodie, or els killing the whole consort of the bodie with the soule, and taking away life from it. These foure ouerthrowes of our bodies and health, olde age, waste, aire, and violence, finde by helpe of nature, and arte, certaine oppositions, which either diuert them quite, if they maye be auoided, or kepe them of longer, if they maye be differred, or mittigate their malice, when it is perceiued. For forreine violence, foresight will looke to, where casualtie commaundes not, and cannot be foreseene. For infection by the aire, that it do not corrupte and marre so much as it would, wisedome will prouide, and defende the bodie from the iniuries, and wronges therof. That olde age grow not on to fast, circunspectnes in diet, consideration in clothes, diligence in well doing, wil easely prouide, both for the minde not to enfect, first it selfe and then the bodie: and for the bodie not to enforce the minde, by too impotent desires. That waste weare not, meat takes in chardge, to supplie that is drye, and decayeth: drinke promiseth to restore moysture, when it doth diminishe: the breath it selfe, and arteriall pulse, looke to heating and cooling. And *Physick* in generall professing foresight to preuent euills, and offering redresse, when they haue done harme, so not incurable, doth direct both those and all other meanes. Now in all these helpes, and most beneficiall aides of our afflicted nature, which deuiseth all meanes to saue her selfe harmelesse, and deliteth therin, when she is discharged of infirmities, to much stuffes and stiffles, to litle straites and pines, both vndoe the naturall. To much meat cloyes, to litle faintes, both perishe the principall. To much liquour drownes, to litle dryes, both corrupt the carcasse. Heat burnes, cold chilles, in excesse both to much, in defect both to litle, and both causes to decaie. Mediocritie preserueth not onely in these but in whatsoeuer els.

Exercise.

But now what place hath exercise here? to helpe nature by motion in all these her workinges, and wayes for health: to encrease and encourage the naturall heat, that it maye digest quickly and expell strongly: to fashion and frame all the partes of the bodie to their naturall and best hauiour: to helpe to rid needelesse, and superfluous humours: reffuse and reiected excrementes, which nature leaues for naught, when she hath sufficiently fed, and wisheth rather they were seene abrode, then felt within. And be not these great benefites? to defend the body by defeating diseases? to stay the minde, by strengthening of her meane? to assist nature being both daily, and daungerously, assailed both within and without? to helpe life to continue long? to force death, to kepe farre a loufe?

Now as all constitutions be not of one and the same mould, and as all partes be not moued alike, with any one thing: so the exercises must alter, and be appropriate to each: that both the constitution may be continued in her best kinde, and all the partes preserued to their best vse, which exercises being compared among themselues one to an other, be more or lesse, but being applyed to the partie kepe alwayes in a meane, when they meane to do good. Concerning students, for whose health my care is greatest, the lesse they eate, the lesse they neede to voide: and therfore small diet in them, best preuenteth all superfluities, which they cannot auoide, if their diet be great and their exercise small. Their exercise must also be very moderate, and not alter to much, for feare of to great distemperature in that, which must continue moderate: and with all it should be ordinarie, that the habit may be holesome, and sudden chaunge giue no cause of greater inconuenience. Wherfore to auoide distemperature the enemie to health, and so consequently to life, and to maintaine the naturall constitution so, as it may serue to the best, wherin her duetie lyeth, and liue to the longest, that in nature it can, besides the diet, which must be small, as nature is a pickler, and requires but small pittaunce: besides clothing which should be thin euen from the first swadling to harden, and thick the flesh: I do take this traine by exercise, which I wishe to be ioyned with learning, to be a marueilous furtherer.

But for diet to auoide inward daungers, and clothing to auert outward iniuries, and all such preuentions, as are not proper to teachers, though in communitie more proper then to any common man: I set them ouer to parentes, and other well willers, which will see to them, that they faile not in those thinges: and if they do, will fly to Physicians, by their helpe to salue that, which themselues may forsee. For exercises I will deale, which to commend more then they will commend them selues, when I shall shew both what they be, and the particular profites of euery one of them, which I chuse from the rest, were me thinke verie needlesse, and cheifly to me, which seeme sufficiently to praise them, in that I do place them among principles of prerogatiue. But as in the soule I did picke out certaine pointes, whervnto I applyed the training principles: so likewise in the bodie, may I not also seuer some certaine partes, whervnto my preceptes must principally be conformed? that shall not neede. For as in the soule the frute of traine doth better and make complete euen that which I tuched not, and so consequently the whole soule: so in the bodie, those exercises which seeme to be appointed for some speciall partes, bycause they stirre those partes most, do qualifie the whole bodie, and make it most actiue. Wherefore as there I did promise not to anatomise the soule, as neither dealing with Diuines nor Philosophers: so do I not here make profession to shew the anatomie of the bodie, as medling neither with Physicians nor Surgeans, otherwise then any of them foure can helpe me in exercise. To the which effect, and ende, I will onely cull out from whence I can, such speciall notes, as both Philosophers, and Phisicians do know to be most true, and both the learned, and vnlearned, will confesse to be for them: and such also, as the training maisters may easely both helpe, and encrease in their owne triall. For both reason, and rule, do alwaye commaunde, that the maister be by, when exercise is vsed, thorough whose ouerlooking the circunstance is kept, which helpeth to health, and the contrarie shunned, which in exercise doth harme. In the elder yeares, reason at the elbow must serue the student, as in these younger, the maisters preference helpes to direct the child.

But to ioyne close with our traine. What partes be they in our bodie, vpon whom exercise is to shew this great effecte? or what be the powers therof, which must still be stirred, so to say, and establish the perpetuitie of health, not in themselues alone, but in the whole bodie, by them? Where ioyntes be to bend, where stringes to tye, where synewes to stirre, where streatchers to straine, there must needes be motion: or els stifnesse will follow, and vnweildynesse withall: where there be conduites to conuey the blood, which warmeth, canales to carie the spirite, which quickneth, pipes to bestow the aire, which cooleth, passage to dismisse excrements which easeth, there must needes be spreding, to kepe the currant large, and eche waie open, for feare of obstructions, and sudden fainting. Where to much must needes marre, there must be forcing out, where to litle must nedes lame, there must be letting in: where thickning threates harme, there thinning fines the substance: where thinning is to much, there thickning must do much, and to knit vp all in short, all those offices, whervnto our bodie serueth naturally, either for inward bestowing of nurriture, and maintenaunce of life: or for outward motion, and executions of vse, must be cherished and nusled so, as that they do by nature well, and truely, they may do by traine, both long, and strongly. I shall not neede to name the partes, all in one ruk, as of set purpose, which be knowen by their effectes: and the exercises also themselues will shew for whom they serue. But for example first in the partes let vs see, whether we can discern them by their working, and properties, that therby the exercise may be pickte, which is most proper to helpe such effectes.

1. Who doth not streight waye conceiue, that the lunges or lightes be ment, when he heareth of an inward part, which prouideth winde for the harte, to allay his heat, and to minister some clammy matter vnto it, whence he may take aire, most fit for his functions, and not at the sudden be forced to vse any forreine?

2. Or who doth not by and by see, that the harte is implyed, when he heareth of an other inward part, which is the spring, and fountaine, of the vitall spirite and facultie, the seat and sender out of naturall heat, the occasion and cause of the arteriall pulse, which by one arterie, and way, receiueth cooling from the lunges, by an other, sendeth the vitall spirite, the hote, and hurling blood, thorough out the whole bodie?

3. Or who is so grosse, as not to gesse at the liuer, when he heareth of an other inward part, which is the cheife instrument of nurriture, the workhouse of thicke and grosse blood: that feedeth the life and soule: when it desireth meat, and drinke, and what is els necessarie: which conueieth blood thorough the veines to nurrish all partes of the bodie, with the naturall spirit in it, if there be any, verie darke and heauie?

He can tel what the parte is.

4. Nay hath he any braine, which seeth not the braine plainly laid before him, when he heareth a part of mans bodie named, which breedeth a sowlish, and life spirite, as most pure, so most precious, and rather a qualitie then a bodie, and vseth it partly to further the working of that princely, and principall part of mans soule, wherby he vnderstandeth and reasoneth: partly to helpe the instrumentes of sense, and motion, by meane of the sineues, neuer suffering them to lacke spirite: which is the cheife and capitall cause, why these instrumentes do their dueties well? And so forth in all the partes aswell without, as within sight, whose properties when one heareth and finding that they be helped by such a motion he can forthwith say, that such an exercise is good for such a part.

1. Now againe for exercises. Who hearing that moderate running doth warme the whole body, strengthneth the naturall motions, prouoketh appetite, helpeth against distilling of humours and catarres, and driueth them some other waie:

2. Or that daunsing beside the warmth, driueth awaye numnesse, and certaine palsies, comforteth the stomacke, being cumbred with weaknes of digestion, and confluence of raw humours, strengtheneth weake hippes, fainting legges, freatishing feete:

3. Or that ryding also is healthfull for the hippes and stomacke: that it cleareth the instrumentes of all the senses, that it thickneth thinne shankes: that it stayeth loose bellies:

4. Or that loud speaking streatcheth the bulke exerciseth the vocalle instrumentes, practiseth the lungues, openeth the bodie, and all the passages therof:

5. Or that loud reading scoureth all the veines, stirreth the spirites thorought out all the entraulles, encreaseth heat, suttileth the blood, openeth the arteries, suffereth not superfluous humours to grow grosse and thicke: who, say I, hearing but of these alone in taste for all, or of all together by these alone, doth not both see the partes, which are preserued, the exercise which preserueth, and the matter wherin?

Wherfore seing exercise is such a thing, that so much enableth the bodie, whom the soule hath for companion in all exploites, a comfort being lightsome, a care being lothesom, a courage being healthy, a clog being heauie, I will, bycause I must, if I meane to do well, plat forth the whole place of exercising the bodie, at ones for all ages.

CHAPTER 7.

THE BRAUNCHING, ORDER, AND METHODE, KEPT IN THIS DISCOURS OF EXERCISES.

BYCAUSE the speciall marke wherat I shoote, is to bring the minde forward to his best, by those meanes which I take to be best, wherin I must of force continue verie long, as in my principall and cheife subiecte, and in no place sauing this, entreat of the bodie, but onely how to apply that to it, which I pitche downe here: I thinke it good therefore in this place to perfit, and handle at full the whole title of exercises with all the cicunstances belonging thervnto, so sufficiently and fully, as my simple skill can aspire vnto: and as the present occasion of a position or passage vseth to require, leauing that which I do not medle with, to those that shall professe the thing, ether for their owne, or for their childrens health, wherin I will kepe this methode and manner of proceeding. 1. First I wil note somewhat, generally concerning all exercises. 2. Secondly I will chuse out some especiall exercises, which vpon good consideration I do take to be most proper, and propitious to schooles, and scholers. 3. Thirdly, I will applye the circunstances, required in exercise to euerie of them, so neare as I can, that there be no error committed in the executing. For the better the thing is, if it hit right, the more dangerous it proueth, if it misse of that right. 4. Last of all I will shew the training maister, how to furnish himselfe thoroughly, in this professed exercising: bycause he must both applie the minde with learning, and the bodie with mouing, at diuerse times, refreshing himselfe, with varietie and chaunge.

But in handling of these foure pointes, I meane to rippe vp no idle question: I terme that idle, where health is the ende, and the question no helpe to it, but cause to discours, and delaye of precept. Such questions be these: who first found out the arte of exercise called *Gymnastice*, or whether it belong to the Physician or no: being a preseruatiue to health: or who first deuised the particular exercises: or who were most famous for the executing therof, and a number of such like discoursory argumentes, which learned men hauing leasure at will, as a schoolemaister hath not, and willing to wade farre, as my selfe could wish, haue mined out of the bowelles of antiquitie, and entraules of authoritie, sometimes sadly, and saing in deede much, vpon euident and apparent testimonies, sometimes simply, and surmising but some such thing, by very light and slight coniectures: oftimes supported by bare guesse, at some silly word, or some more naked warrant. Wherfore to the matter.

CHAPTER 8.

Of exercise in generall and what it is. And that it is Athleticall for games, Martiall for the fielde, Physicall for health, præparatiue before, postparatiue after the standing exercise: some within daores, for foule whether, some without for faire.

The diuision of exercises.

ALL exercises were first deuised, and so in deede serued, either for games and pastime, for warre and seruice, or for suretie of health and length of life, though somtime all the three endes did concurre in one, sometimes they could not. For why might not an healthfull, and a sound body, both serue in the fielde for a soldiar, and in the sand for a wrastler? But we seldom reade, that the *athleticall* constitution whose ende was gaming, whose exercise was pastime, whose diet was vnmeasurable for any man to vse, did either deliuer the world an healthfull body, being strained beyond measure, or a courageous soldiar, being vnweildy to fight, as one compounded and made of fat and fog, brawnie and burdenous.

Athleticall.

The *athleticall* and gaming exercises, were in generall assemblies, to winne some wager, to beare awaie the prise, to be wondered at of the world, or to set foorth the solemnities of their festiuall seruice, and ceremonies in the honour of their idoles: or in publike spectacle to adourne and set foorth, the triumphant and victorious shewes, the sumptuous and costly deuises of their princes and states. Wherin we reade, that particular men haue shewed such effectes of strength, and sturring, by the helpe of exercise, and traine, as nature her selfe could neuer attaine vnto, though she furthered the feat, and got her selfe the worst, both by empairing of health, and hastning on of death, thorough straining to much. It is more then marueilous to thinke on, and yet we finde it of verie good recorde, what and how incredible weight, both of liuing creatures, and massier mettal, one mans force hath bene noted to haue borne, by being only vsed to that burthen. Would any man beleue it, if it were not of good writen credit, that one *Milo* so strutted himselfe, so pitcht his feet, so peysed his bodie, as he remained vnremoueable from his place, being haled at and pulde by a number of people. *Actiuitie* hath wrought wonders, *swiftnesse* incredible thinges, and what propertie what not? where nature and ambition were backt with exercise and good will, to do but one thing well.

Martiall.

For the vse of warre, and defence, it is more then euident, that exercise beares the bell: Can one haue a bodie to abide cold, not to melte with heat, not to starue for hunger, not to dye for thirst, not to shrinke at any hardnesse, almost beyond nature, and aboue common reache, if he neuer haue it trained? will nimblenesse of limmes awaie with all labour, surpasse all difficulties, of neuer so diuers, and dangerous groundes, pursue enemies to vanquish, reskue freinds to saue, retire from danger without harme, thrust it selfe into daunger without daunger, where no traine before made acquaintance with trauell? Whervpon called the *Romaines* their whole armie *Exercitus,* but bycause it consisted of a valiant number of exercised and trained men? which were not to seeke at a sudden, bycause they had vsed armes before? how could common weales where the territory was but small, and the enhabitantes few, haue still deliuered themselues from mightier assailantes, then they seemed defendantes? or in continuall threates, of ieleous neighbours, how could they still haue kept their owne, if that small territorie, had not bene thoroughly employed, and that petie paucitie gallantly trained? wherby it was able for hardnesse and sufferance to abide what not? For actiuitie and manhood, to haue mastered whom not? or at the least had good meanes, not to receiue any foile, where onely the huger number, and the vntrained multitude, were to trie the masterie in fielde against them?

Physicall.

For health it is most manifest that exercise is a mighty great mistresse, whether it be to confirme that which we haue by nature, or to procure that which we haue not by nature: or to recouer that by industrie, and diligence, which we haue almost lost, by misfortune and negligence. The exercises which do serue to this healthy end, do best serue for this my purpose, and though an healthfull body be most apt and actiue, both for gaming to get wagers, and for warring to winne victories, yet in my exercises, I neither meane to dally with the gamester, not to fight with the warrier, but to marke which way I may best saue studentes, who haue most neede of it: being still assailed by those enemies of health, which waxe more eager and hoat, the more weake and cold that exercise is.

What is exercise?

This exercise of ours by forme of definition, is said to be a vehement, and a voluntarie stirring of ones body, which altereth the breathing, whose ende is to maintaine health, and to bring the bodie to a verie good habit. Doth not exercise at this her first entry offer to performe so much as I did vndertake for her? health of the body, and an healthy habit of all the limmes: which two effectes, bycause they be good, who doth not desire them? and being got by exercise, why is it not in price? and being reducible to order, why should it not be in traine? They that write of exercise, make three degrees in it, wherof they call the first a preparatiue, in Greek παρασκευαστικόν, the next simply by the name of exercise γυμνάσιον the third a postparatiue, in Greek ἀποθεραπευτικὸν. The preparatiue serued, not to passe rudely, and roughly into the maine exercise, without qualifying the bodie by degrees before, bycause sudden alteration workes ill disposition. The postparatiue or apotherapeutike followeth the maine exercise, to reduce the body by gentle degrees, to the same quietnesse in constitution, wherin it was, before it was so moued. Which two pointes bycause they rest most in the maisters consideration, which is to ouersee the traine, I commit them to his care: so to applie his cunning as he shall see cause in exercising his charge. And yet herein I entend to helpe him, when I shall handle the circunstances which direct exercises.

γυμνασιον.

The third degree, which is enclosed betwene these two, is that same exercise, which I praise so much, and vpon whom the other two waite, wherof, as writers make to many, and to finely minced distinctions, so I make account but of one at this time, wherof I do make two braunches, or spieces, the one to be vsed within dores, and the other abroade, that whether the weather be faire or fowle, the exercise in some kinde may neuer faile.

CHAPTER 9.

Of the particular exercises. Why I do appoint so manie, and how to iudge of them, or to deuise the like.

I WILL not here runne thorough all the kindes of exercises that be named either by *Galene* or any other writer, wherof many be discontinued, many be yet in vse, but out of the whole heape I haue pickt out these for within dores, *lowd speaking, singing, lowd reading, talking, laughing, weaping, holding the breath, daunsing, wrastling, fensing, and scourging the Top*. And these for without dores, *walking, running, leaping, swimming, riding, hunting, shooting, and playing at the ball*. Wherof though the very most be vsed oftimes, not in nature of exercises, but either of pleasure, or necessitie, yet they be all such, as will serue well that waie, and be so made account of among the best writers, that deale in this kinde: and for that some of them maye be said to be most proper to men, and farre aboue boyes plaie: you must remember, that I deale for all studentes, and not for children alone, to whom it is in choice, besides all these to deuise other for their good, as circunstance shal lead them. There may also be reasons, to perswade some men to mislike of, I do not thinke all, but I suppose some, of these thinges, which I do appoint, as both commendable and profitable exercises, with whom I will not here striue, but desire them to iudge of me, without preiudice, and to stay their sentence, vntill they see in what sorte I allow them. For knowing the cause of offence, I might seeme very simple, if I should simply allow that, which is disallowed vpon reason, and not misliked without manifest shew of probable cause: and so to reserue the thing, as I did not remoue the blame. They must also thinke that nothing is abused, but that both may and ought to be well vsed, which well, they must vse, and refuse the ill: seing where misuse draweth blame, there right vse deserueth praise.

Therfore I wishe those that be of yeares, and abilitie to guide themselues to call circunstance to counsell, and consideration to aduise. For as consideration shapeth the circunstance, so circunstance is a thing, which maketh all that is done, either to please or displease: to be sent awaie with a cutting checke: or to be bid tarie, with a cheary contenaunce. As for the child in whom wisdom wanteth, to way with discretion, what it is that he doeth, the maister alone must supplie all wantes, or beare all blames, though it be but a simple recompence, to blame wante of consideration, when harme is receiued. Some man may also say, what needes so many, and mislike the multitude. Of many to chuse some, is vsuall in all choice, and where store is, why should choice be stinted? he may lessen the number, that alloweth but of one, and I haue pickt out the likest, to satisfie all in diuersities of liking, who so shall like any of these, may vse them with me, or vpon the like ground, may deuise himselfe other. In handling of eche of these, I will first shew for what partes, to what end, and in what manner, they be profitable and holesome being moderatly vsed: then for whom, and with what daunger, they be strained to the contrarie.

CHAPTER 10.

Of lowd speaking. How necessarie, and how proper an exercise it is for a scholler.

THE exercise of the voice which in Latin they name *vociferatio*, in Greek *ἀναφωνησις*, as them *φωνασκόι* which were the training maisters, in English maye be tearmed lowd speaking, of the height: for though it vse all the degrees, which be in the voice, yet is it most properly to take his name, of the lowdest and shrillest, as the most audible in sound, and therfore fittest to giue the name, as all thinges els receiue theirs, of some one qualitie of most especiall note. The auncient *Physicians* entertaine it among exercises, bycause it stirreth the bulke, and all those instrumentes, which serue for the deliuerie of voice, and vtterance of speeche: bycause it aideth, dilateth, and comforteth the lunges in his windworke, it encreaseth, cleanseth, strengtheneth, and fineth the naturall heat: it maketh the sound and soueraigne partes of the bodie strong and pure: and not lightly to be assailed by any disease: it mendeth the colour, and cheareth the countenaunce. Now that it hath these properties they do proue by naturall argumentes. That it practiseth and stirreth the inward partes, and vocall instrumentes, no man may denie, which will confesse, that the mouth alone, is the onely port and passage for speeche. That it encreaseth the naturall heat, the breath it selfe doth most euidently declare, bycause it is alwaye exceeding warme, when one exerciseth the voice, it is so thronged and crusshed with taking in and letting out. That it cleanseth and cleareth, there be two causes to proue: the one is, bycause it maketh the flesh more fine and thinne, and smoother to the hand, not onely thorough stretching and straining the skinne, but by remouing excrementes, which naturally thicken and make rugged. The other is, for that by mouing the vocall instrumentes the inward moysture consumeth and wasteth, as it doeth appeare by that thicke and grosse vapour, which proceedeth out of his mouth that speaketh alowd, and other congealed excrementes resting of olde in other passages, which this exercise expelled from the inward partes. That it both fines and strengthens the naturall heat, hereby it is more then plaine. For that the inward vesselles and pipes be scoured thereby, and sundry superfluities expelled both at the nose, and mouth, which as they darkened, weakned, and thickned the naturall heat, when they were within the bodie: so being dismissed themselues, they leaue it pure, fine, and strong, whereby the partes being sound and cleare more strength groweth on to healthward, and lesse to disease. Hervpon it falleth out, that this exercise of the voice, must needes be a singular helpe for them, which haue their inwarde partes troubled with moysture, and be of cold constitution, as also for such, as be troubled with weaknesse, or pewkishnesse of stomacke, with vomiting, or bytter rifting, with hardnesse of digestion, with lothing of their meat, with feeding that feedes not, with faintnesse, with naughty constitution, that corrupteth the blood, with dropsies, with painfull fetching their breath, or but then easely, when they sit vpright, with consumptions, with any long disease, in the breast or midrife, with apostemes which are broken within the bulke, with quartane agues, with fleame, and also for all those, which be on the mending hand, after sicknesse: for those that are troubled with the scurfe, or Egyptian lepre, called *Elephantiasis*, or whose bellies be so weake, as they cannot avoide, but watry and thin excrementes, for the hikup, for the voice, and her instrumentes, whether naturally resolued, or casually empaired.

Now as this exercise aduisedly, and orderly vsed, is verie good for those effectes in these partes, so rashly and rudely ventured vpon, it is not without daunger of doing harme, and cheifly to those which neuer vsed it before: it filleth the head and makes it heauie, it dulleth the instrumentes of the senses, which are in the head. It hurtes the voice, and breakes the smaller veines, and is verie vnwholesome for such, as are subiect to the falling sicknesse, bycause it shaketh the troubled partes too sore: it is daungerous when one is troubled with ill, and corrupt humours, or when the stomacke is cumbred, with great and euident crudities, and rawnes, bycause thorough much chafing of the breath, and the breath instrumentes, it disperpleth, and scattereth corrupt humours, thorough out the whole bodie. And as the gentle exercising of the voice, who oft enterlacing of graue soundes, is wholesome, so to much shrilnesse straynes the head, causeth the temples pante, the braines to beate, the eyes to swell, the eares to tingle. Further it is verie vnwholesom after meat, bycause the breath being chafed partly by reason of late eating, partly by lowdnesse of the voice as it passeth thorough, gawlleth the throte, and so corrupteth the voice. It is also enemie to repletion, to wearinesse, to sensualitie: for that in those people, which are subiect to those infirmities, the great and forcible straining of the voice, doth oftimes cause ruptures and conuulsions, so that the commodities, and incommodities of the exercise do warne the training maister to vse it wisely and with great discretion. The vse of it for the motion is this, that I haue said, but for the helpe of learning, it is to some other verie good and great purpose, to pronounce without booke, with that kinde of action which the verie propertie of the subiect requireth, orations and other declamatory argumentes, either made by the pronouncer him selfe, or borowed of some other, but cheifly the hoatest *Philippik, Catilinarie,* and *Verrine* argumentes, and the rest of that race, either out of many Greeke oratours, or our one and onely Latin *Tullie,* and whether ye list to prose alone, or to be bold with Poetes, and vse their meeter. *Cælius Aurelianus*[4] an auncient *Romane* Physician, though borne at *Sicca* in *Aphricke* speaking of this exercise vseth these wordes. They did vtter their beginninges or prohemes with a gentle and a moderate voice, their narrations, and reasoning discourses with more straining, and louder: their perorations, and closinges, with a discent, and fall of the voice. And is not that to my saying?

The manner of this exercise, which *Antyllus* a verie olde Physician doth shew in *Oribasius*[5], that wrate his bookes vnto *Iulian* the apostate, whose Physician he

[4] Libro. 1. *Χρονίων*, cap. 5. de furore.

[5] Lib. 6, cap. 8. De sanit. tuen.

was, agreeth also with mine opinion. For hauing appointed certaine preparatiues for nimbling, and spreding the vocall powers, he sayth, that such, as exercised the voice, did first begin lowe, and moderatly, then went on to further strayning, of their speeche: sometimes drawing it out, with as stayed, and graue soundes, as was possible, sometimes bringing it backe, to the sharpest and shrillest, that they could, afterward not tarying long in that shrill sound, they retired backe againe, slacking the straine of their voice, till they fell into that low, and moderate tenour, wherwith they first began. Which wordes do not onely shew, that it was thus vsed, but also how the voice is to be vsed, in this exercise generally. But vpon what matter, and argument was all this paines bestowed? Those which were vnlearned said such things as they could remember, which were to be spoken aloud, and admitted any change of voice in the vttering, now harshe and hard, now smoothe and sweete. Those that were bookish recited either *Iambike* verses or *Elegies*, or such other numbers, which with their currant carie the memorie on, but all without booke, as farre surmounting any kinde of reading. I haue dwelt the longer in this exercise, bycause it is both the first in rancke, and the best meane to make good pronouncing of any thing, in any auditorie, and therfore an exercise not impertinent to scholers.

CHAPTER 11.

Of loude singing, and in what degree it commeth to be one of the exercises.

IT were to much to wishe, that *Musick* were the most healthy exercise, as it is the most pleasaunt profession, bycause either to much delite would drowne men in it alone, or to much cloying would cause it be quite contemned. Wherfore as it may not diminish other of their due, by occupying to much roome, so by change after other, and distance in it selfe, it continueth in her owne credit. For both varietie refresheth, and distance reneweth, where still the same dulles, and continuance wearies. As Musick is compounde of number, melodie, and harmonie, it hath nothing to do with *gymnastick* and *exercise,* but serueth in that sense either for delite and pleasure, and exerciseth desire: or in some respectes concerneth the manering and training vp of youth in matter of knowledge, as I said before. Whervnto I was induced not onely by argument, and nature of the thing, but by great authorities of *Plato,*[6] and *Philo,* of *Aristotle,*[7] and *Galene,*[8] and whom not? out of all antiquitie, which both allow of the thing in nature, and admit it in pollicie, into the best common weales, as a great worker of much good. But for as much as *singing* vseth the voice for her meane, and the voice instrumentes for her vtteraunce, and medleth with all sortes, and degrees in sounde base, meane, and triple, which in deliuerie do labour, and trauell the pipes, it is receiued among exercises of health, though it be not so forcible, nor can pearce so farre, as loude speaking doth, which doth not much care for any fine concent, so it vtter strongly, and straine within compasse: wheras Musick to the contrary standes not much vpon straining or fullnesse of the voice, so it be delicate and fine in concent. And yet in *Aristotles*[9] opinion, it both exerciseth, and preserueth the naturall strength bycause it standeth vpon an ordinate, and degreed motion of the voice. We finde in our owne experience, that it sturreth the voice, spreadeth the instrumentes therof, and craueth a cleare passage, as it also lightneth the laborer, and encreaseth his courage, in carying of burdens. It was vsed in the olde time Physicklike, to stay mourning and greife, for the losse of deare freindes, or desired thinges. In curing diseases, which rise vpon some distemperature of the minde, the temperature of time iudicially applyed, hath bene found both a straunge and a strong remedie. Alwaye prouided, that whether ye say loud, or sing loud, ye neither say to long, nor sing to much, for feare of a worse turne, if any entraill teare, with to much straining, as some times

[6] Pla. 2, 3, 4, de Repub. Phil. περὶ τῆς εἰς τὰ προπαιδεύματα συνόδου.

[7] Aristot. 8, polit.

[8] Galen. 1. De sanit. tuen.

[9] 19 part. probl. 38.

hath proued to true, for the afflicted partie. But to make an ende of *Musick* at this time, though it be neither so strong, nor so stirring an exercise, yet it hath made a great purchace, that it is allowed for one, and therby esteemed a double principle, of more value, where her force is more, in matters of the minde, of very good worth, though of much lesse worke in the health of the bodie. Which seeing it is an exercise within dore, it gaineth with the place a good footing to grow fairer: for whether ye allow it for a cunning exercise, or an exercised cunning, it exerciseth cunning, and encreaseth by exercise.

CHAPTER 12.

Of loude and soft reading.

READING is a thing so familiarly knowne, as there needeth no great proofe, that it exerciseth the voice, and therwith all the health, wherof the Physicians admit two kindes, into the raunge of exercises, which be furtherers to health. The one quicke, cleare, and straining, the other quiet, caulme, and staing. The cleare and straining kinde of *reading*, bycause it stirreth the breath, not sleightly nor superficially, but sheweth what it can do, in the verie fountaine and depth of all the entrailles, it encreaseth the naturall health, maketh the blood suttle and fine, purgeth all the veines, openeth all the arteries, suffereth not superfluous humours to thicken, neither to congeale and freese to a dreggie residence within any of those places, which do either receiue and lodge, or distribute and dispose, the meat and nurriture. Whervpon *Cornelius Celsus*[10] an eloquent Romain Physician accounteth it one of the finest and fairest exercises. To proue that it is holesome for the head, what more credible witnesses neede we, then *Cœlius Aurelianus*[11] a diligent Physician, and *Annæus Seneca*[12] a deepe Philosopher? *Cœlius* holdeth this kinde of *reading* to be verie soueraine not onely in headaches, but also in frensies and troubled mindes. *Seneca* vsed it to stay the rewme, and distillation from the head, which troubled him sore, as a man being both of eager conceit, and earnest studie, where by the waye, *Cœlius* giueth this note, whether ye meane to reskew the patient, from the headache, or the frantike from madnesse, by this exercise of *reading*, that the matter which is read, be pleasaunt and plaine, and nothing hard to vnderstand, to cause the witte to muse. For that such obiectes do no lesse trouble the weake braine, then sore shaking or hard iogging doth the wearied body. Moreouer cleare *reading* and loude, doth refreshe not onely the inward partes of the breast, but the stomack also: and comforteth it in feeblenesse, bycause therby phelgmatike excrementes, are without paine both thinned and consumed: whervpon it is held to be verie holesome, to mend a feeble voice, to helpe the colicke, occasioned by cold humours, and to check some consumptions. And to that ende the young *Plinie* writeth, that his vncle did vse it. When I haue said that it is also good for the drie cowghe, I neede not say any more good of it here. *Auicen*[13] the Arabian and princely Physician speaking herof, sayth that in the beginning, this *reading* must be soft and caulme, then mount by degrees, and when the voice seemeth to be in his strength, growing, and long, that then it is hie time, to staie for that time, nor to

[10] Lib. 1. c. 2.

[11] Libro 1. *Χρονίων*, cap. 1.

[12] Lib. 11. Epist. 97.

[13] Lib. de remed.

straine till ye sticke, but to leaue with some list, and abilitie to do more. The quiet and staid kinde of *reading*, sauing that the working is weaker, doth the best that it can, about all this that is said: and in one pointe it hath obtained a prerogatiue aboue the loude, that it is admitted and allowed streight after meat, when the other is licensed and allowed to depart. The maister may so vse these two exercises of *reading* and *speaking* as besides the health of the bodie, whervnto they are deputed, they may proue excellent and great deliuerers of cunning, and well beseeme the schoole: as to much in either doth trouble the scholer to much, which yet boyes would defend, by the countenaunce of a commended exercise, were it not, that in boyes exercises, I do require the maisters presence, who will refourme that exercise against their will to his owne discretion. Thus much concerning this exercise, wherby the training maister may perceiue, both what the learned haue thought of it, and how much the learners are like to gaine by it.

CHAPTER 13.

Of much talking and silence.

TALKING in Latin *Sermo,* as it is accounted an exercise for succouring some partes, so both for eagernesse, and heat, in the nature of speeche, though not of passion, it comes farre behinde others, and is therfore regestred among the meane, and weake exercises. It is thought verie fit for such, as be drousely giuen: which haue their senses daunted, either thorough dreaming melancholie, or dulling phleame. For such kinde of people by talking be cleared, their mindes awaked, their senses freed from the burden of their bodies. That *talking* spendes phleame there is no plainer proofe, then that they which talke much spit stil, which as it commeth partly from the head, partly from the stomacke, partly from the chest: so it declareth, that those partes delite in speeche, and receiue comfort from speeche, which makes roome for health, where reume kept residence. But as in these cases, it is counted healthfull: so hath it a force to fill the head, with somwhat more then dinne, and to make it dumpishe. And therefore in aches, and distemperatures of the head, clattering is commended to the cloakbag by Physick. It is also a poyson to the pained eyes: ill for them that voide blood either at the nose or from the bulke. Whervpon in any such bleading silence is enioyned. And as silence is a meane both to stay bleading, and to slake thirst, so talking dryes the toungue and prouockes thirst, openeth the passage, and promoteth bleading. In so much as *Pline*[14] writeth, that one *Mecenas Messius,* a noble Romain, betooke him selfe to voluntarie silence, the space of three yeares, to staie the casting of blood, which he fell into by reason of some straine. To be short, as silence remedyeth the cough and hikup: so talking pulleth downe, and paines the patient, when agues grow vpward, and be in the encrease. Herevpon I conclude, that talking hath great meane either to make or marre, not onely for the subiect, wheron the toungue walketh, but also for the obiect, wherin health resteth.

[14] Lib. 27, cap. 6.

CHAPTER 14.

Of laughing, and weeping. And whether children be to be forced toward vertue and learning.

IF *laughing* had no more wherfore to be enrouled in the catalogue of exercises, then *weeping* hath, they might both be crossed out. And yet as they be passions, that tende in some pointes, to the purging of some partes, so some may thinke it, a verie strange conceit, to laugh for exercise, or to weepe for wantonnesse. For as laugh one may, with an hartie good will, so weepe none can, but against their wil, to whom it is allotted in the nature of an exercise, and not quite questuarie, as to those wailing women, which wepte for the deade, whom they knew not aliue. There be manie and very easie, and much desired meanes, to make one laugh though they haue small cause, and lesse deuotion to be mery at all, but to make one weepe, is stil againe the haire. For ill newes or matter to weepe for, neither children, nor olde folkes, will thanke you at all. If you meane to make them weepe for ioye, or crye for kindenesse, that is an other matter. If the maister should beate his boye, and bring no cause why, but that he sought to haue him weepe, so to exercise him to health, and to ridde him of some humours, which made him to moist, the boye would beshrew him, and thinke his maister beate him so, to exercise himselfe, though at the verie conceit of his maisters mad reason, he might brust out in *laughing* streight after his stripes, and so become a patrone to the contrary exercise: a great deale more gracious and more desired in nature, whose enemie greife is, and *weeping* also: as a plaine argument of an vnpleasaunt guest. Howbeit seing they be both set downe, by the name of pettie, and pretie exercises, let them haue that is giuen them, seeing they are thought to stirre, and cleare some partes: *laughing* more and better: *weeping* lesse and worse. And therfore the more children laugh for exercise, the more light some they be, the more they weepe if it be not in ieast, so much the worse in very good earnest. For I can hardly beleue that much *laughter* can auoide a foole, if it be not for exercise, which is also somwhat rare: or that but a foole can weepe for exercise, which deserues the bat, to make him weepe in earnest.

But for *laughing* in the nature of an exercise and that healthful, can there be any better argument, to proue that it warmeth, then the rednesse of the face, and flush of highe colour, when one laugheth from the hart, and smiles not from the teethe? or that it stirreth the hart, and the adiacent partes, then the tickling and panting of those partes themselues? which both beare witnesse, that there is some quicke heat, that so moueth the blood. Therfore it must needs be good for them to vse *laughing*, which haue cold heades, and cold chestes, which are troubled with melancholie, which are light headed by reason of some cold distemperature of the braine, which thorough sadnesse, and sorrow, are subiecte to agues, which haue new dined, or supped: which are troubled with the head ache: for that a cold distemperature being the occasion of the infirmitie, *laughing* must needes helpe them, which moueth much aire in the breast, and sendeth the warmer spirites outward. This kinde of helpe wil be of much more efficacie, if the parties which desire it, can suffer themselues to be tickled vnder the armepittes, for in those partes there is great store of small veines, and litle arteries, which being tickled so, become warme themselues, and from thence disperse heat thorough out the whole bodie. But as moderate *laughing* is holesome, and maketh no too great chaunge, so to much is daungerous, and altereth to sore. For besides the immoderate powring, and pressing out of the spirites: besides to much mouing and heating, it oftimes causeth extreame resolution and faintnesse, bycause the vitall strength and naturall heat driue to much outward. Whervpon they that laugh do sweat so sore, and haue so great a colour, by the ascending of the blood. And as the naturall heat, and fire it selfe do still couet vpward, as to their naturall place, so must it needes be, that the lower roomes lie open, and emptie in their absence, wherby whether soeuer motion be marred, the naturall heat dyeth, and the vitall force faileth. Besides this, no man wil denie, but that this kinde of *laughing*, doth both much offende the head, and the bulke, as oftimes therewith both the papbones be loosed, and the backe it selfe perished. Nay what say ye to them that haue dyed *laughing*? where gladnesse of the minde to much enforcing the bodie, hath bereft it of life.

Weeping.

For *weeping* in the nature of an exercise, there is not much to be said, but that it is accompanied with crying, sobbing groning and teares, wherby the head, and other partes are rid of some needlesse humour: though the disquieting do much more harme, then the purging can do good, and the humour were a great deale better auoided some other waye. Wherof some children seeme to be exceeding full, when feare of beating makes them straine their pipes. *Aristotle* must beare both most blame for this exercise, if it displease any, and most praise, if it profit any, who in the last chapter[15] of the seuenth booke of his politikes writeth thus of it, and for it. That they do not well which take order, that children straine not themselues, with crying and weeping, bycause that is a meane to their growing, in the nature of an exercise. And that as holding the breath doth make one stronger to labour: so crying and weeping in children, do worke the same or the like effectes. And yet me thinke it should be no exercise, by the verie definition. For if it were vehement, yet is it not voluntarie, and though it did alter the breath, yet it bettereth not the bodie, howsoeuer it serue the soule.

But seeing the *gymnastikes* haue it, let vs lend it them for their pleasure, though we like it not for our owne. It is generally banished by all Physicians as being the mother to manie infirmities, both in the eyes and other partes: neither if it could be auoided in schooles were it worthy the looking on: being the heauy signe of torture and trouble. And though it somtime ease the greiued minde to shedde a few teares, as some for extreme anguish cannot let fall one, yet children would be

[15] 7 Polit. cap. vlt.

lesse greiued if they might shedde none, as some hold it a signe of a verie shrewd boye, when he deserues stripes, not to shew one trikle. Some Physicians thinke by waye of a conserue to the minde, that it ought to be vsed in schooles sometimes, though not voluntarie, yet in forme of an exercise to warme shrewd boyes, and to expell the contagious humours of negligence, and wantonnesse, the two springes of many streaming euilles: as playing would be daily, at some certaine houres, then to vse these exercises, when bookes be out of season.

The greatest patron of weeping that I finde, leauing *Heraclitus* to his contemplation of miseries, is a soure centurion in *Xenophon,*[16] which sat at the table with *Cyrus* in his pauilion. He commendeth weeping, wherto he had no great deuotion, to discountenaunce *laughing* which he saw allowed, and his reason is: bycause *awe, feare, correction, punishements,* which commonly haue *weeping,* either companion, or consequent, be vsed in pollicy, to kepe good orders in state, and good manners in stay, wheras *laughing* is neuer, but vpon some foolish ground. And yet both *laughing* for exercise may be for a good obiecte, and occasion to make laughter, may well deserue praise, when the minde being wearied either about great affaires that are alreadie past, or about preuenting of some anquish which is to ensue, doth call *laughing* to helpe, to ease the one, and to auert the other. And this kinde of *weeping,* which the soldiar settes out so, concerneth no exercise, though it commonly follow all vnpleasaunt exercises, where the partie had rather be idle with pleasure, then so occupyed to his paine: but it tendeth to the impression, or continuing of vertue in the minde: which should be so much the worse, bycause that waye it seemeth vnwilling, where feare is the forcer, and not free will. Which free will is the principall standard to know vertue by, which is voluntary, and not violent: as it is not the beast meane, to bring boyes neither to learning, nor to vertue.

Socrates in *Plato*[17] thinketh, that an absolute witte in the best sorted kinde, and aboue all common sorte, for ciuill societie, ought not to be forced, as in deede what needes he, being such a paragon? and that free will in such a one so sifted is the right receit of voluntarie traine. But we neither haue such common weales, as *Socrates* sets forth, nor such people to plant in them, as *Socrates* had, which he made with a wishe: nor any but subiecte to great infirmities, though some more, some lesse, by corruption in nature, which runneth headlong to vnhappinesse, and needeth no beating for not being nought. And therfore we must content our selues with that which we haue, and in our countrey which is not so absolute, in our children which be no *Socraticall* saintes, in our learning which will not proue voluntarie, if the child playe voluntarie we must vse correction and awe, though more in some, then some, bycause in illnesse there be steps, as in excellencie oddes. Wherof there is no better argument then that which this verie place offereth, not for the soldiars saying, which so commendeth awe, bycause his authoritie is to campishe, though he that brought him in, and platted the best prince were himselfe no foole: but for mine owne collection. For if one neede not to beat children to haue them do ill, whervnto they are prone, we must needes then beat them for not doing wel, where nature is corrupt. Onelesse we meete with one, that will runne as swift vphill against nature, to do that which is good, as we all runne downe

[16] Lib. 2 παιδ.

[17] 7 De Rep.

bancke, with the swinge of nature, to do that which is ill. Which when I finde, I will honour him, as I do none, though I do oft beare with some, in whome there appeareth but some shew of such a one. If vnder doing well, ye comprehend not learning, ye must needes comprise vertue, and make her meane violence, against all both heauenly *Diuinitie,* and earthly *Philosophie,* with whom all vertues be voluntarie, when reason is in ruffe: but not in children euen for compassing of the best effectes, whom custome and traine must now and then force foreward, to be ready for reason, when she maketh her entrie, which requireth some yeares. For howsoeuer *religion, wisdome, duetie,* and reasonable *consideration* do worke in riper age, sure if awe be absent, in the younger yeares, it will not be well. And who can tell, what euen he that vnder lawe is most obsequious and ciuill, would of him selfe proue, if lawe, which emportes awe, would leaue him at libertie?

CHAPTER 15.

Of holding the breath.

THOUGH all men can tell, what a singular benefit breathing is, whervnder the vse of our life is comprehended: yet they can best tell, which haue it most at commaundement. For as they liue with others, in societie of common dealinges, so they can execute any thing by the bodie, farre better then others, whether it be politike in the towne, or warlike in the fielde. And all exercises haue this ende, most peculiar and proper, by helping the naturall heat, to digest the good nurriture, and to auoide the offall, thorough out the whole bodie. Which what is it els, but to set the breathing at most libertie, being best discharged of impediment and let? And as the libertie of breathing maketh the soldiar to abide in fight long, the runner to continue his race long, the daunser to endure his labour long, and so forth in the rest, which must either haue breath at their will, or els shrinke in the midest: so the restraint and binding of the breath, euen where it is most at will, (for else it could not abide the restraint,) hath his commoditie, by waye of exercise to assist our health.

Now in breathing there be three thinges to be considered, the taking in, the letting out, and the holding in of the breath, wherof euerie one hath his priuate office to great effect, in the vpholding of health, and maintaining of life. For when we take in our breath, by the working of the lungues thorough such passages, as be appointed for the vse of breathing, we conueigh and fetch in aire into the roomy and large places of the bulke, to coole the harte and fine the spirites. When we let out our breath by those same passages, by which we tooke it in, we discharge the hart of a certaine smoky substance engendred in it, which is conueyed thence, thorough the same hollow, and roomie places of the bulke. When we hold and kepe in our breath which is of iudgement, and not of such neede as the other two, and done vpon cause to helpe nature therby: we must neither fetch aire inward, nor sende those smokie excrementes outwarde, bycause the belly and breast muscles and such fleshy partes as be about the ribbes being violently and vehemently strained and stretched, do for the time as it were mure vp, and stop the passage. This keeping in of the breath, by reason of the straine offered to those partes, and heating of the bowells, is therfore heeld for one of the vehement exercises, as it is also a postparatiue, called before apotherapeutike, bycause after maine stirringes it helpeth to expell those residences, which lynger within the bodie as being lothe to depart: and furthereth those, that are in good waye, and make hast to be gone. They that vsed this exercise by waye of traine to health, did it in two sortes: for either they strayted onely those muskles, which appertaine to the breast and bulke, and let those be at libertie which belong to the midrife and belly, that the excrementes might haue the readier waye downward, being once forced on: or they strayned both all the partes, and all their muscles at one time, that the bowelles also which are beneth the midrife might enioye the benefit of the exercise, and be as ready to discharge, as the other to driue downe. But for the better and more daungerlesse performing therof, they were wont to swadle the chest, the ribbes, and the belly. Bycause the holding of ones breath vnaduisedly and with to much strayning causeth ruptures and diuers other infirmities in the interiour vesseles of the bodie. Their meaning was hereby, sometime to strengthen the inward and naturall heat being encreased by exercise: sometime to helpe the breathing partes: sometime to discharge the breast and bellie of needlesse burden. For the breath being so violently strayted, when it findeth issue forceth his owne passage, and caryeth with him some finish and thinne excrement, either driuing it before, if it lye in his waye, or drawing it with him, if he catch it by the waye. Being of it selfe such a strainer, and expeller, it is good for to open the pipes, to fine the skinne, to driue out moysture from vnder the skinne: to warme, to strengthen and to scoure the spirituall and breathing partes, to make the places of receit more roomy, to encrease strength in labour, to helpe the eare in listening, to remoue coldnes or inflations from the entrailles, to stay the hikup and the cowgh: which commeth of some cold distemperature in the windepipes, to remedie the colick, the weaknesse of stomacke, the want or difficultie of breath. So that all those ought to esteeme of it, which haue their breathing and spirituall partes either cold or weake, or cloyed with excrementes, or whose bodies can either with much adoe or with none at all expell and ridde superfluous humours, or that be cumbred with much gaping and yawning, with resolution or weaknesse of the tongue, or any vocalle instrument. If it were to be perceiued by no waye els, verie children let vs see, that holding of the breath doth stirre and strengthen that power in vs, wherwith we expell superfluities. For let them staye their breath either laughing long, or weeping fiercely, or vpon some such other occasion, and they will either presently or verie shortly after, disburden themselues one waie or other, by ordure, vrine, or some other matter at the nose and eares. Now as this exercise is healthful to manie in good order: so contrariewise to some in disorder it is verie daungerous, bycause oftimes while the breath is to forcibly stopt, the arteries in the iawes, and baulles of the eyes swell so, as they will never come in temper againe. It filleth the head also with a grosse and stuffing humour, as maie easely be seene by the swelling of the vaines and arteries in the neck, by the puffing about the eyes, by the rednesse of the face, and by the strutting of the whole head, all which be manifest signes of repletion. It is daungerous for those which be subiect to the falling sicknesse, bycause it encreaseth the disease by that recourse, which the blood hath vp into the head: as also to them which spit or cast vp blood, for that both the sound and whole inward vesseles do burst with stretching, if they be but weake: or being broken once before, and healed againe, they will then breake out againe, by reason of heat which is encreased in the hollow of the breast, and the ouerstraining of the said vessells withall. Moreouer such as from their birth haue small entraulles and thinne, or the rim of their bellie tender and weake: or that be troubled with renting and ruptures must in no case minde this exercise, bycause it straineth those partes to sore, and lightly teareth them, as it proueth oftimes to pitifull true in young children, which by holding their breath to long, either weeping or otherwise, oftimes breake either the rim of their belly, or the call of their cods, wherby the bowelles and guttes falling downward, they become miserably tormented with incurable ruptures and burstinges: If trumpetters, and those that play vpon winde instruments were asked the question, whether they feele not the effect herof somtime, they would shake the head, and so sooth the demaunde, though they said no more. They do write of *Milo*[18] the *Crotoniate*, a great champion in those achleticall exercises, that he vsed to binde his forehead, his breast, and his ribbes with verie strong tapes, and would neuer let his breath goe, till the vaines were swelled so full, as they burst the tapes. But this fellow had no fellow in any of those pastimes. It was he that bare the bull vpon his shoulder in the *Olympian* assemblie by vsing to cary him of a litle young calfe. So great thinges be easely compassed, if they be set in hand with, when they be but litle, or medled with, by litle and litle. The best waye to auoide perill in this exercise is to beginne gently, and so to grow on by degrees, and to leaue be times before extremitie bidde hoe, and while ye be yet able to do more, neither to force nature to the furthest.

[18] Hier. Mercu. lib. 3, cap. 6.

CHAPTER 16.

Of daunsing, why it is blamed, and how deliuered from blame.

DAUNSING of it selfe declareth mine allowance, in that I name it among the good and healthfull exercises: which I must needes cleare from some offensiue notes, wherwith it is charged by some sterne people: least if I do not so, it both continue it selfe in blame still, and draw me thither also with it, for allowing of a thing, that is disliked, and by me not deliuered from iust cause of misliking, which by my choice do seeme to defend it. And yet I meane not here to rippe vp, what reading hath taught me of it, though it seeme to haue serued for great vses in olde time, both athleticall for spectacle and shew: militare for armour and enemie: and Physicall for health and welfare: so many and so notable writers, make so much and so oftimes mention therof in all these three kindes. Some dedicate whole volumes to this argument onely, some enterlace their brauest discourses with the particularities therof, and those no meane ones. And in deede a man, that neuer red much, and doth but marke the thing cursorily, would scant beleue, that it were either of such antiquitie, or of such account, or so generally entreated of by learned men, all those their writinges stil sounding to the praise and aduancement therof: howsoeuer in our dayes either we embase it in opinion: or it selfe hath giuen cause of iust embasement, by some peoples misvse. Many sortes of it I do reade of, but most discontinued, or rather quite decayed, that onely is reserued, which beareth oftimes blame, machance being corrupted by the kinde of *Musick*, as the olde complaint was: machance bycause it is vsed but for pleasure and delite onely, and beareth no pretense or stile of exercise, directly tending to health, which is our peoples moane now in our dayes. For where honest and profitable reasons be not in the first front, to commend a thing, but onely pleasaunt and deliteful causes, which content not precise surueiours, there groweth misliking, the partie that exerciseth, not pretending the best, which is in the thing, and the partie that accuseth, marking nothing else but that, which maye moue offence.

The sad and sober commodities, which be reaped by *daunsing* in respect of the motion applyed to health be these, by heating and warming, it driueth awaie stifnes from the ioyntes, and some palsilike trembling from the legges and thighes, whom it stirreth most, it is a present remedie to succour the stomacke against weaknesse of digestion, and rawnesse of humours: it so strengtheneth and confirmeth aching hippes thinne shankes, feeble feete, as nothing more: in deliuering the kidneys or bladder from the stone, it is beyond comparison good: but now such as haue weake braines, swimming heades, weeping eyes, simple and sory sight, must take heede of it, and haue an eye to their health, for feare they be disie when they daunce, and trip in their turning, or rather shrinke downe right when they should cinquopasse. Such as haue weake kidneys and ouerheated, may displease them selues, if it please then [them] to daunce, and encrease their diseases, by encreasing their heat.

The blame that daunsing beareth.

The *daunsing* in armour, called by the Greekes πυῤῥιχὴ, as it is of more motion in exercise, so it worketh more nimblenesse in executing, when ye deale in the field with your enemies. These be the frutes which are reaped by *daunsing* well and orderly vsed, for the benefit of health, and the contrary displeasures, which are caught by it, thorough inconsiderate applying of it, by the partie which is not made for it. The blames which it beareth be these. That it reuelleth out of time, wherewith Physick is offended: That it serueth delite to much, whereat good manners repine. For these two faultes there is but one generall aunswere: that daunsing is healthfull, though the daunsers vse it not healthfully, as other things of greater countenaunce be verie good, though the professours do not so, as their professions do enioine them. For the first in particular, the rule of health condemnes not daunsing, but the mistyming of it: that it is vsed after meat, when rest is most holesome: with full stomacke, when digestion should haue all the helpe of naturall heat: that to please the beholders, such as vse daunsing do displease them selues. And sure if *daunsing* be an exercise, as both all antiquitie doth commend it for, and I my selfe do allow of it by that name: it would by rule of Physick go before meat, and not be vsed but long after, as a preparatiue against a new meale: and a disburdener of superfluities, against a surcharge of new diet: Howbeit there be in it some more violent measures then some: and in beginning with the most staydest and most almanlike, and so marching on, till the springing galliard and quicker measures take place, choice in euerie one, vpon knowledge of his owne bodie, and his emptinesse or saturitie maye helpe health, though the custome of eche countrey commaunde not onely health, though to her harme, but euen the verie science which professeth the preseruation of health, if desire egge delite, to shew it selfe in place. Wherevpon the second blame of *daunsing,* doth especially builde, and take her hold.

To keepe thinges in order, there is in the soule of man but one, though a verie honorable meane, which is the direction of reason: to bring things out of order there be two, the one strongheaded, which is the commaundement of courage, the other many headed, which is the enticement of desires. Now *daunsing* hath properties to serue eche of these, *exercise* for health, which *reason* ratifieth, *armour* for agilitie, which *courage* commendeth, *liking* for allowance, which *desire* doth delite in. But bycause it yeildeth most to delite, and in most varietie of pleasures, desire ministreth most matter to blame, *daunsing* by pleasing desire to much, hath pleased reason to litle, and when reason obiecteth inconueniences, it turneth the deafe side, and followeth her owne swinge. For when the tailour hath braued, where nature hath beawtified: when amiablenesse of person hath procured agilitie by cunning, what gallant youthes in whom there is any courage, can abide not to come to shew, hauing such qualities so worthy the beholding? here will courage shew her selfe, though repentance be her port, here will desire throng in prease, though it praise not in parting. All this doth confesse that *daunsing* is become seruant to desire, though not *daunsing* alone: and yet companions in blame be no dischargers of fault. What then? for the generall, seing thinges which man vseth, cannot be quite free from misuse, it is halfe a vertue to winne so much, as there be as litle misuse, as may be: and to charge the partie that deserues blame, with hinderance of health, with corruption of manners, with ill losse of good time: which if he care not for, the precept may passe, though he passe not for it. But howsoeuer *daunsing* be or be thought to be, seing it is held for an exercise, we must thinke there is some great good in it, though we protecte not the ill, if any come by it. Which good we must seeke to get, and praie those maisters, which fashion it with *order* in time, with *reason* in gesture, with *proportion* in number, with *harmonie* in *Musick,* to appoint it so, as it may be thought both seemely and sober, and so best beseeme such persons, as professe sobrietie: and that with all, it may be so full of nimblenesse and actiuitie, as it may proue an exercise of health, being vsed in wholesome times, and not seeking to supplant rest, as the rule of health at this daie complaineth. And generally of all ages, me thinke it beseemeth children best, to enable, and nimble their iointes therby, and to stay their ouermuch deliting therin in further yeares. The very definition of it declareth, what it was then, when it was right, and what it is now, when it seemes to be wronge, if right in such thinges be not creature to vse, and maye change with time, without challenge for the change. They define *daunsing* to be a certaine cunning to resemble the manners, affections, and doinges of men and women, by motions and gestures of the bodie, artificially deuised in number and proportion. This was to them a kinde of deliuerie, to vtter their mindes, by signes and resemblances, of that which came nearest to the thing, and was most intelligible to the lookers on. But now with vs, there is nothing left to the dauncer ordinarily, but the bare motion, without that kinde of hand cunning (for so I terme their χειρονομία) bycause the skill seemed then to rest most in the vse of the vpper partes, and gesturing by the hand. The credit of our *daunsing* now is to represent the Musick right, and to cause the bodye in his kinde of action to resemble and counterfet that liuely, which the instrument in his kinde of composition deliuereth delicately: and with such a grace to vse the legges and feete, as the olde daunsers vsed their armes and handes. And as in the olde time both men, wymen and children did vse *daunsing* to helpe and preserue their health, to purchace good hauiour and bearing of their bodies: so in these our dayes, being vsed in time, by order, and with measure, it will worke the same effectes of health, hauiour and strength, and may well auoide the opinion of either lewdnesse, or lightnesse. Thus much for *daunsing,* as the motion is for health, and the meaning for good.

CHAPTER 17.

Of wrastling.

FOR wrastling as it is olde and was accounted cunning sometimes, so now both by Physicians in arte, and by our countreymen in vse, it seemeth not to be much set by, being contemned by the most, and cared for but by the meanest. Yet the auncient *Palestra* a terme knowen to the learned, and ioined with letters, and Musick, to proue the good bringing vp of youth as a most certaine argument of abilitie well qualified, fetcht that name of the Greeke πάλη, which we in English terme wrastling, and was alwaye of good note, as wrastling it selfe in games gat victories, in warre tried forces, in health helpt hauiour, in the bodye wrought strength, and made it better breathed. *Clemens Alexandrinus*[19] which liued at *Rome* in *Galenes* time in the third booke of his Pædagogue, or training maister, in the title of exercise, reiecting most kindes of wrastling yet reserueth one, as verie well beseeming a ciuill trained man, whom both seemelinesse for grace, and profitablenesse for good health, do seeme to recommende. Then an exercise it is, and healthfully it may be vsed: if discretion ouerlooke it, our countrey will allow it. Let vs therefore vse it so, as *Clement* of *Alexandria* commendes it for, and make choice in our market. Wherfore not to deale with the catching pancraticall kinde of wrastling, which vsed all kindes of hould, to cast and ouercome his aduersarie, nor any other of that sort, which continuance hath reiected, and custome refused, I haue picked out two, which be both ciuill for vse, and in the vsing vpright without any great stouping, the one more vehement, the other more remisse. The vehement vpright wrastling chafeth the outward partes of the bodie most, it warmeth, strengthneth, and encreaseth the fleshe, though it thinne and drie withall. It taketh awaie fatnesse, puffes, and swellinges: it makes the breath firme and strong, the bodie sound and brawnie, it tightes the sinews, and backes all the naturall operations. If they that wrastle do breath betwene whiles, it prouoketh sweat, bycause the humours, which were gathered together by rest, are egde out by exercise. If they go on still without intermission, it dryeth vp the bodie in such sort as the sonne doth. It is good for the head ache, it sharpneth the senses, it is enemie to melancholie, it whetteth the stomacke being troubled with any cold distemperature. And bycause the attemptes to get vantage in wrastling be very eager and earnest wherwith the whole bodie is warmed and set in a heat, it must of force be good for the bellie, being anoyed and cumbred with any kinde of cold. Now contrarie it is daungerous to be delt with in agues, as to vehement and conspiring with the quiuerer, in naturall moysture as to filling, where it spreadeth. For the necke

[19] παιδαγ. 3. De exercitijs.

and iawes perillous whom it harmes by rowgh handling, and strangleth by much ouerstraining. For the breast and bulke not of the best, as either bursting some conduit, or stopping some windcourse. Weake kidneis, and wearie loynes may be but lookers vpon wrastlers. They that be gawled or byled within, may neither runne nor wrastle, for eagering the inward, being in way to amendement, or in will to proue worse. If weake legges become wrastlers, of their owne perill be it, for they do it without warrant. The remisse kinde of vpright wrastling, as it is a more gentle exercise, so it breadeth much flesh, and is therfore verie commodious for such as be vpon the recouerie after sicknesse, as a kinde of motion, which without any danger, bringeth strength and stowtnesse. It is freind to the head, bettereth the bulke, and strengthened the sinewes. Thus much for wrastling, wherin as in all other exercises, the training maister must be both cunning to iugde of the thing: and himselfe present to preuent harme, when the exercise is in hand.

CHAPTER 18.

Of fensing, or the vse of the weapon.

THE vse of the weapon is allowed for an exercise, and may stand vs at this daie now liuing, and our posteritie in great stede, as wel as it did those which went before vs. Who vsed it *warlike* for valiauntnesse in armes, and actiuitie in the field, *gamelike* to winne garlandes and prices, and to please the people in solemne meetinges: *Physicklike* to purchace therby a good hauiour of body and continuance of health. Herof they made three kindes, one to fight against an aduersarie in deede, an other against a stake or piller as a counterfet aduersarie, the third against any thing in imagination, but nothing in sight, which they called σκιομαχία, a fight against a shadow. All these were practised either in armes, or vnarmed. The armed fensing is to vehement for our trade, let them trie it, that entend to be warriers, which shall finde it their freinde, if they meane to follow the fielde, where, as in all other thinges vse worketh maisterie. But we scholers minde peace, as our muses professe that they will not medle, nor haue to do with *Mars*. All these sortes of fensing were vsed in the olde time, and none of them is now to be refused, seing the same effectes remaine, both for the health of our bodies, and the helpe of our countries. That kinde of fensing or rather that misuse of the weapon, which the *Romane* swordplayers vsed, to slash one an other yea euen till they slew, the people and princes to looking on, and deliting in the butcherie, I must needes condemne, as an euident argument of most cruell immanitie, and beyond all barbarous, in cold blood, to be so bloodie. For their allegation, to harten their people against the enemie, and not to feare woundes: no not death it selfe in the verie deadly fight, that caryeth small countenaunce, where the *Athenian*[20] comes in, which in cokfights and quailefightes, did so harten their people: bycause those birdes will fight till they fall: without either embrewing their youth with blood, or acquainting their citisens eyes with such sanguinarie spectacles.

A thing complained on in the time when it was vsed, euen by them which behelde it, as *Plinie*[21] doth note: and by the *Christianes* which abhorred it, as *Cypriane*[22] cryeth out of it in moe places then one. But for the credit and countenaunce of the exercise, that was then vsed, and is now to be continued, *Plato,*[23] a man whose authoritie is sacred among Philosophers and studentes, in his dialogue surnamed *Laches*, where he handleth the argument of fortitude and valiantnesse, en-

---

[20] Solon apud Lucianum in Αναχάρσει.

[21] Lib. 28, cap. 1, & lib. 36. cap. vlt.

[22] Epist., Lib. 2.

[23] Plato in Lachete.

courageth young men to learne the vse of their weapon: as being an exercise which needeth not to make curtsie to go with the very best and brauest in his parish: either for trauelling or strengthening the bodie, besides the cunning of it selfe. The profites which health receiues by all these three kindes be these. He that exerciseth him selfe either against an aduersarie, or against a post or pillar as deputie to his aduersarie heateth himselfe thoroughly, maketh way for excrementes, prouoketh sweat, abateth the abundance of flesh, strengtheneth his armes and shoulders, exerciseth his legges and feet marueilously. He that fighteth against a stake stirreth the bodie, plucketh the flesh downe, and straynes the iuyce awaye, a peculiar freind to the armes and handes: It refresheth the wearied sense, it setleth the roming humours, it redresseth the fainting and trembling of the sinewes, it deliuereth the breast from his ordinarie diseases: it is good for the kidneyes: and the great gutte called κῶλον, it furthereth such cariage as must be conueighed downward. The same effects hath the fight against the shadow or the shadowish nothing, but that it is a litle more valiant to light vpon somwhat then to fight against nothing. But of all these three, the exercise against an aduersarie is both most healthfull, and most naturall to aunswere all assaies: and specially to canuase out a coward, that will neither defend his freinde, nor offend his foe: the cheife frute that should follow fensing. This is the opinion of the best writers concerning fensing, or skill how to handle the weapon: no worse in it selfe, though it be sometimes not worthily vsed, as it is no lesse profitable, then hath bene said afore: though it shake and shiuer weake heades, swimming braynes, and ill kidneys. The mo reasons any man can bring of him selfe for any of these exercises, the more he fortifieth my choice, which point them but out slightly.

CHAPTER 19.

Of the Top, and scourge.

HE that will deny the Top to be an exercise, indifferently capable of all distinctions in stirring, the verie boyes will beate him, and scourge him to, if they light on him about lent, when Tops be in time, as euerie exercise hath his season, both in daie and yeare, after the constitution of bodies, and quantities in measure. Of this kinde of Top, that we vse now a dayes, both for young and olde people, to warme them in cold weather, I finde nothing in writing, bycause hauing no yron ringes, nor pinnes, it can neither be the Greek κρῖκος nor τρόχος, though the running about be bold to borrow the last name *trochus*. For they whirled about, and along, with a marueilous great, though a pretie noyse, and were pastimes for men euen in the midst of sommer, when our Tops be bestowed, and laid vp against the spring. It resembleth the Latin *Turbo* most, and the Greeke βέμβιξ. The place of *Virgil* in the 7. of his *Æneis*, where he compareth *Amata* the Queene in her furie to this *Turbo* which the boyes scourged about the wide haule: declareth both what *Turbo* is, and whose play it was, and that it best resembleth our Top. Of βέμβιξ there was an old Greek *Epigram*, which maketh it either the like or the same with our Top.

Οἵδ᾽ ἄρ ὑπὸ σκυτάλῃσι θοὰς βέμβικας ἔχοντες,
Ἔςρεφον εὐρείῃ παῖδες ἐνὶ τριόδῳ.

Which is to say, that children when they had their whirling gigges vnder the deuotion of their scourges, caused them to troule about the broad streates. The harme this exercise may bring must be to the head and eyes, thorough stouping to much forward, or to the backe and shoulders by bending to much downwardes, otherwise it warmeth the bodie, and worketh all the effectes, which those exercises do that either by mouing the legges or armes most, and with all the whole bodie in degree, enlarge and stirre the naturall heat either to prouoke appetite, or to expel superfluities. The more roome the Top hath to spinne in, the better for the legges and feete, the bigger it is, the better for the armes and handes. The vprighter one scourgeth, the better for all partes, whom neither bending doth crushe, nor moysture corrupt. It were to be wished, that it were whipt with both the handes, in play to traine both the armes, seing vse makes the difference, and no infirmitie in nature. As both *Plato* wishing the same professeth it to be most true and our experience teacheth vs, both in left handed people, which vse but the left, and in double right handed which vse both the handes a like, and beare the name of the right hand as the more common in vse. But bycause the place of *Plato* concerning the left hande is verie pithie to this purpose though I vse not to auouch much in the Greeke toungue, yet me thinke I maye not ouerpasse it. In the seuenth booke of his lawes, allowing the indifferent vse of our feete and legges, he complayneth of to much partialitie vsed towardes the armes and handes, in these wordes, *τάγε περὶ πόδας τε καὶ τὰ κάτω τῶν μελῶν οὐδὲν διαφέροντα πρὸς τοὺς πόνους φαίνεται. Τὰ δὲ κατὰ χεῖρας ἀνοίᾳ τροφῶν καὶ μητέρων οἷον χωλοὶ γεγόναμεν ἕκαστοι. τῆς φύσεως γὰρ ἑκατέρων τῶν μελῶν σχεδὸν ἰσοῤῥοπούσης, αὐτοὶ διὰ τὰ ἤθη διάφορα αὐτὰ πεποιήκαμεν οὔκ ὀρθῶς χρώμενοι*, &c. For the performance of any kinde of labour there is no difference, sayeth he, in the legges, and lower partes. But for our armes, thorough ignoraunt nurses and mothers, we be euery one of vs halfe lamed. For wheras naturally both the armes be almost of equall strength, thorough our owne default we make the difference. And so he passeth on still prouing the vnnaturall handling of the left hande, when it is left weaker then the right hande is.

These be the exercises which I terme within dores, bycause they may be practised at home vnder couert, when we cannot go abroad for the weather: though all may be vsed abroad, if the roome and the weather do serue abroad. Wherein I take it, that I haue kept *Galenes*[24] rule in chusing these exercises, and that they be all both pleasant, profitable and parable, the perfect circunstances of all good and generall exercises, not to be costly to compasse, nor vnpleasant to loth them, nor vnprofitable to leaue them. Those that require more libertie of roome, to raunge at will, or to forrage in the field, be these, which I noted before, *walking, running, leaping, swimming, riding, hunting, shooting,* and *playing at the ball.*

[24] Lib. de parua pila.

CHAPTER 20.

Of walking.

AMONG those exercises which be vsed abroade, what one deserueth to be set before walking, in the order and place of traine: what one haue they more neede to know, which minde, the preseruation and continuaunce of health? what one is there, which is more practised of all men, and at all times, then walking is? I dare saye that there is none, whether young or olde, whether man or woman, but accounteth it not onely the most excellent exercise, but almost alone worthy to beare the name of an exercise. When the weather suffereth, how emptie are the townes and streates, how full be the fieldes and meadowes, of all kindes of folke? which by flocking so abroad, protest themselues to be fauourers of that they do, and delite in for their health. If ye consider but the vse of our legges, how necessarie they be for the performaunce of all our doings, *nature* her selfe seemeth to haue appointed *walking*, as the most naturall traine, that can be, to make them discharge their duetie well. And sure if there be any exercise, which generally can preserue health, which can remedie weaknesse, which can purchace good hauiour, considering it is so generall, and neither excludeth person nor age, certainly that is *walking*. Herevpon Physicians when they entreat of this argument, vse alwaye to giue it, the place of preferment and birthright in this kinde. The auncient Princes, and common weales so highly esteemed of it, as in the places appointed for exercise, whether within their great buildinges, or without, they seemed to minde no one thing more: and still prouided walking roomes, to serue for all seasons and times of the yeare, some couert and close, some vncouert and open, some secret and hidden. The reason why they thus regarded *walking*, was great, for as it seemeth to be, so it is in verie deede wholly consecrate to the vse of health.

Is it euer red that the athlets or gamesters vsed walking for an exercise: either in sportes, or in theaters, or in the solemnising of their sacred ceremonies, whervnto they serued? did either *Plato*[25] handling this argument, or any good writer else saye that walking was any waye to traine vp soldiars withall? Onely *Vegetius*[26] sayeth in his discourse of warfare, that it were good for soldiars to accustome themselues to walke quickly and proportionately, for their better breathing: and *Augustus Cesar*, and *Adrian* the Emperours, did ordeine by constitution, that soldiars both horsemen and footemen should monthly be led abroad to walke and that not only in the plaine fieldes, but in all kindes of soile, to be able by that acquaintaunce with groundes, to make difficultie at none. So that *walking* seemeth to

[25] 3 De Rep.

[26] Lib. 1, cap. 9 & penul.

be onely institute both by nature and custome for the vse of health: and that in the traine of health, no one thing deserueth better place than it doth: bycause no other thing besides health layth claime vnto it.

The vse of slow walking after exercise.

Herof there be two kindes, the one vsed after vehement exercises, the other, which beareth the name of the exercise itselfe. Concerning the former of the two, I haue but thus much to saye: bycause the latter is my peculiar subiect. That it commeth in place, when other exercises are dismissed, and finished, after purgations ministred by counsell of Physick, after great vomiting: that it is good to refresh the wearied minde: to alter and bring in order the spirites: to loose that which is strayted, to scoure the chest: to make one fetch his breath at ease: to strengthen the instrumentes of the senses, to confirme the stomacke, to cleare and fine the bodie: and not to suffer it after trauaile to melt or decaie, but to purge and cleanse it: and that, which is of most account, to dissolue and bannish awaye all affections that procure any feeling of weariesomnes, or disturbaunce to the bodie.

The three principall kindes of walking.

The second kinde of *walking* hath three sortes vnder him. Wherof the first beareth his name of the kinde of motion, how: The second of the place, where: The thrid of the time, when the walking is vsed. Which three also haue particular braunches vnder eche of them, as hereafter shall appeare.

Walking which is named after ye time of mouing.

Walkinges which take their names of the motion now, be either swift or slow, vehement or gentle, much or litle, moderate, or sore, long and outright, or short and turning: now bearing vpon the whole feete, now vpon the toes, now vpon the heeles.

Moderate walking.

Of all these diuersities in *walking* the moderate is most profitable, which alone of all, that I rekened, hath no point either of to much, or of to litle, and yet it is both much, and strayning, which be the two properties of an healthfull walke. It is good for the head, the eyes, the throte, the chest, when they be out of frame: so the partie spit not blood. For distilling from the head, for difficultie of breath, for a moyste and pained stomacke, wherin the nurriture either groweth bitter or corrupteth: for the iaundise, costifnesse, fleeting of the meat in the stomacke, stopping of the vrine, ache of the hippes, and generally for all such, as either neede to prouoke any superfluitie from the vpper partes downward, or to send that packing, which is already in waye to depart. Now to the contrarie it is naught for agues, bycause it encreaseth heat, and so consequently the disease: for the falling euill, for hauking vp of blood: and in the time when one is making water.

Swift and quick walking.

Swift *walking* doth heat sore and abateth the flesh, whervpon to ease the colicke, and to take awaie grossenesse, it is accounted a verie good meane.

Slow walking.

Slow *walking* hath the same effectes, that the apotherapeutike hath. And therfore it is good for sickly weake olde men, and those which delite in, or neede walking after meate, to setle it better in the bottome of their stomacke: or that be newly awaked from sleepe, or that prepare themselues to some greater exercise, or that feele any ache in any part, or that haue drie bodies. When one hath the head ache it is good to walke first slowly, and after a while a litle faster, and stronger, strutting out the legges. Slow *walking* is also good against the falling sicknesse: bycause without any shaking to the head, it fetcheth the humours downward, where it thinneth and disperseth them, and warmes the whole bodie, without endammaging it. Finally in quartane agues, when the fit is past, in leprosies, for tetters, ringewormes, cankars, and to procure easie fetching of ones breath, it is verie soueraine.

Vehement and to sore.

Vehement or to sore and to eager *walking,* is best for cold folkes, and therfore good to driue away trembling or quaking, it encreaseth puffing and blowing, and yet dissolueth, and disperseth winde. But it is ill for weake heades and feete, and such as are in daunger of the gout. For both the gout and the hippe ache do oftimes come of to much and to sore walking. As to the contrarie gentle walking vpon soft straw, or grasse, or vpon euen ground is good for any gout or inward exulceration, before meat, but not after. For wearinesse is their principall enemie: which heateth and enflameth their iointes to sore: and thereby causeth them to draw stil more matter from the partes further of, to feede their continuall fluxe.

Much and oft.

Much and oft *walking* is good for them that haue a distempered bulk or head: that perceiue small nurriture in their lower partes, that in their exercises neede more vehement stirring.

Litle and seldome.

Litle *walking* is good for them, that vse no bathing or washing after exercise, which must needes walke after meate, to send it downe, to the bottom of their stomacke, and for those which finde some heauinesse in their bodies.

Long and outright.

Long and outright *walking* is nothing so troublesome as the short, that maketh many turnes. It is good for the head, and yet it sucketh vp humours, and dryeth to fast.

Long and quicke.

Long and quicke *walking* is goode to staye the hikup or yeaxing.

Short and soone *turning* wearyeth sooner: and troubleth the head sorer.

Circular or *walking* round about maketh one disie, and hurteth the eyes.

In *walking* to strout the legges, and beare vpon the heeles, is verie good for an ill head, a moyst bulke, a strayned bellie, and for such of the lower partes, as prosper not, yea, though the partie feede well: and generally for all those, in whome superfluities steeme vpward.

To beare vpon the toes hath bene proued good for ill eyes, and to staye loose bellies.

Bearing vpon the whole feete is alwaye incident to some of the other kindes, and therefore ioyneth with eche of them in effectes.

Walking which is named after the place.

Walking which taketh the name after the place, is either on hilles and high groundes, or in valleies and lowe groundes: againe the lowe ground is, either euen, or vneuen: either vnder couert, or abroad: in the sunne, or in the shade. When one walketh vp against the hill, the bodie is marueilously wearied, bycause all the sway and poize of it presseth downe those partes, which are first moued. And for all that such motions be heauie and slow, yet they cause one sweat sooner and sorer, and staye the breath more, then the *walking* downhill doeth: bycause heauie thinges bearing naturally downward, are forced vpward against nature. Whervpon heat which beareth the bodie vp, as in comming downe it trauelleth not of his owne nature, so preasing vpward it is burthened with the bodie, whereby it both encreaseth it selfe, prouoketh sweat, and stayeth the breath. This kinde of walke afore meate is good for the bulke, which hath not his breath at commandement. *Demosthenes*[27] strengthened his voice by it, pronouncing his orations alowd, as he walked vp against the hill, whereby he gat the benefit of breathing, to deliuer his long periodes, without paine to himselfe, or breach to his sentence. The knees are most toiled in this kinde of walking, being forced backward contrarie to their nature, and therfore to their griefe.

Walking downhill.

Walking downhill draweth superfluity from the head more than the other doeth: but withall it is enemy to feeble thighes, bycause they both moue the legges, and support all the whole weight of the bodie aboue. The change and varietie of the motion causeth that kinde of walking to be best liked, which is sometime vphill, sometime downhill.

When ye walke vpon euen or vneuen ground, ye walke either in medowes or grassie places, or in rowgh and brambly, or in sandie and soft. If ye walke in a medow, it is without all contradiction most for pleasure, bycause nothing there anoyeth, nothing offendeth the sense, and the head is fed both with varietie of sweet odours, and with the moysture of such humour, as the medow yeeldeth.

Rough, brambly, and bushy groundes stuffe the head.

Walking vpon sande.

Sandie, and cheifly if it be any thing deepe, bycause the walking in it stirreth sore, confirmeth and strengtheneth all the partes of the bodie: and fetcheth superfluities mightily downward. This was one of *Augustus Cæsars* remedies, as

[27] Plut. in Demost.

Suetonius[28] writeth, to helpe his haulting and weake legges. For to cleare the vpper partes of that which cloyeth them, there is nothing better then to trauell in deepe sande.

Walking in a close gallerie.

Walking in a close gallerie is not so good, bycause the ayre there is not so fresh, free, and open, but pent, close, and grosse: and therfore stuffeth the bodie, onelesse the gallerie be in the vppermost buildinges of the house, where neither any vapour from the ground can come: and the ayre that commeth is pure and cleare.

The close *walkes*, which were called *cryptoporticus* were not of choice but of necessitie, when extremitie of weather would not let them walke abroad.

Walking in an open place.

Walking in an open place, and cheifly greene, is much better and more wholesome, then vnder any couert. First of all for the eyes, bycause a fine and subtile ayre comming from the greene to the bodie, which is more penetrable bycause of stirring, scourreth awaye all grosse humours from the eyes, and so leaueth the sight fine and cleare. Further, bycause the bodie in walking waxeth hoat, the aire sucketh humours out of it, and disperseth whatsoeuer is in it more then it can well beare.

Now in *walking* abroad there is consideration to be had to the soile. For *walking* by the sea side ye thinne and drie vp grosse humours, by riuers and standing waters ye moyst. Howbeit both these two last be naught, and specially standing waters. Walking not neare any water, as it is not so good as the walke by the sea, so it is much better, then walking neare any other water. Walking in the dew moystes and harmes.

It is good to walke where birdes haunt.

If ye *walke* in a place where birdes haunt, it is of great efficacie to cleare by the breath, and to disburden the bodie so, as if ye did walke in some higher ground. If there be no winde where ye walke, it cleareth by breath, it disperseth excrements, it slakes and nippes not, and is good for colicks that come of a cold cause. If there be winde, the *Northern* causeth coughing, hurtes the bulke, and yet confirmes the strength, soundes the senses, and strengthens the weake stomacke. The *Southwinde* filles the head, dulles the instrumentes of sense, yet it looseth the bellie, and is good to dissolue. The *Westwinde* passeth all the rest, both for mildenesse and wholesomnesse. The *Eastwinde* is hurtefull and nippes.

It is better to walke in the shade then in the sunne.

Daungerous walking vnder dewy trees.

What effecte the faire and cleare aire hath.

It is better *walking* in the shade then in the sunne: as it is naught for the headache to walke either in the cold or in the heat. And yet it is beter to walke in the sunne, then to stend in it, and better to walke fast, then slowly. Of all shades, those

[28] In Augusti vita. cap. 80.

be the best which be vnder walles or in herboures. It is verie daungerous *walking* neare vnto dewye trees, for feare of infection by the sappie dew: bycause dew in generall is not so wholesome, it abateth the flesh, as wymen that gather it vp with wooll or linnen clothes for some purposes do continually trye. Now if the dew come of any vnwholesome matter, what may it proue to? The best *walking* in shadowes simply is vnder myrtle and baye trees, or among quicke and sweet smelling herbes, as wilde basell, penyroyall, thyme, and mynt, which if they be wild and of their owne growing be better to wholesome the soile, then any that be set by hande: but if the better cannot be, the meaner must serue. Againe in this kinde of *walke* the faire and cleare aire lighteneth, scoureth, fineth, procureth good breathing, and easie mouing. Darke and cloudie aire heauyeth, scoureth not by breath, and stuffeth the head.

Walking which taketh his name after the time.

Walking which is termed after the time, is either in winter or summer: in the morning or in the euening, before meat or after. The most of these differencies will appeare then playnest, when the time for all exercises is generally appointed, in consideration of circunstance, as shall be declared vnder the title of time. In the meane while *walking* whether in the morning or euening, ought still to go before meat.

The good of ye morning walk.

The *morning walke* looseth the belly, dispatcheth sluggishnes, which comes by sleep, thinneth the spirits, encreaseth heat, and prouoketh appetite. It is good for moyst constitutions, it nimbleth and quickneth the head, and all the partes in it.

The good and ill of the euening walk.

The *euening walke* is a preparatiue to sleepe, it disperseth inflations, and yet it is ill for a weake head. Walking after meat is not good but only for such as are vsed vnto it. Yet euen they maye not vse it to much. It is good also for them, which otherwise cannot cause their meat go downe to the bottome of their stomacke.

And thus much for *walking,* both regarding the manner of the motion, the place where, and the time when. Which circunstances though they be many and diuers: yet to purchase the commodities, which walking is confessed to be very full of, they must needes be cared for: considering our whole life is so delt with, as if we hastened on death, against the which, this exercise may be rightly termed an antidote, or counterreceit.

CHAPTER 21.

Of running.

THE manifest seruices which we receiue by our legges and feete, in *warre* for glorie, to pursue or saue, in *game* for pleasure to winne and weare, in *Physick* for health to preserue and heale, do giue parentes to vnderstand, that they do suffer their children to be more then halfe maymed, if they traine them not vp in their youth to the vse and exercise therof. To polishe out this point with those effectuall reasons, which auaunce and set forth nature, when she sayeth in plaine termes, that she meanes to do good: or with those argumentes, wherwith the best authors do amplifie such places, when they finde nature so freindly and forward, (as the anatomistes which suruey the workmanship of our bodie, and histories, which note the effectes of swiftnesse, do wonder at nature, and wish exercise to helpe her, for that which they see) were to me nothing needefull, considering my ende is not the praise, but the practise of that which is praiseworthy: neither to tell you, what *Alexander* the *Macedonian*, nor what *Papyrius* the *Romain* did by swifte foote, nor that *Homere* gaue *Achilles* his epithete of his footmanship, but to tell you that *running* is an exercise for health, which if reason cannot winne, wherof euery one can iudge, sure historie will not, where the authors credit may be called in question as to much fauoring the partie whom he praiseth, wherefore I will leaue of all manner of by ornamentes, wherwith such as be in loue with running do vse, to set it forth, and directly fall to the seuerall kindes there of which differ one from an other, both in the mouing it selfe, and also in the manner of the mouing whervpon the effectes, which follow must needes proue diuers according to that diuersitie. Running of it selfe is helde by the Physicians generally to be a swift exercise which needeth neither much strength, nor great violence, and in what sorte so euer it is vsed, it is ill for agues.

1. The first kinde of *running* which beareth his name of the verie motion vehement swift, and withall outright, hindereth health, rather then helpeth it: and if it helpe it any waye, it is in that it abateth the fleshinesse, and corpulence of the body: which if it chaunce to be moyst, swift running will empty it of humours, and stay it also quickly. It hath bene found so wholesome in some diseases of the splene or mylt, as *Ætius* a learned Physician writeth, that he knew some which by walking and running onely were deliuered from all greife and peine there. But it is verie vnwholesome for such as haue ill heades. Whervpon *Aristotle*[29] in his Problemes, asking the question why running which is thought to driue all excrementes downward, if it be vehement and swift should be offensiue to the head, not in men

[29] 5. para. probl. 9.

and wymen alone, but also in beastes, aunswereth thus: that the swift motion, bycause it strayneth the strength, and stayeth the breath, heates the head with all, and swelles the veines therein: so that they draw vnto them forreine meane as cold or heat: and besides that, it enforceth what so euer is in the breast to ascend vpwarde, whereby the head cannot chuse but ake, which is the cause, that swift running is naught for the falling euill. *Galene*[30] thinketh so basely of this kinde of running, as he termeth it, a thing both an enemie to health, to great a thinner of the whole bodie, and such a one, as hath no manner of manly exercise in it. Besides this, it putteth him which runneth so vehemently in daunger of some great conuulsion, if he fortune to encounter any violent stop by the way.

2. The second kinde of *running* which taketh his name of the gentle and moderate mouing, warmes the body very well, strengthens the naturall actions, prouokes appetite, helpes and turnes rewmes, and catarres, some other waye. And therfore it is commended for a remedie against the swiming of the head, against the drie cough, if ye holde your breath withall, against exulcerations in the inner side of the iawes, and the distortion or writhing of the mouth, which the Greekes call κυνικὸν σπὰσμα. For though at the first it seeme to prouoke defluxions and distilling of humours, yet within a small time it stayeth them: and therfore it is thought to be good for those, which are pained with the *Ischiatica*, which haue much a do to stirre their legges at the first, but after that they haue runne a while, they be so nimble and quicke, as if they had neuer felt any paine in those partes. It strengtheneth the stomacke mightely, and deliuereth the bellie from winde, and cold passions: whereby it is thought, and that not without great cause to be verie good for the colike and dropsie: it delayeth the swelling of the milt. For the gnawing of the guttes, and some diseases of the kidneis it is exceeding good, so the kidneies be not either presently, or haue not bene of late, subiect to some exulceration. To saye that it is wholesome for the legges and feete, were to make a doubt, where none can be, considering *running* is their proper and peculiar action. This exercise for all that it is such a freind to health: yet bringes with it some inconueniences: for it is verie laborious: it cooleth the flesh and furthereth not the feeding. And as naturally of it selfe, it breadeth no great harme, so if it meete with an ill head, or a weake bulke, or burning and hoat vrine, it helpes to draw on diuers diseases. He that hath any rupture in the twiste, or els where, must forbeare running, as those also, which haue infected liuers or gauled kidneies. If the chased deare could speake, he would desire the hunter to giue him leaue to pisse, when he pursueth him sorest, and that for but so litle respite, he would shew him a great deale more pastime: but the hunter which knoweth well that the skalding vrine will not let him runne long, wil not lend him that leasure: bycause he careth more for the frute of his owne praie, then the effect of the deares prayer. All the other kindes of *running* which follow, take their names of the manner of their mouing, wherof the first is the long outright running, which if it continue on gently though long, it warmeth the flesh, and makes it plumpe, and is verie good, for great feeders, though it make the bodie slow and grosse. *Running* streight backward, and withall not hastily, is good for the head, the eyes, the streatchers, the stomacke and the loynes. *Running* round about, thinnes the flesh and streaches it, but cheifly the belly, and bycause

[30] De parua pila. lib.

of the quicke motion, it gathereth moysture quickly. And therefore *Hippocrates*[31] wisheth them to vse it, which dreame of blacke starres, as the fore warning of some forreine disease. It troubleth the head and makes it dizie: it marreth both the bulke and the legges, and therefore would be left. He that runnes vphill straynes him selfe sore, and doth neither his bulke nor his legges any great good. He that runnes downhill makes his head giddy, shakes all within him, and tries the weaknesse, or strength of his hippes. He that runneth in his clothes sweateth sore, and warmes his flesh more: and therefore it is good for them, that haue the head ache to runne so: and those that haue somewhat to do, to fetch their breath. He that runneth out of his clothes single or naked, sweateth much, which is much more healthful how litle so euer it be, then much more, with the clothes on. *Hyppocrates*[32] likes running generally more in winter then sommer. *Oribasius*[33] in both, yea though sommer be in his prime and cheife heat. The resolution is, when most sweating is best, which *Artistotle* sayeth is in sommer.

[31] Lib. de insomnijs languentium.
[32] 3. Lib. de Diæta.
[33] 2. part. proble. 21. 33. 42.

CHAPTER 22.

Of leaping.

LEAPING should seeme to be somewhat naturall, and chearfull, bycause at any pleasant or ioyefull newes, not onely the hart will leape for ioye, but also the body it selfe will spring liuely, to declare his consent, with the delited minde, and that not in young folkes alone, but also in the elder, whom we commonly say that no ground can hold: so that leaping seemes to stand the body in such a steade for vttering of ioy, as the tongue serues the minde to deliuer her delite by speche with laughter. The cattell and brute beastes bewraie their contentment, and well liking, by the selfe same meanes, leaping and galloping of them selues in their pasture when they be lustily disposed and in good health. Though in training of the bodie by waye of exercise, there be not so much regard had to the mirth of the minde, as to the motion of the bodie: and yet being an exercise it may not be vnpleasant. In which kinde it is noted to be vehement, wherein both strength is vsed to make the body spring, and swiftnesse to make it nimble: being naturally an interrupted race, as running is a continued leape. It serued the olde world in *game* for brauerie, and shew of actiuitie: in *warfare* to skip ouer diches and hard passages, in *Physicke* for an exercise of health, whereby it became more stately and imperiall, bycause the first famous Romain Emperor *Augustus Cæsar*,[34] being troubled with the *Ischiatica* and stone in his bladder, and also hauing some weaknesse in his left legge and feet, vsed this running leape, or leaping race to helpe himselfe thereby. There be diuers kindes of leaping wherof I will tuch the most likely.

1. *Leaping* and springing without intermission is good to encrease the naturall heat, to helpe digestion, to dispatche raw humours, though afterward it anoie the head and brest, bycause it shaketh the head verie vehemently: and by reason of much bending and so pressing the backe, it oftimes breaketh some canall in the breast or lungues. 2. To *leape* running is good for such diseases of the head, as haue troubled it long. It helpeth the bulke, bycause it vseth no violent bending, nor pressing of the bodie, it fetcheth downe such needeles fumes, as otherwise would haue ben aspiring vpward: it chearisheth weake legges: which prosper not by nurriture, thorough some trembling and benummed flesh. 3. *Leaping* as we do commonly call it and vse it, doth driue idle superfluities downward thoroghly, but bycause it shaketh the bulke to sore, both by to violent mouing and to forcible strayning, it is not good for it: though it shew a verie deliuer and an actiue bodie: both to stirre and to do anything else. It driueth also the stone from the kidneies into the bladder: yet it hurteth the knees by reason of violent and continuall bend-

[34] Suetonius in Augusto cap. 83.

ing them. The *Lacedemonian* wymen, whose picture *Callimachus* the painter, for his foolish curiosity named κακοχειρότεχνος, as *Plinie*[35] reporteth, vsed to leape so, as their heeles did hitte their hippes, which manner of leaping doth both purge and drie. But me thinke I here some gentlewymen saye, fye vpon them *Rigs*. Not so. The lawes and custome of their countrey did allow, nay did commaunde them to runne, to leape, to wrastle, and to do all such exercises, both as well, as men, and also with men. Their reason was. They did thinke the childe lame of the one side, whose mother was delicate, daintie, tender, neuer stirring, neuer exercising, not withstanding, the father were neuer so naturally strong, neuer so artificially trained. And to preuent that infirmitie in their owne youth, they exercised their wymen also, no lesse then their men. As *Plato*[36] wisheth his people in his common weale, which he patterneth for the best. *Skipping* againe the banck, as it helpeth the hippes, so it hurteth the breast: and the same downhill cleareth the head from superfluities, which it fetcheth downward: It strengtheneth the legges, but it shaketh the bowelles to sore, which is very dangerous, for ruptures anywhere: for the crooked swelling veines in the legge: for all gouttes: for all those, in whom the humours vpon any small occasion will fall downe to the feete: and cause them to swell.[37] Further in cases where it were good to let blood or to purge, if either yeares or some other impediment wil admit neither, to auoide superfluous humours, *leaping* will supply the roome. As it is verie ill for those which pisse blood: or be in a flixe: or haue weake or ouerheated kidneies: or that haue at that time, or not long before had, some gaule or exulceration in the kidneies. And yet though the kidneies be sound, eaping will sometime loose a veine. Eche kinde of *leaping* is better accomplished by holding of some weight in the hand for steddinesse, then with the hand emptie and without his ballace.

[35] 34. Lib. cap. 8.

[36] 4. de Rep.

[37] Gal. 6. epi. commen. 3. aph. 2.

CHAPTER 23.

Of swimming.

IN the old time, when they would point at a fellow, in whom there was nothing to be made account of, they were wont to saye, he neither knoweth letter on the booke, nor yet how to *swimme*: wherby it appeareth that *swimming*, was both in great vse, and of great price in those daies, which either first brought forth that byword or afterward maintained it, seing he was helde for no bodie that could not, or but for a dastard which would not learne the sleight to *swimme*. The traine came bycause it was then best to learne, when the iointes were most pliable, and yet strong withall. The ende was either to saue themselues in fightes by sea, or in flightes by lande, where they were to passe riuers, or to assaile enemies by water, or for other such seruices: as what if *Leander* say it serues for loue, and bring both *Hero* to witnesse, which was partaker of the euill, and *Musæus* the Poete, which described their misfortune? Which considerations may recommende *swimming* to vs also: who may stand in neede of it, vpon the same causes, and in the like euentes that they did. But bycause it is so necessarie, it would not be vncurteously entertained, and therefore regard must be had in what water ye swimme, for if ye swimme in springes which are naturally hoat, it is stuffing, and yet good for the palsie, so he that swimmeth do vse bladders, to ease him selfe withall: and lighten his labour. To *swimme* in marsh waters, and pooles, infecteth both the head and all the residue of the bodie, bycause rotten, and corrupt vapours, enter the pores of the bodie, together with the moysture. It is reasonable good *swimming* in lakes and standing meres, which the larger they be and the clearer, the more commodious and wholesome to swimme in. But no kinde of fresh water is so good to swimme in, as the running riuer is, chiefly for them, which be in health, to whom besides many other commodities, it serueth for a preparative to sleepe. Yet it is not good abiding long in any fresh water, for feare of perishing the sinues both with cold and moysture, whose issues be the crampe, and the swimmers daunger. But nothing at all, be it neuer so good for health, be it neuer so defensible to saue, can be gotten without perill in prouing. And why should *swimming* dreame of securitie, and neuer thinke to drowne? Doth it not deale with water, where there is no warrant, but wisedome to forsee? pointe the place, pointe the fight, pointe the daunger and a pointe for daunger: but where you cannot appointe the particularitie, ye cannot warrant the perill. *Cocles,*[38] scaped, it was in a small riuer, and reskue at hand. *Scœna* the centurion scaped, he was neare both shippe and shoar.

[38] Liuius. C. Cæs.

Nay *Cæsar*[39] himselfe saued him selfe from drowning, and helde his lettres vp drie in the one hand. A signe of courage and cunning as that man had enough; but his shippes were at hand, and it is not writen, that either he swamme alone, or any long waye. But of all daungers to drowne, there is least in the sea, where the swimming is best: for the salt water as it is thicker then the fresh, so it beareth vp the bodie better, that it may fleet with lesse labour. The *swimming* in salt water is very good to remoue the headache, to open the stuffed nosethrilles, and therby to helpe the smelling. It is a good remedie for dropsies, scabbes, and scurfes, small pockes, leprosies, falling awaye of either legge, or any other parte: for such as prosper not so, as they would, though they eate as they wishe, for ill stomackes, liuers, miltes, and corrupt constitutions. Yet all *swimming* must needes be ill for the head, considering the continuall exhalation, which ascendeth still from the water into the head. *Swimming* in hoat waters softeneth that which is hardened, warmeth that which is cooled, nimbleth the iointes which are benummed, thinneth the skinne, which is thickned, and yet it troubleth the head, weakneth the bodie, disperseth humours, but dissolueth them not. *Swimming* in cold water doth strengthen the naturall heat, bycause it beates it in: it maketh verie good and quick digestion: it breaketh superfluous humours, it warmeth the inward partes, yet long tarying in it hurtes the sineues, and takes awaye the hearing. Thus much concerning *swimming*, which can neither do children harme in learning, if the maister be wise, nor the common weale but good, being once learned, if either priuate daunger or publike attempt do bid them auenture. For he that oweth a life to his countrey, if he die on lande, he doeth his duetie, and if he drowne in water, his duetie is not drowned.

[39] Appian.

CHAPTER 24.

Of riding.

IF any wilbe so wilful as to denie *Riding* to be an exercise and that a great one, and fittest also for greatest personages, set him either vpon a trotting iade to iounce him thoroughly or vpon a lame hakney to make him exercise his feete, when his courser failes him. In all times, in all countries, among all degrees of people, it hath euer bene taken, for a great, a worthy, and a gentlemanly exercise. Though *Aristophanes* his testimonie, were naught against honest *Socrates*, yet it is good to proue, that riding was a gentlemanly traine, euen among the principles of education in Athens. And *Virgile* in the legacie sent to *Latinus*, describeth the same traine in the Romain children, which, sayeth he, exercised themselues on horsebacke before the towne. And *Horace* accuseth the young gentleman in his time as not able to hange on a horse. But to deale with stories, either Greeke, or Latin, for the Romain or other nations exercise in riding in a matter of such store, were more then needeles. The *Romains* had their whole citie diuided into partialities, by reason of the foure factions of those exercising horsemen. Who of the foure colours, which they vsed, Russet, White, Greene, and Blew, were named *Russati, Albati, Prasini, Veneti.*[40] For the warres how great a traine riding is, I would no countrey had tried, nor had cause to complaine, nor the subdued people to be sorofull, though the conquerour do vant himselfe, of his valiantnesse on horsebacke. For health it must needes be of some great moment, or els why do the Physicians seeme to make so much of it? They saye that generally it encreaseth naturall heat, and that it purgeth superfluities, as that to the contrarie it is naught for any sicke bodie, or that hath taken Physicke hard before, or that is troubled with infection or inflammation of the kidneies. They vse to deuide it into fiue kindes, *Slow, quicke, trotting, ambling,* and *posting*.

1. Of *Slow riding* they write that it wearieth the grines very sore, that it hurteth the buttokes, and legges, by hanging downe to long, and yet it heateth not much: that it hindreth getting of children, and breadeth aches and lamenesse.

2. Of *quicke riding* they saye, that of all exercises it shaketh the bodie most, and that yet it is good for the head ache, comming of a cold cause: for the falling euill, for deafnesse, for the stomack, for yeaxing or hikup, for clearing and quickning the instrumentes of sense: for dropsies: for thickning of thinne shankes: which was found true in *Germanicus Cæsar*[41] nephew to *Tiberius* the Emperour, which so helped his spindle shankes. Againe quick riding is naught for the bulke: for a weake bladder, which must forebeare all exercises, when it hath any exulceration:

[40] Gal. 7. meth. Pli. epist. 9. lib. 6. Martial. lib. 11. Iuuenal.

[41] Suetonius.

for the *Ischiatica*, bycause the hippes are to much heated and weakned, by the vehementnesse of the motion. Whervpon the humours, which are styrred rest there: and either breede new or augment olde aches.

Of *trotting*, it is said euen as we see, that it shaketh the bodie to violently, that it causeth and encreaseth marueilous aches, that it offendes the head, the necke, the shoulders, the hippes, and disquieteth all the entrailes beyond all measure. And though it may somewhat helpe the digestion of meate, and raw humours, loose the belly, prouoke vrine, driue the stone or grauell from the kidneyes downward, yet it is better forborne for greater euilles, then borne with for some sorie small good.

Ambling as it exerciseth least, so it anoyeth least, and yet looseth it the bellie.

As for *posting*, though it come last in reading, it will be first in riding, though for making such hast, it harme eche part of the bodie, and specially the bulke, the lungues, the bowells generally, the kidneyes: as what doth it not allway anoy, and oftimes either breake or put out of ioynte by falles or straynes? It warmes and paires the body to sore, and therfore abateth grossenes, though a grosse man be ill either to ride post himselfe, or for a iade to beare. It infecteth the head, it dulleth the senses, and especially the sight: euen til it make his eyes that posteth to run with water, not to remember the death of his friendes, but to thinke how sore his saddle shakes him, and the ayer bites him.

CHAPTER 25.

Of hunting.

HVNTING is a copious argument, for a poeticall humour to discours of, whether in verse, with *Homer*, or in prose, with *Heliodorus*. *Dian* would be alleged, as so auoyding *Cupide*. *Hippolytus*, would be vsed in commendation of continence, and what would not poetrie bring in to auaunce it, whose musicke being solitarie and woddishe, must needes be, nay is very well acquainted with the chace. If poets should faint, the *Persians* would fight, both for riding and hunting: so that if patrocinie were in question, we neede not to enquire, they would offer them selues, from all countries, and of all languages. But we need not either for praise, or for prose, to vse forraine aduocats. For hunting hath alway caried a great credit, both for exercising the bodie, and deliting the mynde, as it semes to be verie naturall, because it seeketh to maister, and to take beastes, and byrdes, which are naturally appointed for mans vse, and therefore though they be taken and killed, there is no wrong done them. The courteous *Xenophon*[42] as delited himselfe therein, and all the auncient writers, as subscribing to a truth, commend it marueilously, and chiefly, for a proper elementarie to warlike vses, and *Mars* his schoole, whether for valiauntnes or for pollicy, because the resemblaunces of the chiefe warlike executions do fall out in hunting, as the qualitie or courage of the game offereth cause, either to vse force and manhoode, or to flie to deuise and sutteltie.

The *Romain Emperours* did exhibit publike hunting vnto the whole people in way of pastime and pleasure. The *Physicians* make much of it: as being an exercise, which containeth vnder it most of the other stirring exercises, for they that hunt, walke, runne, leape, shout, hallow, ride, and what may they not do, hauing the whole country for roome, and the whole day for time, to do in what they list? And though *Galene*[43] do restraine it to men of great abilitie, as if hunting were not for euery man to vse, which is one of the markes, whereby to know the best exercises, that they be parable, and purchaceable euen to meane purses: yet we see it in common to most, where restraint by law doth not forbid it. Neither is the charge in respect of the exercise, but in respect of the game, whereon the exercise is employed. To hunt a hare, and course a hart, to chase a bucke, and chase a bore is not all one, neither for prouision, nor for perill though the exercise haue small oddes, which being compounded of those exercises that I named, must nedes haue the same effectes, that those exercises haue besides his owne. To warme the bodie very well, to disperse superfluites, to abate flesh, to lessen ouerflowing moysture, to make

[42] Lib de venat. 1. παιδ.

[43] De par pila lib.

one sleepe soundly, to digest meat, and raw humors, to quicken both the sight and the hearing, to keepe of old age, and finally to make the body most healthfull, and the health most lasting.

Rases[44] a notable Arabicke Physician, writeth that in a great plague there remained almost none aliue in a certaine towne, saue hunters only, which escaped by reason of their preseruing exercise. And *Mitbridates* that famous king vsed hunting so much for his healthes sake, as in seuen yeares space, it is written that he neuer came within house, neither in citie nor countrie. And yet hunting is not good for the head, when it is vsed with vehemence, as no other vehement exercise is.

There be but two kindes of *Hunting* to my purpose, the one on horsebacke, the other one foote.

1. They that *Hunt* on horsebake, for so much as they sometime gallop, sometime ride fast, sometime hallow, sometime be stil, and varie so in most actions, seeme to trauel euery part of their body, and therefore it is thought, that thereby the brest, the stomacke, the entrailes, the backe and legges be strengthened: but it is ill for them, which are troubled with any paine in their head, and daungerous for feare of breaking some veine in the breast: for the stone in the kidneyes, for those that be of hoate constitution of body: for weake bellicawles, and for feare of ruptures, because such thinges fall out oftentimes in hunting on horsebacke: not without losse sometime of life.

2. *Hunting* on foote, hath all the commodities, and incommodities to, that hunting on horsebacke hath, sauing the daunger whereunto it is not so much subiecte. And yet the trauell of the bodie is more, the body hoater, the legges and feete more strengthened, the appetite to meat more, to make children lesse. Neither of then is good but for strong and healthful bodies, neither can hunting be but harmefull vnto them, which vse it vnaduisedly, without consideration how they runne, by way of pleasure and ordinarie exercise, or at the suddaine of a head, for by tarying abroade all day, and feeding so vncertainely, and so vnseasonably, there come sundrie inconueniences.

But of all *Hunting* that is still best, wherein we exercise our selues and our owne bodies most, not our hauks of howndes, because exercises be meanes to make men healthfull, and other thinges be meanes to bring that meane about. Such a kinde of hunting was it which *Chiron, Machaan, Podalyrius, Æsculapius,* the parentes and patrones of physike did vse, whose delite thererin, is our warrant in choyce, bycause they being so great physicians, as physicke went then in *Platoes* opinion, did trie that in their owne persons, which they deliuered to posteritie for the same vse.

[44] 3 Commen. 13 tract. cap. 3.

CHAPTER 26.

Of shooting.

THE physicians seeme to commend shooting for the vse of health sufficiently, in that they make *Apollo* and *Æsculapius* the presidentes and protectors of *Archerie,* which both be the greatest gods, and chiefest patrones of ther owne profession. And that it is a thing to be beloued, and liked, what argument is there that can be alleadged of comparable force to that of *Cupide* himselfe, which in the matter of loue, doth bend with his bow, and enamour with his arrow? But in sadnes to say enough of this exercise in few wordes, which no wordes can praise enough for the commodities which it bringeth to the health of the body: as it hath bene vsed by diuers nations, in diuerse sortes, both on horsebacke and on foote, both for peace and warre, for healthfull exercise and pleasant pastime: so none either now doth vse it, or heretofore hath vsed it, more to health, and bettering of the body then our owne countrimen do. As if it were a thing somewhat naturall to *Ilandes,* bycause they of *Crete* and *Cyprus* in olde stories, they of the *Indian* Ilandes in new stories are noted also for neare *Shooting,* strong *Darting,* and streight *Slinging,* whereof the *Balear Ilandes* seeme to take their name. Nay by all auncient monumentes *Shooting* should seeme to be both the eldest, and the vsuallest defence in fighting a farre of, which though it haue now, and tofore, haue had great place in the fielde for warfare: yet hath it a great deale better place in our fields for wellfare: and therefore the more, because it consisteth both of the best exercises, and the best effectes of the best exercises. For he that shooteth in the free and open fields may chuse, whether betweene his markes he will runne or walke, daunce or leape, hallow or sing or do somewhat els, which belongeth to the other, either vehement or gentle exercises. And whereas *hunting* on foote is so much praised, what mouing of the body hath the foote *hunter* in hilles and dales, which the rouing *Archer* hath not in varietie of growndes? Is his naturall heate more stirred then the *Archers* is? Is his appetite better then the *Archers* is though the prouerbe helpe the hungrie *hunter*? Nay in both these the *Archer* hath the vantage. For both his howers be much better to eate, and all his mouing is more at his choice: because the *hunter* must follow his game of necessitie, the *Archer* neede not but at his owne leasure. For his pastime will tarystil, till he come to it, the hunters game is glad to get from him. In fine what good is there in any particular exercise, either to helpe natural heat, or to cleare the body, or to prouoke appetite, or to fine the senses, or to strengthen the sinewes, or to better all partes, which is not altogither in this one exercise? Onely regard to vse it in a meane doth warrant the *archer* from daunger to himselfe: and an eye to looke about, doth defende the passager from perill by him. I could here speake much, if it were not to much, to say euen so much in such a thing, being so faire a pastime, so pleasant to al people, so profitable to most, so familiar to our country, so euery where in eye, so knowne a defence, such a meane to offende, as there is no man but knoweth it to be a preseruatiue to health, and therefore well to be numbred among the trayning exercises. And chiefly as it is vsed in this Iland, wherein the rouing must nedes be the best and most healthful, both for varieties of motion in diuersities of soile, and by vsing all *archery*, in exercising one kinde. For in rouing, you may vse either the butte, or the pricke by the way for your marke, as your pleasure shalbe. This exercise do I like best generally of any rownde stirring without the dores, vpon the causes before alleadged, which if I did not, that worthy man our late and learned countrieman maister *Askam* would be halfe angrie with me, though he were of a milde disposition, who both for trayning the *Archer* to his bow, and the scholler to his booke, hath shewed him selfe a cunning *Archer*, and a skilfull maister.

In the middest of so many earnest matters, I may be allowed to entermingle one, which hath a relice of mirth, for in praysing of *Archerie*, as a principall exercise, to the preseruing of health, how can I but prayse them, who professe it throughly, and maintaine it nobly, the friendly and franke fellowship of prince *Arthurs* knightes in and about the citie of *London*, which of late yeares haue so reuiued the exercise, so countenaunced the artificers, so enflamed emulation, as in themselues for friendly meting, in workemen for good gayning, in companies for earnest comparing, it is almost growne to an orderly discipline, to cherishe louing society, to enrich labouring pouertie, to maintaine honest actiuity, which their so encouraging the vnder trauellours, and so encreasing the healthfull traine, if I had sacred to silence, would not my good friend in the citie maister *Hewgh Offly*, and the same my noble fellow in that order Syr *Launcelot*, at our next meeting, haue giuen me a sowre nodde, being the chiefe furtherer of the fact, which I commend, and the famosest knight, of the fellowship, which I am of? Nay would not euen prince *Arthur* himselfe maister *Thomas Smith*, and the whole table, of those wel known knights, and most actiue *Archers* haue layd in their chaleng against their fellow knight, if speaking of their pastime, I should haue spared their names? whereuntо I am easily led, bycause the exercise deseruing such praise, they that loue so praiseworthie a thing neither can of them selues, neither ought at my hand to be hudled vp in silence.

CHAPTER 27.

Of the ball.

THE play at the *Ball* seemeth compound, bycause it may be vsed, both within dores, and without. Wherof good writers haue deliuered vs thus much: that in the olde time there were diuers kindes of *balles* and diuers kindes of exercise therwith, according to the diuers vse of the *ball* either small or great: both amongst the *Romaines* and *Greekes*, whose names I vse so much, bycause they were best acquainted both with the thinges, and with the right vse therof. *Galene* in his first booke of maintaining health, speaking of the *Germains*, who vsed then to dippe their new borne children into extreme cold water ouer head and eares, to trie their courage and to harden their skinne, sayeth that he wrate those lessons of health and exercise, no more to the *Dutch* and such rude people as we also were then, then to beares, boares and lyons: but to *Greekes* and such people, as though barbarous in nature, yet by traine and learning, were become greekish as we now are, and the *Romains* then were. So that our examples be fetcht from these two nations, which either vsed the thinges most, and handled them best: or else enriched their owne tongues with all that was best, and when they had so done set them ouer vnto vs. But of all their exercises with the *Ball*, we haue not any so farre as I can gesse, by their notes, though we retaine the name: and yet our playing with the *Ball* worketh the same effectes, which theirs did, as it appeareth by their descriptions. Wherfore seeing they be so farre different from ours, and almost worne out of knowledge euen to curious coniectures, which seeke to sift them out, I will neither trouble my selfe with studying to set downe their names: nor my reader with reading to gesse what they were, and how they were vsed.

Three kindes shall content me, which our time knoweth, wherein all the properties of their *balles*, and all the effectes of their exercises, be most euidently seene. The *hand ball*, the *footeball*, the *armeball*.

1. The litle *hand ball* whether it be of some softer stuffe, and vsed by the hand alone, or of some harder, and vsed with the rackette, whether by tennice play with an other, or against a wall alone, to exercise the bodie with both the handes, in euerie kinde of motion, that concerneth any, or all the other exercises, is generally noted, to be one of the best exercises and the greatest preseruations of health. In so much as *Galene* bestoweth an whole treatise vpon the vse and praise of it, wherein he compareth it with other exercises, and preferreth it before all, for parabilitie, to be all mens game: for profitablenesse, to do all men good: for pleasauntnesse, to quicke all mens spirites, and in short knits vp the some of his conclusion thus.

That the vse of the litle *ball* doth plant in the minde *courage*, in the bodie *health*, in all the limmes a trim and wel proportionate *constitution*: so it be moderately and aduisedly executed. Playing at the *ball* in generall is a strong exercise, and maketh the bodie very nimble, and strengtheneth all the vitall actions. The litle *handball* is counted to be a swift exercise, without violence, and therefore the rakketters in tennyse play, if they vse it in that kinde, which is thought to be most healthfull, must shew them selues nymble without strayning, and yet it falleth out most commonly contrarie, while desire to wynne some wager makes the winners loose a benefit, which they wish for more, and would gladly get to better their health by. This playing abateth grossenes and corpulence, as al other of the same sort do: it maketh the flesh sownd and soft, it is very good for the armes, the greene and growing ribbes, the back, and by reason the legges are mightely stirred ther by, it is a great furtherer to strength, it quickneth the eyes by looking now hither, now thither, now vp, now downe, it helpeth the ridgebone, by stowping, bending and coursing about: it is verie good for bellies and stomakes, that be troubled with winde or any paine which proceedeth from colde. Now to the contrary it is not good for ill and bleare eyes raw stomakes, vndigested meat, which haue more neede of rest then stirring, and for such as will soone be turnesicke, which the oft turning about of the head and eyes cannot but cause. The playing at tennyse is more coastly and strayning to aunswere an aduersary, but the playing against the wall is as healthfull, and the more ready, bycause it needeth no aduersary, and yet practiseth euery kinde of motion, euery ioynt of the body, and all without danger. Children vse this ball diuersly, and euery way healthfully, in regard of the exercise: if accidentarie faultes fall out among children, in the vse of the play, the parties must beare the blame, and not the play.

The second kinde I make the *Footeball* play, which could not possibly haue growne to this greatnes, that it is now at, nor haue bene so much vsed, as it is in all places, if it had not had great helpes, both to health and strength, and to me the abuse of it is a sufficient argument, that it hath a right vse: which being reuoked to his primatiue will both helpe, strength, and comfort nature: though as it is now conmonly vsed, with thronging of a rude multitude, with bursting of shinnes, and breaking of legges, it be neither ciuil, neither worthy the name of any traine to health. Wherin any man may euidently see the use of the trayning maister. For if one stand by, which can iudge of the play, and is iudge ouer the parties, and hath authoritie to commaunde in the place, all those inconueniences haue bene, I know, and wilbe I am sure very lightly redressed, nay they wil neuer entermedle in the matter, neither shall there be complaint, where there is no cause. Some smaller number with such ouerlooking, sorted into sides and standings, not meeting with their bodies so boisterously to trie their strength: nor shouldring or shuffing one an other so barbarously, and vsing to walke after, may vse *footeball* for as much good to the body, by the chiefe vse of the legges, as the *Armeball*, for the same, by the vse of the armes. And being so vsed, the *Footeball* strengtheneth and brawneth the whole body, and by prouoking superfluities downeward, it dischargeth the head, and vpper partes, it is good for the bowells, and to driue downe the stone and grauell from both the bladder and kidneies. It helped weake hammes, by much mouing, beginning at a meane, and simple shankes by thickening of the flesh no lesse then riding doth. Yet rash running and to much force oftentimes breaketh some inward conduit, and bringeth ruptures.

3. The third kind I call the *Armeball* which was inuented in the kingdom of *Naples*, not many yeares agoe, and answereth most of the olde games, with the great ball, which is executed with the armes most, as the other was with the feete, and be both very great helpers vnto health. The arme in this is fensed with a wooden brace, as the shin in the other with some other thing for meeting with a shrew. The *armeball* encreaseth the naturall heate, maketh way for superfluities, causeth sound sleepe, digesteth meate wel, and dispatcheth raw humors, though it stuffe the head, as all vehement exercises do. It exerciseth the armes and backe chiefly, and next to them the legges, and therfore it must needs be good for such, as desire to haue those partes strong and perfit, to digest their meate at will, to distribute profitable iuice to the whole body, and to auoide needelesse matter, as well by sweate, as by any other kinde of secret euacuation. And yet it is very ill for a naughtie backe, for hoat kidneyes, for sharp vrine, and generally for any that is troubled with infirmities and diseases in those parts which are strained with stirring.

Thus much concerning the particular exercises, which I haue pickt out from the rest, as most reducible to our time and countrie, wherein I haue not followed the ordinarie diuision, which the training maisters and Physicians do vse, but I deuised such a one, as I tooke to be fittest for myne owne purpose regarding our soyle and our seasons. Neither haue I rekened vp the other *antique* exercises, but haue let them rest with their friends and fauorers, which be long ago at rest. For the tumbling *Cybistike*, the thumping *Pugillate*, the buffeting *Cestus*, the wrastling *Pancrace*, the quayting *Discus*, the barlike *Halteres*, the swinging *Petawre*, and such old memorandums, they are to auncient and to farre worne from the vse of our youth: the considering whereof may rather stirre coniecture, then stai assurance, what they were, when they were. And of these which I haue named, many be farre beyond boyes plaie, for whom alone I do not deale, but for all studentes in generall, neither yet do I exclude either any age, or any person, if I may profit any else beside studentes and scholers. Neither do I tie the trayne to these exercises alone, but alway to some though not alway to one kinde. The cause and consideration must leade all, which may bring forth the like, and why not the better vpon due and wel obserued circunstance? For though the general cause do direct much, yet the particular circunstance directeth more, being it self enformed in the generall iudgement. The most of these notes, which I haue alleaged, were giuen in *Italie, Greece & Spaine*, and that climate farre distant, and much differing from our degree. Wherefore our traine vpon consideration of the degrees in soyle, in temperature, in constitution, and such like, must appropriate it selfe where the difference is apparent. Therefore both to vse these exercises which I haue named, to the best, and to deuise other by comparison and circumstance, as cause shal offer, I will runne thorough those particularities, which either make by right, or marre by wrong applying, both all that I haue said, or that can be deuised in this kinde, to preserue health.

CHAPTER 28.

Of the circumstances, which are to be considered in exercise.

THERE be six circumstances, which leade and direct all exercises, and are carefully to be considered of, by the trayning maister. For either the missing or mistaking of any one of them, may do harme to more then one, and the vsing of them with circumspection and warynes, doth procure that good to health, which this whole discourse hitherto hath promised.

The sixe circumstances be these, the *nature* of the exercise which ye entend to vse: the *person* and *body* which is to be exercised, the *place* wherin, the *time* when, the *quantitie* how much, the *maner* how, whereof I do meane to giue some particular aduertisements so as I do finde the learned physicianes, and wise health maisters to haue handled them in their writings, yet by the way least any man either dispaire of the good, and therefore spare the prouing, because the forme of exercise doth seeme so intricate, and there with all to much: or if he be entred in triall, and thinke he shall faile, if he misse in some litle, bycause the charge is giuen so precisely, to keepe al that is enioyned: I wish him not to thinke either the errour vnpardonable, to regard, or the thing vnauailable to health, if either all, or any one of these circumstances be not absolutely hyt. For as a perfit healthfull body is not to be found by enquirie, which is not to be hoped for in nature, bycause in so continuall a chaunge such a perfitnes cannot chaunce, our bodyes being subiect to so many imperfections: so is it no wonder for men to do what they may, and to wish for the best, though still beyond their reach. If any can come neare them, he breakes no right of vse, though he misse the rule of art, which alwaye enioyneth in the precisest sort, but yet resteth content with that which falleth within compasse of ordynarie circumstance. The reason is, *art* weyeth the matter abstracte, and free from circumstaunce, and therefore hauing the whole obiect at commaundemet, she may set downe her precept, according to that perfitnes, which she doth conceiue: but the execution being chekt with a number of accidentarie occurrences, which *art* cannot comprehend, as being to infinite to collect, must haue one eye to her precept, and an other to hir power, and aske consideration counsell, how to performe that with a number of lettes, and thwartings which, art did prescribe, either without any, or at the lest, with not so many.

CHAPTER 29.

The nature and qualitie of the exercise.

THE *nature* of the exercise which we vse, either to recouer health and strength, if they be feebled: or to preserue them, that they feeble not, as it is verie forcible to worke this healthfull effect: so it deserueth verie circumspect consideration, in applying and fitting it to the effect: that the exercise in his degree of motion may aunswere the partie in his kinde of constitution: least by iarring that way too farre, they fall into a greater discord. *Galene*[45] examining the thinges, which do please the displeased infantes, findes out that all their naturall vnquietnesse is appeased by three natural meanes, which the nurse vseth, the *pappe* to feede, the *voice* to still, the *arme* to moue. Whervpon he concludeth that *meat* to nourish, *Musicke* to delite, *motion* to exercise be most naturall, which being so, then for the preseruation of nature, she must needes haue her owne motion, which agreeth best with her owne disposition. For as some exercises go before the maine to prepare the bodie, and some follow to retourne it by degrees into his former state and temper: so some be verie vehement, strong, and strainable: other verie gentle, curteous, and remisse: which must haue echone their application, according vnto the qualitie, and state of the bodie, wherunto they are to be applyed. They be also as far distinct and different, as particular circunstance can worke alteration in any respect, as their particular titles before did shew in their particular braunching and diuision. And yet therein they swarue not from the generalitie of Physicke, which leaning vpon some vnfallible groundes, yet lighteth still vpon some fallible euentes, which make the whole profession to seeme coniecturall, though in the best and surest kinde of coniecture, if the professour haue studied to sufficiencie and obserued so long, till discretion haue saide, the thing is thus. I will not therfore spend any more labour, about a matter of so great confusion, but as they shall fall out, so will I apply them, that by their proper vse, their propertie maye appeare.

[45] 1. Sanit. tuen.

CHAPTER 30.

Of the bodies which are to be exercised.

IN the bodie which is to take good of exercise, there be three pointes to be considered: 1. for either it is *sickly* hauing his operations tainted and weake: 2. or it is *healthy* and without any extraordinarie and sensible taint: 3. or it is *valetudinarie,* neither pure sicke nor perfit whole.

To speake first of the weake and sickish bodie, it is to be noted, as hath bene already in parte marked before, that sicknesse assaileth vs three wayes: By distemperature, when either the whole bodie, or some parte therof is anoyed with vnproportionate heat, cold, drynesse, or moysture: or by misfashioning, when either the whole bodie, or some parte therof, wanteth his due forme, his iumpe quantitie, his iust number, his naturall seat: or by diuision, when any part of the bodie being naturally vnited vpon some weaknesse is dissolued and sundred. And as diseases come by one, or all these three wayes, so health doth defend it selfe by the contrarie, good temperature, good forme, good vniting of partes. It is graunted by the best though contraried by some of the soryest Physicians, that sicke bodies may be put to exercise: so it be well considered before, what kinde of weaknesse the body is in: and what kinde of helpe may be hoped for by the exercise. As for example in sicknesse which commeth by distemperature: if a bodie be distempered with to much heat, it may not be put to any great or earnest exercise, for ouer heating. If it be to drie and withered, it must forbeare much exercise for feare of ouerdrying. If it be to hoat and dry both, or to hoat and to moyste both, it must quite abandon exercise, as in the first kinde enflaming, in the second choking. If it be cold and drie it must either neuer be exercised or verie gently. If it be cold or moyst, then exercise can do it no harme. If it be cold and moyst, it maye boldly abide exercise: which variety commeth vpon the effectes, that are wrought by exercises, either in augmenting heat, and stirring humours, or auoiding superfluities. Whervpon the generall conclusion is: that no distempered bodie may vse, any great or vehement exercise though some there be, which may venture vp on some meane and gentle kinde of stirring, whether the infirmitie concerne the whole bodie, or be so in some parte, as it shake not the whole. If the infirmitie in *fashion* be casuall and come by late misfortune, (for in this kinde naturall weaknesse is euer excepted) exercise maye do good, bycause it will make that streight, which was croked, that smooth, which was rugged, lay that which was swollen, raise that which was layd, emptie that which was full, fill that which was emptie, open that which was close and shut: and so forth, still working the contrarie to the defect, and thereby the amendment. If the faulte be in *quantitie,* great and swift exercises will abate, and pull downe the flesh, small and slow will fat and thicken it. If the fault be in *number*, exercise helpeth, as vehement mouing driueth the stone and grauell from the straite passages of the kidneyes to the broader, and from thence downe into the bladder. If the fault be in *seat*, no exercise is good, bycause till the part be restored to his place and site, there is no mouing to be vsed, nor yet long after, for feare of displacing it againe. If the fault come by *disvnion*, *exulration*, or *gaule*, the disvniting of the nobler partes, as the braine, the stomacke, the liuer, and such other, specially if it be ioyned with any ague excludeth all exercises. The baser partes refuse not meane stirring, as the skinne being deuided and disvnited with scabbes, which come of salt and sharp humours, by motion is freed and deliuered of them. This consideration is to be had in the exercising of sicke bodies, whether the sicknesse come by distemperature of humours, by deformitie in composition, or by disvnion of partes.

Valetudinarie.

Concerning *valetudinarie* bodies, which be neither alwaye sicke, nor euer whole, and such as be vpon recouerie after sicknesse, and aged men, whom yeares make weake and sickish, thus I read: that exercise is verie necessarie for the two first, to strengthen their limmes, to dispatche superfluities, to stirre heat, to restore the bodie to his best habite, alwaye prouided that the exercise rise from some mediocritie and slownes by degrees to that height, which the parties may well abide. For to earnest and rash exercise will empaire their health more. Olde men, as by want of naturall heat, they grow full of superfluities, so they must haue some pleasant and gentle kinde of exercise, both to stirre the heat, and to ridde awaye those needlesse necessities, which of force inferre sicknes, if they be not enforced awaye. And as they be naturally drie, so they must vse no exercise, which dryeth to much. Wherein these foure circunstances are to be considered, 1. First their strength, which being not great, requireth but quiet and gentle exercises. For though *Prodicus* the warie Philosopher in *Plato, Antiochus* the healthy Physician in *Galene, Spurina* the considerate counsellour in *Plinie,* could do straunge thinges in their olde age, by good forsight in their former yeares, yet they be no generall presidentes. 2. Secondly the forme of their bodies. For as good constitutions, can do that meanly and pretily well in their olde age, which they did strongly and stowtly in their youth, so the weake and misfashioned are vnfit for exercise. For loude speaking will hurt to narrow bulkes, and any walking fainteth weake legges, and so forth in all imperfections of the like sorte. 3. Thirdly how they haue bene vsed: bycause they will better awaie with their acquainted exercises, then with other, wherunto they haue neuer bene vsed, the vehemencie and courage of their yong dayes onely excepted. 4. Fourthly what infirmities they be subiect vnto, as if their heades will soone be giddy, or their eyes sore, or if they be in daunger of sudden falling, then they must auoide all exercises which be offensiue to the head. And this rule is generally to be obserued in all bodies, that the partes pacient maye not be pressed to sore.

Healthy bodyes.

As for healthy and strong bodies, they are to be esteemed not by absolute perfitnesse in measure and rule, which will not be found, but by performing all naturall functions, without any greife or painfull let: wherof in some places there is good plentie. For as generally in so many wayes to weaknesse, our bodies neuer continuyng any one minute in the same state, perfit health in the absolutest degree is not to be hoped for: so in the second degree of perfection, where no sensible let is, no felt feeblenesse, but all ordinaries excellent, though no excellent extraordinarie, there be many bodies to be found healthfull, lustie, and lasting verie long: as the soile wherin they brede and be is of healthfulnesse, and wholesomnesse. Such a praise doth *Galene* giue to his owne, and *Hipocrates*[46] his country: Nay that is the common proofe, where small diet, and much labour accompanieth necessitie in state and good constitution in body. Now these healthfull bodyes, as they dayly feede, and digest well, so to auoide superfluities, which come thereby, bycause no meat is so meete with the body, as it turneth all into nurriture, they must of necessitie pray ayde of exercise, which must be neither to violent, nor to immoderate, but sutable to their constitution, as in the priuate description the particular exercise bewrayeth it selfe, and generally the generall reason suffiseth such a trayner, as can vse the consideration of circumstance wisely. In exercising of healthy bodies, there be fiue speciall thinges to be obserued. 1. The first is how they haue bene vsed, for looke wherewith they haue bene most acquainted, and therein, or in the like they will best continew, and with most ease. 2. The second is what age they be of, for old men must haue gentle exercises, children somewhat more stirring, yong men more then they, and yet but in a meane, bycause they are subiect to more harme by violence then either children or old men, for that hauing strong and drie bodyes, thicke and stiffe flesh, fast cleauing to the bone, and the skinne stretched accordingly, they are in great daunger of strong conuulsions, and diuers ruptures, both of flesh and veines, through extremities of exercise. 3. The third is the state of their body, because fat and grosse men, may abyde much more exercise, then leane may and so in other. 4. The fourth is their kinde of liuing, for he that eateth much, and sleepeth much, must either exercise much or liue but a while. And to the contrary, the spare feeder or great waker, needeth not any such kinde of physicke. 5. The fift is the temperature of their bodyes, for small exercise satisfieth drie or hoat bodyes, in any degree of eager heat. Againe colde bodyes may away with both vehement and very much, for moyst bodyes to auoide superfluities, exercise and labour is very good, so the bodies be not hoat withall, the humor very much and very soone turned into vapour, and that also neare to the lungues for feare of choking after much stirring. Hoat and dry admit no exercise, hoat and moyste, cold and dry admit some litle. But of all constitutions none is more helpt by exercise then the colde and moyst: because heat and clearing, the two effectes of exercise haue their owne subiect whereon to worke, which must be weyed in complexions, and states of the body.

[46] 2. De tu. vali.

CHAPTER 31.

Of the exercising places.

THAT the place, wherein any thing is done, is of great force to the well or ill performing therof, and specially in natural executions, there can be no better profe, then that we se, not onely plantes and trees, not onely brute beastes and cattell, but also euen the bodies and myndes of men to be altered and chaunged, with the varietie and alteration of the place and soyle, so that for the better exercising of the bodies to the preseruing or recouering of health, it is verie materiall to limit some certainety concerning the place. Wherin not to dwell long at this time, bycause in the common place both for learning and exercising togither, I shall haue occasion to say more of this matter: these foure qualities are to be obserued in the place. 1. First the place where ye exercise, must haue his ground flowred so, as it be not offensiue to the body, as in wrastling not hard to fall on, in daunsing soft, and not slipperie. How angrie would a boie be to be driuen to scourge his *top* in sand, grauell, or deepe rushes? and so forth in the rest: as is most fit for the body exercised, with lest daunger and best dispatch. 2. The second, that the place be either free from any wind at all, or if be not possible to auoide some, that it be not subiect to any sharpe and byting winde: which may do the body some wrong, being open, and therefore ready to receiue forreine harme by the ayer. 3. Thirdly that the place be open, and not close nor couered, to haue the best and purest ayre at will, whereby the body becommeth more quicke and liuely, and after voyding noysom superfluities, may proue lightsome by the very ayer and soyle. 4. Fourthly that there be no contagious nor noysome stenche neare the place of exercise, for feare of infecting that by new corruption, which was lately cleared by healthful motion. Generally if the place connot be so fit and fauourable to exercise, as wish would it were, yet wisedom may win thus much, that he may be as well appointed, to preuent the ill of euery both season and circumstance, as possibility can commonly performe. When great conquests had made states almost, nay in deede to wealthie, and libertie of soyle giuen them place to chuse, they builded to this end meruelous and sumptuous monuments, which time and warres haue wasted, but we which must doe as we may, must be content with that, which our power can compasse, and if the worst fall, thinke that he which placed vs in the world, hath appointed the world for vs for an exercising place, not onely for the body against infections, but also for the mynde against affections, which being herselfe well trayned, doth make the bodie yeelde to the bent of her choice.

CHAPTER 32.

Of the exercising time.

TIME is deuided into *accidentarie* and *naturall,* and *naturall* againe into *generall* and *particular*. The *naturall time* generally construed is ment by the spring, the summer, the haruest and the wynter: particularly by the howers of the day and night. The *accidentarie time* chaungeth his name still, sometime faire, sometime foule, sometime hoat, sometime colde and so forth. Of this *accidentary time* this rule is giuen, that in exercise we chuse, as neare as we can, faire weather, cleare and lightsome to confirme the spirites, which naturally reioice in light and are refreshed thereby: not cloudy, darke and thicke, wherein grosse humours make the bodie dull and heauie: againe when there is either no great, or no verie noysome winde to pearce the open pored body, nor to much forreine heat to enflame the naturall: nor to much cold to stiffen it to sore.

For the *naturall* time generally taken, *Aristotle*[47] would haue the bodie most exercised in sommer, bycause the naturall heat being then least, and the bodie therefore most burdened with superfluities, then exercise most helpes: both to encrease the inward heat, and to send out those outward dettes. *Hippocrates*[48] againe giuing three principall rules to be kept in exercise, to auoide wearinesse, to walke in the morning, maketh this the third to vse both more and longer exercise in the winter and cold weather, and most of his fauourites hold that opinion. The reason is, bycause in sommer the heat of the time dryeth the bodie enough, so that it needeth no exercise to wither it to much, where the aire it selfe doth drie it enough. *Galene*[49] a man of great authoritie in his profession, pronounceth thus in generall, that as temperate bodies are to be exercised in a temperate season which he countes to be spring: so cold bodies are in hoat weather: hoat in cold, moyst in drie, drie in moyst: meaning thereby that whensoeuer the bodie seemeth to yeeld towardes any distemperature, then the contrarie both time and place must be fled to for succour. Of these opinions iudgement is to chuse, which it best liketh. Me thinke vpon diuers considerations, they maye all stand well without any repugnance, seing neither *Hippocrates* nor *Galene,* deny exercise in sommer simply, and *Aristotle* doth shew what it worketh in sommer.

For the *naturall time* particularly taken, thus much is said, that it is vnwholesome to exercise after meat, bycause it hindereth digestion by dispersing the heat, which should be assembled wholly to further and helpe digestion. And yet both

[47] 2. Part. proble. 21. 33. 42.

[48] 3. De diæta.

[49] 2. De tuen. vali.

Aristotle and *Auicene*, allow some gentle walking after meat, to cause it so much the sooner setle downe in the stomacke, specially if one meane to sleepe shortly after. But for exercise before meate, that is excedingly and generally commended, bycause it maketh the naturall heat strong against digesting time, and driuing away vnprofitable humours, disperseth the better and more wholesome, thorough out the whole bodie, whereas after meate it filleth it with rawnesse, and want of digestion: bycause mouing marres concoction, and lets the boyling of the stomacke. Now in this place there be three thinges to be considered.

1. First that none venture vpon any exercise, before the bodie be purged naturally, by the nose, the mouth, the belly, the bladder, bycause the contrarie disperseth that into the bodie, which should be dismissed and sent awaie: nor before the ouernightes diet be thoroughly digested, for feare of to much superfluitie, besides crudity and cholere. Belching and vrine be argmentes of perfit or vnperfit digestion. The whiter vrine the worse and weaker digestion, the yealower, the better.

2. The second consideration is, that no exercise be medled withall the stomacke being verie emptie, and wearie hungrie, least rauening cause ouerreaching, and *Hippocrates*[50] condemne you, for linking labour with hunger, a thing by him in his *aphorismes* forbid.

The third consideration is not to eate streight after the exercise, before the bodie be reasonably setled. Yet corpulent carcases, which labour to be lightened of their cariage, be allowed their vittail, though they be puffing hoat. The cause why this distance betwene mouing and meate is enioyned, is this, for that the bodie is still a clearing, while it is yet hoat: and the excrementes be but fleeting: so that neither the partie can yet be hungrie, nor the heat entend digestion. Whervpon they counsell him that is yet hoat after exercise, neither to washe himselfe in cold water: nor to drinke wine, nor cold water. Bycause washing will hurt the open body, wine will streight way steeme vp into the head, cold water will offend the belly and lyver, yea sometime gaule the sinewes, nay sometime call for death.

Houres.

What *houres* of the daie were best for exercise, the auncient *Physicians* for their soile, in their time, and to their reason, appointed it thus. In the spring about noone, for the temperatenesse of the aire: in sommer in the *morning*, to preuent the heat of the daie: in haruest and winter towardes night: bycause the *morninges* be cold, the dayes short, and to be employed otherwise: and the meat before that time will lightly be well digested. But now in our time, the diet being so farre altered, and neuer a circumstance the same, no time is fitter for exercise then the *Muses* not to wonder and muse at it, that we be so boulde with our and their common friend, I meane the *morning*, seeing we seeke to haue learning and health ioyned together. Which falling both most fit in the *morning*, doth lend vs an argument to proue that they were ill sundred, whom the samenes of time so vniteth together. In the *morning* the bodie is light, being deliuered of excrementes, strong after sleepe, free from common lettes and without any perill of indigestion, all which fall out quite contrarie in the *euening*. If any writer allow any other houre after meate, it is

[50] 2. Aph. 16.

in some extremitie of sicknesse, not in respect of exercise: as when the weather is most lowring, and children most heauie and dumpish, why is not then the fittest time to play, by chearing the minde, to lighthen the bodie?

CHAPTER 33.

Of the quantitie that is to be kept in exercise.

ALL they which vse exercises vse them either not so much as they should, and that doeth small good, or more then they should, and that doeth much harme, or so as they should, and that doeth much good. Wherupon he that hath skill to crie ho, when he is at the height of his exercise, wherwith nature feeleth her selfe to be best content, knoweth best wherein the best measure consisteth. But how may one know the verie pitche in exercise, and when it were best for one to crie ho? principally by these two generall limittes. 1. Wherof the first is, when a *vapour* mingled with sweat is sensibly perceiued to proceede from the bodie: when the *vaines* begin to swell, and the *breathing* to alter. For wheras the ende of exercise is to strengthen the bodie, and to encrease the naturall heat, whereby the wholesome iuyce is digested, and distributed to the nurriture of the other partes: and vnprofitable residences discharged: if the exercise come not to these degrees of *sweat, swelling*, and *breathing*, it is to weake to worke those effectes, which it doth vndertake. 2. The second generall limit is, to continue the *exercise* so long, as the *face* and bodie shall haue a fresh colour, the *motion* shalbe quicke and in proportion, and no *wearynesse* worth the speaking shalbe felt. For if the *colour* begin to faint, or the bodie to be gaunt, or *wearynesse* to wring, or the *motion* to shrinke, or the sweat to alter in *qualitie* from hoat to cold, in *quantitie* from more to lesse, which should naturally encrease with the exercise, then crie ho, for feare of thinning the bodye to much, of consuming the good and ill iuyces together, of weakning the naturall heat, of destroying in steade of strengthning: bycause these be euident shewes, that the bodie wasteth, cooleth and dryeth more then it should.

Now as these be generall staies not to proceede further, but to rest when we are well: so there be other more particuler, wherein there is regard to be had, to the *strength* or *weakenes* of the partie, to the *age*, to the *time* of the yeare, to the *temperature* of the body, to the *kinde* of life. For in all these measure is a mery meane, and immoderatenes a remeadilesse harme.

They that be of good *strength* may continue longer in exercise, then any other, without some great occasion to the contrary: though they faint, and feele some litle *lassitude* and *wearines*, bycause they will quickly recouer themselues. Those that be but *weake* must exercise but a while, bycause any small taint in them, is long and hard to be recouered, and therefore their limit is to be warme, and to be ware of sweating.

2. As touching the difference in age. Olde men, yea though they vse the same exercises, wherewith they were acquainted when they were yong, yet must leaue ear they either sweat or begin to be wearie, bycause they are drye and wythered. Men of middle *age* must of necessitie keepe the meane lymit, bycause too much offendes them, to litle doth them litle good, both hinder the state of their bodies. *Youth* from seuen till one and twenty, will abyde much exercising, very well: wherefore they are allowed without daunger to be hoat and chafe, to puffe and blow, to sweat, to be wearie also to some degree of *lassitude*: for being full of excrementes by reason of ther reacheles diet, they finde great ease in labour and sweat: and being strong withall, a litle *wearines* makes them litle worse. And yet there must be great eye had to them, that they keepe within compasse, and so much the more, the lesse they be aboue seuen yeare old. For too much exercise in those yeares marres their growing, and alters the constitution of their bodies to the worse.

3. For the *time* of the yeare. In *Winter* the exercise may be great, till the body be hotte: but yet sweat not, lest the cold do harme. In the *Spring* more euen till it sweat, in the *Haruest* lesse, in the *Sommer* least: because the ayre which enuironeth the body, doth then of it selfe so wearie and weaken it, as it needeth neither sweating, nor heating, nor wearying with exercise, wherein *Hippocrates* and his *Phisicke* will preuaile against *Aristotle* and his *Philosophie*.

4. For the temperature of the body: *Moyst* bodies may abide much exercise, by much stirring to drie vp much moisture, so that they may sweat, and yet they must take heede of wearynes. Dry *bodies* may very ill away with any exercise, and if with any, it must be such as will neither cause heat nor sweat. Could *bodies* may moue till they be throughly warme. Hoat *bodies* must be deintily dealt withall. For *heat, sweat,* and great chaunge of their breathing be enemies to their complexion. Hoat and dry for feare of encreasing their qualities to much must be content with either no exercise at all, or with verie litle. Cold and dry may abyde stirring in respect of their coldnes, till they be warme: but for feare of ouerdrying they must not venture vpon sweat. Hoat and moyst must vse moderate exercise, bycause to litle dyminisheth not their superfluous moysture: to much melteth to fast, and warmth to much. Whereupon daungerous flixes ensue: so that they must needes auoid great alteration of breath, and to much warmeth. Cold and moyst may exercise them selues till they blow, till they be hoat, and till they sweat. To be short, of any constitution this may best abide exercise, to emptie it of needlesse humors, to stirre the natural heat, and to procure perfit digestion. *Sicke-men* may not dreame of any definite *quantitie* in their exercises, bycause according to the variety of their infirmities, both their exercises, and the quantities thereof must be proportionally applyed: so that there can be no certaine rule set for them.

Such as be newly recouered from sicknes, or that be on the mending hand, bycause their strength is feeble, their heat weake, their lymes dried vp, must content themselues with small and competent exercise, for feare of no small inconuenience. Their limit therefore must be to stirre, but not to change breath, to warme, but not to heat, to labour, but not to be wearie: yet as their health growes, their exercise may encrease.

5. For the kinde of life. Such as liue moderately and with great continencie, though they be not full of superfluities, and therefore neede not exercise much: yet they must not abandon it quite, least their bodies for want therof, becomming vnweildie, lease both the benefit of naturall heat, and good constitution, and auoid not such residence, as of force breedes in them, and in the ende will cause some sicknes crepe on, which comes without warning, bycause *Iupiter*, as both *Hesiode* sayeth, and *Plutarch* subscribeth, hath cut her tongue out, least she tell, when she comes, for that he would haue her come stealing, eare she be perceiued, as *Galene* also maketh the litle vnperceiued, or for the smallnesse contemned to be mother to all illes both of bodie and soule. *Incontinence* breedes much matter for exercise: and therefore requireth much, cheifly to procure sound sleepe, the captaine cause of good digestion. Such as haue not vsed exercises before, and be nouices in the trade, must first be purged, then by *meane* and *moderate* ascents, day by day be well applyed, till they come to that degree, wherein those are, which haue bene acquainted therewith before. But in all those *degrees* and *mediocrities*, *immoderate* exercise must alway be eschewed, as a very capitall enemie to health causing *children* not to prosper nor grow: *lustie men* to fall into vnequall distemperatures, and oftimes agues: *oldmen* to become dry and ouerwearied. To conclude who is it, to whom it doth not some harme, and from whom it keepeth not some great good. These be the tokens, whereby immoderate exercises be discerned, if ye feele your ioyntes to be very hoat: if you perceiue your body to be drie and vnequall: if in your trauell you feele some pricking in your flesh, as if it were of some angrie push: if after sweating your colour become pale: if you finde your selfe faint and wearie more than ordinary, which wearines, fayntnesse and pricking, occupy the credit of a great circumstance in physicke, of *Galene*,[51] and greeke physicianes called κόπος of the *latines* and our *Linacer lassitudines*, and come vpon dissolution and thinning of grosse humours, being to many at that time to cleare the body of, and pricking as they passe like some angrie bile within the body, whereby the body is both forced to make an end of exercise, and withall is verie wearysome, and stif oftymes after.

[51] 4. De tuenda sanita.

CHAPTER 34.

Of the manner of exercising.

GALENE in the second booke of his preseruatiue to health knitteth vp three great thinges in verie few wordes, that who so can handle the exercises in due *maner*, with the *apotherapeutike*, or gouerning the body after exercise, and his *frictions* to rubbe it and chafe it as it should be, is an absolute trayner in his kinde. Wherein we may see the vse of *chafing*, and rubbing the body both to be verie auncient, and very healthfull, to warme the outward partes, to open the passages for superfluitie, and to make one actiue and chearie to deale with any thing afterward. It hath his place euery day at tymes, euery yeare in seasons, altering vpon circumstance, but still both needefull and healthfull, and clearith where it chafeth. For the *apotherapeutike* much hath bene saide already: wherefore this place must serue peculiarly for the *maner* of exercising.

They of old time to whom these rules were first giuen hauing all thinges at their will, and sparing for no cost, neither straited for want of time, which they disposed as they listed, and to whom the traine bycause of their libertie and leasure was properly bequeathed, did vse many circumstances both ear they entred into their exercise, and when they were in it, and also after that they had ended it, ear they went to meat. Which their curious course, I will briefly runne through, onely to let them see it, which can do no more but see it, bycause the circumstances of our time will skant suffer any to assay it. After that they felt their former meat fully digested, and had at leysure performed what belonged to the purging of their bodies, they disrobed themselues, and were chafed with a gentle kinde of rubber, till that the freshnes of their colour, and agilytie of their ioyntes seemed to call for exercise. Then were they oynted with sweete oyle so neatly and with such cunning, as it might sooke into their bodies, and search euerie ioynt. That being done if they ment to wrastle, they threw dust vpon the oyntment: if not, they went to the exercise, which they had most fansie vnto, which being ended they rested a while, then with certaine scrapers called *Strigiles*, they had all their filth scrapte of their bodies: afterward they were chafed and rubbed againe, then oynted also againe, either in the *Sunne* or by the *fire*. Then to the *bath*, last of all apparelling themselues they fell to their meat. And this was not one or two, nor men of might alone, but euery one and of euery sort, nay, shall I say it? euen of euery sex. A long and laboriouse trauell, and an argument of much ease, and to much adoe in that, which should be more common.

But in these our dayes, considering we neither haue such places wherin, nor the persons by whose helpe, nor the leasure by whose sufferance we maye entend so delicate a tendring of our selues, and yet for all that may not neglect so great a misterie for our owne health, as exercise is, though we cannot reatch to the olde, which perhaps we neede not, smaller prouision and simpler fourniture, will serue our turne, and worke the same effectes, nay may fortune better by helpe of some circunstance peculiar to our selues. Therefore for our *maner* and *order* of exercise, these few and easie considerations may seeme to be sufficient: To *cleare* our bodies from superfluities echewaye, to *combe* our heades, to *wash* our handes and face, to *apparell* our selues for the purpose, to *begin* our exercise first slowly, and so grow on quicker, to *rebate* softly, and by gentle degrees, to *change* our sweatie clothes, to *walke* a litle after, last of all our bodies being setled, to *go* to our meate. This is that which I promised to note concerning the six circunstances of exercise.

CHAPTER 35.

An adurtisement to the training maister. Why both the teaching of the minde, and the training of the bodie be assigned to the same maister. The inconueniences which ensue, where the bodie and soule be made particular subiectes to severall professions. That who so will execute anything well, must of force be fully resolued of the excellency of his owne subiect. Out of what kinde of writers the exercising maister may store himselfe with cunning. That the first groundes would be laid by the cunningest workeman. That priuate discretion in any executor is of more efficacie then his skill.

I HAUE already spoken of the parties, which are to be exercised, and what they are to obserue: nowe must I saye somwhat of him, and to him, which is to direct the exercise, and how he may procure sufficient knowledge, wherby to do it exceeding well. And yet the trainers person is but a parcell of that person, whom I do charge with the whole. For I do assigne both the framing of the minde, and the training of the bodie to one mans charge, whose sufficiencie may verie well satisfie both, being so neare companions in linke, and not to be vncoupled in learning. The causes why I medle in this place with the training maister, or rather the training parte of the common maister, be these: first I did promise in my methode of exercises so to do: secondly the late discours of exercise will somwhat lighten this matter, and whatsoeuer shall be said here, may easely be reuiued there, where I deale with the generall maister. Beside this, exercise being so great a braunche of education as the sole traine of the whole bodie, maye well commaunde such a particular labour, though in deede I seuer not the persons, where I ioine the properties. For in appointing seuerall executions, where the knowledge is vnited, and the successe followeth by the continuall comparing of the partes, how they both maye, or how they both do best procede in their best way, how can that man iudge wel of the soule, whose trauell consisteth in the bodie alone? or how shall he perceiue what is the bodies best, which hauing the soule onely committed to his care, posteth ouer the bodie as to an other mans reckening? In these cases both *fantsie* workes *affection*, and *affection* ouer-weyneth, either best liking where it fantsieth most, or most following, where it affecteth best, as it doth appeare in *Diuines*, who punish the bodie, to haue the soule better, and in *Physicians*, who looke a side at the soule, bycause the bodie is there best. Where by the way I obserue, the different effectes which these two subiectes, being seuered in charge, do offer vnto their professours. For the health of the soule is the *Diuines* best, both for his honest delite, that it doth so well, and for his best ease, that himselfe faires so well. For an honest, vertuous, godly and well disposed soule, doth highly esteeme and honorably thinke of the professour of diuinitie, and teacher of his religion, bycause vertuous dealinges, godly meditations, heauently thoughtes, which the one importeth, be the others portion, and the best food, to a well affected minde: Whervpon in such a healthy disposition of a well both informed and reformed soule, the *Diuine* can neither lacke honor for his person, nor substance for his purse.

Now to the contrarie the health of the bodie, which is the *Physicians* subiect, is generally his worst, though it be the ende of his profession, which though he be glad of his owne good nature, as he is a man, or of his good conscience, as he is a Christian, that the bodie doth wel, yet his chymny doth not smoke where no pacient smartes. For the healthfull bodie commonly careth not for the *Physician*, it is neede that makes him sought. And as the *Philosopher* sayeth, if all men were freindes, then iustice should not neede, bycause no wrong would be offered: so if all bodies were whole that no distemperature enforced: or if the *Diuine* were well and duetifully heard, that no intemperance distempered, *Physick* should haue small place: Now the contrary dealinges, bycause the diuine is not heard, and distemperature not auoided, do enforce *Physick*, for the healing parte of it, as the mother of the professours gaine: where as the preseruing part neither will be kept by the one, neither enricheth the other. In these two professions we do generally see what the seuering of such neare neighbours doth bring to passe, like two tenantes in one house belonging to seuerall lordes. And yet the affections of the one so tuch the other, as they cause sometimes, both the *Diuine* to thinke of the body, for the better support of the soule: and the *Physician* to thinke of the soule to helpe him in his cure with comfort and courage. The seuering of those two, sometime shew vs verie pitifull conclusions, when the *Diuine* diliuers the desperate sicke soule, ouer to the secular magistrate, and a forcible death by waye of punishement: and the *Physician* deliuereth the desperate sicke bodie to the *Diuines* care, and a forced ende by extremitie of disease. I dare not saye that these professions might ioyne in one person, and yet *Galene*[52] examining the force which a good or ill soule hath to imprint the like affections in the bodie, would not haue the *Physician* to tarie for the *Phylosopher* but to play the parte himselfe. Where to much distraction is, and subalterne professions be made seuerall heads, there the professions make the most of their subiectes, and the subiectes receiue least good, though they parte from most. And seuerall professing makes the seuerall trades to swell beyond proportion, euerie one seeking to make the most of his owne, nay rather vanting his owne, as simply the highest, though it creepe very low. And therefore in this my traine I couch both the partes vnder one maister's care. For while the bodie is committed to one, and the soul commended to an other, it falleth out most times, that the poore bodie is miserably neglected, while nothing is cared for but onely the soule, as it proueth true in very zealous *Diuines*: and that the soule it selfe is but sillyly looked to, while the bodie is in price, and to much borne with, as is generally seene: and that in this conflicte the diligent scholer in great strength of soule, beares mostwhat about him, but a feeble, weake, and a sickish bodie. Wherefore

[52] 1. De san. tu.

to haue the care equally distributed which is due to both the partes, I make him but one, which dealeth with both. For I finde no such difficultie, but that either for the cunning he may compasse it: or for the trauell he maye beare it, hauing all circunstances free by succession in houres. Moreouer as the temperature of the soule smelleth of the temperature of the bodie, so the soule being well affected, will draw on the bodie to her bent. For will a modest and a moderate soule but cause the body obey the rule of her temperance? or if the soule it selfe be reclaymed from follie, doth it not constraine the bodie forth with to follow? So that it were to much to sunder them in charge, whose dispositions be so ioyned, and the skill of such facilitie, as may easely be attained, and so much the sooner, bycause it is the preseruing parte, which requireth most care in the partie, and but small in the trainer, as the healinge part of Physicke requireth most cunning in the professour, and some obedience in the patient.

I do make great account of the parties skill, that is to execute matters which besides diligence require skill: for if he be skilfull himselfe, it almost needes not to giue precept. If he be not, it altogither bootes not. If he be skillfull he will execute well, bycause he can helpe the thing, which he must execute if particular occurrence pray aide at the sudden: if he want skill he will lightly mangle that, which is wel set downe, if he be a medler. Wherefore seing I wish the executors cunning, and yet must be content to take him as I finde him: I will do my best both to instruct infirmitie, and to content cunning. I must therefore haue him to thinke, that there be two properties which he must take to be of most efficacie to make a cunning executor. The one is to be rauished with the excellencie and worthynes of the thing which he is to execute. The other is, if he may very easily attaine vnto some singuler knowledge in so noble a subiect, which both concur in this present execution.

The liking of the executors subiect.

1. For graunting the soule simply the preheminence both in substance of being, and in traine to be bettered, can there be any other single subiect, (which I say in respect of a communitie directed by diuine and humaine law, that is compound, and the principall subiect of any mans dealing,) can there be any single subiect I say of greater nobilitie, and more worthy to be in loue with, either by the partie, that is to finde it, or by him that is to frame it, then healthfullnes of body? which so toucheth the soule as it shakes it withall, if it selfe be not sownd?

What a treasure health is, they that haue it do finde, though they feele it not till it faile, when want bewrayes what a iewell they haue lost, and their cost discouers how they mynde the recouerie. The ende of our being here is to serue God and our country, in obedience to persons, and perfourmance of duties: If that may be done with health of bodie, it is effectual and pithie: if not, then with sorow we must shift the soner, and let other succede, with no more assurance of life, then we had made vs, without this healthfull misterie: in perpetuall change to let the world see, that multitude doth supply with number the defect of a great deale better, but to sone decaying paucity.

To liue and that long of whom is it not longed for, as Gods blessing if he know God: as the benefit of nature, if he be but a naturall man.

The state of our bodie, when we are in good health, so liuely and lusty, so comfortable and cleare, so quicke and chearie, in part and in hole, doth it not paint vs, and point vs the valew of so preciouse a iewell, as health is to be esteemed?

The pitifull grones, the lamentable shrikes, the lothsome lookes, the image of death, nay of a pyning death, yea in hope of recouery: the rufull heauines, the wringing handes, the wayling friendes, all blacke before blacke, when health is in despaire, do they not crie and tell vs, what a goodly thing health is, themselues being so griesy?

So many monuments left by learned men, so much sumptuousnes of the mightiest princes, so many inuentions of the noblest wittes bestowed vpon exercises to maintaine this diamond, are they not sufficient to enflame the executour, being a partaker him selfe, and a distributer to others, that the subiect wherein he dealeth is both massie, most worth, and most meruelous? let him thinke it to be so, bycause he seeth it is so, and vpon that presumption proceede to his so healthfull, and so honorable an execution. In whom his owne iudgement is of speciall force to further his good speede. For being well resolued in the excellencie of his owne subiect he will both himselfe execute the better, and perswade other sooner to embrace that with zeale, which he professeth with iudgement. If you will haue me weepe for you, saith the *Poet*, then weepe you first: he shall hardly perswade an other to like of that, which is his owne choice, who shall himselfe not seeme to set by it, where himselfe hath set his choise.

How to become a skillfull exercising maister.

2. The knowledge wherewith, and how to deale therein is so much the easier, bycause it is so generall, and so many wayes to be wonne. I will not seeme to raise vp the memorie which can neuer dye, giuen to this traine by all both old and new histories: which prayse those vertues and valiances, which they found, but had neuer had matter to praise, nor vertues to finde, if exercises had not made the personages praiseworthy, whereby they did such thinges, and of so great admiration, as had bene vnpossible to any not so trained as they were. What *Philosopher* describeth the fairest forme of the worthiest common weale, either by patterne of one person, as allowing that state best, where one steares all: or by some greater multitude, as preferring that gouernment, where many make much stirre: but he doth alwaye, when he dealeth with the youth, and first trayning of that state, not onely make mention, but a most speciall matter of exercise for health?

Who is it in any language that handleth the *Padagogicall* argument, how to bring vp youth, but he is arrested there, where exercise is enfraunchised? As for the *Physicians*, it is a principall parcell of their fairest patrimonie, bycause it is naturally subiect, and so learnedly proued to be by *Galene* in his booke intitled *Thrasybulus*, to that parte of their profession which seeketh to preserue health, and not to tarie till it come to ruine, with their gaine to repare it, though it still remaine ruinous and rotten, which is so repared. Therefore whensoeuer the maintenance of health, is the inscription of the booke, this title of exercise hath some euidence to shew. Further in the discours of *Exercises* we finde eche where the names of diet, of *waking*, of *sleeping*, of *mouing*, of *resting*, of *distemperature*, of *temperature*, of *humours*, of *elementes*, of *places*, of *times*, of *partes* of the *bodie*, of the *vses* therof, of *frictions* and *chafings*, of *lassitude* and *wearinesse*, and a number such, which when the training maister meeteth with among the *Physicians*, or naturall *Philosophers*, what els say they vnto him, but that where ye finde vs before the dore, ye may be bold to come in? As for naturall *Philosophy* the ground mistresse to *Physik* it must needes be the foundation to this whole traine. Hence the causes be set, which proue eche thing either good or bad, either noysome or needefull to health. All naturall *problemataries, dipnosophistes, symposiakes, antiquaries, warmaisters,* and such as deale with any particular occurence of exercise, if ye appose them well: you shall finde them yours freindes. This terme *Gymnastice,* which emplyeth in name, and professeth in deede the arte of exercise, is the verie seat, wheron the trainer must builde. And therefore all either whole bookes, or particular discourses in any writer by the waie, concerning this argument, do will him to rest there. In which kinde, for the professed argument of the whole booke, I know not any comparable to *Hieronymus Mercurialis,* a verie learned *Italian Physician* now in our time, which hath taken great paines to sift out of all writers, what so euer concerneth the whole *Gymnasticall* and exercising argument, whose aduice in this question I haue my selfe much vsed, where he did fit my purpose.

By these reasons I do see, and by some proofe I haue found, that the waye to be skilfull in the preseruatiue part of *Physick,* and so consequently in exercises, as the greatest member therof, is very ready and direct, bycause it is so plaine, so large, and with all so pleasant: as it is also most honorable, bycause it seekes to saue vs from that, which desireth our spoile. And therefore this execution requireth a liberall courage, where the gaine is not great, but the disposition much praised. The repairers get the pence, the preseruers reason faire. And as the effect commendes the knowledge: so being of it selfe thus necessarie for all, a student may with great credit trauell in the cunning, if it were for no more but to helpe his owne health, and vpon better affection, or some gainfull offer to empart it with other. For to helpe himselfe he is bound in *nature,* and will do it in deede: to do good to all if he may, he is bound by *dutie,* and so sure he ought. But to helpe as many as he may, and himselfe to, what *nature* can but loue? what *dutie* can but like? chiefly where the thing which he must do, may be done with ease, and the good which he shall do, shall gaine him praise, besides the surplus of profit. Some will say perhaps to traine vp children, what needes so much cunning: or in so petie a matter what needes so much labour? Though I entreat of it here, where it first beginnes, yet it stretcheth vnto all, both ages and persons: neither is the matter so meane, which is the readiest meane to so great a good, but if it were meane, the meanest matter requireth not the meanest maister, to haue it well done: and the first groundworke would be layd by the best workeman. For who can better teach to reade, then he which for skill can commaund the language? And what had more neede to be exactly done then that principle, which either marreth the whole sequele, with insufficiencie, or maketh all sound, being it selfe well layd? The thing you will graunt to be of such efficacie, such an excutor you despaire of: such a man may be had, nay a number of such may be had, if recompence be prouided to answere such sufficiencie. The common not opinion but error is, he hath cunning enough for such a small trifle. It is not that small which he hath that can do the thing well, but your skill is small, to thinke that any small skill, can do anything well. He must know a great deale more then he doth, which must do that well, which he doth: bycause *store* is the deliuerer of the best effectes, *neede* which sheweth all at once, is but a sorie steward, and must put in band, that he hath some credit, though verie smal substance.

For the skill of the trayner I take it to be verie euident, both whence it may be had, and how plentiful a store house he hath for his prouision. Thence he may haue the generall groundes, and causes of his cunning.

Discretion in the trayner.

3. But there is a third thing yet besides these two, which is proper to his owne person, which if he haue not, his cunning is worth nought. For though he see and embrace the worthines of his subiect, though he haue gathered in his whole haruest from out of all writers, yet if he want *discretion* how to apply it according vnto that, which is most fit to the verie meanest not bowghes and braunches, but euen the twigges and sprigges of the petiest circumstances, he is no skillfull trayner: but so much the more daungerous, the more helpe of learning he hath, which will bolden him to much. Therefore of these two other pointes, the one being throughly resolued on, the other perfitly obtained, and all the contemplatiue reasons well vnderstoode, he must bend his wittes to wey the particularities, whereby both the generall conclusions be brought to be profitable, and his owne iudgement to be thought discrete. The want of this is the cause of such a number of discoursers, which swarm ech where, and both like their owne choice, and can say pretily well to the generall position, which is not denyed to any toward youthe, but they shew themselues altogither lame in the particular applying, which is a thing that attendeth onely vpon experience and yeares. The hauing of it will prouide vs notable store of excellent executours, to all their profites, vpon whom they shall execute. *Aristotle* the great *philosopher* in all his *morall* discourses tieth all those vertues which make mens maners praiseworthie, and be subiect to circumstances, to the rule of foresight and *discretion,* whose commendation he placeth in skill of speciallities to direct mens doinges. Therefore it is no dishonour to the trayner, to be reclaymed vnto *discretion,* which hath all those so many and so manerly vertues to attend vpon her traine. Is not death commendable, and ascribed to valiancie, when it is voluntary for the common good, by reason of the circumstance? and the sauing of life is it not basely thought of, when it had bene better spent, considering the circumstance? Which circumstance is the line to liue by, the guide to all our doinges, the tuchestone to try a contemplatiue creature from an actiue courage.

In the course of training, a thousand difficulties not possible to be forseene by the generall direction, will offer themselues, and appose the maister, and at the sudden must be salued. What will the trainer do? runne to his booke? nay to his braines. He must remember his rule, that indiuisibles and circunstances be beyond the reach of *arte*: and are committed to the *Artificer* whose *discretion* must helpe, where *arte* is to weake: though she giue him great light, by fitting this to that, when he hath found wherfore. *Arte* setteth downe the exercise and all the knowen circunstances. The person bringes with it some difficultie in execution, where is the succour? *Arte* will not relent, she can not make curtsie, her knees be groune stiffe, and her iointes fast knit, and yet curtsie there must be. The *Artificer* must make it, and assist his ladie, which if she had not had a man to be her meane, she herselfe would haue done all, and trusting to man whom she hath made her meane, why should she be deceyued, and her clyentes be abused, where she commendes them of trust? Children that come to schoole dwel not in one house, not in the same streate, nay not in the same towne, they cannot lightly come at one houre, they be not of one age, nor fit for one exercise, and yet they must haue some. The *arte* knoweth my child no more then my neighbours, but the trainer must, and stay those vncertainties vpon the arrest of *discretion*: being enstructed afore hand in the generall skill though bound but of voluntarie: as the like cause shall lead the like case.

The rule is, no noysome sauour neare the newly exercised: how shall the poore boye do, that is to go home thorough stinking streates, and filthy lanes.

The rule is, change apparell after sweat: what if he haue none other? or not there where he sweateth? Here must the trainers *discretion* shew it selfe, either to chuse exercises that be not subiect to any such extremities, or to vse them with the fewest. But I am to long, neither neede I to doubt of mens discretion, though I say thus much of it, which many haue and moe wishe for, I shall haue occasion to supplie the rest in the generall teacher.

Thus haue I runne thorough the whole argument of exercises, and shewed not onely what I thinke of them in generall, but also what be the cheife particulars, and the circunstances belonging thereunto: and according to my promise I haue delt with the training maister, and ouertreated him to thinke honorably of his profession, to gather knowledge, where it is abundantly to be got: and last of all to ioine *discretion* as a third companion to his owne admiration and sufficiency.

CHAPTER 36.

That both young boyes, and young maidens are to be put to learne. Whether all boyes be to be set to schoole. That to many learned be to burdenous: to few to bare: wittes well sorted ciuill, missorted seditious. That all may learne to write and read without daunger. The good of choice, and ill of confusion. The children which are set to learne, hauing either riche or poore freindes, what order and choice is to be vsed in admitting either of them to learne. Of the time to chuse.

NOW that the thinges be appointed, wherwith the minde must be first furnished, to make it learned, and the bodie best exercised, to keepe it healthfull, we are next to consider of those persons, which are to be instructed in this furniture, and to be preserued by this exercise: which I take to be children of both sortes, *male* and *female*, young *boyes* and young *maidens*, which though I admit here generally, without difference of sex, yet I restraine particularly vpon difference in cause, as herafter shall appeare. But young *maidens* must giue me leaue to speake of *boyes* first: bycause naturally the *male* is more worthy, and politikely he is more employed, and therfore that side claimeth this learned education, as first framed for their vse, and most properly belonging to their kinde: though of curtsie and kindnesse they be content to lend their *female* in youth, the vse of their traine in part, vpon whom in age they bestow both themselues, and all the frute of their whole traine.

It might seeme sufficient for the determining of this case to say onely thus much: that they must needes be *boyes* which are to be trayned in this sorte, as I haue declared, bycause the bringing vp of young *maidens* in any kynd of learning, is but an accessory by the waye. But for so much as there be many considerations in the persons, both of *boyes* and *maidens* worthy the deciding, I meane to entreat of them both somwhat largely: and as neare as I can, to resolue both my selfe and my reader in some pointes of controuersie and necessitie, or rather in some pointes of apparent necessities, being out of all controuersie. For the *male* side, that doubt is long ago out of doubt, that they be to be set to schoole, to qualifie themselues, to learne how to be religious and louing, how to gouerne and obey, how to fore cast and preuent, how to defende and assaile, and in short, how to performe that excellently by labour, wherunto they are borne but rudely by nature. For the very excellency of executions and effectes where by we do so great things, as we vonder at our selues in all histories and recordes of time, (which be but stages for people to gase on, and one to maruell at an others doings) testifieth and confirmeth that it were great pitie, that such towardnesse should be drowned in vs for lacke of education, which neuer comes to proofe, but where education is the meane. That we can proue learned, the effect doth shew, but that not vnlesse we learne, the defect declares. That our bodies can do great thinges, healthfull strength is witnesse to it selfe: but where weaknesse is, what doinges there be, verie want will pronounce. But now in the way of this so commended a traine, there be two great doubtes which crosse me. 1. The first is, whether all children be to be set to schoole, without restraint to diminish the number. 2. The second is, how to worke restraint, if it be thought needefull. Touching the first question, whether all children be to be set to schoole or no, without repressing the infinitie of multitude, it is a matter of great weight, and not only in knowledge to be resolued vpon, but also in deede so to be executed, as the resolution shall probably giue sentence. For the bodie of a common weale in proportion is like vnto a naturall bodie. In a naturall bodie, if any one parte be to great, or to small, besides the eye sore it is mother to some euill by the verie misfourming, wherupon great distemperature must needes follow in time, and disquiet the whole bodie. And in a bodie politike if the like proportion be not kept in all partes, the like disturbance will crepe thorough out all partes. Some by to much will seeke to bite to sore, some by to litle will be trode on to much: as both will distemper: which if it fortune not to kill in the ende, yet it will disquiet where it greiues, and hast forward the ende. But though the pestering of number do ouerlaie the most professions and partes of any common weale, and harme there where it doth so ouercharge, yet I will not medle with any, but this of learning and the learner, which I haue chosen to be my peculiar subiect. Wherof I saye thus, that to many learned be to burdenous, that to few be to bare, that wittes well sorted be most ciuill, that the same misplaced be most vnquiet and seditious.

To many learned.

1. To many burdens any state to farre: for want of prouision. For the rowmes which are to be supplyed by learning being within number, if they that are to supply them, grow on beyound number how can yt be but too great a burden for any state to beare? To haue so many gaping for preferment, as no goulfe hath stoore enough to suffise, and to let them rome helpeles, whom nothing else can helpe, how can it be but that such shifters must needes shake the verie strongest piller in that state where they liue, and loyter without liuing? which needeles superfluitie fleeting without seat, what ill can it but breede? A dangerous residence it is at hoome, still seeking shiftes to liue as they may, though with enemitie to order, which neede cannot see. A perilous searcher it is abroode, to seeke to fish in a troubled water, if any cause promote their quarrell, bycause the cleare is not for them, which they haue sounded allready. Sure *neede* is an imperious mistres to force conclusions, whether shee build vpon *fantsie* and *desire,* which is a *mani-headed neede,* euen before *neede,* and mostwhat without *neede*: or vpon meere *lacke* and *want* in deede, which though it haue but one head, yet that one is exceeding strong, importunate, and furiouse. And shee hath at hand to salue her mischiefes, a ready and an ordinarie excuse, wherewith she will seeme to craue pardon for all that is done by needy men, as there vnto enforced by her ineuitable violence. A

violent remedy, which doth not heale infections, but will alleage cause, where to haue mischiefes excused and foregiuen.

Wherfore if these mens misdemeanour come of their owne ill, which prouision cannot preuent, bycause in best prouision ill will be ill, so farre as it dare shew, where wealth workes wantonnes, it deserues correction and punishment. If it come of necessitie, for want of foresight in publike gouernment, to helpe the common, from common blame, and to prouide for the priuate: it would be amended and not suffered to runne, till the harme being receiued and felt, cause the question be moued, whether such a mischiefe proceede from priuate insolence, or publike negligence. For as the priuate is to pay, if it do not performe, when the publike hath prouided: so the publike must pardon, if for insufficient foresight, the priuate proue dissolute, and lend the state a blow. But for my number I neede not to dwell any longer in to many, for troubling all with to many wordes, seeing all wise men see, and all learned men say, that it is most necessary to disburden a common weale of vnnecessary number, and multitude in generall, which in some countries they compassed by brothelry, and common stewes, to let the yong spring: in some by exposition and spoile of enfantes, both contrary to nature, and countermaunded by religion: but according to their pollicie and commaunded by their countries. In particular disposing of them that liued, they cast their account, and as the proportion of their states did suffer: so did they allote them with choice, and constrained them to obey. If such regard for multitude be to be had in any one braunche of the common weale, it is most needefull in schollers. For they professe learning, that is to say the soule of a state: and it is to perilous to haue the soule of a state to be troubled with their soules, that is necessary *learning* with vnnecessary *learners*, or the publike body with their priuate, which is the common *wealth* with their priuate want. For in all proportion, to much is to bad, and to much out of all proportion, and to haue to much euen of the soule, is not the soundest, where her offices be appointed and lymited in certaine. *Superfluitie* and *residence* bring sickenes to the body, and must not to much then infect the soule sore, being in a *sympathie* with the body? Scholers by reason of their conceit which learning inflameth, as no meane authority saith,[53] become to imperiall to rest upon a litle: and by their kinde of life which is allway idle they proue to disdainefull to deale with labour, vnlesse neede make them trot, or the *Turkish captiuitie* catch them, the greatest foe that can fall vpon idle people, where labour is looked for, and they not vsed to it. *Contentment* in *aspiring*, which is hard to such wittes, and *patience* in *paines* which they neuer learned, be the two cognisances, whereby to discerne a ciuill wit, and fit to enioye the benefit of his countrie. Now of all ouerflush in number, is not that most dangerous, which in conceit is loftie, and in life loytering, as the vnbestowed scoller by profession is?

To few learned.

To few be to bare and naked: bycause necessities must be supplyed, and that by the fittest. For whereas the defect of the fit enforceth supplement of the lookers on, though not the most likely, but whosoeuer they be, without further respect, then that they stand by, bycause neede bides no choyce where there is no *pluralitie*,

[53] S. Paul.

and yet biddes *pluralitie* make choyce: there the vnsufficient seruice of necessarie seruices breedes much miscontentment, and more shaking to any state. And that chiefly in such pointes, as the state embraseth, and the feeble minister doth nothing but deface. So that the defeat of the generall purpose must be most imputed to the bare defect of insufficient persons. For as to many bringes surfettes, so to few breedes consumptions.

Wittes well sorted.

3. Wittes well sorted be most ciuill: This I say bycause to auoyd excessiue number, choice is one principall helpe: for in admitting to vses onely such as be fit, and seeme to be made for them, pares of the vnfit, and lesseneth the number, which yet would be lookt vnto, euen at the verie first. For euen he that is thought most vnfit, and is so in deede, yet will grieue at repulse, vnles ye repell him by preuention, ear he come to the sense and judgement to discerne what a heauie thing a flat repulse is. Which *miscontentment* if it range in a number, cannot be without daunger to the common body. As to the contrarie such wittes as be placed where the place needes them more then they the place, do performe with sufficiencie, and proceede with *contentment* of the state that enstawled them. The chiefe signes of *ciuilitie* be *quietnesse, concord, agrement, fellowship* and *friendship,* which *likenesse* doth lincke, *vnliknesse,* vndoeth: *fitnesse* maketh fast, *vnfitnesse* doth loose: *proprietie* beares vp, *impropr ietie* pulleth downe: *right matching* makes, *mismatching* marres. How then can ciuill societie be preserued, where wittes of vnfit humours for seruice, are in places of seruice, by appointment, either vnaduisedly made, or aduisedly marred. Is there any picture so ill fauoured, being compound of incompatible natures, as an execution is, being committed to a contrarie constitution? If fire be to enflame, and cause thinges burne, where water should coole, and be meane to quench, is the place not in danger? If that wit fall to preach, which were fitter for the plough, and he to clime a pulpit, which is made to scale a walle, is not a good *carter* ill lost, and a good *souldier* ill placed? If he will needes lawe it, which careth for no lawe, and professe *iustice* that professeth no *right,* hath not *right* an ill *caruer,* and *iustice* a worse *maister*? If he will deale with *physicke* whose braines can not beare the infinite circumstances which belong thereunto, whether to maintaine health, or to restore it: doth he any thing else, but seeke to hasten death, for helping the disease? to make way to murther, in steede of amendement? to be a *butchars prentice* for a *maister* in *physike*? And so is it in all kindes of life, in all trades of liuing, where fitnes and right placing of wittes doth worke agreement and ease, vnfitnes and misplacing haue the contrarie companions, disagreement and disease.

Wittes misplaced.

4. Againe wittes misplaced most vnquiet and seditious: as any thing else strayned against nature: light thinges prease vpward, and will ye force *Fire* downe? Heauie thinges beare downeward: and will ye haue *Leade* to leape vp? An imperiall witte for want of education and abilitie, being placed in a meane calling will trouble the whole companie, if he haue not his will, as winde in the stomacke: and if he haue his will, then shall ye see what his naturall did shoote at. He that beareth a tankarde by meanesse of degree, and was borne for a cokhorse by sharpenes of

witte, will keepe a canuase at the Conduites, tyll he be Maister of his companie. Such a stirring thing it is to haue wittes misplaced, and their degrees mislotted by the iniquitie of *Fortune*, which the equitie of *nature* did seeme to meane vnto them.

Plato in his wished common weale, and his defining of naturall dignities, appointeth his degrees and honors, where *nature* deserueth by *abilitie* and *worth*, not where *fortune* freindeth by *byrth* and *boldnes*, though where both do ioyne *singularitie* in *nature*, and successe in *fortune*, there be some rare iewell. Hereupon I conclude, that as it necessary to preuent to great a number for the *quantitie* thereof: so it is more then necessarie, to prouide in the necessarie number for the *qualitie* thereof, wherein *restraint* it selfe will do much good for the one, and *choice* in restraint will do more for the other. Sure all children may not be set to schole, nay not though priuate circumstance say yea. And therefore scholes may not be set vp for all, though great good will finde neuer so many founders, both for the place wherein to learne, and for the number also which is for to learne: that the state may be serued with sufficiencie enough, and not be pestered with more than enough. And yet by the way for writing and reading so they rested there, what if euerie one had them, for *religion* sake, and their necessarie *affaires*? Besides that in the long time of their whole youth, if they minded no more, these two were easely learned, at their leasure times by extraordinary meanes, if the ordinarie be daintie and no schoole nigh. Euerie parish hath a minister, if none else in the parish, which can helpe writing and reading.

Of riche and poore children.

Some doubt may rise here betwene the *riche* and *poore*, whether all *riche* and none *poore*, or but some in both maye and ought to be set to learning. For all in both that is decided alreadie, No: bycause the whole question concerneth these two kindes, as the whole common weale standeth vpon these two kindes. If all *riche* be excluded, *abilitie* will snuffe, if all *poore* be restrained, then will *towardnesse* repine. If *abilitie* set out some *riche*, by priuate purses for priuate preferment: *towardnesse* will commende some *poore* to publike prouision for publike seruice: so that if neither publike in the *poore*, nor priuate in the *riche* do marre their owne market, me thinke that were best, nay that will be best, being ruled by their wittes to conceiue learning, and their disposition to proue vertuous. But how may the publike in the *poore*, and the priuate in the *riche*, make their owne market in the education of those whom they preferre to learning? I will tell ye how. The *riche* not to haue to much, the *poore* not to lacke to much, the one by ouerplus breadeth a loose and dissolute braine: the other by vnder minus a base and seruile conceit. For he that neuer needeth by supplie of freindes, neuer strayneth his wittes to be freind to himselfe, but commonly proues retchelesse till the blacke oxe tread vpon his toes, and neede make him trie what mettle he is made of. And he that still needeth for want of freindes being still in pinche holdes that for his heauen, which riddes him from neede, and serues that Saint, which serues his turne best, euen *Neptune* in shipwrackie. Wherby he maketh the right of his iudgement become bond for wealth: and the sight of his witte blinde for desire, such slauerie workes want, vnlesse Gods grace proue the staye, which is no line to common direction, though it be our onely hope, by waye of refuge. Now then if the wealthy parentes of their priuate patrimonie, and publike patrones of their supererogatorie wealth, will but driue to a meane in both these two mains, neither shall wealth make the one to wanton, nor want make the other to seruile: neither the one to leape to fast, for feare he loose some time, nor the other to hast to fast, for feare he misse some liuing. Sure to prouide for poore scholers but a poore patche of a leane liuing, or but some meane halfe, is more then halfe a maime, the desire to supplie that which wanteth, distracting the studie more by many partes, then that petie helpe, which they haue can possibly further it: bycause the charge to maintaine a scholer is great, the time to proue well learned, long, and when ripenesse is ready, there would be staye to chuse and time to take aduice, where neede turnes the deafe eare. The paterne of to prodigall wealth oftimes causeth the toward student to ouershoote himselfe by corrupt imitation, as brauerie and libertie be great allurers, where studie and staye pretend restraint. And therfore neither must to much be butte to allurementes, nor to litle a burden: to iudgement the one the meane to lewdnesse the other a maime to libertie. The midle sorte of parentes which neither welter in to much wealth, nor wrastle with to much want, seemeth fitteth of all, if the childrens capacitie be aunswerable to their parentes state and qualitie: which must be the leuell for the fattest to fall downe to, and the leanest to leape up to, to bring forth that student, which must serue his countrey best. *Religion* and *learning* will frame them in iudgement, when *wealth* and *abilitie* haue set them once on foote.

The choosing time.

For the choice of wittes definitely, till they come to the time, or verie neare to it, when they are themselues naturally and for ripenesse of yeares to chuse their owne kinde of life, how so euer circunstance free, or binde their choice, I cannot say much, though I do see what other haue said in that behalfe. A quicke witte will take soone, a staid memorie will hold fast, a dull head may proue somwhat, a meane witte offers faire, *praise* bewrayeth some courage, *awe* some, in eche kinde there is likelyhood, and yet error in eche. For as there be faire blossomes, so there be nipping frostes. And till the daunger of reuolt be past, the quicke must be helde in hope, the dull without dispaire, the meane the meetest, if the sequele do aunswere. I can limit no one thing, though I see great shewes, where there is such vncertaine motion, both in soule and body, as there is in children. The maisters *discretion* in time and vpon triall, may see and say much, and in a number there will some leaders appeare of themselues, as some speciall deare in the whole heard. Where great appearance is, there one may prophecie, and yet the lying spirite may sit in his lippes. For God hath reserued, his calling and discouering houres, as all other future euentes to his owne peculiar and priuate knowledge: probabilities be our guides, and our coniectures be great, though not without exception. What kinde of witte I like best for my countrey, as most proper to be the instrument for learning, it shall appeare herafter. But for the first question of the two, it seemeth to me verie plaine that all children be not to be set to schoole, but onely such as for naturall wittes, and sufficient maintenance, either of their naturall parentes, or ciuill patrones, shall be honestly and wel supported in their study, till the common weale minding to vse their seruice, appoint their prouision, not in hast for *neede*, but at leasure with *choice*.

CHAPTER 37.

The meanes to restraine the ouerflowing multitude of scholers. The cause why euerie one desireth to haue his childe learned, and yet must yelde ouer his owne desire to the disposition of his countrie. That necessitie and choyce be the best restrayners. that necessitie restrayneth by lacke and lawe. Why it may be admitted, that all may write and read that can, but no further. What is to be thought of the speaking and vnderstanding of Latine, and in what degree of learning that is. That considering our time and the state of religion in our time, lawe must needes helpe this restraint: with the answere to such obiections as are made to the contrary. That in choice of wittes, which must deale with learning, that wit is fittest for our state, which aunswereth best the monarchie, and how such a wit is to be knowne. That choice is to helpe in scholing, in admission into colledges, in proceeding to degrees, in preferring to liuinges, where the right and wrong of all the foure pointes be handled at full.

IN the last title we haue concluded, that there must be a *restraint*, and that all may not passe on to learning which throng thitherward, bycause of the inconueniences, which may ensue, by want of preferment for such a multitude, and by defeating other trades of their necessarie trauellours. Our next labour therefore must be, how to handle this *restraint*, that the tide ouerflow not the common, with to great a spring of bookish people, if ye crie come who will, or ring out all in. Euerie one desireth to haue his childe learned: the reason is, for that how hardly soeuer either *fortune* frowne, or *casualtie* chastice, yet *learning* hath some strength to shore vp the person, bycause it is incorporate in the person, till the soule dislodge, neither lyeth it so open for mischaunce to mangle, in any degree, as forren and fortunes *patrimonie* doth. But though euerie parent be thus affected toward his owne child, as nature leades him to wish his owne best, yet for all that euerie parent must beare in memorie that he is more bound to his country, then to his child, as his child must renounce him in countermatch with his countrie. And that country which claymeth this prerogatiue of the father aboue the child, and of the child aboue the father, as it maintained the father eare he was a father, and will maintaine the child, when he is without a father: so generally it prouideth for all, as it doth require a dutie aboue all. And therefore parentes in disposing of their children may vpon good warrant surrender their interest to the generall consideration of their common countrie, and thinke that it is not best to haue their children bookish, notwithstanding their owne desire, be it neuer so earnestly bent: if their countrie say either they shall serue in this trade, without the booke: or if shee say I may not allow any more booke men without my to much trouble. I pray thee good parent haue pacience, and appoint some other course for thy childe, there be many good meanes to liue by, besides the booke, and I wilbe thy childes friend, if thou wilt fit in some order for me. This verie consideration of the countrie, vttered with so milde a speach, spoken by her that is able to performe it, may moue the reasonable parent, to yealde to her desire as best, as she can tell the headstrong in plaine termes, that he shall yeelde perforce, if he will not by entreatie, for priuate affection though supported by reason of strength whatsoeuer, must either voluntarily bend, or forcibly breake, when the common good yeeldeth to the contrary side.

Seeing therefore the disposition of wittes according to the proportion of ech state is resigned ouer to the countrie: and she sayth all may not be set to schole, bycause ech trade must be furnished, to performe all duties belonging to all parts: it falleth out in this case of *restraint* which bridles desire, that two speciall groundes are to be considered, which strip away excessiue number, *necessitie* and *choice*, the one perforce, the other by your leaue.

Necessity.

As for *necessitie*, when the parent is ouer charged with defect in circumstance, though desire carie him on, it then restraineth most, and lesseneth this number when desire would encrease it, and straines to the contrary. You would haue your childe learned, but your purse will not streatch, your remedy is pacience, deuise some other way, wherein your abilitie will serue. You are not able to spare him from your elbow, for your neede, and learning must haue leysure, a scholers booke must be his onely busines, without forreine lettes, you may be bold of your owne, let booking alone, for such as can entend it, from being called away by domesticall affaires, and necessarie busines, for the scholers name will not be a cypherlike subiect, as he is termed of leasure, so must he haue it. And that they cannot spare their children so, must forebeare their scholing, by the olde *Persian*[54] ordinance, bycause leasure is the foregoer to liberall profession: *necessitie* compelleth and bastardeth the conceit, a venom to learning, whom freedom should direct. You haue no schole neare you, and you cannot pay for teaching further of, let your owne trade content you: keepe your childe at home. Your childe is weake tymbred, let scholing alone, make play his physician and health his midle end. Which way soeuer *neede* driues you perforce, that way must ye trot, if he will not amble, and bid Will thinke that well. He that gouerneth all seeth what is your best, your selfe may be misseled either by *ignorance* in *choice*, or *affection* in blood. In these and the like cases *lacke* is the leader, which way soeuer she straineth. Whereby if the restrained childe cannot get the skil to write and read: I lament that lacke, bycause I haue allowed him somuch before, vpon some reasonable perswasion euen for necessary dealings. For these two pointes concerne euery man neare, bycause they submit themselues to euerie mans seruice: yea in his basest busines and secretest

[54] Xenop. 1. κυρ παιδ.

affaires. I dare not venture to allow so many the lattine tongue nor any other language, vnlesse it be in cases, where their trades be knowne, and those toungues be founde to be necessarie for them. For all the feare is, though it be more then feare, where it still falleth out so, least hauing such benefits of schole, they will not be content with the state which is for them, but bycause they haue some petie smake of their booke, they will thinke any state be it neuer so high to be low ynough for them. Which petie bookemen do not consider, that both clounes in the countrie, and artificers in townes be allowed lattine in well gouerned states, which yet rest in their calling, without *pride* or *ambition,* for that small knowledge, whereby they be better able to furnish out their trades, without further aspiring. Neither measure they the meaner qualities, as the thinges be in nature, but as themselues be in conceit: neither can they consider that at this daye it is not the toungue, but the treasure of learning and knowledge, which is laid vp in the toungue whereunto they neuer came, which giueth the toungue credit, and the speaker authoritie. For want of this right iudgement there ensueth in them a miscontentment of minde, not liking their owne state, and a cumbersome conceit, still aspiring higher, that disquieteth the whole state. Wherefore *necessitie* is a good meane to preuent this in many, which would if they could, now may not, bycause they cannot.

Lawe.

The second point of *necessitie* I do assigne to *lawe* and *ordinaunce* vpon consideration to cut of this flocking multitude, which will needes to schoole. Whereupon two great goods must needes ensue. *Contentment* of minde in the partie restrained, when he shall perceiue publike prouision to be the checke to his fantsie: and timely *preuenting,* eare conceit take roote, and thinke it selfe wronged. Bycause it is much better to nip misorder in the verie ground, that it may not take hold, then when it is growen vp, then to hacke it downe. He that neuer conceiued great thinges maye be helde there with ease, but being once entred in the waye to mount, and then throwne backward, he will be in some greife and seeke how to returne gaule, whence he receiued greife, if he chaunce to proue peuish, as repulse in great hope is a perillous grater. Yet in both these cases of necessarie *restraint,* I could wish prouision were had to some singular wittes, found worthy the auauncement: either by priuate patronage, or publike: and yet againe if they passe on, and bewtifie some other trade: that also is verie good, seeing they serue their countrey, whersoeuer they be loated, and in those also whom libertie of circunstance doth set to schoole *pouertie* will appeare, and *towardnesse* call for helpe: and yet the number will neuerthelesse proue still with the most.

Two obiections against restraint by lawe.

1. It is no obiection to alleadge against such a lawful restraint, the abilitie of good wittes, and great learning in men, that either now be, or heretofore haue bene, which we might haue lackt if so strait a *lawe* had bene then: 2. or that it were pitie by seueritie of an vnkinde *lawe* to hynder that excellencie, which God commonly giues to the poorer sort. To the first I aunswere, besides that, which euen *lawe* to that ende will aunswere for it selfe. As in time to come we know not, who shall serue the state, if the *lawe* be made straite, and yet we know well, that

he which defendes states will prouide sufficient persons, by whom they shalbe serued: so in time past or present, if these were not, or those had not bene, whom we now see or of whom we haue heard, God would haue raised vp other, whose benefites in seruing gouernmentes may not be restrained to any degree of men, as they be men, but to the appointment of a ciuill societie, which hath direction ouer men: as a thing which God doth most cherish, both in respect of this Church which is of number, and in regard of societie it selfe, which is the naturall ende of mans being here, and not to liue alone. And I warrant you whensoeuer such an orderly *restraint* shalbe put in practise that there wilbe as good foresight had to haue necessarie functions serued, as there will be regard to draine away the vnnecessarie ouerflow. A thing not new faingled, but euer in vse, where the common weales, had an eye to distribute their multitude to the best and easiest proportion of their owne state: which otherwise improportionate would breade an *aposteme*. And therefore if the generall iudgement appoint it so, it is best to yeelde. And priuate opinion in politike cases will proue an errour, if the generall liking contrarie it flat. I do not now meane, where the generall is blinded by common errour, but where priuate conceit can take no exception, sauing that, which he bredeth from out of his owne braine. If the state of my countrey take order, that my child shall not go to schoole, sure I will obay, and prouide some other course, though I like learning exceeding well, and be verie farre in loue with it, besides the affection to my child, bycause the squaring with the generall, is to farre out of square for any particular. And I pray you may it not be, that for want of such an ordinance we mist better wittes, then those were, or are, which we either had or haue, though we thinke very well of both the sortes, whether now liuing with vs, or tofore parted from vs? And doth not *negligence* for want of looking to, ouerthrow as gaie and gallant heades, as *diligence* by doing euen her verie best, hath euer brought to light? Aduised and considerate planting is like enough to receiue verie good encrease and euentes in such cases, by authoritie and testimonie of two the greatest oratours in both the best tongues, be but foolish maisters, and febler argumentes.

As for pytying the poore, it is no pitie, not to wish a begger to become a prince, though ye allow him a pennie, and pitie his needefull want. Is he poore? prouide for him, that he may liue by trade, but let him not loyter. Is he wittie? why? be artificers fooles? and do not all trades occupie wit? sometimes to much, and thereby both straine their owne heades to the worse, and proue to suttle for a great deale their betters. Is he verie likely to proue singuler in learning? I do not reiect him, for whom I prouide a publike helpe in common patronage. But he doth not well to oppose his owne particular, against the publike good, let his countrie thinke of him enough, and not he of him selfe to much. If *nobilitie* and *gentlemen* would fall to diligence, and recouer the execution of learning, where were this obiection? The greatest assurers of it affirme, that learning was wont to be proper to *nobilitie*, and that through their negligence it is left for a pray to the meaner sort, and a bootie to corruption, where the professours neede offereth wrongfull violence to the liberalitie of the thing. Do they not therein confesse, where the right of the thing lyeth and themselues to be vsurpers, if they should enter vpon their owne, whose the interest is, and whom in so many discourses of nobilitie, they themselues blame so much for their so great negligence? They must needes here yeelde without law to their owne confession. But we see God hath shewed himselfe meruelous munificent and beneficiall this way to the poorer sort. I grant, yet that proues not, but that he bestowed as great giftes of them which shewed not. And that as *diligence* in the one did shew that they had, to the glorie of the giuer, and their owne praise: so *negligence* in the other, did suppresse that they had to their owne shame, who neither honoured the giuer, nor honested themselues, nor profited their countrie. So that here not the *gift*, but the *shew* is brought in allegation. And why not the greater *talent* hid seeing it is no noueltie? But the other shew. Nomore then that they haue. And the other shew not. No argument that they haue not. Take order then, that they shew, which haue and hide, and then make comparisons. Be great giftes tied to the meane, or banished from the mighty? be there not as good wittes in wealth, though oftimes choked with *dissolutenes* and *negligence*, as there be in pouertie appearing thorough *paines* and *diligence*? Nay be there not as vntoward *poorelinges*, as there be wanton *wealthlinges*? I know yes, and when vntowardnes and an ill inclynation hittes in a base condition, it proues more vile. So that this thing turnes about to my other conclusion, that neither pouertie is to be pitied more then the countrey, if pitie must needes take place: neither riches more to be esteemed then the common weale, if wealth must needes be wayed: but that the value in wittes must be heelde of most worth, which hath her hauen already appointed, where to harbour her selfe, in maintenaunce to studie, either by priuate helpe, if the parents be wealthy, or by publike ayde, if pouertie praie for it.

Certainly there is great reason (if euen the terme, great, be not to small, when the thing is more then needfull, and the time to preuent it, is almost runne to farre) why order should be taken, to restraine the number, that will needes to the booke. For while the Church was an harbour for all men to ride in, which knew any letter, there needed no *restraint*, the liuinges there were infinite and capable of that number, the more drew that waye, and found reliefe that way, the better for that state, which encroached still on, and by clasping all persons, would haue graspid all liuinges. The *state* is now altered, that *book-maintenance* maimed, the *preferment* that waye hath turned a new leafe. And will ye let the *fry* encrease, where the *feeding* failes? Will ye haue the *multitude* waxe, where the *maintenance* waines? Sure I conceiue of it thus, that there is as great difference in ground, betwene the suffring all to booke it in these dayes, and the like libertie to the same number, in the ruffe of the papacy amongst vs: as there is betwene the two religions, the one expelled and the other retained, in the grounds of their kinde. The expelled religion was supported by multitude, and the moe had interest, the moe stood for it: the retained must pitch the defence of her truth, in some paucity of choice: seeing the liuinges are shred, which should serue the great number. So that our time, of necessitie must restraine: if not: what you breede and feede not, the aduersarie part will allure by liuing, and arme by corrupting, against their vnwise countrey, which either bestowed them not at first, or despised them at last. Where your thankes shalbe lost, which brought vp, and forsooke their desert shall sinke deepe, which fed the forsaken. And is it not meere folly by *sufferance* to encrease your enemies force, which you might by *ordinance* supplant at ease? it is the booke, which bredes vs enemies, and causeth corruption to creepe, where cunning neuer came. The enemy state cared not so much for many well learned, as for the multitude though vnlearned, which backt much bould ignorance, with a gaie surface of some small learning: our state then must reiect the multitude, and rempare with the cunning. Our owne time is our surest touch, and our owne trouble our rightest triall, if wisedome in time do not preuent it, folly in triall will surely repent. It is to no purpose to alledge, when people see, that there is no preferment to be had for all learners, that then the number will decay, and abate of it selfe without any *lawe*: onelesse ye can worke so, as no moe may hope, though but one can hit: or els, if ye can appoint vs, how long the controuersie for *religion* is like to endure. For while hope is indifferent, eche one will croud: and while *religion* is in brake, eche one vnder hand, will furnish where he fauoreth. The aduersarie of our religion, as in deede he needed none, so dreamed he not of any defense, while he was rockt in ease, and his state vnassailed by any *miscontentment*: but now that he is skirmished with so much, and so sore gauled, he is driuen to studie, and seeketh by new coined distinctions to recouer, that credite and reputation which he lost by intruding: wherin as he dealeth more cunningly with the person of his aduersarie, so he bewrayeth still the great auantage, which his aduersaries cause hath wonne ouer his. For in disputing, good *Logicians* know that it is an euident shift, to auoide manifest foile, when the disputer in dispaire of his cause is forced to bend against his aduersaries person. And therefore prouision must be, to defend by a learned *paucitie*, where the *flocking number* by reason of ingenerate wantes, will proue but a scare crow, and by apparent defection doth encrease the embush, which lyeth still in waite to intercept our possession. Thus much of *Necessitie*, which stayeth the multitude of learners either by *defect* in *circunstance*, or by *law* in *ordinance*, when the parties be letted, either by *lack* that they can not, or by *law* that they may not, lay claime to the booke.

Choice.

Now are we come to a larger compasse, where libertie giues leaue to learne if he can, where forraine circumstances be free, and no let for any to be learned but either his wit, if he be dull, or his will, if he be stubborne. In this kinde, *choise* is a great prince, which by great reason and good aduice, abridgeth that which is to much, and culs owt the best. Which choice, as it begins at the entrie of the elementarie schole, so it proceedeth on, till the last preferment be bestowed, which either the state hath in store for any person, or any person can derserue, for seruice in the state. And therefore as it keepeth in an ordinate course, so it may full well be orderly handled, and by conuenient degrees.

What wit is fittest for learning in a monarchie.

But bycause the *choice* is to be made by the wit, and the wit is to be applied to the frame and state of the countrie, where it continueth: I will first seeke out, what kinde of wit is euen from the infantcie to be thought most fit, to serue for this state in the learned kinde. Which if it be to stirring, troubleth, if it be well staied, setleth the countrie where it lyueth, so farre as it dealeth. And yet oftymes that wit maketh least show at the first, to be so plyable, which at the last doth best agree with the pollicy. And therefore it is then to be taken, when it beginnes first to shew, that it will proue such: wherefore precise reiecting of any wit, which is in way to go onward, before due ripenes, as it is harmefull to the partie reiected, so it bewraieth some rashnes in him that reiecteth: bycause the varietie is exceeding great, though the coniectures be as great, and the most likelyhood must needes leade, where certaintie is denied. But to the wittes: wherein as lacke and law do guide necessitie so the qualitie of the witte, conformable to the state directeth *choice*.

There be three kindes of gouernment most noted among all writers, 1. whereof the first is called a *monarchie,* bycause one prince beareth the sway, by whose circumspection the common good is shielded, and the common harme shouldred: 2. the second an *oligarchie*: where some few beare all the swinge: 3. the third a *democratie,* where euery one of the people hath his interest in the direction, and his voice in elections. Now all these three be best maintained by those kindes of wit, which are most proper for that kinde of gouernment, wherein they liue. But bycause the gouernment of our countrie is a *monarchie*: I will in *choise* seeke out that kinde of wit, which best agreeth with the *monarchie,* neither will I touch the other two, vnles I fortune to trip vpon them by chaunce. And for as much as I haue made the yong child my first subiect, I will continue therein still: bycause that which beginneth to shew it selfe neare vpon infancie, will so commonly continue, though alteration creepe in sometime. But lightly these wittes alter not, bycause the tokens be so fast and firme in nature, and tend to so certaine and so resolute a iudgement.

A wit for learning in a monarchie.

The child therefore is like to proue in further yeares, the fittest subiect for learning in a *monarchie,* which in his tender age sheweth himselfe obedient to scholeorders, and either will not lightly offend, or if he do, will take his punishment gently: without either much repyning, or great stomaking. In behauiour towardes his companions he is gentle and curteous, not wrangling, not quarelling, not complaining, but will put to his helping hand, and vse all perswasions, rather then to haue either his maister disquieted, or his fellowes punished. And therefore he either receiueth like curtesie againe of his scholefellowes: or who so sheweth him any discurtesie must abyde both chalenge and combate with all the rest.

If he haue any excellent towardnes by nature, as commonly such wittes haue, whereby he passeth the residue in learning, it will shew it selfe so orderly, and with such modestie, as it shall soone appeare, to haue no loftines of minde, no aspiring ambition, no odiouse comparisons ioyned withall.

At home he will be so obsequious to parentes, so curteous among seruauntes, so dutiefull toward all, with whom he hath to deale: as there will be contention, who may praise him most behinde his backe, who may cherish him most before his face: with prayer that he may go on, with feare of too hastie death, in so od a towardnes of wit and demeanour. These thinges will not lightly make any euident shew, til the childe be either in the *grammar schole,* by orderly ascent, and not by two forewardly hast, or vpon his passage from the perfited *elementarie,* bycause his yeares by that time, and his contynuaunce vnder gouernment, will somwhat discouer his inclination. Before that time we pardon many thinges, and vse pointes of ambition and courage, to enflame the litle ones onward, which we cut of afterward, for making them to malapart, as in their apparell frise is successour to silke.

When of them selues without any either great feare, or much hartening, they begin to make some muster and shew of their learning to this more then that, then is coniecture on foote to finde, what they willbe most likely to proue.

But now to examine these signes more nearely and narowly, which I noted to be in the child that is like to proue so fit a subiect for a *monarchie,* in matters of learning: Is not obedience the best sacrifice, that he can offer vp to his prince and gouernour, being directed and ruled by his countrie lawes? And in the principles of gouernment, is not his maister his *monarchie*? and the scholelawes his countrey lawes? wherunto if he submit himselfe both orderly in *perfourmance,* and patiently in *penaunce,* doth he not shew a mynde already armed, not to start from his dutie? and so much the more, bycause his obedience to his maister is more voluntarie, then that to his prince, which is meere necessarie. For in perswasions of children, which the parentes will give eare to: in desire to chaunge, where their wills be chekt: in multitude of teachers, who thriue by such chaunges: all meanes be good, where there is such plentie, to offer such parentes as be tikelish, and such scholers as be shifting, remouing from maisters and renouncing of obedience. The child hath many shadowes to shift in vpon any pretence, and as many baites, to winne his parentes beleefe, and specially if he stand in feare of beating. Whereas neither he, ne yet his parentes, can forsake their prince, vpon any colour without forfaiting more then a quarters scholehire. And therfore in so many meanes to change, and some perhaps offered, bycause who will not very willingly deale with such a witte, where his trauell will make shew, that child which notwithstanding all these entisementes, will continue both on, and one, and digest dyscurtesies, though his mayster sometyme chaunce to proue churlish, is the peculiar and proper witte, which I commende for obedience, and that is like to proue both honestly learned, and earnestly beloued. 2. In his owne demeanour towardes his fellowes and freindes, and all sortes of people generally, either at home, or abroade, either in schoole, or elsewhere and in their loue and liking of him againe, doth he not shew forth an euident sociabilitie and liklyhood, that he will be very well to be liued withall? and proue a very curteous man, which is so louing, and so beloued while he is yet a boye? 3. In letting nature shew her owne excellencie without vnsweetning it with his owne sawcinesse doth he not argue that he hath stuffe towards preferment, without any sparke of ambition to moue further flame? or to prease to fast forwarde? which shall neuer neede: bycause all men that know him, will either willingly helpe to preferre him, if their voice be in it: or will reioyce at his preferment, if they be but beholders. For who will not be glad to see vertue, which he loueth, auaunced to rewarde? or what can enuie do, in so plausible a case, but set forth the partie, by declaring his desert, in that she is there? There be many consequentes, which hange vpon these, as neither vertue nor vice be single where they be, but are alwaie accompanied with the whoule troupe of the like retinue. And one conuenience graunted draweth on a number of the like kinde, as well as one inconuenience draweth on his like traine.

But these be the maine as I conceiue at the first blush: obedience to superiours and superioritie, freindlynesse and fellowship toward companions, and equalles: substance to deserue well and winne it, desire to auoide ill and flie it. What duetie either towardes God or man, either in publike or priuate societie, in any either hie or low kinde of life is there, wherv nto God hath not seemed in nature to haue framed and fashioned this so toward a youth? and therefore to haue appointed him for the vse of learning to be ruled by his betters, and to rule his inferiours, nothing offensiue nor vnpleasant to any? Many such wittes there be, and at them must choice first begin. And as those be the best, and first to be chosen, in whom there is so rare metall, so the second or third after these be vnworthy the refusall, in whom the same qualities do appeare, though not in the same, but in some meaner degree. For wheras great ill is oft in place, and proues the generall foe to that which would be better, there meane good, if it may haue place, will be generall freind to preferre the better: as euen this second mediocritie, if it may be had, as choice will finde it out, will proue verie freindly to set forward all good. Now these properties and signes appeare in some, verie soone, in some verie late, yea oftimes when they are least looked for: as either iudgement in yeares, or experience in dealinges do frame the parties.

The plat for the *monarchicall* learner being alwaye reseant in the chusers head, concerning the propertie of his witte: and appearance towardes proofe: the rest is to be bestowed vpon the consideration of learning, and towardnesse in children generally (wherof these wittes be still both the first and best frutes) where to stay, or how farre to proceede in the ascent of learning. Whether he be riche or poore, that makes no matter, and is already decided, whether he be quicke or slow, therein is somwhat, and requireth good regard.

Schoole choice.

Wherfore when sufficient abilitie in circunstances bids open the schoole dore, the admission and continuaunce be generall, till vpon some proofe the maister, whom I make the first chuser of the finest, and the first clipper of the refuse, begin to finde and be able to discerne, where abilitie is to go on forward, and where naturall weaknesse biddes remoue by times. For if negligence worke weaknesse, that is an other disease, and requires an other medecine, to heale it withall. Now when the maister hath spied the strength or infirmitie in nature, as by lightsomnesse or heauinesse in learning, by easinesse or hardnesse in retaining, by comparing of contrarie or the like wittes, he shall easely sound both, then as his delite wilbe to haue the toward continue, so must his desire be, how to procure the diuerting and remouing of the duller and lesse toward, to some other course, more agreeing with their naturall, then learning is: wherin they are like to go forward verie litle, though their fortune be to go to schoole very long: but here two considerations are to be had: neither to soone to seeke their diuerting, till some good ripenesse in time, though with some great paines to the teacher in the meane time, wish them to be weined from booking: neither yet before their bodies be of strength to abide the paines of some more laborious prenticeship. For it may so proue, that those wittes, which at the first were found to be exceeding hard and blunt, may soften, and proue sharp in time and shew a finer edge, though that be not to be made a generall caution, to cover dullardes with all. For the naturall dulnesse will disclose it selfe generally in all pointes, that concerne memorie and conceit: that dulnesse which will once breake out sharp, will shew it selfe by glaunces, as a clowdy day vseth, which will proue faire, when all shrews haue dined. Wherefore peremptorie iudgement to soone, may proue perillous to some: and againe he that is fit for nothing else, for the tendernesse of his bodie, may abide in the schoole a litle while longer, where though he do but litle good, yet he may be sure to take litle harme.

Moreouer if the parentes abilitie be such, as he may, and his desire such, as he will maintaine his child at schoole, till he grow to some yeares, though he grow to small learning, the maister must haue pacience, and measure his paines by the parentes purse, where he knowes there is plentie, and not by the childes profit, which he seeth will be small. Wherein yet he must impart his opinion continually with the parent both for his duetie sake, and for auoiding of displeasure. But in the meaner sorte the case altereth, for that as a good witte in a poore child, deserues direct punishment, if by negligence he for slow the obtaining of learning, which is the patrimonie to wittie pouertie: so a dull witte in that degree would not be dalyed with all to long, but be furthered to some trade, which is the fairest portion to the slow witted poore. Now bycause the maister to whose iudgement I commend the choice, is no absolute potentate in our common weale, to dispose of wittes, and to sorte mens children, as he liketh best, but in nature of a counsellour, to ioine with the parent, if he will be aduised: therfore to haue this thing perfectly accomplished, I wish the parentes and maisters to be freindly acquainted, and domestically familiar. And though some parentes neede no counsell, as some maisters can giue but litle, yet the wise parent will heare, and can iudge: and the skilfull maister can iudge, and should be heard. Where neither of these be, neither skill in the teacher to tell it, nor will in the parente to heare it, and lesse affection to follow it, the poore child is wrung to the worse in the meane while, and the parent receiues small comfort in conclusion.

This course for the maister to keepe in iudging of his scholer, and the parent to follow in bestowing of his child, according to his wit, continueth so long as the child shalbe either vnder maistership in schole, or tutorship in colledge. During the which time, a great number may be verie wisely and fitly bestowed, vnlearned trades sufficiently appointed, the proceding in letters reserued to them, to whom for wit and iudgement they seeme naturally vowed: and finally the whole common weale in euery braunch well furnished with number, and the number it selfe discharged of to much. Bycause this tyme vnder the maisters gouerment, is the time wherin youth is to be bestowed by forraine direction: for afterward in a more daungerous age, and a more ieoperdouse time, they grow on to their owne choice, and these vnfitnesses in nature, or frailtes in maners, being not foreseene to, may cause the friendes forthinke it, and the parties sore rue it. And though the maister shall not allway haue his counsell followed in this case, yet if he do signifie his opinion to the parent, his dutie is discharged, and that which I require is orderly performed. For if the parent shew himselfe vnwilling to be directed that way, which the maister shall allow, vpon great ground, and be blynded by affection, measuring his childes wit to learning, by his doing of some errand, or by telling of some tale, or by marking of some pretie toy, as such argumentes there be vsed, which yet be no argumentes of a towarde learner, but of a no foolish obseruer: in this case though the maister to his owne gaine draw on vnder his hand a desparate wit, the fault is his that would not see, if he that saw did honestly tell it. Whereby it still proueth true, that parentes and maisters should be familiarly lynked in amitie, and contynual conference, for their common care, and that the one should haue a good affiance of iudgement in the thing, and of goodwill towards himselfe, reposed in the other. Which will proue so, when the maister is chosen with iudgement, and continued with conference, and not bycause my neighbours children go to schole with you, you shall haue myne to. A common commendation among common coursiters, which post about still to suruey all scholes, and neuer staie in one: and reape as much learning, as the rowling stone doth gather mosse.

But concerning scholes, and such particularities, as belong thereunto I will then deale, when I shall take in hand the peculiar argumentes, of schooles and schooling, both for the elementarie and the grammarian. Wherein we are no lesse troubled with number and confusion in our petie kingdomes, then the verie common weale is molested with the same in greater yeares, and larger scope.

But bycause it were not orderly delt, to rip the faultes, and not to heale them, I wil post all these pointes ouer to their owne treatises, in my particuler discourses hereafter, where I will presently helpe, whatsoeuer I shall blame. The other meanes wherby choice lesseneth number, be admissions into colleges, prefermentes to degrees, aduauncement vnto liuings, wherein the common weale receiueth the greater blow, the nearer these thinges be to publike execution, and therefore the playner dealing to preuent mischiefe before it infect, is the more praiseworthy.

Admission into colleges.

As concerning *colleges* I do not thinke the liuinges in them to be peculiar, or of purpose ment to the poorer sort onely, whose want that small helpe could neuer suffice, though there be some prerogatiue reserued vnto them, in consideration of some great towardnes, which might otherwise be trod down, and that way is held vp: but that they be simply preferments for learning, and auauncementes to vertue, as wel in the wealthy for reward of wel doing, as in the poorer for necessarie support. And therefore as I giue *admission* scope to chuse of both the sortes, so I do restraine it to honest and ciuill towardnes. For if fauour and friendship not for these furnitures, but for priuate respectes, carie away elections though with some enterlarding of towardnes and learning, and some few to giue countenaunce to some equitie of choice, and theerby to maintaine the credit of such places, surely the scholers and heades which deuised the sleight, and conceiued they were not seene, shall repent without recouerie, and finde themselues bound, and their colleges bowelled, when they shal fele themselues ouerruled by their owne deuise: bycause such as come in so, will communicate the like with others, and neuer care for the common, which were helpt by the priuate. For where fauour bringes in almost in despite of order, there must fauour be returned with meruelous disorder, and yet I do not mislike fauour, which helpeth desert, which otherwise might be foiled, if fauour friended not. But when the ground wherupon fauour buildes is not so commendable, *founders* be discouraged, common *prouision* supplanted, *learning* set ouer to *loytering, brauerie* made enheritour to *bookes*. Stirringe wittes haue their will for the time, and repentance at leasure. The fault hereof commeth from scholers themselues, which first make way to sinister meanes, and afterward blame, the verie meane which they vsed themselues. For finding some ease at first in working their owne will, either more cunningly to hide some indirect dealing, or more subtilly to supplant some contrary faction: or in deede desiring rather by commaundement to force, and so to seeme somebodie, then of dutie to entreat, and so seeme abiect to honestie: they stumble at the last vpon the blocke of bondage, being bridled of their owne will, euen when they are in ruffe, by the selfe same meanes, which brought them vnto it, and thought so to staule them, as themselues would commaund where they caused the speed. These fellowes be like to *Horaces* horse, which to ouercome the stag, vsed man for his meane once, and his maister alway: neither refusing the saddle on his ridg, to be rid on, nether the bit in his mouth, to be bridled by. A braue victory so dearely bought, to the victours bondage, and perpetuall slauerie. Whereas if learning and those conditions which I did lymit to a ciuill wit in this state, were the end in elections, the vnfit should be set ouer to some other course, in conuenient time: the fittest should be chosen, the founders mynde fulfilled: some periurie for non perfourmaunce of statutes auoided: new *patrones* procured, *religion* auaunced, good studentes encouraged, and fauour vpon extreame and importunate sute disfranchised: which neuer will oppose it selfe to so honest considerations, so constantly kept: neither euer doth intrude, without some such sollicitours, as should be sorie for it, and vse no meane to haue it, which oftimes vse this meane, to do il by warrant, as if they were forced to that, which in deede they ment before, and sought fauour but for a shadow to hide their deuise. Now if you that are to chuse, yeeld so much to your selues, and your owne conceit to bring your deuises to passe, though ye wring by the waie, and your state in the ende, why should you not in good truth relent, and giue place your selues being in places, to your betters and bidders, which gaiue you the roome, and yet would haue left all to you, if you would haue left any place to reason: or haue bene led by right, as ye leaned all to the wronge? you had your will by them, and why not they haue theirs of you? requitall among equalles is of common curtesie, recompence in inequalities is enforced of necessitie.

If any metall be to massie, and way downe the ballance, or if any metallish meane, where money will scale, do enter that fort, where is small resistance, that is solde, which ought not, the enheritaunce of vertue: that is bought, which should not, the liuelihood of learning: that is betrayed, which neither should for feare, nor ought for freindship, the treasure of the state, and prouision of the countrey. And if there be neede, which enforceth such dealing, yet deale, where it is due, and let neede be remedyed, with her owne prouision, not by vnhonest intrusion. I do not blame any one, bycause my selfe know none, and I thinke well of most, bycause I know some sincere. But some thing there is that feedeth the generall complaint, and some contentious factions there be, that bring catchers into colleges. For both these two inconueniences, worse then mischeifes as our common law termeth them, I haue nothing to say more then to renue the memorie of two accidentes, which happened to the *Romain* common weale, and may be vnderstood by scholers that will marke and applie them. 1. The first is, that in *Tullie*,[55] when *Pontius* the *Samnite* wished that he either had not bene borne vntill, or but

[55] Offic. 2.

then borne, when the *Romaines* would haue receiued giftes and rewardes, Why? what if? I would not haue suffred them to haue reigned one day longer, by selling their libertie, they should haue become bond. The fellow said much, and that state felt more, when they fell to fingering.

The main rot of the Romaine empire.

2. The second is this, not noted in any one, but obserued by all, that marke and write of the declining and ruine of the *Romain Empire*. The principall cause among many, to raze that state, which did rise in the blood of other nations and fell in their owne, was, when their generalls vsed the helpe of forreine and barbarous fellowes, late foes, new freindes, to ouerthrow the contrarie factions in their ciuill warres, both before and in their Emperours time, and let them both smell and taste of the *Romish* wealth and fatnesse of *Italie*. Wherwith the horesons being rauished, euer as they went home sent more of their countreymen to serue in seditious or necessarie defenses: till at the last their whole nations ouerflew that flourishing towne, and that fertile countrey. Wherby that great abundance, that vnspeakeable wealth, those inestimable riches, which the whether conquering or rauening *Romaines* had gathered together in so many hundred yeares, from so many seuerall countries, in a verie small time, became a bootie to that barbarous offall of all kinde of people, which neuer had any, till they became lordes, both of the *Romain* substance and the soile of *Italie*. A glasse for those to gase on, which will rather stirre to fall, then be still to stand. If ye shew a child an apple, he will crye for it, but if you make a mightier then your selfe priuie to your pleasures, if he be desirous to haue, and speede not, he will make you crye for it.

But now as fauour founded not vpon desert, but vpon some fetch, is foe to all choice, enforcing for the fauorite, so free admissions into colledges, by but mildely and honestly replying: vpon fauour may helpe it in sufficiency, and lighten the booke of some needlesse burthen, which hurtes not onely in the admission, but also by sending abroade such broad dealers, which corrupt where they go, and poison more incurably, bycause of their meane, which is mothered vpon learning, which the cunninger it is, the craftyer meane it is: and of the more credit it is, the more conueiance it hath to corrupt with good colour, though it be to bad, when it is bewrayed. If hope were cut of to speede by disorder, such wittes would streight waye sorte themselues to order, as they be not the most blockheades, which offer violence to order: wherin I must needes say somwhat in plaine truth, and plausible to.

The abusing of great personages.

Those great personages, which be so tempted by the importunity of such petie companions, as seeke them for protection, to force good and godly statutes, are litle bound to them. For what do they? Their owne obscuritie comes in no daunger, as being but vnderlinges, neither much seene, nor whit cared for, though they cause the mischeife: but they force good, and well giuen dispositions, excellent and noble natures, by false and coloured informations, to serue their owne turnes, and to beguile their great freindes: they bring them in hatred of all those, which builde vpon the good zeale of vertuous founders. Which thing reacheth so farre, and to so many, as either the possibilitie to enioye their benefit doth, or the praise of their doing, to procure the like: or the protection of posteritie, which cannot but lament the great misuse, and foull ouerthrow of their ancestours good and most godly meaning. They cast all men in feare of them to be likewise forced in their best interest, as a principle to tyrannie, and make them to be odious to all, whom they would seeme to honour aboue all. The worst kinde of *caterpillours*, in *countenaunce* fine and neate, in *speeche* delicate and diuine, in *pretence* holy and heauenly, in *meaning* verie furies, and diuells: to themselues scraping howsoeuer they couer: to nobilitie and countenaunce, whatsoeuer shew they make, the verie seminarie of most daungerous dishonour, and therfore worthy to be thrust out, bycause they thirst so much. For if loue and honour be the treasures of nobility, the contrarie meane howsoeuer it be coloured deserues coudgelling out, when it croutcheth most. It is no dishonour to nobilitie, not to haue their will, but it is their greatest disgrace to yielde to that, by vnreasonable desire, which they ought not to will, and so make a diuorse betwene honestie and honour, which is vnseemely, seeing honestie, how basely soeuer some ruffians regard it, is the verie mother to honour of greatest moment, and in the best kinde. That such honorable natures yeelde to such importunate promoters, halfe against their will, bycause otherwise they cannot be rid of them: their owne and honorable contentment doth oftimes proue, when they haue bene aunswered truely and duetifully, by such either companies, or particulars, as haue preferred plaine trueth, before painted colours, whereby noble dispositions do well declare to the world, how vnwilling they be to force order by fauour, if they be enfourmed of the truth: which will alway proue the enfourmers warrant, and foile such fetchers, when it comes to the hearing. And as the learned *Quintilian* sayth, that in a grammarian it is a vertue not to seeme to know all: so sayth pollicy that in the verie highest, it is not good to do all, that authoritie and interest in the extremitie of right maie do, with some warrant to it selfe, though with small liking, where it goeth. Mine antecedent is of mine owne profession, which beareth blame of to much boldnesse, and hath bene thought to presumptuous for knowledg, as *Rhemmius Palæmon* one of our coate, was wont to brag, that learning began to liue, and should die with him: My consequent concerneth my countrey, and good will to nobilitie, which as in degree can do most, so were it great pitie that it should be vsed, but to worke the best. My chalenge is to those infamous meanes, which dishonour their honorable patrones, defeat honest men of best education, disturbe the state euen while they liue, poison the posteritie by their president, euen when they are dead.

Now if *choice* had taken place in the beginning, such impudent wittes had wonne no place, and noble patrones had shaked of such sutes. For as deepe waters do seeme not to runne bycause of their stillnesse: so true vertue and honest learning will tary their calling, and not stirre to soone, to set forth their stuffe, though they be the deepest and most worthy the place. I must craue pardon: a well affected maister speaketh for all poore and toward scholers, well nusled in learning, well giuen in liuing, and ill thwarted in liuinges, by such visardes of counterfect countenaunces, which one may more then halfe gesse, what they will receiue, when none seeth but the offerer: which dare themselues offer such dishonorable requestes to those personages, at whose countenaunces, they ought in conscience to tremble, if that impudencie, which first hath reiected God secretly, and all goodnesse openly, had not tyrannised them to much, so vilely to abuse, where they ought to honour. The consideration of the good, the canuasing for the ill, hath caryed me from colledges, though not from colleginers, where for necessarie roomes there must be boursares, and why not of the learned sorte? Which the more towarde they be, the more trusty they will proue, and cheifly to that colledge, which auaunced them for value. Neuer wonder if he do sacrifice to the purse, which was admitted either for it, or by it. And yet there is some wrong, to fill priuate purses for entring, and to punish the common, when they be entred. If they could vse it so, as to still it from those, which strayned it from them, when they were to enter, the cunning were great, and the deceit not amisse, where craft is allowed to deceiue the deceiuer. But the common wrings, for the priuate wrong, and there the iniury is.

Preferment to degrees.

2. Preferment to degrees in schole may, nay in deede ought to be a mightier stripper of insufficiencie, bycause that way, the whole countrie is made either a lamentable spoile to bould ignorance, or a laudable soyle to sober knowledge. When a scholer is allowed by authoritie of the vniuersitie, to professe that qualitie, whereof he beares the title, and is sent abroad with the warrant of his commencement, and want of his cunning, who made either fauour and friendship, either countenaunce or canuase, or some other sleight the meane to enstawle him, what must our common countrie then say, when she heareth the bragge of the vniuersities title sound in her eares, and findes not the benefit of the vniuersitie learning to serue her in neede? Shee must needes thinke that the vnlearned and ignorant creature is free from blame, bycause he sought to countenaunce himselfe, as the customarie led him: but she must needes thinke her selfe not onely not bound to the vniuersitie, but shamefully abused, nay most vnnaturally offered to the spoile of ignorance and insufficiencie by the vniuersitie, to whom committing her sight shee is dealt with so blindly, in whom reposing her trust, she is betrayed so vntruely. For what is it to say in common collection, when the vniuersitie preferreth any, to degree: but as if she should protest thus much. Before God and my countrie, to whom I owe my selfe and my seruice, whereof the one I cannot deceiue, the other I ought not, I do knowe this man, whom I now prefer to this degree, in this facultie, in the sufficiencie of abilitie, which his title pretendeth, not perfunctorilie taken knowledge of, but thoroughly examined by me, to be well able to execute in the common weale of my countrie, that qualitie in art and profession, which his degree endoweth him with: and that my countrie may rest vpon my credit in securitie for his sufficiencie: and betrust her selfe vnto him vpon my warrant, which I do seale with the publike acknowledging of him to be such a one, as his title emporteth, being consideratly and aduisedly bestowed vpon him by me, as I will answere almightie God in iudgement, and my countrie in my conscience and vpon my credit. Now what if he be not such a one? where then is your aduisednesse? where then is your credit? where then is then your conscience? nay where then is your God, whom ye called to witnesse? What if the vniuersitie knew before, that he neither was such a one, neither like euer to proue any such? let him that weyeth

this, if it be to light, reiect it as counterfect. Let the earnest professours of the truest religion in the vniuersities at this day call their consciences to counsell, and redresse the defect, for their owne credit, and the good of their countrie. If it shall please the vniuersities, to preferre these considerations of countrie and conscience, before any priuate persuasion (which if it were roundly repelled a while, would neuer be so impudent, as so to intrude it selfe) the matter were ended, and despaire that way would leaue rowme to learning: and send such fellowes to those faculties, which were fitter for them: and not suffer them vnder the titles of learning, to supplant the learned, and forstaull away their liuinges: to the discouraging of the right student in deede, and the defeating of the state. For if ye rip the cause why they seeke to set foorth then selues, with such forraine feathers, being vnlikely to looke on, in their owne coloures, if the eye might behold that which the minde conceiueth, ye shall finde that their desire to gaine vnder honorable titles, is the verie grounde whereupon they goe: which they seeke by indirect wayes, bycause they feele them selues to be of no direct worth. But what fooles be good scholers in deede, to lende such dawes their dignities, vnder that borrowed habit, to rob them of preheminence, and to seeme to be *eagles*, where they be but *bussardes*? Nay do they not discredit the vniuersitie more? as if they there were either so simple, as they could not descrie a *calfe*, or so easie to be entreated, as when they had discried it, they would sweare by perswasion, that the *calfe* were a *camell?* good my maisters make not all priestes that stand vpon the bridge as the *Poope* passeth. For then the cobler as one consecrated, bycause his person was in compasse, and his showes with in hearing, will sure be a priest, and set nothing by his naule, and as good as you and as fit for a benefice, as those that came to take orders in deede, and deserued them in doing. Looke to it betimes and lende not your garmentes to set forth *bastardt* and bold suters, for feare your selues be excluded, when ye entend to sue, both your labour and your loue being lost, through your owne follie.

To seeme is not so much in weight as to be, but in paines it is much more. To counterfeat vertue, and to auoide spying, requireth a long labour, and daily new deuises: to be vertuouse in deede, and learned in deede, craues labour at the first, and lendes leysure in the end, borne out by it selfe, neuer needing any vele. And therefore great warines must be vsed to discerne and shake of the counterfeat smaller consideration will soone finde, and sooner content sufficient stuffe. Let deepe dissembling and dubling *hypocrisie* leape the ladder, and honest *learning* be beholder the while. In these pointes to haue worthinesse preferred, and to haue choice to seeke, and saue it, if a teacher deale thus earnestly, as methinke I do now, he may deserue pardon as I hope I shall haue, considering his end, to him selfe ward is delite, to his charge is their profit: to his countrie is sound stuffe sent from him. And can he be but grieued to see the effect so disorderly defeated, wherunto with infinite toile, with inconparable care, with incredible paines, he did so orderly proceed? I take it very tollerable for any, that hath charge of number and multitude to be carefull for their good, not only in priuate gouernment, but also in publike protection, so farre, as either the honestie of the cause, or the dutie to magistrate, will maintaine his attempt. As truely in learning and learned executions, me thinke it concerneth all men to be very carefull, bycause the thing tucheth themselues so neare in age, and theirs so much in youth.

Auauncement to liuinges.

3. For the third part which consisteth in *auauncement* to liuinges, as it is commonly handled by the highest in state, and eldest in yeares, which haue best skill to iudge, and least neede to be misled: so it needes least precept: bycause the misse there is mostwhat without amendes, being made by great warrant: and the hitting right is the blessed *fortune* of ech kinde of state, when value is in place, whence there is no appeale but pleasure in the perfit: pitie in imperfection: the common good either carried to ruine by intrusion of insufficiencie, or strongly supported by sufficient staie. *Repulse* here is a miserable stripp, that insufficiencie should be suffered to growe vp so high, and not be hewed downe before. And some great iniurie is offered to the bestowers of prefermentes, that they are made obiectes to the danger of insufficient boldnes, which ought to be cut of by sufficient modestie, who pretendeth the claime to be her owne of dutie, and to whom the patrones, would rediliest yeild, if they could discerne and were not abused by the worthy themselues, which lend the vnworthy the worth of their countenance to deceiue the disposers, and to beguile their owne selues. But blind bayard, if he haue any burden that is worth the taking downe, and bestowing somwhere else, wilbe farre bolder then a better horse, and so farre from shame, as he will not shrinke to offer himselfe to the richest sadle, being in deede no better then a blinde iade and seeking to occupie the stawle where *Bucephalus* the braue horse of duety ought to stand. And in this case of preferrement, store is lightely the greatest enemie to the best choice, bycause in number no condition wilbe offered, which will not be admitted, though some do refuse. The preuenting of all or most of these inconueniences, I do take to be in the right sorting of wittes at the first, when learning shall be left to them alone, whom nature doth allow by euident signes, and such sent awaye to some other trades, as are made to that ende. Wherby the sorters are to haue thankes in the ende of both the parties, which finding themselues fitted in the best kinde of their naturall calling, must of necessitie honour them, which vsed such foresight in their first bestowing.

Thus much haue I marked in clipping of, of that multitude which oppresseth learning with too too many, as too too many wheresoeuer they be, ouercharge the soile in all professions. For the matter wheron to liue iustly and truly being within compasse, and the men which must liue vpon it, being still without ende, must not desire of maintenaunce specially if it be ioyned with a porte, wring a number to the wall, to get wheron to liue? I neede pinch no particular wherethe generall is so sore gauled. Marke but those professions and occupations, which be most cloyed vp with number, whether they be bookish or not, and waye the poorer sort, wheron at the last the pinching doth light, though it passe many handes before, if to great a multitude making to great a state do not proue a shrew, then am I deceyued: so that it were good there were stripping vsed, and that be time in yonger yeares. For youth being let go forward vpon hope, and chekt with dispaire while it rometh without purueyaunce, makes marueilous a doe before it will die. And if no miserable shift will serue at home, verie defection to the foe, and common enemie will send them abrode, to seeke for that, which in such a case they are sure to finde. Wherefore as countenaunce in the ouerflowing number, which findeth place in a state doth infect extremely, by seeking out vnlawfull and corrosiue maintenaunce: so roming in the vnbestowed offaull, which findes no place in a state, doth festure fellonly, by seeking to shake it, with most rebellious enterprises.

CHAPTER 38.

That young maidens are to be set to learning, which is proued, by the custome of our countrey, by our duetie towardes them, by their naturall abilities, and by the worthy effectes of such as haue bene well trained. The ende wheryvnto their education serueth which is the cause why and how much they learne. Which of them are to learne, when they are to begin to learne. What and how much they may learne. Of whom and where they ought to be taught.

The necessitie of this title.

WHEN I did appoint the persons, which were to receiue the benefit of education: I did not exclude young *maidens*, and therefore seeing I made them one braunche of my diuision, I must of force say somwhat more of them. A thing perhaps which some will thinke might wel enough haue bene past ouer with silence, as not belonging to my purpose, which professe the education of boyes, and the generall traine in that kinde. But seeing I begin so low as the first *Elementarie*, wherin we see that young *maidens* be ordinarily trained, how could I seeme not to see them, being so apparently taught?

The proofes why they are to learne.

And to proue that they are to be trained, I finde foure speciall reasons, wherof any one, much more all may perswade any their most aduersarie, much more me, which am for them toothe and naile. 1. The first is the *maner* and *custome* of my countrey, which allowing them to learne, wil be lothe to be contraried by any of her countreymen. 2. The second is the *duetie*, which we owe vnto them, whereby we are charged in conscience, not to leaue them lame, in that which is for them. 3. The third is their owne *towardnesse*, which God by nature would neuer haue giuen them to remaine idle, or to small purpose. 4. The fourth is the excellent *effectes* in that sex, when they haue had the helpe of good bringing vp: which commendeth the cause of such excellencie, and wisheth vs to cherishe that tree, whose frute is both so pleasaunt in taste, and so profitable in triall. What can be said more? our *countrey* doth allow it, our *duetie* doth enforce it, their *aptnesse* calls for it, their *excellencie* commandes it: and dare priuate *conceit*, once seeme to withstand where so great, and so rare circunstances do so earnestly commende.

The custome of our countrey.

But for the better vnderstanding of these foure reasons, I will examine euerie of them, somwhat nearer, as inducers to the truth, ear I deale with the traine. For the first: If I should seeme to enforce any noueltie, I might seeme ridiculous, and neuer se that thing take place, which I tender so much: but considering, the *custome* of my countrie hath deliuered me of that care, which hath made the *maidens* traine her owne approued trauell, what absurditie am I in, to say that is true, which my countrie dare auow, and daily doth trie? I set not yong *maidens* to publike grammer scholes, a thing not vsed in my countrie, I send them not to the vniuersities, hauing no president thereof in my countrie, I allow them learning with distinction in degrees, with difference of their calling, with respect to their endes, wherefore they learne, wherein my countrie confirmeth my opinion. We see yong *maidens* be taught to read and write, and can do both with praise: we heare them sing and playe: and both passing well, we know that they learne the best, and finest of our learned languages, to the admiration of all men. For the daiely spoken tongues and of best reputation in our time, who so shall denie that they may not compare euen with our kinde in the best degree, they will claime no other combate, then to talke with him in that verie tongue, who shall seeke to taunt them for it. These things our country doth stand to, these qualities their parentes procure them, as either opportunitie of circunstance will serue, or their owne power wil extend vnto, or their daughters towardnesse doth offer hope, to be preferred by, for singularitie of endowment, either in marriage, or some other meane. Nay do we not see in our countrey, some of that sex so excellently well trained, and so rarely qualified, either for the toungues themselues, or for the matter in the toungues: as they may be opposed by way of comparison, if not preferred as beyond comparison, euen to the best *Romaines* or *Greekish paragonnes* be they neuer so much praised: to the *Germaine* or *French* gentlewymen, by late writers so wel liked: to the *Italian* ladies who dare write themselues, and deserue fame for so doing? whose excellencie is so geason, as they be rather wonders to gaze at, then presidentes to follow. And is that to be called in question, which we both dayly see in many, and wonder at in some? I dare be bould therefore to admit yong *maidens* to learne, seeing my countrie giues me leaue, and her *custome* standes for me.

Duetie.

For the second point. The duetie which we owe them doth straitly commaund vs to see them well brought vp. For what be young *maidens* in respect of our sex? Are they not the seminary of our succession? the naturall frye, from whence we are to chuse our naturall, next, and most necessarie freindes? The very selfe same creatures, which were made for our comfort, the onely good to garnish our alonenesse, the nearest companions in our weale or wo? the peculiar and priuiest partakers in all our fortunes? borne for vs to life, bound to vs till death? And can we in conscience but carefully thinke of them, which are so many wayes linked vnto vs? Is it either nothing, or but some small thing, to haue our childrens mothers well furnished in minde, well strengthened in bodie? which desire by them to maintaine our succession? or is it not their good to be so well garnished, which good being defeated in them by our indiligence, of whom they are to haue it, doth it not charge vs with breache of duetie, bycause they haue it not? They are committed and commended vnto vs, as pupilles vnto tutours, as bodies vnto heades, nay as bodies vnto soules: so that if we tender not their education duetifully, they maye vrge that against vs, if at any time either by their owne right, or by our default, they winne the vpper roome and make vs stand bare head, or be bolder with vs to.

They that write of the vse of our bodies, do greatly blame such parentes, as suffer not their children to vse the left hand, as well as the right, bycause therby they weaken their strength and the vse of their limmes: and can we be without blame, who seeke not to strengthen that, which was once taken from vs, and yet taryeth with vs, as a part of vs still: knowing it to be the weaker? Or is there any better meane to strengthen their minde, then that knowledge of God, of religion, of ciuil, of domesticall dueties, which we haue by our traine, and ought not to denie them, being comprised in bookes, and is to be compassed in youth?

That some exercise of bodie ought to be vsed, some ordinarie stirring ought to be enioyned, some prouision for priuate and peculiar trainers ought to be made: not onely the ladies of *Lacedæmon* will sweare, but all the world will sooth, if they do but wey, that it is to much to weaken our owne selues by not strengthning their side. That cunning poet for iudgement in matter, and great philosopher for secrecie in nature, our well knowen *Virgill*, saw in a goodly horse that was offered vnto *Augustus Cæsar* an infirmitie vnperceaued by either looker on or any of his stable, which came as he said by some weaknes in the damme, and was confessed to be true. *Galene* and the whole familie of Physicians ripping vp our infirmities, which be not to be auoided, placeth the seminarie and originall, engraffed in nature, as our greatest and nearest foes. And therfore to be preuented by the parentes, thorough considerate traine, the best and fairest meane, to better weake nature: so that of *duety* they are to be cared for. And what care in *duetie* is greater, then this in traine?

Naturall Towardnesse.

3. Their *naturall towardnesse* which was my third reason doth most manifestly call vpon vs, to see them well brought vp. If nature haue giuen them abilities to proue excellent in their kinde, and yet thereby in no point to let their most laudable dueties in mariage and matche, but rather to bewtifie them, with most singular ornamentes, are not we to be condemned of extreme vnnaturallnes, if we gay not that by discipline, which is giuen them by *nature*? That naturally they are so richly endowed, all *Philosophie* is full, no *Diuinitie* denyes, *Plato*[56] and his *Academikes* say, that all vertues be indifferent, nay all one in man and woman: sauing that they be more strong and more durable in men, weaker and more variable in wymen. *Xeno* and his *Stoikes* though they esteeme the ods betwene man and woman naturally to be as great as the difference, betwene an heauenly and an earthly creature, which *Plato* did not, making them both of one mould, yet they graunt them equalitie and samenesse in vertue, though they deliuer the strength and constancie ouer vnto men, as properly belonging vnto that side. *Aristotle* and *his Peripatetikes* confessing them both to be of one kinde, though to different vses

[56] Proclus vpon Platoes common weale, and Theodorus Asinæus vpon the question, whether men and wymen haue all vertues common.

in *nature*, according to those differences in *condition*, appointeth them differences in *vertue*, and yet wherin they agree: alloateth them the same. When they haue concluded thus of their naturall abilities, and so absolutely entitled them vnto all vertues, they rest not there, but proceede on further to their education in this sorte. That as naturally euery one hath some good assigned him, whervnto he is to aspire, and not to cease vntill he haue obtained it, onlesse he will by his owne negligence reiect that benefit, which the munificence of *nature* hath liberally bestowed on him: so there is a certaine meane, wherby to winne that perfitly, which *nature* of her selfe doth wish vs franckly. This meane they call *education*, whereby the naturall inclinations be gently caryed on, if they will curteously follow, or otherwise be hastened, if they must needes be forced, vntill they ariue at that same best, which *nature* bendeth vnto with full saile, in those fairer, which follow the traine willingly, in those meaner, which must be bet vnto it. And yet euen there where it is sorest laboured, it worketh some effecte vnworthy of repentaunce, and is better forced on in youth, then forgon in age: rather in children with feare, then not in men with greife. Now as the inclinations be common to both the kindes, so they deuide the meane of education indifferently betwene both. Which being thus, as both the truth tells the ignorant, and reading shewes the learned, we do wel then perceaue by *naturall men*, and *Philosophicall reasons*, that young *maidens* deserue the traine: bycause they haue that treasure, which belongeth vnto it, bestowed on them by *nature*, to be bettered in them by *nurture*. Neither doth *religion* contrarie religious *nature*. For the *Lorde* of *nature*, which created that motion to continue the consequence of all liuing creatures, by succession to the like, by education to the best, appointing either kinde the limittes of their duetie, and requiring of either the perfourmaunce therof, alloweth all such ordinarie and orderly meanes, as by his direction in his word may bring them both from his appointment to their perfourmaunce, from the first starting place, to the outmost gole: that is vnto that good, which he hath assigned them, by such wayes, as he hath willed them: so that both by *nature* the most obedient seruant, and by the *Lorde* of *nature* our most bountifull *God*, we haue it in commandement not onely to traine vp our owne sex, but also our female, seeing he hath to require an account for naturall talentes of both the parties, vs for directing them: them for perfourmance of our direction.

Excellent effectes.

4. The excellent effectes of those women, which haue bene verie well trained, do well declare, that they deserue the best training: which reason was my last in order, but not my least in force, to proue their more then common excellencie. This is a point of such galancie, if my purpose were to praise them, as it is but to giue precept, how to make them praiseworthie, as I might soner weary my selfe with reckening vp of writers, and calling worthie wymen to be witnesses in their owne cause then worthely to expresse their weight and worth, bycause I beleeue that to be most true, which is cronicled of them. I will not medle with any moe writers to whom wymen are most bound, for best speaking of them, and most spreading of their vertues, then with one onely man a single witnes in person, but aboue all singularitie in profe: the learned and honest *Plutarch*, whose name emporteth a princis treasure, whose writings witnes an vnwearied trauel, whose plaine truth

was neuer tainted. Would he so learned, so honest, so true, so sterne, haue become such a trumpet for their fame, to triumph by, so haue gratified that sex, whom he stood not in awe of: so haue beutified their doings, whom he might not haue medled with, so haue auaunced their honour, to hasard his owne sex, by setting them so hie, if he had not resolutely knowne the truth of his subiect? he durst be so bould with his owne Emperour the good *Traian*, to fore his scholer, in his epistle to him before his booke of gouerning the comon weale, as to say and call his booke to witnes thereof, that if he went to gouerne, and ouerthrew the state, he did it not by the authoritie of *Plutarch*, as disauowing his scholer, if he departed from his lessons. And would that courage haue bene forced to frame a false argument? or is so great a truth not to haue so great a credit? howsouer some of the lighter heades haue lewdly belyed them, or vainly accused them: yet the verie best and grauest writers thinke worthely of them, and make report of them with honour. *Ariosto* and *Boccacio* will beloth to be tearmed light, being so great doctours in their diuinitie, yet they be somwhat ouer heauie to wymen, without any great weight as in generall the *Italian* writers be, which in the middest of their louing leuities still glaunce at their lightnes, and that so beyound all manhoode, as they feele their owne fault, and dispaire of reconcilement, though they crie still for pardon. As those men know well, which will rather meruell, that I haue red those bookes, then mistrust my report, which they know to be true. In all good and generally authorised histories, and in many particuler discourses, it is most euident, that not onely priuate and particular wymen, being very well trained, but also great princesses and gallant troupes of the same sex haue shewed fourth in them selues meruelous effectes of vertue and valure. And good reason why. For where naturally they haue to shew, if education procure shew, is it a thing to be wondered at? Or is their singularitie lesse in nature, bycause wymen be lesse accustomed to shew it, and not so commonly employed, as we men be? Yet whensoeuer they be, by their dealinges they shew vs that they haue no dead flesh nor any base mettle. Well, I will knit vp this conclusion and burne day light no longer, to proue that carefully, which all men may see clearely, and ther aduersaries grieue at, bycause it confutes their follie, which vpon some priuate errour of their owne, to seeme fautles in wordes, where they be faithles in deedes, blame silly wymen as being the onely cause why they went awrie.

That yong *maidens* can learne, nature doth giue them, and that they haue learned, our experience doth teach vs, with what care to themselues, them selues can best witnes, with what comfort to vs, what forraine example can more assure the world, then our diamond at home? our most deare soueraine lady and princesse, by nature a woman, by vertue a worthy, not one of the nyne, but the tenth aboue the nyne, to perfit in her person that absolute number, which is no fitter to comprehend all absolutnes in Arithmetike, then she is knowne to containe al perfections in nature, all degrees in valure, and to become a president: to those nyne worthy men, as *Apollo*[57] is accounted to the nyne famouse wymen, she to vertues and vertuous men, he to muses, and learned wymen: thereby to proue *Plutarches* conclusion true, that oppositions of vertues by way of comparison is

[57] Philo Iudæus in his discours of the ten commaundementes rips out the perfitnes of that number.

their chiefe commendation. Is *Anacreon* a good poet, what say you to *Sappho*? Is *Bacis* a good prophet, what say you to *Sibill*? was *Sesostris* a famouse prince, what say you to *Semiramis*? was *Seruius* a noble king, what say you to *Tanaquill*? was *Brutus* a stowt man, what say you to *Porcia*? Thus reasoneth *Plutarch*,[58] and so do I, is it honorable for *Apollo* a man to haue the presidencie ouer nyne wymen, the resemblers of learning? then more honorable it is for our most worthy *Princesse* to haue the presidencie ouer nyne men, the paragons of vertue: and yet to be so familiarly acquainted with the nyne *muses*, as they are in strife who may loue her best, for being best learned? for whose excellent knowledge and learning, we haue most cause to reioyce, who tast of the frute: and posteritie to praise, which shall maintaine her memorie: though I wish their memorie abridged, to haue our tast enlarged: our prouing lengthened, to haue their praising shortened: to be glad that we haue her, not to greue, that we had her: as that omnipotent god, which gaue her vnto vs, when we had more neede of such a prince, then shee of such a people, will preserue her for vs, I do nothing dout, that we both may serue him, she as our carefull soueraine, to set forth his glory, we as her faithfull subiectes, to submit our selues to it.

If no storie did tell it, if no state did allow it, if no example did confirme it, that yong *maidens* deserue the trayning, this our owne myrour, the maiestie of her sex, doth proue it in her owne person, and commendes it to our reason. We haue besides her highnes as vndershining starres, many singuler ladies and gentlewymen, so skilfull in all cunning, of the most laudable, and loueworthy qualities of learning, as they may well be alleadged for a president to prayse, not for a pattern to proue like by: though hope haue a head, and nature be no nigard, if education do her dutie, and will seeke to resemble euen where presidentes be passing, both hope to attaine to, and possibilitie to seeme to. Wherefore by these profes, I take it to be very clear, that I am not farre ouershot, in admitting them to traine being so traineable by nature, and so notable by effectes.

The ende of learning in yong maides.

But now hauing graunted them the benefit and society of our education, we must assigne the end, wherfore their traine shall serue, whereby we may apply it the better. Our owne traine is without restraint for either matter or maner, bycause our employment is so generall in all thinges: theirs is within limit, and so must their traine be. If a yong *maiden* be to be trained in respect of mariage, obedience to her head, and the qualities which looke that way, must needes be her best way: if in regard of necessitie to learne how to liue, artificiall traine must furnish out her trade: if in respect of ornament to beawtifie her birth, and to honour her place, rareties in that kinde and seemly for that kinde do best beseeme such: if for gouernment, not denyed them by God, and deuised them by men, the greatnes of their calling doth call for great giftes, and generall excellencies for generall occurrences. Wherefore hauing these different endes alwayes in eye, we may point them their traine in different degrees. But some *Timon* will say, what should wymen do with learning? Such a churlish carper will neuer picke out the best, but be alway ready to blame the worst. If all men vsed all pointes of learning well, we had

[58] Plutarch in his booke of wymens vertues.

some reason to alleadge against wymen, but seeing misuse is common to both the kinds, why blame we their infirmitie, whence we free not our selues? Some wymen abuse writing to that end, some reading to this, some all that they learne any waye, to some other ill some waye. And I praie you what do we? I do not excuse ill: but barre them from accusing, which be as bad themselues: vnlesse they will first condemne themselues, and so proceede in their plea with more discretion after a repentant discouerie. But they will not deale thus, they will rather retire for shame and proue to be nonsuite, then confesse themselues faulty and blush for their blaming. Wherfore as the communitie of vertues, argueth the communitie of vices naturally in both: so let vs in that point enterchaunge forgiuenesse, and in hope of the vertues direct to the best, not for feare of the vices, make an open gap for them. Wherefore in directing of that traine, which I do assigne vnto young maidens, I will follow this methode, and shew which of them be to learne, and when, what and how much, where and of whom.

Which and when.

As concerning those which are to be trained, and when they are to begin their traine, this is my opinion. The same restraint in cases of necessitie, where they conueniently cannot, and the same freedom in cases of libertie, when they commodiously may, being reserued to parentes in their daughters, which I allowed them in their sonnes, and the same regard to the weaknesse and strength of their witts and bodies, the same care for their womanly exercises, for helpe of their health, and strength of their limmes, being remitted to their considerations, which I assigned them in their sonnes, I do thinke the same time fit for both, not determinable by yeares, but by ripenesse of witte to conceiue without tiring, and strength of bodie to trauell without wearying. For though the girles seeme commonly to haue a quicker ripening in witte, then boyes haue, for all that seeming, yet it is not so. Their naturall weaknesse which cannot holde long, deliuers very soone, and yet there be as prating boyes, as there be pratling wenches. Besides, their braines be not so much charged, neither with weight nor with multitude of matters, as boyes heades be, and therefore like empty caske they make the greater noise. As those men which seeme to be very quicke witted by some sudden pretie aunswere, or some sharp replie, be not alwaye most burthened, neither with lettes, nor learning, but out of small store, they offer vs still the floore, and holde most of the mother. Which sharpnesse of witte though it be within them, as it bewraeth it selfe: yet it might dwell within them a great while, without bewraying of it selfe, if studie kept them still, or great doinges did dull them: as slight dealinges and imperious, do commonly maintaine that kinde of courage. Boyes haue it alwaye, but oftimes hide it, bycause their stuffe admitteth time: wenches haue it alwaye, and alwaye bewray it, bycause their timber abides no tarying. And seeing it is in both, it deserues care in both, neither to timely to stirre them, nor let them loyter to long. As for bodies the *maidens* be more weake, most commonly euen by nature, as of a moonish influence, and all our whole kinde is weake of the mother side, which when she was first made, euen then weakned the mans side. Therefore great regard must be had to them, no lesse, nay rather more then to boyes in that time. For in proces of time, if they be of worth themselues, they may so matche, as the parent may take more pleasure in his sonnes by law, then in his heires by nature. They are to be the principall pillers in the vpholding of housholdes, and so they are likely to proue, if they proue well in training. The dearest comfort that man can haue, if they encline to good: the nearest corrosiue if they tread awry. And therfore charilie to be cared for, bearing a iewell of such worth, in a vessel of such weaknesse. Thus much for there persons whom I turne ouer to the parentes abilitie for charge: to their owne capacitie for conceit: in eche degree some, from the lowest in menaltie, to the highest in mistriship.

The time hath tied it selfe to strength in both parts, for the bodie to trauell, for the soule to conceiue. The exercises pray in no case to be forgot as a preseruatiue to the body, and a conserue for the soule.

What.

For the matter what they shall learne, thus I thinke, following the custome of my countrie, which in that that is vsuall doth lead me on boldly, and in that also which is most rare, doth shew me my path, to be already troden. So that I shall not neede to erre, if I marke but my guide wel. Where rare excellencies in some wymen, do but shew vs some one or two parentes good successe, in their daughters learning, there is neither president to be fetcht, nor precept to be framed. For preceptes be to conduct the common, but these singularities be aboue the common, presidentes be for hope, those pictures passe beyond al hope. And yet they serue for profe to proceede by in way of argument, that wymen can learne if they will, and may learne what they list, when they bend their wittes to it. To learne to read is very common, where conuenientnes doth serue, and *writing* is not refused, where oportunitie will yeild it.

Reading.

Reading if for nothing else it were, as for many thinges else it is, is verie needefull for religion, to read that which they must know, and ought to performe, if they haue not whom to heare, in that matter which they read: or if their memorie be not stedfast, by reading to reuiue it. If they heare first and after read of the selfe same argument, reading confirmes their memorie. Here I may not omit many and great contentmentes, many and sound comfortes, many and manifoulde delites, which those wymen that haue skill and time to reade, without hindering their houswifery, do continually receiue by reading of some comfortable and wise discourses, penned either in forme of historie, or for direction to liue by.

Writing.

As for *writing*, though it be discommended for some priuate cariages, wherein we men also, no lesse then wymen, beare oftentimes blame, if that were a sufficient exception why we should not learne to write, it hath his commoditie where it filleth in match, and helpes to enrich the goodmans mercerie. Many good occasions are oftentimes offered, where it were better for them to haue the vse of their pen, for the good that comes by it, then to wish they had it, when the default is felt: and for feare of euill, which cannot be auoided in some, to auert that good, which may be commodious to many.

Musike.

Musicke is much vsed, where it is to be had, to the parentes delite, while the daughters be yong, more then to their owne, which commonly proueth true, when the yong wenches become yong wiues. For then lightly forgetting *Musicke* when they learne to be mothers, they giue it in manifest euidence, that in their learning of it, they did more seeke to please their parentes, then to pleasure themselues. But howsoeuer it is, seeing the thing is not reiected, if with the learning of it once, it may be retained still (as by order it may) it is ill let go, which is got with great paines, and bought with some cost. The learninge to sing and plaie by the booke, a matter soone had, when *Musike* is first minded, which still preserue the cunning, though discontinuance disturbe. And seeing it is but litle which they learne, and the time as litle wherein they learne, bycause they haste still on toward husbandes, it were expedient, that they learned perfitly, and that with the losse of their pennie, they lost not their pennieworth also, besides the losse of their time, which is the greatest losse of all. I medle not with *nedles*, nor yet with *houswiferie*, though I thinke it, and know it, to be a principall commendation in a woman: to be able to gouerne and direct her houshold, to looke to her house and familie, to prouide and keepe necessaries, though the goodman pay, to know the force of her kitchen, for sicknes and health, in her selfe and her charge: bycause I deale onely with such thinges as be incident to their learning. Which seeing the custome of my country doth permit, I may not mislike, nay I may wish it with warrant, the thing being good and well beseeming their sex. This is the most so farre as I remember, which they commonly vse in youth, and participate with vs in. If any parent do priuately traine vp his children of either sex in any other priuate fantsie of his owne, I cannot commend it, bycause I do not know it, and if it fortune to die within his priuate walles, I cannot giue it life by publike rehearsall. The common and most knowne is that, which I haue saide.

How much.

The next pointe *how much,* is a question of more enquirie, and therefore requireth aduised handling. To appoint besides these thinges, which are already spoken of, how much further any *maide* maye proceede in matter of learning and traine, is a matter of some moment, and concerneth no meane ones. And yet some petie lowlinges, do sometimes seeke to resemble, where they haue small reason, and will needes seeme like, where their petieship cannot light, vsing shew for a shadow, where they haue no fitter shift. And therfore in so doing, they passe beyond the boundes both of their birth, and their best beseeming. Which then discouereth a verie meere follie, when a meane parent traineth vp his daughter hie in those properties, which I shall streight waye speake of, and she matcheth lowe, but within her owne compasse. For in such a case those ouerraught qualities for the toyousnesse therof being misplaced in her, do cause the young woman rather to be toyed withall, as by them giuing signe of some idle conceit otherwise, then to be thought verie well of, as one wisely brought vp. There is a comlynesse in eche kinde, and a decentnesse in degree, which is best obserued, when eche one prouides according to his power, without ouerreaching. If some odde property do worke preferrement beyond proportion, it commonly stayes there, and who so shootes at the like, in hope to hit, may sooner misse: bycause the wayes to misse be so many, and to hit is but one, and wounders which be but onse seene, be no examples to resemble. Euery *maide* maye not hope to speede, as she would wishe, bycause some one hath sped better then she could wishe.

Where the question is *how much* a woman ought to learne, the aunswere may be, so much as shall be needefull. If that also come in doubt, the returne may be, either so much as her parentes conceiue of her in hope, if her parentage be meane, or prouide for her in state, if her birth beare a saile. For if the parentes be of calling, and in great account, and the daughters capable of some singular qualities, many commendable effects may be wrought therby, and the young maidens being well trained are verie soone commended to right honorable matches, whom they may well beseeme, and aunswere much better, their qualities in state hauing good correspondence, with their matches of state, and their wisedoms also putting to helping hand, for the procuring of their common good. Not here to note, what frute the common weale may reape, by such witts so worthily aduaunced, besides their owne priuate. If the parentes be meane, and the *maidens* in their training shew forth at the verie first some singular rarenesse like to ensue, if they florish but their naturall, there hope maye grow great, that some great matche may as well like of a young maiden excellently qualified, as most do delite in brute or brutish thinges for some straunge qualitie, either in nature to embrase, or in art to maruell. And yet this hope may faile. For neither haue great personages alwaye that iudgement, nor young *maidens* alwaye that fortune, though the *maidens* remaine the gainers, for they haue the qualities to comfort their mediocrity, and those great ones want iudgement to set forth their nobilitie.

This *how much* consisteth either in perfiting of those forenamed foure, *reading* well, *writing* faire, *singing* sweete, *playing* fine, beyond all cry and aboue all comparison, that pure excellencie in things but ordinarie may cause extraordinarie liking: or else in skill of languages annexed to these foure, that moe good giftes may worke more wounder. "For meane is a maime where excellencie is the maruell." To hope for hie mariages, is good meat, but not for mowers, to haue leasure to take delite in these gentlewomanly qualities, is no worke for who will: Nay to be a paragon among princes, to vse such singularities, for the singular good of the general state, and the wonder of her person, were a wish in dispaire, were not true proofe the iust warrant, that such a thing may be wished, bycause in our time we haue found it, euen then, when we did wish it most, and in the ende more maruellous, then at first we durst haue wished. The euentes in these wymen which we see in our dayes, to haue bene brought vp in learning, do rule this conclusion. That such personages as be borne to be princes, or matches to great peeres, or to furnish out such traines, for some peculiar ornamentes to their place and calling, are to receiue this kinde of education in the highest degree, that is conuenient for their kinde. But princely *maidens* aboue all: bycause occasion of their height standes in neede of such giftes, both to honour themselues, and to discharge the duetie, which the countries, conmitted to their hands, do daily call for, and besides what matche is more honorable, then when desert for rare qualities, doth ioine it selfe, with highnesse in degree? I feare no workmanship in wymen to giue them *Geom-*

etrie and her sister sciencies: to make them *Mathematicalls,* though I meane them *Musicke*: nor yet barres to plead at, to leaue them the lawes: nor vrinalls to looke on, to lend them some Physicke, though the skil of herbes haue bene the studie of nobilitie, by the *Persian* storie, and much commended in wymen: nor pulpittes to preach in, to vtter their *Diuinitie*: though by learning of some language, they can talke of the lining: and for direction of their life, they must be afforded some, though not as preachers and leaders: yet as honest perfourmers, and vertuous liuers. *Philosophie* would furnish their generall discourses, if their leasure could entend it: but the knowledge of some toungues, either of substaunce in respect of deeper learning, or account for the present time may verie well be wisht them: and those faculties also, which do belong to the furniture of speache, may be verie well allowed them, bycause toungues be most proper, where they do naturally arme. If I should allow them the *pencill* to draw, as the penne to write, and thereby entitle them to all my Elementarie principles, I might haue reason for me. For it neither requireth any great labour to fraye young maidens from it, and it would helpe their nedle, to beautifie their workes: and it is maintainable by very good examples euen of their owne kinde. *Timarete*[59] the vertuous, daughter to *Mycon*: *Irene* the curteous, daughter to *Cratinus*: *Aristarete* the absolute, daughter to *Nearchus*: *Lala* the eloquent, and euer maide of *Cyzicus*: *Martia* the couragious, daughter to *Varro* the best learned and most loued of any *Romain,* and many mo besides, did so vse the *pencill,* as their fame therefore is so much the fairer, bycause the fact in that sex is so seldome and rare.

And is not a young gentlewoman, thinke you, thoroughly furnished, which can reade plainly and distinctly, write faire and swiftly, sing cleare and sweetely, play wel and finely, vnderstand and speake the learned languages, and those toungues also which the time most embraseth, with some *Logicall* helpe to chop, and some *Rhetoricke* to braue. Besides the matter which is gathered, while these toungues be either learned, or lookt on, as wordes must haue seates, no lesse then rayment bodies. Were it any argument of an vnfurnished maiden, besides these qualities to draw cleane in good proportion, and with good symmetrie? Now if she be an honest woman, and a good housewife to, were she not worth the wishing, and worthy the shryning? and yet such there be, and such we know. Or is it likely that her children shalbe eare a whit the worse brought vp, if she be a *Lælia,* an *Hortensia,* or a *Cornelia,* which were so endued and noted for so doing? It is written of *Eurydice* the *Epirote*[60] that after she began to haue children, she sought to haue learning, to bring then vp skilfully, whom she brought forth naturally. Which thing she perfourmed in deede, a most carefull mother, and a most skilfull mistresse. For which her well doing, she hath wonne the reward, to be enrowled among the most rare matrones.

Where and when.

Now there is nothing left to ende this treatise of young *maidens,* but where and vnder whom, they are to learne, which question will be sufficiently resolued, vpon consideration of the time how long they are to learne, which time is commonly till

[59] Plin. lib. 35. cap. 11.
[60] Plut. *περὶ παιδ. ἀγωγ.*

they be about thirtene or fouretene yeares old, wherein as the matter, which they must deale with all, cannot be very much in so litle time, so the perfitting thereof requireth much trauel, though their time be so litle, and there would be some shew afterward, wherein their trayning did auaile them. They that may continue some long time at learning, thorough the state and abilitie of their parentes haue also their time and place sutably appointed, by the foresight of their parentes. So that the time resting in priuate forecast, I can not reduce it to generall precept, but onely thus farre, that in perfitnes it may shew, how well it was employed.

The places.

The places wherein they learne be either *publike,* if they go forth to the *Elementarie* schole, or *priuate* if they be taught at home. The teacher either of their owne sex or of ours.

For *publike* places, bycause in that kinde there is no publike prouision, but such as the professours of their training do make of them selues, I can say little, but leaue them to that and to their parentes circumspection, which both in their being abroad, during their minority, and in bringing them vp at home after their minoritie, I know will be very diligent to haue all thinges well. For their teachers, their owne sex were fittest in some respectes, but ours frame them best, and with good regard to some circumstances will bring them vp excellently well, specially if their parentes be either of learning to iudge, or of authoritie to commaund, or of both, to do both, as experience hath taught vs in those, which haue proued so well. The greater borne Ladyes and gentlewymen, as they are to enioy the benefit of this education most, so they haue best meanes to prosecute it best, being neither restrained in wealth, but to haue the best teachers, and greatest helpes: neither abbridged in time, but to ply all at full. And thus I take my leaue of yong maidens and gentlewymen, to whom I wish as well, as I haue saide well of them.

CHAPTER 39.

Of the traning vp of yong gentlemen. Of priuate and publike education, with their generall goods and illes. That there is no better way for gentlemen to be trained by in any respect then the common is being well appointed. Of rich-mens children which be no gentlemen. Of nobilitie in generall. Of gentlemanlie exercises. What it is to be a nobleman, or a gentleman. That infirmities in noble houses be not to be triumphed ouer. The causes and groundes of nobilitie. Why so many desire to be gentlemen. That gentlemen ought to professe learning and liberall sciences for many good and honorable effectes. Of trauelling into forraine countries: with all the braunches allowance and disallowance thereof: and that it were to be wished, that gentlemen would professe, to make sciences liberall in vse, which are liberall in name. Of the trayning vp of a yong prince.

IN the last title I did declare at large, how yong maidens in ech degree were to be auaunced in learning, which me thought was verie incident to my purpose, bycause they be counter-braunches to vs in the kinde of mortall and reasonable creatures, and also for that in eche degree of life, they be still our mates, and sometime our mistresses, through the benefit of law, and honorablenes of birth. Now considering they ioyne allway with vs in number and nearenes, and sometime exceede vs in dignitie and calling: as they communicate with vs in all qualities, and all honours euen vp to the scepter, so why ought they not in any wise but be made communicantes with vs in education and traine, to performe that part well, which they are to play, for either equalitie with vs, or soueraintie aboue vs? Here now ensueth another title of meruelous importaunce, for the kinde of people, whereof I am to entreat: bycause their state is still in the superlatiue, and the greatest executions be theirs by degree, though sometime they leese them by their owne default, and set them ouer to such, as nature maketh noble by ingenerate vertues. I meane the trayning vp of yong *gentlemen* in euery degree and to what so euer ascent, bycause euen the crowne and kingdome is their height, though it come to the female, when their side faileth. For *gentlemen* will commonly be exempt from the common, as in title, so also in traine, refrayning the publike, though they hold of the male, and preferring the priuate, to be liker to maidens, whose education is most priuate, bycause of their kinde, and therefore not misliked: whereas yong gentlemen should be publike, bycause of their vse. And for not being such, they beare some blame, as therein contrarying both all the best ordered common weales, and all the most excellent and the learnedest writers, which bring vp euen the best princes allway with great company.

But seeing they wilbe priuate, and I take vpon me not to leap ouer any, which light within my compasse, and chiefly yong gentlemen, whose ordinarie greatnes is to gouerne our state, and to be publike pillers for the prince to leane on, and the people to staie by: their priuate choice commaundes me a priuate consideration, which in yong gentlewymen needed not any handling, bycause it beseemeth them to be taught in priuate: in *gentlemen* it needeth, the case being doubtfull, whether priuate trayning be their best or no. And though this argument succede yong maidens in order of methode, I hope yong gentlemen will not be offended neither with me for the placing, seeing the other sex is in possesssion of prerogatiue, nor with them for being so placed, which haue wone the best place.

Of priuate education.

Priuate.

Education.

This question for the bringing vp of yong gentlemen offereth the deciding of an other ordinarie controuersie, betwene *publike* education and *priuate*, which verie name in nature is enemy to publike, as inclosure is to common, and swelling to much ouerlayeth the common, not onely in *education*, where it both corrupteth by planting a to priuate habit, and is corrupted it selfe by a degenerate forme, but also in most thinges else. Yet do I not deny both personall properties and priuate realities, which law doth allow in priuate possessions, euen there, where friendship makes thinges to be most common by participation. I will therefore speake a litle of this *priuate* traine, before I passe to the *education* of *gentlemen*. What doe these two wordes import, *priuate education*? *Priuate* is that, which hath respect in all circumstances to some one of choice: as *publike* in all circumstances regardeth euery one alike. *Education* is the bringing vp of one, not to liue alone, but amongest others, (bycause companie is our naturall cognisaunce) whereby he shall be best able to execute those doings in life, which the state of his calling shall employ him vnto, whether *publike* abrode, or *priuate* at home, according vnto the direction of his countrie, whereunto he is borne, and oweth his whole seruice. All the functions here be publike and regard euery one, euen where the thinges do seeme to be most priuate, bycause the maine direction remaineth in the publike, and the priuate must be squared, as it will best ioyne with that: and yet we restraine *education* to *priuate*, all whose circumstaunces be singular to one. As if he that were brought vp alone, should also euer liue alone, as if one should say, I will haue you to deale with all, but neuer to see all: your end shalbe *publike*, your meane shalbe *priuate*, that is to say, such a meane as hath no minde to bring you to that end, which you seeme to pretend: Bycause naturally *priuate* is sworne enemy to *publike* in all euentes, as it doth appeare when *priuate* gaine vndoeth the common, though *publike* still pretend friendship to all that is *priuate* in distributiue effects, as it is plainely seene when the *publike* care doth helpe ech *priuate*, and by cherishing the singuler maintaineth the generall, whereas the priuate letteth the publike drowne, so it selfe may flete aboue. For in deed they march mostwhat from seuerall groundes to seuerall issues by most seuerall and least sutable meanes, the one in nature a rowmy *pallace* full of most varietie to content the minde, the other a close *prison,* tedious to be tied to, where the sense is shackled: the one in her kinde, a *libertie*, a broade *feild,* an open *aire*, the other in the contrarie kinde, a *pinfold*, a *cage*, a *cloister*: Neither do I take these tearmes to make a fit diuision, where the end is still *common* and the abuse *priuate*. For how can *education* be *priuate*? it abuseth the name as it abuseth the thing. If they will say *education* is either good or ill, and vse the naturall name, then methinke the disembling which is shadowed in the tearme *priuate* would soone appeare: though there can be no worse name then *priuate,* sauing where the publike doth appoint it, which in education it will not, thereby to foster her owne foe: though in possessions it do, to haue subsidies to sustaine, and paiements to maintaine her great common charge.

And though in communities of kinde which naturally is deuided into spieces, *nature* engraffe *priuate* differences for distinction sake, as *reason* in man to part him from a beast, yet that difference remaineth one still, bycause there is none better: which countenaunce of best cannot here be pretended, bycause in *education priuate* is the worst. This *priuate* renting in sunder of persons, for a pretended best *education,* which must passe on togither after *education* is verie daungerous in all daies, for many priuate pushes, while euery parent can serue his owne humour, be it neuer so distempered: by the secrecie of his owne house, not to be discouered: by the choyce of his teacher, which will be ready to follow, if he forgoe not in folley: by the obedience of his child, which must learne as he is led, or else be beaten for not learning: which must obey as he is bid, or else lease his parent blessing. In *publicke* schooles this swaruing in affection from the *publicke* choice in no case can be. The master is in eye, what he saith is in eare: the doctrine is examined: the childe is not alone, and there must he learne that which is laid vnto him in the hearing of all and censure of all. Whatsoeuer inconueniences do grow in *common* schooles, (as where the dealers be men, how can there be but maimes?) yet the *priuate* is much worse, and hatcheth moe odde ills. Naturally it is not built vpon vnitie, brad by disunion, to seeme to see more then the common man doth, to seeme to preuent that by *priuate* wit, which the common doth incurre by vnaduised follie: to seeme to gaine more in secrecie, then the common giues in ciuilitie. By cloistering from the common it will seeme to keepe a countenaunce farre aboue the common, euen from the first cradle. Wherby it becomes the *puffer* vp to *pride* in the recluse, and the *direction* to *disdaine,* by dreaming still of bettership: the enemie to vnitie, betwene the vnequall: the ouerwayning of ones selfe, not compared with others, the disiointing of agreement, where the higher contemneth his inferiour with skorne, and the lower doth stomacke his superiour with spite: the one gathering snuffe, the other grudge.

This kinde of traine which soweth the corne of dissension by difference, where the haruest of consent is the harbour of common loue, the indissoluble chaine of countriemens comfort, may very well be bettered, and much better be forborne, bycause by the way it tempereth still the poyson of a creeping spite. And certainly the nature of the thing doth tend this way, though chaunging bytimes to better choice, or the common check, which will not be controwled, do many and often times interrupt the course. And though the child in proces proue better, and shew himselfe curteous, contrarie to my note, and the verie nature of priuate education, thanke naturall goodnesse or experience seene abroad, not the kinde of education, which in her owne sternnesse alloweth no such curtesie, though the childe see it in his parentes, and finde it in his bookes. And somtimes also it maketh him to shepish bashfull, when he comes to the light: as being vnacquainted with resort: though generally he be somwhat to childish bold, by noting nothing, but that which he breedes of himselfe in his solitarie traine, where he is best himselfe, and hath none to controwle him, no not his maister himselfe, but vnder confession, how so euer the title of maister do pretend authoritie and the name of scholer, make shew of obedience in priuate cloistring. I neede not saie all, but in this short manner, I seeke to giue occasion for them to see all, which desire to sift more, both for the matter of their learning, and the manner of their liuing.

Do ye know what it is for one to be acquainted with all children in his childhood, which must liue with them being men in his manhood? Is the common bringing vp being well appointed good for the common man, and not for him of more height? and doth not that deserue to be liked on in priuate, which is thoroughly tryed being showed forth in common, and sifted by the seeing? which without any great alteration, for the matter of traine will be very well content to be pent vp within priuate dores, though it mislike the cloistring, in priuating the person. Sure that common which is well cast, must needes helpe the priuate, as one of her partes and feede one child very well being a generall mother to all: but priuate be it neuer so well cast in the sternnesse of his kinde, still drawes from the publike. I count not that priuate which is executed at home for a publike vse, in respect of the place, for so all doinges be priuate, but that which will be at home, as better so. And why? for the priuate parties good. But it should seeme generally that the question is not so much for the manner of education, nor for the matter, wherin, but for the place where, as if that, which is good for all in common, should not be good for some but in priuate. I must speake it vnder pardon. The effect commendes the common: for that the common education in the middest of common mediocritie bringeth vp such wittes to such excellencie, as serue in all degrees, yea euen next to the hyest, wheras priuate education in the middest of most wealth, if it maintaine it selfe with any more then bare mediocritie both of learning and iudgement, when it is at the hyest, let him that hath shewed more, giue charge to the chalenge. And yet some one young mans odnesse, though it be odde in deed, ouerthroweth not the question. And oftimes the report of that odnesse which we see not in effect, but heare of in speeche, falles out very lame, if the reporters iudgement be aduisedly considered, though for the authoritie and countenaunce of the man, skill giue place to boldnesse, and silence to ciuilitie: which otherwise would replie against it. There is no comparison betwene the two kindes, set affection apart. If the priuate pupill chaunce to come to speake, it falleth out mostwhat dreamingly, bycause priuitie in traine is a punishment to the tongue: and in teaching of a language to exclude companions of speeche, is to seeke to quenche thrist, and yet to close the mouth so, as no moysture can get in. If he come to write, it is leane, and nothing but skinne, and commonly bewrayes great paines in the maister, which brought forth euen so much, being quite reft of all helping circunstance, to ease his great labour, by his pupilles conference, with more companie. Which is but a small benefit to the child, that might haue had much more if his course had bene chaunged. He can but vtter that, which he heares, and he heares none but one, which one though he know all, yet can vtter but litle, bycause what one auditorie is two or three boyes for a learned man to prouoke him to vtteraunce? If he trauelled to vtter, and one of iudgement should stand behinde a couert to heare him, methinke he should heare a straunge orator straining his pipes, to perswade straunge people, and the boye if he were alone, fast a sleepe, or if he had a fellow, playing vnder the bourd, with his hand or feete, hauing one eye vpon his talking maister, and the other eye on his playing mate. If the nyne *Muses* and *Apollo* their president were painted vpon the wall, he might talke to them with out either laughing or lowring, they would serue him for places of memorie, or for hieroglyphicall partitions. If he that is taught alone misse, as he must often, hauing either none, or verie small companie to helpe his memorie, which multitude serues for in common scholes, where the hearing of many confirmes the sitter by, shall he runne to his maister? if he do that boldly, it will breede contempt in the ende: if he do it with feare, it will dull him for not daring. And though it be verie good for the child, not to be afrayd to aske counsell of his maister in that, where he doubteth, yet if he finde easie entertainment he will doubt still, rather then do his diligence, not to haue cause to doubt. If the priuate scholer proue cunninger afterward, then I conceiue he can be by priuate education, there was some forreine helpe which auaunced him abroad, it was not his traine within being tyed to the stake, which offereth that violence to my assertion.

Why is priuate teaching so much vsed?

But what leades the priuate, and why is it so much vsed? There must needes be some reason, which alieneth the particular parente from the publike discipline, which I do graunt to very great ones, bycause the further they rise from the multitude in number, and aboue them in degree, the more priuate they grow as in person, so in traine: and the prince himselfe being one and singular must needes embrace the priuate discipline, wherin he sheweth great valure in his person, if by priuate meanes, he mount aboue the publike. And yet if euen the greatest, could haue his traine so cast, as he might haue the companie of a good choice number, wherein to see all differences of wittes, how to discerne of all, which must deale with all, were it any sacrilege?

But for the gentleman generally, which flyeth not so high, but fluttereth some litle aboue the ordinarie common, why doth he make his choice rather to be like them aboue, which still grow priuater, then to like of them below, which can grow no lower, and yet be supporters, to stay vp the whole, and liker to himselfe, then he is to the highest? To haue his child learne better maners, and more vertuous conditions? As bad at home as abroad, and brought into schooles, not bred there. To auoide confusion and multitude? His child shall marke more, and so proue the wiser: the multitude of examples being the meanes to discretion. Nay in a number, though he finde some lewd, whom to flie, he shall spie many toward, whom to follow: and withall in schooles he shall perceaue that vice is punished, and vertue praised, which where it is not, there is daunger to good manners, but not in schooles, where it is very diligently obserued, bycause in publike view, necessitie is the spurre. To keepe him in health by biding at home for feare of infection abroad? Death is within dores, and dainties at home haue destroyed more children then daunger abroad. Doth affection worke stay, and can ye not parte from your childes presence? That is to fond. And any cause else admittes controwlement, sauing onely state in princes children, and princelike personages, which are to farre aboue the common: by reason of great circunstance. And yet their circunstance were better, if they saw the common, ouer whom they command, and with due circumspectnesse could auoid all daungers, wherv nto the greatest be commonly subiect, by great desires, not in themselues to haue, but in others that hope, which make the greatnesse of their gaine their colour against iustice, where they iniurie most. It is enough that is ment, though I say no more: besides that by a *Persian* principle, the seldome seing in princes, workes admiration the more, when they are to be seene.

Send your priuate M. with your child to the common schoole.

Vse common scholes to the best, ioyne a tutor to your childe, let *Quintilian* be your guide, all thinges will be well done, where such care is at hand, and that is much better done, which is done before witnes to encourage the childe. *Comparisons* inspire vertues, *hearing* spreads learning: one is none and if he do something at home, what would he do with company? It is neuer settled, that wanteth an aduersarie, to quicken the spirites, to stirre courage, to finde out affections.

For the maisters valew, which is content to be cloistered, I will say nothing, entertainement makes digressions euen to that, which we like not. But if it would please the priuate parent, to send his sonne with his priuate maister to a common schoole, that might do all parties very much good. For the schole being well ordered, and appointed for matter and maner to learne, where number is pretended to cumber the maister, and to mince his labour so, as ech one can haue but some litle, though his voice be like the *Sunne*, which at one time with one light shineth vpon all: yet the priuate scholer, by the helpe of his priuate maister in the common place hath his full applying, and the whole *Sunne*, if no lesse will content him. The common maister thereby will be carefull to haue the best: the priuate teacher willbe curiouse to come but to the very best: wherby both the priuate and publike scholers shall be sure to receiue the best. And if the publike maister be chosen accordingly, as allowance will allure euen the principall best, priuate cunning will not disdaine to be one degree beneth, where he knoweth himselfe bettered. And thereby disagreement betwene the two teachers will be quite excluded which onely might be the meane to marre both my meaning and *Qintilianes* counsell. Sure my resolution is, which if it winne no liking abroade may returne againe homeward, and be wellcome to his maister, that that which must be continued and exercised in publike, the residue of ones life, were best to be learned in publike, from the beginning of ones life. And if ye will needes be priuate, make your priuate publike, and drawe as many to your priuate maister, for your priuate sonnes sake, seeing you are able to prouide rowme, bycause that will proue to be best for your child, as shalbe able to keepe some forme of our multitude, that he may haue one companie before him to follow and learne of, an other beneth to teach and vaunt ouer, the third of his owne standing, with whom to striue for praise of forwardnes. Whereby it falleth out still, that that priuate is best, which consisteth of some chosen number for a priuate ende: and that multitude best, where choice restraines number, for the publike seruice: for in deede the common scholes be as much ouercharged with too many, as any priuate is with to few. Which how it may either be helpt, or in that confusion be better handled, I will hereafter in my priuate executions declare, seeing I haue noted the defect.

To knit vp this question therefore of priuate and publike *education*, I do take publike to be simply the better: as being more vpon the stage, where faultes be more seene, and so sooner amended, as being the best meane both for vertue and learning, which follow in such sort, as they be first planted. What *vertue* is private? *wisedome* to forsee, what is good for a desert? *courage* to defend, where there is no assailant? *temperance* to be modest, where none is to chaleng? *Iustice* to do right, where none is to demaunde it? what *learning* is for alonnesse? did it not come from collection in publike dealinges, and can it shew her force in priuate affaires, which seeme affraid of the publike? Compare the best in both the kinds, there the ods wil appeare. If ye compare a priuate scholer, of a very fine capacity, and worthy the open field, so well trayned by a diligent and a discreat maister as that traine will yeald: with a blockhead brought vp under a publike teacher, not of the best sort, or if in comparison ye march a toward priuate teacher with a weake publike maister, ye say somwhat to the persons but smallie to the thing, which in *equalitie* shewes the difference, in *inequalitie* deceiues the doubter, and then most, when to augment his owne liking, he wil make the conference odde, to seeme to auaunce errour, where the truth is against him. And to saye all in one, the publike pestring with any reasonable consideration, though it be not the best, yet in good sooth, it farre exceedeth the priuate alonenesse, though sometime a diligent priuate teacher shew some great effect of his maine endeuour.

That the circunstance is one in gentlemen and common mens children.

But to the education of *gentlemen* and *gentlemanly* fellowes. What time shal I appoint them to begin to learne? Their witts be as the common, their bodies oftimes worse. The same circunstance, the same consideration for time must direct all degrees. What thing shall they learne? I know none other, neither can I appoint better, then that which I did appoint for all. The common and priuate concurre herin. Neither shall the priuate scholer go any faster on, nay perhaps not so fast, for all the helpe of his whole maister, then our boyes shall, with the bare helpe, that is in number and multitude, euery boye being either a maister for his fellow to learne by, or an example to set him on, to better him if he be negligent, to be like him, if he be diligent.

Onely this, young *gentlemen* must haue some choice of peculiar matter, still appropriat vnto them, bycause they be to gouerne vnder their prince in principall places: those vertues and vertuous lessons must be still layd before them, which do appertaine to gouernement, to direct others well, and belong to obedience, to guide themselues wisely. For being in good place, and hauing good to leese, it will proue their ill, by vndiscrete attemptes to become prayes to distresse. And yet for all this, the generall matter of duetie being commonly taught, eche one may applie the generall to his owne priuate, without drawing any priuate argument into a schoole, for the priuitie not to be communicate but with those of the same calling: considering the property of that argument falleth as oft to the good of the common, whom vertue auaunceth, as the *gentlemens* credit, whom negligence abaseth. What exercises shall they haue? The verie same. What maisters? The same What circunstance else? All one and the same: but that for their place and time, their choice makes them priuate, though nothing the better for want of good fellowship. And if they proue so well trained, as the generall plat for all infancie doth promise, and so well exercised, as the thing is well ment them, they shall haue no cause, much to complaine of the publike, nor any matter at all why to couet to be priuate. For it is no meane stuffe, which is prouided euen for the meanest to be stored with.

These thinges gentlemen haue, and are much bound to God for them, which may make them proue excellent, if they vse them well: *great abilitie* to go thorough withall, where the poorer must giue ouer, eare he come to the ende: *great leasure* to vse libertie, where the meaner must labour: *all oportunities* at will, where the common is restrained: so that singularitie in them if it be missed, discommendes them, bycause they haue such meanes and yet misse: if it hit in the meaner, it makes their account more, bycause their meane was small, but their diligence exceeding. Whereby negligence in gentlemen is euer more blamed, bycause of great helpes, which helpe nothing: diligence in the meaner is alway more praised, bycause of great wantes, which hinder nothing: and those prefermentes, which by degree are due vnto gentlemen, thorough their negligence being by them forsaken, are bestowed vpon the meaner, whose diligent endeuour made meane to enioy them.

Riche men no gentlemen.

1. As for *riche* men which being no *gentlemen*, but growing to wealth by what meanes soeuer, will counterfeat *gentlemen* in the education of their children, as if money made equalitie, and the purse were the preferrer, and no further regard: which contemne the common from whence they came, which cloister vp their youth, as boding further state: they be in the same case for *abilitie*, though farre behinde for *gentilitie*. But as they came from the common, so they might with more commendacion, continue their children in that kinde, which brought vp the parentes and made them so wealthy, and not to impatronise themselues vnto a degree to farre beyond the dounghill. For of all the meanes to make a gentleman, it is the most vile, to be made for money. Bycause all other meanes beare some signe of vertue, this onely meane is to bad a meane, either to matche with great birth, or to mate great worth. For the most parte it is miserably scraped to the murthering of many a poore magot, while liuely cheese is lusty cheare, to spare expenses, that *Iacke* maye be a gentleman. If sparing were the worst, though in the worst degree, that were not the worst, nay it hath shew of witte: The rest which I tuch not, be so shamefull and so knowen to be such, and deserue so great hatred as nothing more. Besides the insolencie of the people, triumphing ouer them in their cuppes, by whom they buy their drinke: which shiftes be shamefull to the world, and hatefull to heauen: and too too filthy to be honored vpon earth with either armes by

harold, or honour by any. He that will reade but *Aristophanes* his blinde *Plutus* the God of richesse, and marke the old fellowes fashions shall see his humour naturally, as that poete was not the worst resembler though he were not the best man.

For to become a *gentleman* is to beare the cognisance of vertue, wherto honour is companion: the vilest diuises be the readiest meanes to become most wealthy, and ought not to looke honour in the face, bycause it ioynes not with iustice, which greate wealth by the Greeke verse, οὐδεὶς ἐπλούτησε ταχέως, δίκαιος ὤν, is noted to refuse, and commonly dare not name the meane right, whereby it groweth great. And though witte be pretended to haue made their way, it is not denied but that witte may serue euen to the worst effectes, and to wring many a thousand to make one a gentleman. It is not witte, that carieth the praise, but the matter, wheron, and the manner how it is, or hath bene ill or well employed. Witte bestowed vpon the common good with wise demeanour, deserueth well: the same holy giuen to fill a priuate purse, by any meane, so it be secrete: by any misdemeanour, so it be not seene: deserueth no prais for that which is seen, but is to be suspected, for that which is not seene. These people by their generall trades, will make thousandes poore: and for giuing one penie to any one poore of those many thousandes will be counted charitable. They will giue a scholer some petie poore exhibition to seeme to be religious, and vnder a sclender veale of counterfeat liberalitie, hide the spoile of the ransaked pouertie. And though they do not professe the impouershing of purpose, yet their kinde of dealing doth pierce as it passeth: and a thousand pound gaines bowelles twentie thousand persons. Of these kinde of folkes I entend not to speake, bycause their state is both casuall, and belongeth to the common: and their gentilitie bastardise: and yet while I frame a gentleman, if any of them take the benefit of my aduice, gentle men must beare with me, if my precepts be vsurped on, where their state is intruded on.

My purpose is to employ my paines vpon such as are *gentlemen* in deede, and in right iudgement of their vnbewitched countrie do serue in best place: neither will I rip vp what some write of nobilitie in generall, whether by birth or by discent: nor what other write of true nobilitie, as disclayming in that which vertue auaunceth not: nor what other write of learned nobilitie, as accounting that simply the best, where vertue and learning do beawtifie the subiect. One might talke beyond enough, and write beyond measure, that would examine what such a one saith of nobilitie in greeke, such a one in latin, such in other seuerall toungues, bycause the argument is so large, the vse of nobilitie streaching so farre, and so braue a subiect cannot chuse but minister passing braue discourses. There be so many vertues to commend it, all the brymmer in sight the clearer their subiect is: so many vices to assaile it whose disfiguring is foulest, where it falleth in the face, and must needes be sene.

All these offered occasions, to enlarge and amplyfie this so honorable an argument, I meane to forbeare, and giue onely this note vnto yong gentlemen: That if their calling had not bene of very great worth in deede, as it is of most shew in place, it could neuer haue wone so many learned workes, it could neuer haue perced so many excellent wittes, to reioyce with it in good, to mourn with it in ill, and to make the meditation of nobilitie, to be matter for them to maruell. And that therfore it doth stand *nobilitie* vpon, to maintaine that glorie in their families with prayse, which learned men in so many languages, do charge them with in precept. My friend to be carefull, that I keepe all well, and my selfe to be carelesse and consume all ill? an honest friend and an honorable care. But what am I? my auncetours to auaunce my howse to honour, my selfe to spoile it, and bring it to decaye? The auauncement vertuous, the aduauncer commendable. But what am I? a *gentleman* in birth and nothing else but brauerie. A sory shew which shameth, where it shapeth. It is value that giues name and note to *nobilitie,* it is vertue must endow it, or vice will vndoe it. The more high the more heynouse, if it fortune to faile: the more bruted the more brutish if it fatall vnder fame. Which seeing it is so, as I wish the race well, so I wish their traine were good, and if it were possible euen better then the common, but that cannot be. For the common well appointed is simply the best, and euen fittest, for them, bycause they may haue it full, where the meaner haue it maimed. Their sufficiencie is so able to wyn it with perfection, for leasure at will, for labour at ease, for want the least, for wealth the most, in all thinges absolute, in nothing vnperfit, if they faile not themselues.

But bycause I meane briefly to runne through this title of nobilitie, which concerneth the worthiest part of our state and country, whatsoeuer cauelling the enemies of *nobility* pretend, whose good education must be applied according vnto their degrees and endes, to the commoditie and honour of our state and countrie: Before that I do meddle with their traine, and shew what is most for them, and best liked in them, I will examine those pointes which by good education be best got, and being once got do beawtifie them most, which two considerations be not impertinent to my purpose, bycause I tender their education, to haue them proue best.

The method of the discourse that followeth.

My first note in nature of methode must needes be, what it is to be a *gentleman,* or a *nobleman,* and what force the tearmes of *nobilitie* or *gentrie* do infer to be in the persons, to whom they are proper. Then what be the groundes and causes of *gentrie* and *nobilitie*: both the efficient which make them, and the finall why they serue, wherein the rightnes of their being consisteth, and why there is such thronging of all people that way.

Gentlemanly exercise.

But ear I begine to deale with any of these pointes, once for all I must recommend vnto them exercise of the bodie, and chiefly such as besides their health shall best serue their calling, and place in their countrie. Whereof I haue saide, methinke, sufficiently before. And as those qualities, which I haue set out for the generall traine in their perfection being best compassed by them, may verie well beseeme a gentlemanly minde: so may the exercises without all exception: either to make an healthfull bodie, seeing our mould is all one: or to prepare them for seruice, wherein their vse is more. Is it not for a *gentleman* to vse the chase and hunt? doth their place reproue them if they haue skill to daunce? Is the skill in sitting of an horse no honour at home, no helpe abroad? Is the vse of their weapon with choice, for their calling, any blemish vnto them? For all these and what else beside, there is furniture for them, if they do but looke backe: and the rather for them, bycause in deede those great exercises be most proper to such persons, and not for the meaner. Wherefore I remit them to that place.

What is it to be a nobleman or a gentleman?

What is it to be a *nobleman* or a *gentleman*? and what force do those termes of *nobilitie* and *gentilitie* infer to be in those persons, whereunto they are proper? All the people which be in our countrie be either *gentlemen* or of the *commonalty*. The common is deuided into *marchauntes* and *manuaries* generally, what partition soeuer is the subdiuident. *Marchandize* containeth vnder it all those which liue any way by buying or selling: *Manuarie* those whose handyworke is their ware, and labour their liuing. Their distinction is by wealth: for some of them be called rich men, which haue enough and more, some poore men, which haue no more then enough: some beggers which haue lesse then enough: There be also three kindes in *gentilitie*, the *gentlemen*, which be the *creame* of the common: the *noblemen*, which be the *flowre* of *gentilitie*, and the *prince* which is the *primate* and *pearle* of *nobilitie*. Their difference is in *authoritie*, the *prince* most, the *nobleman* next, the *gentleman* vnder both. And as in the baser degree, the *begger* is beneth all for want of both abilitie to do with, and vertue to deserue with: so the *prince* being opposite to him, as the meere best, to the pure worst, is of most abilitie to do good, and of most vertue to deserue best. The limiting of either sort to their owne lystes, will bewray either an vsurping intruder vpon superioritie, or a base degenerat to inferioritie, either being rauished with the others dealinges, and neither deseruing the degree that he is in. To be vertuous or vicious to be rich or poore, be no peculiar badges to either sort, but common to both, for both a gentleman, and a common man may be vertuous or vicious, both of them may be either rich or poore: landed or vnlanded, which is either the hauing or wanting of the most statarie substance: Examples neede not in familiar knowledge. And as the gentleman in any degree must haue forreine abilitie for the better executing of his lawfull authoritie: so there be some vertues which seeme to be wedded properly to that side: As great wisedom in great affaires: great valiancy in great attemptes: great iustice in great executions and all thinges excellent, in a great and excellent degree of people. The same vertues but in a meaner degree in respect of the subiect, whereon they be employed: in respect of the persons, which are to employ: in respect of circumstance, wherefore they are employed: and all thinges meaner be reserued for the common: of whom I will speake no more now, bycause this title is not for them, though they become the keepers of vertues and learning, when nobilitie becomes degenerate. Hereby it is euident that the tearme of nobilitie amongst vs, is restrained to one order, which I named the flowre of gentilitie: and that the gentlemen be in degree next vnto them. Whereof where either beginneth, none can dout, which can call him a nobleman that is aboue a knight. So that whosoeuer shall vse the tearme of gentilitie, speaking of the whole order opposite to the common, doth vse the ground whence all the rest doth spring, bycause a gentleman in nature of his degree is before a nobleman, though not in the height: as nobilitie employeth the flowre of the gentlemen, which name is taken of the primacie and excellencie of the oddes, and where it is vsed in discourse it comprehendeth all aboue the common. When the *Romaine* speaketh of the gentleman in generall, nobilitie is his terme, being in that state opposite to the common, wherein they acknowledged no prince, when that opposition was made. For *generosus* which is our common tearme signifieth the inward valure, not the outward note, and reacheth to any actiue liuing creature though without reason, wherein there doth appeare any praisworthy valiance or courage in that kinde more then ordinarie, as in *Alexanders* horse and *Porus* his dog. Therefore whether I vse the terme of nobilitie hereafter or of gentilitie, the matter is all one, both the names signifying the whole order, though not one of ground, *nobilitie* being the flower and *gentilitie* the roote. The account wherof how great it is, we may verie well perceaue by that opinion, which the nobilitie it selfe hath vsually of it. For *truth* being the priuate protest of a gentleman, *honour* of a noble man, *fayth* of a Prince, yet generally they do all ioine in this. *As they be true gentlemen.* Such a reputacion hath the name reserued euen from his originall.

Now then nobilitie emplying the outward note of inward value, and gentilitie signifying the inward value of the outward note, it is verie easie to determine, what it is to be a *nobleman*, in excellencie of vertue shewed, and what it is to be a *gentleman* to haue excellent vertue to shew. Whereby it appeareth that vertue is the ground to that whole race, by whether name so euer ye call it, *wisedome* in *pollicie, valiance* in *execution, iustice* in *deciding, modestie* in *demeanour*. There shall not neede any allegations of the contraries, to grace out these vertues, which be well content with their owne gaines and desire not to glister by comparison with vices, though different colours in contarietie do commend, and thinges contrarie be knowne in the same moment. For if true nobilitie haue vertue for her ground, he that knoweth vice, can tell what it bringes forth. Whether *nobilitie* come by discent or desert it maketh no matter, he that giueth the first fame to his familie, or he that deserueth such honour, or he that enlargeth his parentage by noble meanes, is the man whom I meane. He that continueth it in discent from his auncestrie by desert in his owne person hath much to thanke God for, and doth well deserue double honour among men, as bearing the true coate of right and best nobilitie, where desert for vertue is quartered with discent in blood, seeing aunciencie of linage, and deriuation of nobilitie is in such credit among vs and alwaye hath bene.

Of infirmities in nobility by discent.

And as it is most honorable in deede thus to aunswere auncestry in all laudable vertues, and noble qualities of a well affected minde: so the defect in sufficiencie where some of a noble succession haue not the same successe in pointes of praise and worthinesse, either naturally by simplenesse, or casually, by fortune: though it be to be moaned in respect of their place, yet it is to be excused in respect of the person. Bycause the person is, as his parentes begate him, who had not at commaundement the discent of their vertues, which made them noble, as they had the begetting of a child to enherite their landes. For if they had, their nobilitie had continued on the nobler side. But vertues and worthinesse be not tyed to the person, they be Gods meere and voluntarie giftes to bestow there, wheras he entendes that nobilitie shall either rise or continue, and not to bestow, where he meanes to abase, and bring a linage lowe. Wherefore to blame such wantes, and raile vpon nobilitie as to much degenerate, is to intrude vpon prouidence. Where we cannot make our selves, and may clearly see, that he which maketh, hath some misterie in hande, where he setts such markes.

To exhort young men to those qualities, which do make noble and gentlemen, is to haue them so excellently qualified, as they maye honest their countrey, and honour themselues. To encourage noble young gentlemen to maintaine the honour of their houses, is to wish them to apply such vertues, as both make base houses bigge in any degree, and tofore did make their families renowmed in theirs. If abilitie will attaine, and idlenesse do neglecte, the ignominie is theirs: if want of abilitie appeare to be so great, as no endeuour can preuaile, God hath set his seale and men must cease to muse, where the infirmitie is euident, and thinke that euery beginning is to haue an ende. Hereby I take it to be very plaine both what the termes of noble and gentle do meane, and what they infer to be in those parties to whom they are proper. For as *gentility* argueth a courteous, ciuill, well disposed, sociable constitution of minde in a superior degree: so doth *nobilitie* import all these, and much more in an higher estate nothing bastarded by great authoritie. And do not these singularities deserue helpe by good and vertuous education?

The causes and rgoundes of nobilitie.

What be the groundes and causes of *nobilitie,* both the *efficient* which make it, and the *finall* for whom it serues? Concerning the *efficient*. Though the chiefe and soueraigne Prince, of whom for his education I will saye somwhat herafter, be the best and fairest blossom of *nobilitie,* yet I will not medle any further with the meane to attaine vnto the dignitie of the crowne, then that it is either come by, by conquest, which in meaner people is called purchace, and hangeth altogether of the conquerours disposition: or else by discent, which in other conueyances continueth the same name, and in that highnesse continueth the same lawes, or altereth with consent. Neither will I speake of such, as the Prince vpon some priuate affection doth extraordinarily prefer. *Alexander* may auaunce *Hephestio* for great good liking, *Assuerus Hester,* for great good loue, *Ptolome Galetes* for secret vertue.[61] And vpon whom soeuer the Prince doth bestow any extraordinarie preferment, it is to be thought that there is in them some great singularity, wherewith their princes, which can iudge be so extraordinarily moued. Neither will I say any more then I haue said of *nobilitie* by discent, which enioyeth the benefite of the predecessours vertue, if it haue no priuate stuffe: but if it haue, it doth double and treble the honour and praise of auncestrie.

But concerning other causes, that come by authoritie, which make noble and gentlemen vnder their Prince, who be therefore auaunced by their Prince, bycause they do assist him in necessarie functions of his gouernment, they be either single or compound, and depend either holy of learning: or but only for the groundes of their execution. Excellent *wisedome* which is the meane to auaunce graue and politike counsellors, is but a single cause of preferment: likewise *valiancie* of *courage* which is the meane to make a noble and a warrious captaine is but a single cause of auauncement: but where *wisedome* for counsell, doth coucurre with *valiancie* of *courage* in the same man, the cause is compound and the deserte doubled. The

[61] Plutarch. Alexand. Hester lib. Ælianus ποικίλ. 2.

meanes of preferment, which depend vpon learning for the ground of their execution be either *Martiall* for warre and defence abroad, or *politike*, for peace and tranquilitie at home. For the man of warre will seeme to hange most of his owne courage and experience, which without any learning or reading at all hath oftimes brought forth excellent leaders, but with those helpes to, most rare and famous generalles, as the reason is great, why he should proue an excellent man that waye with the assistance of learning which without all learning could attaine vnto so much, *Sylla*[62] the cruell in deede, though surnamed the fortunate of such, as he fauored, was a noble generall without any learning. But *Cæsar* which wondered at him for it, as a thing scant possible to do any great matter without good learning, himselfe with the helpe of learning, did farre exceede him.

Such as vse the penne most in helping for their parte, the direction of publike gouemment, or execute offices of either necessarie seruice for the state, or iusticiarie, for the common peace and quietnesse, without profession of further learning, though they haue their cheife instrument of credit from the booke, yet they are not meere dettours to the booke, bycause priuate *industrie* considerate *experience*, and stayed *aduisement* seeme to chalendge some interest, in their praiseworthie dealing. The other which depend wholly vpon learning be most incident to my purpose, and best beseeme the place, where the question is, how gentlemen must be trained to haue them learned.

A politike counsellour.

The highest degree whervnto learned valure doth prefer, is a wise *counsellour*, whose learning is learned pollicie: not as pollicie is commonly restrayned, and opposed to plainnesse, but as we terme it in learning and philosophie, the generall skill to iudge either of all, or of most thinges rightly, and to marshall them to their places, and strait them by circunstance, as shall best beseeme the present gouernment, with least disturbance, and most contentment to the setled state, of what sorte soeuer the thinges be, diuine or humaine, publike or priuate, professions of minde, or occupations of hande. This man for religion is a *Diuine*, and well able to iudge of the generalities, and application of *Diuinitie*, for gouernement, a *lawyer*, as one that first setts *lawes*, and knowes best how to haue them kept: generally for all thinges, he is simply the soundest, whether he be choosen of the Ecclesiasticall or Temporall, out of whatsoeuer degree, or whatsoeuer profession: so able as I say, and so sufficient in all pointes. And though the particular professour know more then he in euery particular, which his leasure will not suffer him to runne thorough, like the particular student: yet of himselfe he will enquire so considerat-ly, and so methodically of the particuler professour, as he will enter into the very depth of the knowledge, which the other hath, and when he hath done so, handle it better, and more for the common good, then the priuate professour can, for all his cunning in all his particuler: Nay he will direct him in the vse, which enformed him in the skill. Of all them that depend wholy vpon learning, I take this kinde of man worthyest to be preferred, and most worthily preferred for his learned iudgement, the first and chiefe naturally in *diuinitie* among *diuines* though he do not preach: in *law* among *lawyers* though he do not pleade: and so throughout in all

[62] Plut. Sylla. Cæsar.

other thinges that require any publike direction.

The diuine.

2. Of the secondary and particuler professions, the worthynes of the subiect, and the authoritie of the argument preferreth the *diuines*. For they dealing carefully with the charge of soules, the principall part of our composition, and the fairest matter that is dealt in, beside the soule of a ciuill societie, which is compounded of infinite particular soules: and being the miniters and trumpettes of the allmightie God, auancing vertue, and suppressing vice, denouncing death and pronouncing life, which be both most sure, and that euerlastingly to ensue according to demeanour: do well deserue to be honoured of men, with the simple benefit of their temporall estimation, as what they can do, where they cannot do enough. For what reward for vertue is an olyue braunch, though it signifie the rewarders good will, confessing the thing to be farre aboue any mortall reward? which estimation yet is not to be desired of them, though it be deserued by them. For humilitie of minde in auauncing the *diuine* draweth him still backeward, as officious thankefullnes in the profited hearer doth worthely and well push him still on forward. And as the temporall braunche of the common weale being so many in number hath distinction in degrees, for the better methode in gouernment, which function doth honour the executours: so likewise with proportionate estimation for the parties executours, the church consisting of many, and hauing charge ouer all hath her distinction in dignities and degrees to stay that state the better, which would soone be shaken, if there were no such stay: the argument of religion being vsed mostwhat contemplatiue, and in nature of opinion, and therefore a verie large field to bring forth matter of controuersies, specially in yong men, whose naturall is not staied, though their resolution seeme to be, and their zeale carie them on, to the profit of their hearer, their owne commendation, and the honour of him, whose messengers they are. Howbeit in the middle of all these contradictions, the particular execution to beleeue this, and to do that, according to ones calling, which is but one in all, to beleeue truely, and to do honestly, by that same one, doth check the diuersities of all difference in saying. Which great difference in saying, and diuersities in opinion, the church may most thanke the *Grecian* for, who ioyning with religion after diuorce with philosophie, was as bold to be factious in the one, as he had bene in the other, and could not rest in one, still deuided into numbers, as it still appeareth in the ecclesiasticall historie where factious heresies assaile the firme catholike. Neither doth this difference in publike degrees empaire that opinion, that all be but ministers, and in that point equal any more, then that both the prince and the plowman be one, in respect of their humanitie, and first creation. And yet the prince is a thought aboue him for all he be his brother in respect of old *Adam*. The matter of both these two, the wise *counsellour*, and the graue *diuines* honour is best proued to be in the worthynes of their owne persons, which is the true ensigne of right *nobilitie*, bycause both their places and lyuinges, in respect of their degree depart and die with them (though their honorable memorie remaine after) and be not transported to their heires, as the inheritaunce of blood, but to their successours, as the reward of vertue. If it so chaunce that the same person for worthynes be successour both in place, and patrimonie, it is most honorable to

himselfe, and most comfortable to his friendes, and reioyced at of all men.

The lawyer.

3. The peace, and quietnes of ciuill societie, by composing and taking vp of quarrelles, and by directing iustice, makes the *lawyer* next, whose publike honour dyeth also with him: and declareth the substaunce of his worthines, though his priuate name remaine, and his children enioy the benefit of his getting. As why may not the *diuines* to, enioy that, which their parentes haue honestly saued, if they haue any surplus, whereon to saue, for necessarie reliefe of their necessarie charge in succession? Which among the Iewes was of such countenaunce, as *Josephus*, vaunteth himselfe of his nobilitie that way. And. But it were to large a roming place, to runne ouer the port that the churchmen haue kept, not among christians and Iewes onely.

The Physician.

4. The *Physician* is next, and his circumstaunce like, and so furth in learning, where the preferment dying with the partie, and transposed to other, not by line in nature but by choice in valure, is the euidentest argument, that those thinges be most worthiely tearmed the best matter of honour, which die with the partie, and yet make him liue through honorable remembraunce, though he haue no successour but the common weale, which is generally surest, bycause priuate succession in blood is oftimes some blemish. And yet succession in state, is not allway so steddie, but that the old house may haue a very odde maister. These do I take to be the truest, and most worthy causes of nobilitie, lymited not by wealth, but by worth, which accompany the party, and expire with his breath. For sure that which one leaueth behinde him besides an honorable remembraunce of his owne worthynes, cannot noble him while he hath it, nor his, when he leaues it, bycause it bettereth not the owner, but oftimes makes him worse, though it be a necessary stay for that person which is of good worthynes to shew his worth the better. Therefore when wealth is made the way to *gentilitie*: or if it be exceeding great, the gap to *nobilitie*, it is like to some vniuersitie men, which for fauour or feasting lend their schole degrees to doltes to intercept those liuinges by borrowed titles which them selues should haue for learning, and might haue without let, if they hindered not them selues. But both gentlemen and scholers be well enough serued, for ouershooting them selues so farre: *nobilitie* being empaired in note, though encreased in number by such intruders, and learning empouerished in purses, though replenished in putfurthes by such interceptours.

Why so many desire to be gentlemen.

Yet it is no meruell if the base couet his best, as his perfection in nature, and his honour in opinion: no more then that the *asse* doth desire the *lions* skin, to be thought though but a while, very terrible to behold. But counterfeat mettall for all his best shew will neuer be so naturall, as that is, which it doth counterfeat: neither will naturall mettalles euer enterchaunge natures, though the finest be seuered, and the *Alcumist* do his best: And for all the *lions* skin, sure the *asse* is an *asse* as his owne eares will bewray him, if ye fortune to see them: or your eares will discerne him, if you fortune to hear him: he will bray so like a beast. I can say no better, though this may seeme bitter, where I see *nobilitie* betraid to donghillrie, and learning to doultrie. You *gentlemen* must beare with me, for I wish you your owne: you scholers must pardon me, I pity your abuse. Your *apes* do you harme, and scratch you by the face, for all the friendship they finde, which if they found not, they might tarie *apes* still. Their suttletie supplantes you, and your simplenes lettes them see, what fellowes you are. Call vertue to aide, and put slauerie in pin-fold, let learning leade you, and send loselles to labour, more fit for the shouell, then to shuffle vp your cardes. Thus much for the causes which make *nobilitie,* whose leader is learning, and honour is vertue, not to vse more discourse to proue by particular, where the matter is so plaine, as either vertue will admit praise, or historie bring proofe.

For the finall cause it is most euident, that if some sufficiencie this way be the meane to *nobilitie,* the effect of such sufficiencie doth crowne the man, and accomplish the matter. But wherefore is all this? to shew how necessarie a thing it is to haue yong gentlemen well brought vp. For if these causes do make the meane man noble, what will they do in him, whose honour is augmented with perpetuall encrease, if with his *nobilitie* in blood he do ioyne in match the worthines of his owne person? Wherefore the necessitie of the traine appearing to be so great, I will handle that as well as I can in generall precept, for this present place, as hauing to deale with such personages, whose *wisedom* is their weight, *learning* their line, *iustice* their balance, *armour* their honour, and all *vertues* in all kindes their best furniture in all executions, and their greatest ornamentes in the eies of all men, all this tending directly to the common good.

The gentlemens train.

As concerning the traine it selfe, wherof I said somwhat before, I know none better then the common well appointed, which the common man doth learne for necessitie at first, and auauncement after: the greater personage ought to learne for his credit, and honour, besides necessarie vses. For which be gentlemanly qualities, if these be not, to *reade,* to *write,* to *draw,* to *sing,* to *play,* to haue *language,* to haue *learning,* to haue *health,* and *actiuitie,* nay euen to professe *Diuinitie, Lawe, Physicke,* and any trade else commendable for cunning? Which as gentlemen maye get with most leasure, and best furniture, so maye they execute them without any corruption, where they neede not to craue. And be not sciences liberall in terme, that waye to be recouered from illiberalitie in trade, and can those great liuinges be better employed, then in sparing the pillage of the poore people? which are to sore gleaned: by the needie and neuer contented professours? which making their ende as to do good, and their entent but to gaine, do pluk the poore shrewdly, while they couet that they haue not, by a meane that they should not. Bicause though the professours neede do seeke such a supplie, yet the thing which they professe protesteth the contrarie: and prayes for ability in the professour to deale franckely himselfe in the freedome of his cunning, and not to straine her for neede. Doth *Diuinitie* teache to scrape, or *Lawe* to scratche, or any other *learning,* whose epithet is liberall? *Diuines* do vse it, *lawyers* do vse it, *learned men* do vse it. But their profession is free and liberall, though the execution be seruile and corrupt, and cryeth for helpe of *nobilitie* to raunsome it from necessity, which hath emprisoned it so, by the negligence of *nobilitie* who thinke any thing farre more seemly to bestow their time and wealth on, then professions of learning. But if it would please toward young gentlemen to be so wel affected towards their naturall countrey, or to suffer her to ouertreat them so farre, as to shoulder out corruption, by professing themselues, who neede not to be couetous for want of any thing, which haue all thinges at will, how blessed were our state, nay how fortunate were euen the gentlemen them selues? They may spare number enough that way, besides such furniture, as they do affoord vnto the court, to all *martiall* and *militare* affaires to all *iusticiarie* functions by reason of their multitude, which groweth on dayly to farre and to fast, and lessen the middle commoner to much: whose bignes is the best meane, if *Aristotle* say true, as his reason seemes great, for peace and quietnes in any publicke estate, to desire the rich gentlemen, which haue most, and the poore meany, which haue least, to holde their handes, and put vp their weapons, when they would be seditious, as the two extremities in a publicke body. If the couragious gentlemen took them selues to armes, and mynded more exercise: if the quieter tooke bookes, and fell vnto learning, calling home to them againe by their laudable diligence all those faculties, which they haue so long deliuered ouer for prayes to the poorer, thorough their to great negligence, were not the returne to be receiued with sacrifice? and would not the other aswell prouide for them selues by other trades, wherwith to liue? Whereby the honestie of that subiect, wherein they should trauell, would in the meane while, deliuer the honest gentlemen from such faultes, as they be now subiect vnto, while intending so good, they auoided so euill. This were better than brauerie, and more triumphant then trauelling, to remaine at home with their prince, not to rome abroad with the pilgrime, to see farre in other countries, and be starke blinde in their owne.

Trauelling beyond sea.

For what is it to trauell, seeing that word hath so sodainly crossed me? I will not here make any *Epitome* of other mens trauell, which haue set downe whole treaties against this trauelling in diuerse languages: neither will I amplyfie the thing with any earnest aggrauations, which though they may be true, and so may somewhat taint the vnaduised trauellour, yet they be not worthy the rehearsall here. For what reason carieth it, to finde fault with the forraine, and to foster the fault at home? or for particular misdemener, to condemne some whole nations? or for some error in some few to wish a general restraint? and by to sharp blaming to bitterly to eager not the meanest wittes: as commonly dawes be not most desirous to trauell. It is lightly the quintessence which will be a ranging. Silence in thinges peraduenture blameworthy, and friendly entertainement where there is no sting, by curtesie wil call, and by liking will winne such dispositions sooner to come to the lure where we would wish to haue them, then any either launsing, their woundes by to bytter speches, or aliening their hartes by too much harping on one firing: chieflie considering that trauell and going abroad for knowledge in learning, and skill in language haue for their protection much antiquitie, long time, and great number, though still chekt as either needeles or harmfull: and oftimes countermaunded, not onely by priuate mens argumentes, but by publike constitutions, of the best common weales, which were very vnwilling to haue their people to wander.

But what is this trauelling? I meane it not in marchauntes, whom necessitie for their owne trade, and oftentimes neede for our vse, enforceth to trauell, and tarie long from home. Neither yet in souldiers, whom peace at home sendes abroad for skill, in forraine warres to learne how to fend at home, when peace is displeased: which yet both haue their owne, and ouergreat inconueniences, to the wringing of their countrie. For marchauntes by forcing their naturall soile beyond her proportion to some gainefull commoditie verie vtterable abroade, do breede gaules at home, and by bringing in also beyond proportion to serue pleasure and feede fantsie, proue great vndoers to a great number, which can neither temper their tast, nor restraine the fashion.

The souldier likewise, which is trained in hoat blood abroad will hardly be but troublesome in cold blood at home: vnlesse he be such a one as followed the warres for conscience to his countrie, and of iudgement to learne skil, and not vpon bare courage, or hardines of nature, or sinisterly to supply some other want. I meane not any of these, ne yet such trauellers as *Solon*, to preuent a mischiefe in mutabilitie of his countrie mens mindes, whom he had tyed to his lawes, not reuocable till his returne, when acquaintance for that time had wone allowance for euer: neither as *Pythagoras*, or *Plato* were, who sought cunning where it was, to bring it where it was not. For *Platoes* iourney into *Sicile* proceeded not of his minde to trauell, but vp on hope to do some good on *Dionisius* the tyrant, who did send for him by *Diones* meane. We neede not to trauell in their kinde for learning. We haue in that kind thankes be to God for the pen and print, as much at this day as any countrie needes to haue: nay euen as full if we will follow it well, as any antiquitie it selfe euer had. And yong gentlemen with that wealth, or their parentes in that wealth, might procure, and maintaine so excellent maisters and ioine vnto them so choise companions, and furnish them out with such libraries, being able to beare the charge, as they might learne all the best farre better at home in their standing studies, then they euer shall in their stirring residence, yea though the desire of learning were the cause of their trauell. Which rule serueth euen in the meaner personages, which loue to looke abroade, and alleadge learning for their shew, which might be better had at home, with their good diligence, and confirmeth it selfe by sufficient persons, which neuer crossed the sea. Let them fauour their owne fantsies neuer so much, and defende that stoutly, which they haue begone youthfully: yet the thing will proue in the end as I haue said. And if there be defect, we should deuise, as those philosopher trauellours did, to helpe it here at hoome in our owne countrie, that we be not allway borrowers, where it is but of wantonnesse, bycause we are vnwilling to straine out our owne, which of it selfe is able enough to breede, and needeth no more helpes then the generall studie, if it be studied in deede, and not be dalyed with for shew, as I wish it were not, and not I alone. Here lyeth a padde to be pitied though not to be published, they that may amend the thing are in conscience to thinke of it. But what is trauell, as it is to be constrewed in this place, where it interrupteth traine, and bringes it in question, whether yong gentlemen, while they vse trauelling, do vse that, which is best both for their countrie, and themselues. What is it to trauell? It is to see countries abroad, to marke their singularities, to learne their languages, to returne from thence better able to serue their owne countrie here with much fourniture, as they prouided, and such wisedom, as they gathered by obseruing things there.

Sure a good countenaunce to helpe trauelling withall, and to hide her skars, which in some may proue so in deede. But those some be not any generall patternes: in whom, some excellencie in nature, and vertuousnesse in disposition doth turne that to profit and good, which the thing of it selfe doth assure to be dangerous: bycause it may proue to be both perillous and pernicious in those and to those, which for heat are impetuous, for yeares to foreward, for wealth to rachelesse: and proceeding from them may be contagious to others, as cankers will creepe, and the ill taches of euery countrey do more easely allure, and obteine quicker cariage to enlarge them selues, then the good and vertuous do. But while they trauell thus, as sure me thinke I see, it is but of some errour caryed with the streame, which enwraps them so (onelesse some miscontentment at home in busie and displeased humours, vse the colour of language and learning, to absent themselues the better from that, against the which they haue conceyued some stomacke) what might they haue gained at home in the meane while? sounder learning, the same language, besides the loue and liking of their owne countrey soile which breed them, and beares them: by familiaritie, and continuance at home encreased, by discontinuance, and strangenesse mightely empared: while enamouring and liking of forreine warres doth cause lothing, and misliking of that they finde at home. Whereby our countrey receiueth a great blow, thorough alienation of their fantsies, by whom she should be gouerned, which will rather deale in nothing, then not force in the forreine.

What is the very naturall end, of being borne a countryman of such a countrey? To serue and saue the countrey. What? with forreine fashions? they wil not fit. For euery countrey setts downe her owne due by her owne lawes, and ordinaunces appropriate to her selfe, and her priuate circunstance vpon information giuen by continuers at home, and carefull countreymen.

The verie diuision of lawes, into naturall, nationall, and ciuill emport a distinction in applying, though the reason runne thorough, and continue generally one. That which is very excellent good abroad, and were to be wished in our countrey vpon circunstance which either will not admit it, or not but so troublesomly, as will not quite the coast, nor agree with the state is and must be forborne here, though it leaue a miscontentment in the trauellours heade, who likes the thing most, and thinkes light of the circunstance, which he sayth will yelde to it, though experience say no: and in some but petie toyes do shew him, how leaning to the forreine hath misfashioned our owne home. I do not deny but trauelling is good, if it hap to hit right, but I think the same trauel, with minde to do good, as it alwaye pretendeth, might helpe much more, being bestowed well at home. He that rometh abroade hath no such line to lead him, as the taryer at home hath, onlesse his conceit, yeares, and experience be of better stay, then theirs is, which be causes of this question, and bring trauelling in doubt. For the ground of his vyage being priuate, though taken to the best, is vnfreindly to our common. It is like to an idle, lasie, young *gentlewoman*, which hath a very faire heire of her owne, and for idlenesse, bycause she wil not looke to it, combe it, picke it, wash it, makes it a cluster of knottes, and a feltryd borough for white footed beastes: and therfore must needes haue an vnnaturall perug, to set forth her fauour, where her owne had been best, if it had bene best applied. Is not he worse then mad, that hath an excellent piece of ground, made for fertilitie, and suffereth it to be ouergrowen with wedes, while he wandreth abroade, and beholdes with delite, the good housbandes and housbandrie in other men and other soiles? The president of a copie makes a child resemble wel, and a certaine pitch to deale within a mans owne countrey in such a kinde of life, to his and her auauncement, is the surest and soundest direction to any young gentleman: first to learne by, and then to liue by: and to leuell all that waye without any forreine longing.

If he take pleasure in trauelling, and no care in expending, both the expense will bring repentaunce, when reason shall reclame, if euer she do, (as in some desperate cases, fantsie is froward, and wil bide no fronting:) and the pleasure bringes some greife, when the gentleman which in youth so much pleased himselfe, in his age shall not be able to pleasure his countrey, whom he cared for so litle, while he so counted of the forreine. Forreine matters fit vs not, and though our backes, yet not our braines, if we be not sicke there. Forreine thinges be for vs in some cases, but we were better to call home one forreine maister to vs, then they should cause vs to be forreine scholers, to such a forraging maister, as a whole forreine countrey is, to learne so by trauelling, and not by teaching.

Our *ladies* at home can do all this, and that with commendacion of the verie trauelled gentlemen: bycause it is not that, which they haue seene, that makes them of worth, but that which they haue brought home in language and learning, which they do finde here at their retourne. Our *ladie mistresse*, whom I must needes remember, when excellencies will haue hearing, a *woman*, a *gentlewoman*, a *ladye*, a *Princesse*, in the middest of many other businesses, in that infirmitie of sexe, and sundrie impedimentes to a free minde, such as learning requireth, can do all these things to the wonder of all hearers, which I say young *gentlemen* may learne better at home, as her *Maiestie* did, and compare themselues with the best, when they haue learned so much, as her *Maiestie* hath by domesticall discipline. It may be said that her *Maiestie* is not to be vsed for a president, which of a princely courage would not be ouerthrowne with any difficulty in learning that, which might auaunce her person beyond all praise, and profit her state beyond expectation. But yet withall it may be said, why may not young gentlemen, which can alledge no let to the contrarie, obtaine so much with more libertie, which her highnesse gat with so litle? It is wealth at will which egges them on to wander, and it is the same, which causeth them continue in the same humour, though they heare it misliked. If they went abroad as *Embassadours*, that their Princes authoritie might make their entrie to great knowledge in greatest dealinges: or if they were excellent knowen learned men, that all cunning would crepe to them, and honour them with intelligence, and notes of importance: or if they went in the traine of the one, or in the tuition of the other, where authoritie and awe might enforce their benefit, and saue them from harme, I would not mislike it, to breede vp such fellowes, as might follow them in seruice: but for any of the particular endes, which be better had at home, I cast of comparisons. Good, plaine, and well meaning young *gentlemen* in purse strong, in yeares weake, to trauell at a venture in places of danger to bodie, to life, to liuing, though our owne countrey be also subiect to all the same perills, but not so farre from succour, and reskue. Driue me to such a traunse, as I know not what to saye. Commende them I cannot bycause of my countrey: offend them I dare not, bycause of them selues, which may by discretion in themselues, and wisedome of their freindes prouide well for themselues, as I do confesse, though I feare nothing so much, as the ouerliking of forreine, and so consequently some vnderliking at home, which will neuer let them staye. Olde lawes in some countries enacted the contrarie, and sillie *Socrates* in *Plato* being offered to be helpt out of prison, as vniustely condemned by the furie of the people, and persuasion of his vnfreindes: would not go out of his countrey to saue his owne life, as resolued to die by commandment of that lawe, thorough whose prouision he had liued at home so long. Diuisions for religion, and quarrells of state may worke that which is not well for generall quiet, by being hartned abroade with the sight, and hearing of that, which some could be content to see, and heare at home.

Plato[63] in his twelfth booke of lawes, seemeth to rule the case of trauelling, which moueth this controuersie. Where he alloweth both the sending out of his countrymen, into forreine landes, and the receiuing of forreine people into his countrey. For to medle neither with forreine actions, nor forreine agentes might sauour of disdaine, and to suffer good home orders to be corrupted by our forreine trauellers, or their forreine trafficquers might smell of small discretion. Wherfore both to build vpon discretion to preuent harme at home, and to banish disdaine to be thought well on abroad: he taketh this order both for such as shall trauell abroad into forreine countries from his, and for such as shall repare, from forreine countries vnto his. For his owne trauellers he enacteth first. That none vnder fourtie yeares in any case trauell abroad. Then restraining still all priuate occasions, for the which he will not dispense with his lawe, neither graunt any trauelling at all: he alloweth the state in publike to send abroad, embassadours, messagers, obseruers, for so I turne *Plato* his *θεωρούς*.

Such as are sent abroad to warre for the countrie, though foorth of the countrie, he holdes for no trauellers, as being still of, and in the state: the cause of their absence continuing their presence, and the place of their abyding, not altering the nature of their being. And the like rekening he maketh of those solemne embassadors, which they sent to communicate in sacrifice with their neighbours, at *Delphi*, to *Apollo*, in *Olympus*, to *Iupiter*, at *Nemea* to *Hercules*, in *Isthmos* to *Neptune*: where he appointed the pacificque, and friendly Embassages to be furnished out of the most, the best, and brauest citisens, which with their port, their presence, their magnificence, might honest, and honour their countrie most: as to the contrary he requireth in his martiall lieuetenant, which in the camp, and fielde shall represent the state of his country, credit, estimation, honour, purchased before by vertue and valure. His obseruer, whom he alloweth to go abroad to see fashions: he will haue not to be aboue threescore, nor vnder fiftie yeares old, and such a one, as shall be

[63] Plato 12 de leg.

of good credit in his countrie, for great dealinges, both in warre and peace. For the occasion of his trauell pretending to see the manners of men abroad, to marke what is well and them that are good, which be most times there, where the place is least likely: and not to be marred by that which is ill, and them that are naught, which be there oftest, where good orders be rifest: to correct his countrie lawes by the better forreine: or to confirme them by the worse: how can he iudge of any of these thinges, which hath not dealt in great affaires, and shewed himselfe there to be a man of iudgement? or how is he able to auoide the euill, and cleaue to the good, whom yeares haue not stayed and giuen reason the raine, to bridle all desires, that might turne him awry? Such a man, of such a credit, of so many yeares, but no man yonger doth *Plato* send abroad, to learne in forreine countries, and to see forreine fashions, so many of those ten yeares betwene fiftie and sixtie, as shall please him selfe best. But what must this trauellour do at his returne? There is a counsell appointed of the grauest diuines for religion, of ten iustices for law, of the new and old ouerseers for education, whereof ech one taketh with him one younger man, aboue thirtie and vnder fourtie. This counsell hath commission to deale in matters of lawe, either to make new, or to mend the olde: to consider of education and learning, what is good and quickneth, what is ill and darckeneth. And what the elder men determine that the yonger must execute. If any of these young men behaue himselfe not well, the elder that brought him into the parlament, beareth blame of the whole house: those that behaue themselues well, are made honorable presidentes to their countrey to behold: as they are most dishonored if they proue worse then other. Where by the waye I note these three thinges. 1. First the care they had to education, and learning euen in their cheife parlament. 2. Secondly the reason they had to traine, and vse young men in their parlament. 3. Thirdly their three speciall pointes of gouernement, according to the three kindes of persons, which were present in the parlament, *religion, lawe, education*. How to traine before *lawe*, how to rule by *lawe*, how to temper both traine, and *lawe* by *diuinitie*, and *religion*.

Before this counsell, the obseruer presenteth himselfe at his returning home, and there declareth, what he hath either learned of them abroad, or deuised by their doinges, for the helpe of his countrey lawes, of his countrey education, of his countries prouision. And if he seemed neither better nor worse, neither cunninger, nor ignoranter, at his returne home, then he was at his departure from home: he was commended for his good will, and no more was said to him. If he seemed better and more skilfull, he was not only honored by the present parlament, while he liued, but by the whole countrey after his death. If he seemed to returne worse, he was commaunded to vse companie, neither with young, nor olde, as one like to corrupt vnder colour of wisedom. And if he obayed that order, he might liue still, howbeit but a priuate life. If he did not obay, he was put to death. As he was also if he vere found to be busie headed, and innouating any thing after the forreine concerning either *lawe, liuing,* or *education*. Beholde the patterne of a trauellour, rewarded for his well, punished for his ill: neither ill requited, where he meant but well.

Then for reparers from forreine countries into his, whom he will haue well entertained in any case, he appointeth foure kindes. 1. The first wherof be *merchantes*, whose mercates, hauens, and lodging, he assigneth to be without the citie but very neare to it: and certain officers to see, that they innouate nothing in the state, that they do, and receaue right, that they haue all thinges necessarie, but without ouerplus.

2. The second kinde of straungers he appointeth to be such as arriue for *religion*, for *philosophie*, for *learning* sake, whom he willeth the *Diuines*, and church *treasurers*, to entertaine, to lodge, to care for, as the presidentes of true hospitalitie for straungers. That when they shall haue taryed some conuenient time, when they shall haue seene, and heard, what they will desire to see or heare: they may depart without either doing, or suffering any iniurie or wrong. And that during their abode for any plea vnder fiftie drammes, the *Diuines* shalbe iudges betwene them, and the other partie: if it be aboue that summe, that then the maior of the citie shall determine the matter.

3. The third sorte were *Embassadours*, sent from forreine Princes, and states, vpon publike affaires. Their entertainment he commendeth to the common purse, their lodging to some generall, some coronell, or some captaine onely. The care of them was committed to the hie *treasurer*, and their host, where they lodged.

4. The fourth kinde was such *obseruers* from some other place, as his countrey did send abroad before, aboue fiftie yeares old, pretending a desire to see some good thing among them, or to saye some good thing vnto them. This kinde of man he excludeth from none, as being comparable with the best, bycause of his person so aduisedly choosen. Who so was wise, wealthy, learned, valiant might entertaine, and entreat him. When he minded to depart after he had seene, and obserued all thinges at full, he was sent away honorablely, with great presentes, and rewardes. Thus thinketh *Plato* both of comers in, and goers out of one countrey into another. But you will say this was a deuise of *Plato* in his lawes, as other be in his common weale. Yet it is a wisemans deuise, that findes the harme, and would auoide it, and in this our case is well worthy the weying. But as *Plato* neede not to blush for the deuise, which is grounded vpon incorruption, whervnto we say that trauelling is a foe: so if such a lawe were in very deede, politikly planted in any common weale, as it is naturally engraffed in any honest witte: there would be exception notwithstanding against it. In all this *Platonicall* prouision, we may easely obserue, that his cheife care is by trauelling, either to amend the countrey, or not to marre it: and that the forreine vsually is a steppemother to a strange countrey. Therefore as young gentlemen maye trauell, both for their pleasure, to see forreine countries, and for their profit, to returne wise home: so their owne countrey desires them, to minde that profit in deede, and not to marre it with to much pleasure, which is the cause why that all ages haue misliked *trauelling*, as the occasion of corruption in most, and thinke it better forborne for hindring of so many, then to be allowed, for the good of some few, which is hasarded at the first, and vncertaine to proue well. The reason of all this is, both for the forreine euill, which may corrupt, and for the very good, which will not fit, be it neuer so fit their, from whence it is fetcht.

But to my purpose, and the training at home for home. I remit this trauelling abroad to their consideration, which vse it, which I dare not quite mislike, bycause I see very many honest people, which haue trauelled, and the argument of misliking receiueth instance, that the thing may be well vsed, euen bycause some do misuse it, whervnto all other indifferences else be also subiect. Nay I dare scant but thinke well of it, bycause my Prince doth allow it, thorough whose licence their trauelling is warranted. I say but thus much generally though some traueller do some good to his countrey, euen by the frute of his trauell, and most in best places: that yet the statarie countrieman doth a great deale more. The reason why is this. The continuall residenciarie at home hath his eye still bent vpon some one thing: where he meanes to light, and makes the direct and naturall meane vnto it: which though the trauellers do alledge to be their minde to, yet their meane is not so fit, as that is, which ordinarily, and orderly is made for the thing. Neither is this allegation generall. For we see the course which the most do vse after their returne, to bewraie a passage for pleasure, rather then any sound, and aduised enterprise. And therefore I do wish the domesticall traine to be well trauelled to better vs with our owne, and that we did not so much trie how forraine effects do make vs out of fashion, though they feede our fantsies, and that it would please well disposed yong gentlemen to sort them selues betimes to some kinde of learning to make them in deede liberall, their abilitie being throughly fensed against feare of corruption, to serue their country honorably that way which doth so honour them.

For as all will be lawyers, or in houses of law, and court, to some priuate end: so what if some of choice became both diuines, and physicianes, and so furth in other learned sciences, as I said before? If there be any gentleman in our countrie so qualified at this daie in any kind of learning, is he not therefore praysed, esteemed, and honoured of all others, and aboue all others of his calling, and somewhat higher to which are: not comparably qualyfied? Whence I gather this argument: That the worthynes of the thing is confessed by the honour giuen vnto it, and that such as desire honour ought to seeke for such worthinesse, as enforceth the assured confession of the best deserued honour. And I pray you be not these faculties for their subiect to be reuerenced, as they are? and for their effectes to be esteemed of speciall account? which haue bene allway the very groundes of the best, and most beneficiall nobilitie? I do not hold *Tamerlane*, or any barbarous, and bloody inuasions to be meanes to true nobilitie, which come for scourges: but such as be pacifike most, and warlike but vpon defense, if the country be assailed: or to offend, if reueng be to be made, and former wrong to be awraked. Neither take I wealth to be any worthy cause to renowme the owner, vnlesse it be both got by laudable meanes, and likewise be employed vpon commendable workes: neither any qualitie or gift, which beawtifieth the body vnlesse vertue do commende it, as seruiceable to good vse, neither yet any endewement of the minde, but onely such as keepe residence in reason, hauing authoritie in hand, and direction to rule, by the philosophers termed το ἡγεμονικὸν.[64] Wherein those qualities do claime a tenure, which I haue assigned as foundations to honour, and notes of nobilitie, worthy the esteeming, and of inestimable worth. Who dare abase diuinitie for the thing it selfe; or who is so impudent, as not to confesse that profession honorable

[64] Philo.

which hath God himselfe to father, and friend, our most louing, and mercifull maker: the deuill himselfe to enemie and foe, our most suttle, and despitefull marrer, the doctrine of life, the daunter of death? Some scruple there is now, which was not sometime when the allurement was larger, the liuing fatter, and the countenaunce greater: but the matter is now better, though the man be brought both to more basenes in opinion, and barenesse in prouision, and will honour a good gentleman, which will seeke honour by it, and ought so to do. The time was when the great *Cesar,*[65] at his going furth from his house in his sute for the great pontificate sayd to his mother, that she should either see her sonne at his returne the great bishop, or else no body. Such a step was that state to his whole preferment after. *Isocrates*[66] in his oration, where he frameth a prince, ioyneth priesthood with the prince, as two thinges of like care, requiring like sufficiencie in persons, like skill in well handling, which two sayth he, euery one thinkes, he can cunningly weild, but hardly anie one can handle them well.

If gentlemen wil not trauel and professe *physicke,* let them feele the price of ignorance, and punish their carcasses besides the consumption of their cofers, as all learning being refused by them hath no other way to reueng her selfe, then only to leaue them to ignorance, which will still attend to flatter and fawne there where small stuffing is, and that which is most miserable, bycause themselues see it not, will cause them selues to be their owne *Gnatoes,* a most vnproper part, to be seene vpon a stage, when the same person plaieth *Thraso,* and answereth himselfe, as if he were two. Were it not most honorable for them to see these effectes in their owne persons? *singuler knowledge* where studie is for knowledge and knowledge for no neede? *liberall execution,* where desire to do good, and good for gramercie be the true ends of most honour? where the promises from heauen, the princes vpon earth, the perpetuall prayer, and neuer dying prayse of the profited people will remember, and requite that honorable labour, so honestly employed, that fortunate reuenew so blessedly bestowed, not for priuate pleasure, but for common profit?

Albeit there is one note here necessarily to be obserued in yong *gentlemen* that it were a great deale better that they had no learning at all and knew their owne ignorance, then any litle smattering, vnperfit in his kinde, and fleeting in their heades. For their knowne ignorance doth but harme them selues, where other that be cunning may supply their rowmes: but their vnripe learning though pretie in the degree, and very like to haue proued good, if it had taryed the pulling, and hung the full haruest, doth keepe such a rumbling in their heades, as it will not suffer them to rest, such a wonder it is to see the quickesiluer. For the greatnes of their place emboldeneth the rash vnripenes of their studie, in what degree so euer it be, whether in not digesting that which they haue read, or in not reading sufficiently, or in chusing of absurdities to seeme to be able to defende where their state makes them spared, and meaner mens regard doth procure them reuerence, though their rashnes be seene, or in not resting vpon any one thing, but desultorie ouer all. A matter that may seeme to be somewhat in scholes, euen amongst good scholers: and very much in that state, where least learning is conmonly best liked, though best learning be most aduanced, when it ioynes with birth in sowndnes, and ad-

[65] Plut. in Cæs.

[66] Ad Nicoclem.

miration. As the contrary troubleth all the world, with most peruerse opinions, beginning at the insufficient, though stout *gentleman,* and so marching forward still among such, as make more account of the person whence the ground comes, then of the reason which the thing carieth. Wherefore to conclude, I wish yong *gentlemen* to be better then the common in the best kinde of learning, as their meane to come to it, is euery way better. I wish them in exercise, and the frutes thereof to be their defendours, bycause they are able to beare out the charge, wherevnder the common of necessitie must shrinke: That both those wayes they may helpe their countrie in all needes, and themselues, to all honour.

The Princes traine.

The *prince* and *soueraigne* being the tippe of *nobilitie*: and growing in person most priuate for traine, though in office most publike for rule, doth claime of me that priuate note, which I promised before. The greatest *prince* in that he is a childe, is, as other children be, for soule sometimes fine, sometimes grosse: for body, sometimes strong, sometimes weake: of mould sometime faire, sometime meane: so that for the time to beginne to learne, and the matter which to learne, and all other circumstances, wherein he communicateth with his subiectes, he is no lesse subiect, then his subiectes be. For exercise to health, the same: to honour, much aboue: as he is best able to beare it, where coast is the burden, and honour the ease. We must take him as God sendes him, bycause we cannot chuse, as we could wish: as he must make the best of his people, though his people be not the best. Our dutie is to obey him, and to pray for him: his care will be to rule ouer vs, and to prouide for vs, the most in safetie the least in perill. Which seeing we finde it proue true in the female, why should we mistrust to find it in the male? If the prince his naturall constitution be but feeble, and weake, yet good traine as it helpeth forwardnes, so it strengthneth infirmitie: and is some restraint euen to the worst giuen, if it be well applyed, and against the libertie of high calling oppose the infamie of ill doing. Which made euen *Nero* stay the fiue first yeares of his gouernment, and to seeme incomparable good. When the yong princes elementarie is past, and greater reading comes on, such matter must be pikt, as may plant humilitie in such height, and sufficiencie in such neede, that curtesie be the meane to winne, as abilitie to wonder. Continuall dealing with forraine *Embassadours,* and conferring at home with his owne counsellours require both tongues to speake with, and stuffe to speake of.

And wheras he gouerneth his state by his two armes, the *Ecclesiasticke,* to keepe, and cleare religion, which is the maine piller to voluntarie obedience: and the *Politike,* to preserue, and maintaine the ciuill gouernment, which doth bridle will, and enforceth contentment: if he lacke knowledge to handle both his armes, or want good aduice to assist them in their dealing, is he not more then lame? and doth not the helpe hereof consist in learning? Martiall skill is needfull: But it would be to defend, bycause a sturring *Prince* still redye to assaile, is a plague to his people, and a punishment to him selfe, and in his most gaine, doth but get that, which either he or his must one daye loose againe, if the losse rest there, and pull not more with it. But religious skill is farre more massiue: bycause religion as it is most necessarie for all, so to a *Prince* it is more then most of all, who fearing no man, as aboue mans reache, and commanding ouer all as vnder his commission, if he feare not God his verie next both auditour, and iudge, in whose hand is his hart? and what a feare must men be in for feare of most ill, when the *Prince* feares not him, who can do him most good? Almighty God be thanked, who hath at this day lent vs such a *Princesse,* as in deede feareth him, that we neede not feare her which deseruing to be loued desires not to be feared. I wish this education to be liked of the *Prince,* to pull the people onward, by example that they like of, though they cannot aspire to: as I pray God long preserue her, whose good education doth teach vs, what education can do, wherby neither this lande shal euer repent, that education of it selfe did so much good in her: and I haue good cause to reioice that this my labour concerning education comes abroad in her time.

CHAPTER 40.

Of the generall place, and time of education. Publike places, Elementarie, Grammaticall, Collegiate. Of bourding of children abroad from their parentes houses, and whether that be best. The vse and commoditie of a large, and well situate training place. Obseruations to be kept in the generall time.

THESE two circumstances for the generall place, and the generall time, concerne both the exercise of the bodie, and the training of the minde iointly, bycause they both are to be put in execution in the same place, and at the same time, though not at the same howres. For the particular times, and places I will deale in myne other treatises, where I will accomodate the particular circumstance to the particular argument. Priuate places, where euery parent hath his children taught within his doares, haue but small interest in this place: bycause such a parent, as he may take or leaue of the generall traine, what it shall please him, his owne liking being the measure to leade him: so for exercise, or any other thing he is the appointer of his owne circumstance, and his house is his castle.

Diuision of publike places. Collegiat.

Publike places be either elementarie, grammaticall, or collegiate. For the collegiate places, whether they be in the vniuersities, or without, they be lightly well situate, and for both the traines resonably well builded, specially such as haue a cloysture or galerie for exercise in foule weather, and the open fieldes at hand for the faire. If there be any fault in that kinde, it may be set downe, in hope sooner to haue it amended in new erections, when such founders shalbe found: then to be redressed in those which be erected already: bicause these buildinges be restrained to the soile, where on they stand. Yet wish for the better may take place, when the want is found, though the effect do follow a long while after, if it euer do at all.

Elementarie.

The elementarie places, admit no great counsell, bycause such as enter the yong ones, do prouide the rowmes of them selues, and the litle people be not as yet capable of any great exercise: so that there is no more to be said herein but this, that the Elementarie teachers prouide their rowmes as large as they may, and that the parentes domesticall care supply: where the maisters prouision is not sufficient. For as the collegiate yeares must direct themselues most, bycause they are after a certaine degree set ouer to their owne gouernment: so the elementarie, bycause of their weakenes and youth must be ioyntly helpt betwene the maister and the parent, this point for the petie ones being altogither priuate, and vpon priuate charge, as the other collegiate is altogither publicke and vpon publicke erection though alway proceeding from some priuat meane. But if any well disposed wealthie man for the honour that he beareth to the murthered infantes, (as all our erections haue some respect that way,) would beginne some building euen for the litle yong ons, which were no encrease to schooles, but an helpe to the elementarie degree, all they would pray for him, and he himselfe should be much bound to the memorie of the yong infantes, which put him in remembraunce of so vertuous an act. And rich men which haue much more then necessary enough, though none of them thinke he haue simply enough, would be stirred forward by all good and earnest people, which fauour the publicke weale, whose foundation is laid in these petie infantes, to spend the supererogation of their wealth that waie, where it will do most good to other, and least harme to themselues.

Grammaticall.

3. The places where the toungues be taught, by order and art of grammer, require more obseruation, bycause the yeares that be or at the least ought to be emploied that way be fittest, both for the fashioning of the body, and for framing of the minde: most subiect to the maisters direction, and consist of a compound care, publicke erection, which prouideth them places wherein to learne: and priuate maintenaunce which furnisheth out the rest. The scholers either come daily from their fathers houses to schoole, or be bourded at their charges somewhere verie nigh to the schoole.

Of boarding abroad.

Where there riseth a question whether it be better for the childe to boord abroad with his maister, or some where else: or to come from home daily to schoole. If the place where the parentes dwell, be neare to the schoole, that the nighnes of his maisters house can be no great vantage: or but so farre of, as the very walke may be for the boyes health: and the parent himselfe be carefull and wise withall, to be as good a furtherer in the training, as he is a father to the being of his owne chield: certainely the parentes house is much better, if for nothing else, yet bycause the parent may more easily at all times entend the goodnes of his owne, being but one or few, then the maister can, at such extraordinarie times as the bourding with him, doth seeme to begge his diligence, being both tired before, and distracted among many. Further, all the considerations which do perswade men rather to haue their children taught at home, then among the multitude abroad, for the bettering of their behauiour, do speake for their bourding at home, if the parentes will consider the thing well: Bycause the parent may both see to the entertainement of his childe, when he is from schoole, and withall examine, what good he doth at schoole. For vndoubtedly the maisters be wearied with trauelling all the day, so that the priuate helpe within their houses, can be but litle, without both ouertyring the maister, and shortening his life, and the dulling of the childe, if he still pore vpon his booke. Times of recreation must be had, and are as requisite to doe thinges well any long time, as studying is necessarie to do any thing well at any time. For can any man but thinke it a great deale more, then a sufficient time for the maister to teach, and the scholer to learne dayly from six in the morning till eleuen, and from one in the afternoone till well nigh six at night, if these houres be well applied? nay if they were a great deale fewer? And may not the residew be well enough bestowed vpon solace and recreation in some chaunge to the more pleasant for either partie? In the maisters house, I graunt children may keepe schoolehowers better, and be lesse subiect to loytering and trewantrie. The maisters care in his generall teaching may eye them nearer, bycause they be in his so neare tuition, and in place of his owne children, being committed vnto his priuate care by their owne parentes and friendes, he may more easily dispence with their howers, if they fortune to minde many elementarie pointes at one time: and sooner finde out their inclination, then in the generall multitude. And if any particular preferment be incident to his house, without the common wearying both of the scholer and maister, some thing may be done. There be also many priuate considerations, which some parentes follow in the displacing of their children from their owne houses, which I remit to their thoughtes, as I reserue some to myne owne. If the maister do entend onely such scholers as he bourdeth, and haue both in himselfe abilitie to performe, what is needefull for the best traine: and haue such a conuenient number as will rise to some hight in the traine, I know none better, so the place where he dwelleth, and teacheth do answere in conuenientnes, and situation and some circumstances, else. But while he careth to haue his bourders learne, sure some slow paying parentes will keepe him leane, if he looke not well to it, and his gaine will go backeward, besides the continuall miscontentmentes. At home spoiles, soilthes, twentie things, are nothing in the parentes homely eye, which selfe same be death abroad, where the parent hath another eye: and yet the things misliked not auoidable euen at home. But what if sickenes, nay what if death come in deede, then all things be constrewed to the worst, as if death did not know where the parent dwells. And though the maister doe that which the ciuill law requireth in deposing, and vse not onely so much diligence to preserue, but much more then in his owne, yet all that is nothing. Wherefore as parentes must beware of boording out for their owne good: so maisters must be warie of admitting any for their owne harme. And sure to set downe my resolution, me thinke it enough for the maister to take vpon him the traine alone, being so great both for exercise and learning, as I wish him well considered, that can do both well. If parentes dwell not neare the schoole, let some neighbours be hostes, which may and will entend it, and deliuer the maister of the parentes care, whom euen they will fauour more, if they find profit by his schooling. They be distinct offices, to be a parent and a maister, and the difficulties in training do eager sore enough, though the same man be troubled with no more. Boording, that is the vndertaking of both a fathers and a maisters charge requireth many circumstances of conuenientnes in place, of prouision for necessities, of trustie and diligent seruauntes, and a number moe: besides indifferencie in the parent to be armed against accidentes, where there is no euident default, and to content truely where there is great desert: as the maister is to giue a great account of two seuerall cures, a personage for his teaching, and a vicarage for his boording. The maisters charge is great of it selfe, but this composition of a duble office is a meruelous matter. If the maister minde his boorders eitheer only or most, where his charge is ouer moe, where then is his dutie? if not, what gaine haue those boorders, by their maisters priuate? If he teach but boorders let him looke to himselfe, for his charge will proue chargeable moe wayes then one: and those that be best able to put forth to boord, are alway most strait in making all audittes, and to amplifie offences before they be proued, without eitheir conference or contentment. I wish parentes therefore to be warie, ear they set ouer their owne person for more then the training: and the maisters to be as warie for feare of had I wist. But to the grammer schooles. As the elementaries of force must be neare vnto their parentes bycause of their youth, and therefore are not to be denied the middle of cities and townes: so I could wish that grammer schooles were planted in the skirtes and suburbes of townes, neare to the fieldes, where partely by enclosure of some priuate ground, for the closer exercises both in couert and open: partely for the benefit of the open fieldes for exercises of more raunge, there might not be much want of roome, if there were any at all. To haue a faire schoole house aboue with freedome of aire for the toungues, and an other beneath for other pointes of learning, and perfiting or continuyng the Elementarie entrances, which will hardly be kept, if they be posted ouer to priuate practising at home: to haue the maister and his familie though of some good number conueniently well lodged: to haue a pretie close adioyning to the schoole walled round about, and one quarter if no more couered aboue cloisture like, for the childrens exercise in the rainie weather, as it will require a good minde and no mean purse: so it needs neither the conference of a countrey, as *Lacedemon* did in *Athenæus*, and *Plato*, as *Athens* did in *Pausanius*, *Suidas* and *Philostratus*, as *Corinth* did in *Diogenes Laertius*: nor yet the reuenue of a Romain Emperour, whose buildinges in this kinde, were most sumptuous and magnificent, as *Adrian* the Emperours *Athenæum*, *Hermæum* and *Panathænaicum* at *Tibur*, and *Neroes Thermæ* at *Rome*, which in one building furnished out both learning and exercise as it appeareth by the descriptions of their places called *Gymnasia*, *xysta*, and *Palæstræ*.

There is wealth enough in priuate possession, if there were will enough to publike education. And yet we haue no great cause to complaine for number of schooles and founders. For during the time of her *Maiesties* most fortunate raigne already, there hath bene mo schooles erected, then all the rest be, that were before her time in the whole Realme. My meaning is not to haue so many, but better appointed both for the maisters entertainment, and the commoditie of the places. Small helpe will make most of our roomes serue, and small studie with great good will and honest salarie to maintaine a sufficient man, will make our teachers able both to enstructe well and to exercise better. The places of learning and exercise, ought to be ioint tenementes, and neare neigbours capable of number, which must be limited by the neede of the countrey, where the schoole standeth, and the maisters maintenaunce, which way it must rise. For if it rise by the number, better for him few and choice, so they consider his paines accordingly. And sure experience hath taught me, that where the maister is left to the vncertaintie of his stipende to encrease or decrease with his diligence, that there he will do best, and the children profit most, allway prouided that he deale with no more, then he can bring vp vnder himselfe, and hasard not his owne credit, nor his childrens profit vpon any absolute vnderteacher. Whose vse is not, as we now practise it in schooles, where indeede vshers be maisters of them selues, but to assist the maister in the easier pointes of his charge, which ought to haue all vnder his owne teaching, for the cheife pointes, and the same vnder the vshers, for more vsuall and easie, as in the teaching of the Latin toungue, I will declare more at large. Where the very practise wil confirme my wordes, and proue them to be true.

Againe, it is halfe a wonder euer to bring forth a good scholer in the hart of a great towne: where there be chaunge of schooles, and many straunge circunstances to procure chaunge, as it shall please the child. Who notwithstanding he haue his will followed in the chaunge, yet seldome winneth very much by the chaunge: though the second maister oftimes make shew of the formers ground worke, which is made but light of, bycause it kepeth lowe.

If the maisters stipend do rise by foundacion, and standing payment, yet the place may not be ouercharged with number: nor the maister with care to prouide things needfull any other wayes then onely by his trade. For what reason is it to haue a mans whole labour, and to allow him liuing stant [scant?] sufficient for a quarter? or what pollicie is it, to haue him that should teache well, to be enforced for neede, to meddle with some trade, quite different from the schoole. In this pointe the *Pope,* and Canon lawe weare merueilous freindly to maisters, and helped them still with some Ecclesiasticall maintenaunce, as it appeareth in *Gregories* Decretales, the fifth title of the fifth booke, *De Magistris*. And the Glose ripping further then the text, is yet more freindly. And our owne countrey also, in benefit of priuiledge, by the common lawe at this day, doth not frowne vpon vs, and for certaine immunities, letteth vs enioye that benefit, which the *Canonist* meant vs. And the good Emperour *Frederick* did further by his freindly and favourable constitution, which he caused to be placed in the fourth booke of *Iustinians* new Codex, the thirtenth title, *Ne filius, pro patre,* where the Glosse, making an anatomie of the Emperours meaning, and desirous to do vs good, helpeth vs particularly and properly to.

Among many causes which make schooles so vnsufficiently appointed, I know not any, nay is there any? that so weakneth the profession as the very nakednesse of allowance doth. The good that commeth from and by schooles is great and infinite: the qualities required in the teacher many and resolute: the charges which his freindes haue bene at in his bringing vp much and heauy: and in the way of preferment, will ye wish any of any worth to set downe his staffe at some petie portion, which euen they that praise it, would not be content to haue their owne sit downe with, though the founder follow his president, and the time haue bene, when with the Church helpe some litle would haue serued? but the case now is quite altered. In these our dayes eche man will enhaunce in his owne, without reason or remorse: but in professions of greatest neede and most account, they will yeelde no more allowance, then the auncient rent, where all thinges be improued. Yet oftimes they meete with bookmen in some kinds, which wil bite them coursdly. But those bookmen be neither Elementarie teachers, nor yet Grammarians. Our calling creepes low and hath paine for companion, stil thrust to the wall, though still confessed good: Our comfort perforce is in the generall conclusion, that those thinges be good thinges, which want no praising,[67] though they go a cold, for want of happing. For our schoole places, which I do know, the most are either commodiously situate already, or being in the hart of townes might easely be chopt for some field situation, farre from disturbaunce, and neare to all necessaries. It were no small part of a great and good erection, euen to translate roumes to more conuenient places, either by exchaunge or by new purchace: and I do thinke that licences to that ende, will be more easely graunted then to build moe schooles. The inconueniences which I my selfe haue felt that waye, both for mine owne, and for my scholers health, and the checking of that, which of long I haue wished for: I meane some traine in exercise, do cause me so much to commend field roome. Though I my selfe be not the worst appointed within a citie for roome, thorough the great good will towardes the furtherance of learning, and the great cost, in the purchasing, and apparelling the roome to that vse, done by the worshipfull companie of the *marchaunt tailours* in London. In whose schoole I haue bene both the first, and onely maister sence the erection, and their haue continued now twenty yeares.

If ye consider, what is to be done in these roomes which I require, ye shall better iudge what roomes will serue. In the schoole the tongues be taught, and the Elementarie traine continued at times thervnto appointed, for those, two roomes will serue. An vpper, with some conuenient discharging the place from noysome ayre, which the verie children cause: and from to great noise if the place be vawted vnder, or enclosed with other building: and an other beneath likewise appointed, to serue for what else is to be done. They that will haue their children learne all that I haue assigned them vpon good warrant of the best writers, and most commendable custome, if their capacities be according, may haue their turne serued so: and those that will not, need not, but the opportunity of the place, and the commoditie of such trainers, wherof a smal time wil bring forth a great meany, will draw many on, and procure good exhibitours to haue the thing go forward. I could wish we had fewer schooles, so they were more sufficient, and that vpon consideration of the most conuenient seates for the countries, and shires, there were many put together to make some few good. *Insufficiencie* by distraction dismembers, and weakens: *sufficiencie* by vniting strengthens, and doth much good. To conclude I wishe the roome commodious for situacion, which in training vp of youth hath bene an old care, as it appeareth by *Xenophon* in the schooling of *Cyrus* and the *Persian* order: large to holde, and conuenient to holde handsomely. For as *reading* and thinges of that motion do require small elbow roome: so *writing*, and her appendentes may not be straited. *Musicke* will cumber if it be confounded. Where *writing* wilbe allowed, there *drawing* will not be driuen out. But exercise must haue scope. And such kinde of roomes, if the multitude be not to bigge, or the waye to schoole not to farre for the infant, with some litle distinctions, and parting of places, will serue conueniently both for the *Elementarie*, and the *Grammarian*, and so much the better.

The time.

For the time there is but litle to be said at this time: bycause in the Elementarie

[67] Probitas laudatur et alget.

and so onward, I meane by the grace of God to apply all circunstances so neare, and so precisely to schoole vses, as the maister shalbe able streight way to execute: if he do but follow that which shalbe set before him, for *matter* wherin: for *manner* how: for *time* when to do eche thing best. For the generall exercising time. These two groundes of *Hippocrates*, must be still kept in remembraunce, to vse no exercise when ye be very hungrie: neither yet to eate before ye haue vsed some exercise.

For the generall learning times: to begin, the strength of body, and conceit of minde were made the generall meanes: to continue, perfectnesse, and vse were appointed the limittes: for the midle houres this I thinke, that it were not good, to go to your booke streight after ye rise, but to giue some time to the clearing of your body. As also studie after meate, and fast before ye sleepe beareth great blame for great harmes to health, and to much shortning of life. From seuen of the cloke, though ye rise sooner, (as the *lambe* and the *larke* be the prouerbiale leaders, when to rise and when to go to bead) till tenne before noone, and from two till almost fiue in the after noone, be the best and fittest houres, and enough for children wherin to learne. The morening houres will best serue for the memorie and conceiuing: the after noone for repetitions, and stuffe for memorie to worke on. The reasons be the freenesse, or fulnesse of the head. The other times before meat be for exercises, as hath bene fully handled heretofore. The houres before learning, and after meate, are to be bestowed, vpon either neating of the bodie, or solacing of the minde, without to much motion: wherin as I said before the greatest part, and the best to be plaid consisteth vsually in the trainers discretion, to apply thinges according to the circunstances of person, place, and time. To conclude we must be content with those places, which be already founded, and vse those houres which be already pointed to the best that we can, and yet prepare our selues towardes the better, when soeuer it shall please God to send them. And by perswasion some maisters maye well enough bring wise parentes to yeelde vnto this note, and to giue it the triall. In the meane time some excellent man hauing the commoditie of a well situate house, and being able to commaund his owne circunstance, neither depending of other mens helpe, wherof he cannot iudge, and so that way leasing some authoritie in direction, may put many excellent conclusions in triall.

CHAPTER 41.

Of teachers and trainers in generall, and that they be either Elementarie, Grammaticall, or Academicall. Of the Elementarie teachers abilitie, and entertaiment. Of the Grammer maisters abilitie, and his entertaiment. A meane to haue both excellent teachers, and cunning professors in all kindes of learning, by the diuision of colleges according to professions: by sorting like yeares into the same roumes: by bettering the studentes allowance and liuing: by prouiding and maintaining notable well learned readers. That for bringing learning forward in his right and best course, there would be seuen ordinarie ascending colleges for Toungues, for Mathematikes, for Philosophie, for Teachers, for Physicians, for Lawyers, for Diuines, and that the generall studie of Lawe would be but one studie: Euery of these pointes with his particular proofes, sufficient for a position. Of the admission of teachers.

ALTHOVGH I deuided the traine of education into two partes, the one for learning to enrich the minde: the other for exercise to enable the body: yet I reserued the execution of both to one and the same maister: bycause neither the knowledge of both is so excessiue great, but it may easely be come by: neither the execution so troublesome, but that one man may see to it: neither do the subiectes by nature receiue partition seeing the soule and body ioyne so freindly in lincke, and the one must needes serue the others turne: and he that seeth the necessitie of both, can best discerne what is best for both. As concerning the trainers abilitie, whereby he is made sufficient to medle with exercises, I haue already in my conceit sufficiently enstructed him, both for the exercises themselues, and for the manner of handling them according to the rules and considerations of *Physick* and *Gymnastick*, besides some aduertisements giuen peculiarly to his owne person: wherin I dwelt the longer, and delt the larger, bycause I ment not to medle with that argument any more then once, and for that point so to satisfie the trainer, wheresoeuer he dwelt, or of what abilitie soeuer he were, as if he listed he might rest vpon my rules being painfully gathered from the best in that kinde. If he were desierous to make further search, and had oportunity of time, and store of bookes: I gaue him some light where to bestow his studie.

Teachers.

Elementarie.

Grammaticall.

Academicall.

Now am I to deale with the teaching maister, or rather that propertie in the common maister, which concerneth teaching, which is either *Elementarie* and dealeth with the first principles: or *Gramaticall* and entreth to the toungues: or *Academicall,* and becomes a reader, or tutour to youth in the vniuersity.

Academicall.

For the *tutour* bycause he is in the vniuersitie, where his daily conuersation among a number of studentes, and the opinion of learning, which the vniuersitie hath of him: wil direct choice and assure desire: I haue nothing to saye, but leaue the parentes to those helpes, which the place doth promise.

Elementarie.

2. For the *Elementarie* bycause good scholers will not abase themselues to it, it is left to the meanest, and therfore to the worst. For that the first grounding would be handled by the best, and his reward would be greatest, bycause both his paines and his iudgement should be with the greatest. And it would easily allure sufficient men to come downe so lowe, if they might perceaue that reward would rise vp. No man of iudgement will contrarie this pointe, neither can any ignorant be blamed for the contrarie: the one seeth the thing to be but low in order, the other knoweth the ground to be great in laying, not onely for the matter which the child doth learne: which is very small in shew, though great for proces: but also for the manner of handling his witte, to harten him for afterward, which is of great moment.

Of the Elementary teachers entertainment.

But to say somwhat concerning the teachers reward, which is the encouragement to good teaching, what reason is it, though still pretended, and sometimes perfourmed, to encrease wages, as the child waxeth in learning? Is it to cause the maister to take more paines, and vpon such promise, to set his pupille more forward? Nay surely that cannot be. The present payment would set that more forward, then the hope in promise, bycause in such varietie and inconstancie of the parentes mindes, what assurance is there, that the child shall continue with the same maister: that he maye receiue greater allowance with lesse paines, which tooke greater paines, with lesse allowance? Besides this if the reward were good, he would hast to gaine more, which new and fresh repare of scholers would bring, vpon report of the furthering his olde, and his diligent trauell. What reason caryeth it, when the labour is lesse, then to enlarge the allowance? the latter maister to reape the benefit of the formers labour, bycause the child makes more shew with him? why? It is the foundacion well and soundly laid, which makes all the vpper building muster, with countenaunce and continuaunce. If I were to strike the stroke, as I am but to giue counsell, the first paines truely taken, should in good truth be most liberally recompensed: and lesse allowed still vpward, as the paines diminish, and the ease encreaseth. Wherat no maister hath cause to repine, so he maye haue his children well grounded in the *Elementarie*. Whose imperfection at this day doth marueilously trouble both maisters and scholers, so that we can hardly do any good, nay scantly tell how to place the too too raw boyes in any certaine forme, with hope to go forward orderly, the ground worke of their entrie being so rotten vnderneth. Which weaknes if the vpper maister do redresse, when the child commeth vnder his hand, he cannot but deserue triple wages, both for his owne making, and for mending that, which the *Elementarie* either marred with ignoraunce, or made not for haste, which is both the commonest, and the corruptest kinde of marring in my opinion. For the next maisters wages, I do conceiue, that the number in ripenesse vnder him, will requite the *Elementarie* allowance, be it neuer so great. For the first maister can deale but with a few, the next with moe, and so still vpward, as reason groweth on, and receiues without forcing. For the inequalitie of children, it were good a whole companie remoued still togither, and that there were no admission into schooles, but foure times in the yeare quarterly, that the children of foresight might be matched, and not hurled hand ouer head into one forme as now we are forced, not by substaunce, but by similitude and coniecture at the sudden, which thing the conference betwene the maisters in a resolued plat will helpe wonderfully well forward, when the one saith this haue I taught, and this can the child do: the other knoweth this ye should teach, and this your childe should do. Thus much for the *elementarie* maister, that he be sufficiently appointed in himselfe for abilitie, and sufficiently prouided for, by parentes for maintenaunce. Now whether one man, or moe shalbe able to perfourme all the *elementarie* pointes, at diuers houres, or of force there must be more teachers, that shalbe handled in the *elementarie* it selfe hereafter. Once fore all good entertainement by way of reward, will make very able men to leane this way, and one course of training will breed, a meruelous number of sufficient trainers, whose insufficiencie may now be obiected, that such cannot presently be had, though in short time they may. And if there must be moe executours, entertainement will worke that to, and conuenientnes of rowme will bring all togither.

Grammer maisters.

The Grammer maisters entertainement and his sufficiencie.

3. My greatest trauell must be about the *grammer* maister, as ech parent ought to be verie circumspect for his owne priuate that way. For he is to deale with those yeares, whereupon all the residew do build their likelyhoode to proue well or ill. Wherein by reason of the naturall agilitie of the soule and body, being both vnsettled, there is most stirre, and least stay: he perfiteth the *Elementarie* in course of learning: he offereth hope or despaire of perfection to the *tutour* and vniuersitie, in their proceeding further. For whom in consideration of sufficient abilitie, and faithfull trauell I must still pray for good entertainement, which will always procure most able persons. For it is a great daunting to the best able man, and a great cutting of his diligent paynes, when he shall finde his whole dayes trauell not able to furnish him of necessarie prouision: to do good with the best, and to gaine

with the basest, nay much lesse than the lowest, who may entend to shift, when he must entend his charge: and enrich himselfe, nay hardly feede himselfe, with a pure, and poore conscience. But ye will perhaps say what shall this man be able to performe, for whom you are so carefull, to haue him so well entertained? to whose charge the youth of our country is to be committed? If there were no more said, euen this last point were enough to craue enough, for that charge is great: and if he do discharge it well, he must be well able to do it, and ought to be very well requited for doing it so well. Besides his maners and behauiour, which require testimonie and assurance: besides his skill in exercising and trayning of the body, he must be able to teach the three learned toungues, the *latin*, the *greeke*, the *hebrew*, if the place require so much, if not, so much as is required. Wherin assuredly a mediocritie in knowledge, will proue to meane, to emplant, that in another which he hath in himselfe. For he that meaneth to plant but some litle well: must himselfe farre exceede any degree of mediocrite. He must be able to vnderstand his writer, to maister false printes, vnskilfull dictionaries, simple coniectures of some smattering writers concerning the matter of his traine, and be so appointed ear he begine to teach, as he may execute readyly, and not make his owne imperfection, to be a torture to his scooler, and a schooling to him selfe. For it is an ill ground to grow vp from ignoraunce by teaching, in that place, where no ignorance of matter at least should be, at the very first: though time and experience do polish out the maner. He must haue the knowledge of all the best grammers, to giue notes by the way still, though he burden not the childes memorie of course, with any more then shalbe set downe. There are required in him besides these, and further pointes of learning to, as I will note hereafter, *hardnes* to take paines: *constancie* to continew and not to shrinke from his trade: *discretion* to iudge of circumstances: *lightsomnes* to delite in the successe of his labour: *hartines* to encourage a toward youth: *regard* to thinke ech childe an *Alexander*: *courteous lowlines* in himselfe, as if he were the meanest thoug he were knowne to be the best. For the verie least thing in learning, will not be well done, but onely by him, which knoweth the most, and doth that which he doth with pleasure and ease, by reason of his former store. These qualities deserue much, and in our scooles they be not generally found, bycause the rewardes for labour there be so base and simple, yet the most neare is best in choice, and many there be which would come neare, if entertainement were answerable. Let the parentes, and founders prouide for the one: and certainely they shall finde no default in the other.

A meane to haue excellent teachers and professours generally.

The foure particular meanes.

There were a way in the nature of a seminarie for excellent maisters in my conceit, if reward were abroad, and such an order might be had within the vniuersitie: which I must touch with licence and for touching craue pardon, if it be not well thought of, as I know it will seeme straunge at the first, bycause of some difficultie in perfourming the deuise. And yet there had neuer bene any alteration to the better, if the name of alteration had bene the obiect to repulse. This my note but by the way, though it presently parhapes doe make some men muse, yet hereafter vpon better consideration, it may proue verie familiar to some good fantasies, and be exceeding well liked of, both by my maisters of the vniuersities them selues, and by their maisters abroad. Whereby not onely schoolemaisters, but all other professours also shalbe made excellently able to performe that in the common weale which she looketh for at their handes, when they come from the vniuersitie. But by the way I protest simply, that I do not tender this wish, as hauing any great cause to mislike the currant, which the vniuersities be now in: but graunting thinges there to be well done already, I offer no discourtesie in wishing that good to be a great deale better. My conceit resteth in these foure pointes: 1. what if the colleges were deuided by professions and faculties? 2. what if they of the like yeares, and the like profession, were all bestowed in one house? 3. what if the liuings by vniting were made better, and the colleges not so many: though farre greater? 4. what if in euery house there were great pensions, and allowances for continuall and most learned readers: which would end their liues there? what harme could our countrie receiue thereby? nay, what good were not in great forwardnes to be done, if this thing were done? And may not the state of the realme do this by authoritie, which gaue authoritie to founders to do the other, with reseruation of prerogatiue to alter vpon cause? or is not this question as worthy the debating to mend the vniuersities, and to plant sownd learning: as to deuise the taking away landes from colleges, and put the studentes to pension, bycause they cannot vse them without iarring among themselues? Were there any way better to cut away all the misliking, wherewith the vniuersities be now charged, and to bring in a new face of thinges both rarer and fayrer?

In the first erection of schooles and colleges, *priuat zeale* enflamed good founders: in altering to the better, *publicke consideration* may cause a commoner good, and yet keepe the good founders meaning, who would very gladly embrace any auauncement to the better in any their buildinges. The nature of *time* is vpon sting of necessitie, to enfourme what were best: and the dutie of *pollicie* is, aduisedly to consider how to bring that about which time doth aduertise. And if time do his dutie to tell, can *pollicie* auoide blame in sparing to trie? And why should not *publike consideration* be as carefull to thinke of altering to fortifie the state now, as *priuat zeale* was hoat then to strengthen that which was then in liking?

But I will open these foure interrogations better, that the considerations which leade me, may winne others vnto me, or at the least let them see, that it is no meere noueltie which moueth me thus farre.

Of the diuision of colleges.

The college of toungues.

Touching the *diuision* of *colleges* by professions and faculties, I alleege no president from other nations, though I could do diuerse, begining euen at *Lycæum, Stoa, Academia*, themselues, and so downeward, and in other nations east and southeast ascending vpwarde, where studentes cloystured them selues together, as their choice in learning lay: but priuate examples in their applying to our country may be controuled by generall exception. If there were one college, where nothing should be professed, but languages onely, (as there be some people which will proceede no further) to serue the realme abroad, and studies in the vniuersitie, in that point excellently and absolutelie, were it not conuenient? nay were it not most profitable? That being the ende of their profession, and nothing dealt withall there but that, would not sufficiencie be discried by witnes of a number? and would not dayly conference and continuall applying in the same thing procure sufficiencie? Wheras now euery one dealing with euery thing confusedly none can assuredly say, thus much can such a one do in any one thing, but either vpon coniecture which oftentimes deceiueth euen him that affirmes: or else vpon curtesie which as oft beguiles euen him that beleueth. These reasons hold not in this point for toungues onely: but in all other distributions, where the like matter and the like men be likewise to be matched. For where all *exercises*, all *conferences*, all both priuate and publike, *colloquies*, be of the same argument, bycause the soile bringeth foorth no other stuffe, there must needes follow great perfection. When toungues, and learning be so seuered, it will soone appeare, what ods there is betwene one that can but speake, and him that can do more, whereas now some few finish wordes, will beare away the glorie from knowledge without consideration, that the gate is without the towne as dismantling bewraies, though it be the entrie into it.

The colledge for the mathematikes.

If an other colledge were for the *Mathematicall* sciences, I dare say it were good, I will not say it were best, for that some good wittes, and in some thinges not vnseene, not knowing the force of these faculties bycause they neuer thought them worthey their studie as being without preferment, and within contempt, do vse to abase them, and to mocke at *mathematicall* heades, bycause in deede the studie thereof requireth attentiuenes, and such a minde, as will not be soone caried to any publike shew, before his full ripenes, but will rest in solitarie contemplation, till he finde himselfe flidge. Now this their meditation if they be studentes in deede: or the shadow of meditation, if they be but counterfettes, do these men plaie with all, and mocke such mathematicall heades, to solace themselues with.

Wherein they haue some reason to mocke at mathematicall heades, as they do tearme them, though they should haue greater reason, why to cherish, and make much of the mathematicall sciences, if they will not discredit *Socrates* his authoritie, and wisedome in *Plato*,[68] which in the same booke auaunceth these sciences aboue the moone, whence some learned men fetch his opinion, and force his iudgement, as the wisest maister against such as allow of correction in schooles: which they would seeme to banishe, till their owne rod beat them. The very end of that booke is the course that is to be kept in learning in the perfitest kinde, which beginneth at the mathematikes, and it dealeth more with the necessitie of them, then with the whole argument besides: as it is no noueltie to heare that *Plato* esteemed of them, who forbad any to enter his *Academie*, which was not a *Geometrician*, whereunder he contained the other, but specially her sister *Arithmetike*.

For the men which professe these sciences, and giue cause to their discountenaunce, they be either meere ignorant, and maintaine their credit with the vse of some tearmes, propositions, and particularities which be in ordinarie courses that way, and neuer came nigh the kernell: or hauing some knowledge in them

[68] Plato 7, de rep.

in deede, rather employe their time, and knowledge aboute the degenerate, and sophisticall partes of them, applyed by vaine heades to meere collusions though they promise great consequences: then to the true vse, and auauncement of art. Howbeit in the meane time, though the one disgrace them with contempt, and the other make them contemptible, by both their leaues I do thinke thus of them: but what a poore thing is my thought? yet some thing it is where it shalbe beleeued. In time all learning may be brought into one toungue, and that naturall to the inhabitant, so that schooling for toungues, may proue nedeles, as once they were not needed: but it can neuer fall out, that artes and sciences in their right nature, shalbe but most necessarie for any common weale, that is not giuen ouer vnto to to much barbarousnes. We do attribute to much to toungues, which do minde them more then we do matter chiefly in a monarchie: and esteeme it more honorable to speake finely, then to reason wisely: where wordes be but praised for the time, and wisedom winnes at length. For while the *Athenian*, and *Romaine* popular gouernementes, did yeald so much vnto eloquence, as one mans perswasion might make the whole assembly to sway with him, it was no meruell if the thing were in price, which commaunded: if wordes were of weight, which did rauish: if force of sentence were in credit, which ruled the fantsie, and bridled the hearer. Then was the toungue imperiall bycause it dealt with the people: now must it obey, bycause it deales with a prince, and be seruaunt vnto learned matter, acknowledging it to be her liege, and mistresse. All those great obseruations of eloquence, are either halfe drowned, for want of a democratie: or halfe douted of for discredit of diuinitie: which following the substance of matter, commendeth vnto vs the like in all studies.

For the credit of these *mathematicall* sciences, I must needes vse one authoritie of great, and well deserued countenaunce among vs, and so much the rather, bycause his iudgement is so often, and so plausibly vouched by the curteouse maister *Askam* in his booke, which I wish he had not himselfe, neither any other for him entitled the *scoolemaister*, bycause myselfe dealing in that argument must needes sometime dissent to farre from him, with some hasard of myne owne credit, seeing his is hallowed. The worthy, and well learned gentleman *Sir Iohn Cheeke*[69] in the middest of all his great learning, his rare eloquence, his sownd iudgement, his graue modestie, feared the blame of a *mathematicall* head so litle in himselfe, and thought the profession to be so farre from any such taint, being soundly and sadly studied by others, as he bewraid his great affection towards them most euidently in this his doing. Being himselfe prouost of the kings colledge in *Cambridge*, in the time of his most honored prince, and his best hoped pupill, the good *king Edward*, brother to our gracious soueraine *Queene Elizabeth*, he sent downe from the court one maister *Bukley* somtime fellow of the saide colledge, and very well studyed in the *mathematicalls* to reade *Arithmeticke*, and *Geometrie* to the youth of the colledge: and for the better encouraging of them to that studie gaue them a number of *Euclides* of his owne coast. Maister *Bukley* had drawne the rules of *Arithmeticke* into verses, and gaue the copies abroad to his hearers. My selfe am to honour the memorie of that learned knight, being partaker my selfe of his liberall distribution of those *Euclides*, with whom he ioyned *Xenophon*, which booke he wished, and

[69] Sir Iohn Cheeke.

caused to be red in the same house, and gaue them to the studentes, to encourage them aswell to the greeke toungue, as he did to the *mathematikes*. He did I take it as much for the studentes in S. *Iohns* colledge, whose pupill he had once bene, as he did for vs of the kinges colledge whose prouost he then was. Can he then mislike the *mathematicall* sciences, which will seeme to honour Syr *Iohn Cheeke*, and reuerence his iudgement? can he but thinke the opinion to proceede from wisedom, which counteth *Socrates* the wisest maister? Nay how dare he take vpon him to be a maister, not of art, but of artes (for so is the name,) which hath not studyed them, ear he proceeded? Are not the proceeders to reade in any of those sciences publickely, by the vice chauncelours appointment, after they haue commenced? and do they not promise, and professe the things, when they seeke to procure the titles? And with what face dare ignorance open her mouth, or but vtter some sounde of words, where she hath professed the weight of matter? So that the very vniuersity her selfe doth highly esteeme of them if she could entreat her people to esteeme of their mothers iudgement. These sciences bewray them selues in many professions and trades which beare not the titles of learning, whereby it is well seene, that they are no prating, but profitable grounds: not gay to the shew, but good to be shewed, and such meanes of vse, as the vse of our life were quite maimed without them. Then gather I, if bare experience, and ordinarie imitation do cause so great thinges to be done by the meere shadow, and roat of these sciences, what would iudiciall cunning do, being ioyned with so well affected experience? Neither is it any obiection of account to say what should marchauntes, carpentars, masons, shippmaisters, maryners, deuisours, architectes, and a number such do with latin, and learning? do they not well enough without, to serue the turne in our countrie? If they do well with out might they not do better with? And why may not an English carpentar, and his companions speake that toungue to helpe their countrie the more, being gotten in youth, eare they can be set to other labour, which the *Romaine* artificer did naturally vse, seing it is more commendable in ours, where labour is the conquerour, then in the Romain where nature was commendour? As if none should haue Latin but those which were for further degrees in learning.

The tounges be helpes indifferent to all trades as well as to learning. Neither is the speaking of Latin any necessarie argument of deeper learning, as the Mathematicall sciences be the olde rudimentes of young children, and the certaine directours to all those artificers, which without them go by roate, and with them might shew cunning. I maye not at this time prosecute this position, as to fremd for this place: but after my Elementarie and toungue schoole, I meane to search it to the very bottom, with the whole profession of those faculties, if God send me life, and health. 1. For the while this shall suffise that these sciences, which we terme the Mathematicalles in their effectual nature, do worke still some good thing, sensible euen to the simple, by number, figure, sound, or motion: 2. In the manner of their teaching they do plant in the minde of the learner, an habite inexpungable by bare probabilities, and not to be brought to beleeue vpon light coniectures, in any other knowledge, being still drawne on by vnfallible demonstrations: 3. In their similitudinarie applications, they let one see by them in sense the like affection in contemplatiue, and intelligible thinges, and be the surest groundes to retourne vnto in replies and instances, either vpon defect in memorie, or in checke of aduersarie, contrarie to the common similitudes. For when ye compare the common weale to a ship, and the people to the passagers, the application being vnder saile, maye be out of sight, when ye seeke for your proofe. But in these sciences the similitudinarie teaching is so certain in applying, and so confirmed by effectes: as there is nothing so farre from sense, and so secret in vnderstanding, but it will make it palpable. They be taken from the sense, and trauell the thought, but they resolue the minde. And though such as vnderstand them not, do mislike them, which yet is no reason in them, nor any disgrace to the thing misliked by them, seeing ignoraunce misliketh: yet those that vnderstand them, may boldly mislike the mislikers, and oppose the whole auncient Philosophie, and all well appointed common weales against such mockmathematicalles, without whose helpe they could not liue, nor haue houses to hide their heades, though they thanke not their founders.

The colledge for Philosophie.

3. If *Philosophie* with her three kindes had the third colledge, were it thinke you vnproper? Then the naturall might afterward proceede to *Physick,* whom she fitteth: the Politicke to *Lawe,* whom she groundeth: the morall to *Diuinitie,* whom she helpeth in discourse. Which three professions, *Diuinitie, Lawe, Physick* should euery one be endowed with their particular colledges, and liuinges. 4. To haue the *Physician* thus learned, it were nothing to much, considering his absolutenesse is learning, and his ignoraunce butcherie, if he do but marke his owne maister *Galene*[70] in his booke of the best profession. 5. For the *Diuine* to tarie time, and to haue the handmaiden sciences to attend vpon their mistres profession, were it any hindrance to his credit, where discretion the daughter of time is his fairest conusance, and if he come without her, what sternesse so euer he pretend in countenance, we will measure the man, though we marke his sayinges? 6. The *Lawyers* best note in the best iudgementes is contentment, not to couet to much, and for that desire not to striue to gaine to much: not beyond the extremitie of lawe, but farre on this side the extremitie of right. And can digesting time be but commodious in this case, and contempt of toyes eare he enter into them, be but mother to contentment? Time to bread sufficiencie, and sufficiencie to bring sound iudgement, cut of all matter of blame, and leaue all matter to praise. But in this distribution where is *Logicke* and *Rethoricke,* some will saye? Where is *Grammer* then will I saye? A directour to language. And so *Logicke,* for her demonstratiue part, plaieth the *Grammer* to the *Mathematicalles,* and naturall *Philosophie*: for her probabilitie to morall, and politike, and such other as depend not vpon necessitie of matter. *Rhetoricke* for puritie without passion doth ioyne with the writer in any kinde, for perswasion with passion, with the speaker in all kindes, and yet both the speaker dealeth sometime quietly, and the plaine writer waxeth very hoate.

The necessitie of the college for toungues.

1. Of these colledges, that which is for *toungues* is so necessary as scant any thing more. For the toungues being receites for matter, without the perfect vnderstanding of them, what hope is there to vnderstand matter? and seeing wordes be names of thinges applyed and giuen according to their properties, how can thing-

[70] Gal. περὶ ἀρίστης αἱρέσεως.

es be properly vnderstood by vs, which vse the ministrie and seruice of wordes to know them by, onelesse the force of speeche be thoroughly knowen? And do you not thinke that euery profession hath neede to haue a title of the signification of wordes, as well as the ciuill lawyer? I do see in writers, and I do heare in speakers great defectes in the mistaking of meaninges: and euident errours thorough insufficiencie herin. And as *toungues* cannot be better perfitted, then streight after their entrie by the grammer schoole: so they must be more perfitted, then they can be there. And what if some will neuer proceede any further, but rest in those pleasaunt kinde of writers, which delite most in gaing of their language as poetes, histories, discourses, and such, as will be counted generall men?

The necessitie of the Mathematicall colledge.

2. As for the *Mathematicalles*, they had the place before the toungues were taught, which though they be now some necessarie helpes, bycause we vse forreine language for conueaunce of knowledge: yet they push vs one degree further of from knowledge. That the *Mathematicalles* had the place, and were proposed still to children, he that hath read any thing in Philosophie cannot be ignorant. *Plato* is full of it, and termeth them commonly the *childrens entrance*, but cheifly in the seuenth booke of his common weale. So is his scholer though long after his death *Philo* the *Iewe* (whom euen his countrieman *Iosephus*, a man somewhat parciall in praising other, yet calleth a singular man for eloquence and wisedome, speaking of his embassage to *Caius* the Emperour) but specially in that treatise, which he maketh of the foretraine, for so I turne *Platoes* πϱοπαιδεία, and *Philoes* πϱοπαίδευμα.[71] There he deuiseth, as he is a perpetuall allegoriser, *Sara* to be the *image* of *Diuinitie*, and *Agar* the figure of all other handmaiden sciences, wherein he wisheth a young man to deale very long, or he venture vpon *Sara*, which will not be fertil but in late, and ripe yeares. He construeth both in that place, and in *Moses* his life also, those wordes of the bringing vp of *Moses* in all the doctrine of the *Ægyptians*, to be meant in the *Mathematicalles*, which was the traine of that time, and the brood of that soile, or there about. And to saye the trueth let any man marke the course of all auncient learning, and he shall finde, that it could not be possibly otherwise, but that the *Mathematicall* was their rudiment, though no historie, no describer of common weale, no setter forth of Philosophers life, no Philosopher himselfe had tolde it vs? Is not *Aristotles* first booke of all in course of his teaching, his *Organum*, which conteineth his whole *Logicke*? and in his proofes for the piking out of his *syllogismes* doth he not bewraie, wherin he was brought vp? I vse *Aristotle* alone for example, bycause our studentes be best acquainted with him: whom yet they cannot vnderstand without these helpes, as one *Brauardine* espied well, though not he alone, who tooke the paines to gather out of *Euclide* two bookes purposely for the vnderstanding of *Aristotle*. Can his bookes of Demonstration, the *Analytica prosteriora* be vnderstood without this helpe? His whole treatise of Motion wheresoeuer, commonly fetcht from the verie forme of the thing moued: His confutation of others by the nature of Motion, and site: His *Mathematicall* discriptions in many places: His naturall *Theoremes* echwhere can they be conceiued, much lesse vnderstood by any ignorant in this pointe? Wherin *Aristotle* sheweth vs his owne edu-

[71] Philo. πεϱὶ τῆς εὶς τὰ πϱοπαιδεύματα συνόδου.

cation, to whom he commendeth the like, if we like of him, whose liking will not fall, though fooles oftimes shake it. It were to infinite to vse proofes in so generall, and so knowne a case, which the whole antiquitie still allowed of, and the famous *Athenian* common weale vsed euen then, when she had the great brood of the most excellent persons, for her ordinary traine to her youth as *Socrates* still alledgeth in *Plato*: or rather *Plato* fathering the speach vpon *Socrates* sayth so himselfe. *Aristippus* after his shipwrake found releise thorough that train, and encoraged his companions vpon sight of Geometricall figures in the sande. He that will iudge of these sciences in generall, what degree they haue in the course of learning, and wherin they be profitable to all other studies whatsoever, let him read but either *Proclus* his foure bookes vpon *Euclides* first in Greeke, or bycause the greeke is ill, and corruptly printed: *Io. Barocius*, a young gentleman of *Venice* which hath turned them into Latin, and corrected the copie. Though many haue delt in the argument they be but secondarie to *Proclus*. For he handleth euery question that either makes for them, or against them cheifly in his first booke. It were to much for me to stand vpon enumeration of testimonies in this place, that the auncient schoole did begin at the *Mathematicall* after the first *Elementarie*, while they minded sound learning in deede, and sequestred their thoughtes from other dealinges in the world. He that marketh but the ordinary metaphores in the eloquentest Greeke writers of that time, whence we prescribe, shall easily bewray, where in the auncient discipline trauelled. To alledge the *Romain* for learning is to alledge nothing, whose cunning *Virgile*[72] describeth to lye in gouernement, and conquests, remitting other faculties to other people. For till the forreine learning in latter yeares, was translated into their toungue, of themselues they had litle. *Rhetoricke, poetrie, historie, ciuill lawe*, and some petie treatises of *Philosophie*, and *Physicke* were the *Romaines* learning. Some one, or two as *Gallus*, and *Figulus* were noted for the *Mathematicalles*, as many yeares after them *Iulius Firmicus*, and some architecture *Mathematicke* in *Vitruuius*. But their owne stories can tell, what an afterdeale in the wynning of *Syracusæ Archimedes* by those faculties put *Marcellus* their generall vnto, which yet was as carefull to haue saued *Archimedes*, if the rashnesse of a rude soldiar had not preuented his proclamation: as *Demetrius* πολιορκητής was to saue *Protogenes* at *Rhodes*. After the state was brought to a monarchie, the Greekes ouerlaid their learning, as it appeareth, from *Dionysius* of *Halycarnassus*, and *Strabo*, which were in *Augustus Cæsars* time, downe still in a number of most notable Grecians, which serued that state continually both for training vp their young Emperours, and for all other kinde of learning: so that the authoritie of the *Mathematicall* must be fetcht from the Grekes, though they themselues borrowed the matter of other nations, and were founders onely to language, methode, and those faculties, which serue for the direction of language.

The necessitie of the colledge for Philosophie.

3. For *Philosophie* to haue the third place it will be easily obtained, though there be some pretended doubt in the order of the partes for the training. We vse to set young ones to the morall and politike first and reason against *Aristotles* conclusion, that a young stripling is a fit hearer of morall *Philosophie*. But *Aristotle* himselfe be-

[72] 6 Æneid.

ing well brought vp in the *Mathematicalles* placeth naturall *Philosophie* next vnto them, as very intelligible vnto very young heades, by reason of their necessarie consequence, and *Theoreticall* consideration. Wheras the other partes being subiect to particular circunstance in life are to be reserued for elder yeares. For not onely the *Philosophicall* resolution, but also the very religious was in the best, and eldest time to cause youth abide long in study, and to forbeare publike shew, till it were very late. To make *Logicke,* and *Rhetoricke* serue to those vses, and in those places, where I appointed them, was no absurdity. For *Rhetoricke,* there will be small contradiction, though declamations, and such exercises seeme to make some further claime. *Pythagoras* his fiue yeares silence, hath a meaning that ye heare sufficiently, eare ye speake boldly. And *Socrates* that great maister in *Plato* calleth *Logicke* the ridge, or toppe of the *Mathematicalles,* as then to succeede, when they were gotten: and good reason, why, bycause their methode in teaching, and order in prouing did bring forth *Logicke.* As he that will make *Plato* the example to *Aristotles* preceptes shall easily perceaue.

***The necessitie of three colledges peculiar for* Diuinitie, Law, Physicke.**

3, 4, 5. For *Diuinitie, Lawe,* and *Physicke* to haue their owne colledges, for their full exercises, and better learning, then now thus to haue their studentes scattered, it is a thing that implyeth no great repugnaunce with any reason, and is not without president. As for the *Lawe,* if the whole studie were made one and whatsoeuer appertaineth to that profession, for either Ecclesiasticall, or Temporall vse were reduced into one body, had our countrey any cause to complaine? or but great cause to be very glad? wheras now three seuerall professions in lawe, bewraye a three headed state, one *English* and *French,* an other, Romish Imperiall, the third Romish ecclesiasticall, where meere *English* were simply our best. I shall not neede to say any more herein, but onely giue occasion to those which can iudge, and helpe it, to thinke of the position: the distraction of temporall, ciuill, and Canon lawe being in many pointes very offensiue to our countrey.

6. Some difficultie there will be to winne a colledge for such as shall afterward passe to teach in schooles.

The seuenth colledge for training maisters, and the necessitie therof.

7. There is no diuerting to any profession till the student depart from the colledge of *Philosophie,* thence he that will go to *Diuinitie,* to *Lawe,* to *Physicke,* may, yet with great choise, to haue the fittest according to the subiect. He that will to the schoole is then to diuert. In whom I require so much learning to do so much good, as none of the other three, (honour alway reserued to the worthinesse of the subiect which they professe,) can chalenge to himselfe more: either for paines which is great: or for profit which is sure: or for helpe to the professions: which haue their passage so much the pleasaunter, the forwarder studentes be sent vnto them, and the better subiects be made to obay them: as the scholing traine is the trak to obedience. And why should not these men haue both this sufficiencie in learning, and such roome to rest in, thence to be chosen and set forth for the common seruice? be either children, or schooles so small a portion of our multitude? or is the framing of young mindes, and the training of their bodies so meane a point of cunning? be

schoolemaisters in this Realme such a paucitie, as they are not euen in good sadnesse to be soundly thought on? If the chancell haue a minister, the belfray hath a maister: and where youth is, as it is eachwhere, there must be trainers, or there will be worse. He that will not allow of this carefull prouision for such a seminarie of maisters, is most vnworthy either to haue had a good maister him selfe, or herafter to haue a good one for his. Why should not teachers be well prouided for, to continue their whole life in the schoole, as *Diuines, Lawyers, Physicians* do in their seuerall professions? Thereby iudgement, cunning, and discretion will grow in them: and maisters would proue olde men, and such as *Xenophon* setteth ouer children in the schooling of *Cyrus*. Wheras now, the schoole being vsed but for a shift, afterward to passe thence to the other professions, though it send out very sufficient men to them, it selfe remaineth too too naked, considering the necessitie of the thing. I conclude therfore that this trade requireth a particular college, for these foure causes. 1. First for the subiect being the meane to make or mar the whole frye of our state. 2. Secondly for the number, whether of them that are to learne, or of them that are to teache. 3. Thirdly for the necessitie of the profession which maye not be spared. 4. Fourthly for the matter of their studie which is comparable to the greatest professions, for language, for iudgement, for skil how to traine, for varietie in all pointes of learning, wherin the framing of the minde, and the exercising of the bodie craueth exquisite consideration, beside the staidnes of the person.

1. These seuen colledges being so set vp, and bearing the names of the thinges which they professe, for *Toungues*, for *Mathematickes*, for *Philosophie*, for *Traine*, for *Physicke*, for *Lawe*, for *Diuinitie* were there any great absurditie committed either in the thing if it were so, or in me for wishing it so? If it had bene thus appointed at the first, as he might, if the whole building had bene made at once, which is scant possible where thinges grow by degrees, and buildinges by patches: it would haue bene liked very well, and the Vniuersities in their commencementes, and publike actes would haue commended their pollicy, and wisedome, which first did appoint it. And maye not that be now toucht without blame, which if it had bene then done, had deserued great honour, and when soeuer it shall be done will deserue euerlasting memorie? and maye now be well done, seeing we haue all thinges needful for the well doing redie: And why should it seeme straunge to wish such an alteration, seeing greater chaunges haue bene both wished, and wrought within this our time? Sad, and lingring thoughts, which measure common weales as buildinges grounded vpon some rocke of marble, finde many, and sober difficulties: resolute mindes make no bones: there is stuffe enough, the places be ready, the landes be neither to be begd, ne yet to be purchased, they be got, and giuen already: they maye be easily brought into order, seeing our time is the time of reformation. Before my wish be condemned, I desire my reader to consider it well, and marke if it maye take place, and whether it maye not with great facilitie.

The second meane, to sorte like yeares into ye same roomes.

2. For sorting like yeares into one roome, which was my second interrogatorie, it is no new deuice, nor mine: All good common weales not fained by fantsie, but being in deede such haue vsed it both for likenes of education in like yeares, and for trying out where most excellencie lodged, to bestow prefermentes vpon appar-

ent desert, besides that it is most fit, and emulation to the better doth best beseeme like yeares. The greeke poet saith, that God draweth allway the like to the like, and therefore men may well follow the president.

The third meane to better the studentes maintenaunce.

3. For vniting of colledges, enlarging of the vnited, and bettering studentes liuinges, I dare say none of them wilbe against me, which for a better liuing will chaung his colledge. Neither will he thinke it any great losse to leaue his old poore place, for a fatter rowme, which for such a one will abandon the vniuersitie and all. Sure the liuings in colledges be now to to leane, and of necessitie force good wittes to fly ear they be well feathered. More sufficiencie of liuing will yeald more conuenient time and furniture to studie, which two be the onely meanes to procure more sufficiencie in learning, more ripenes in iudgement, more stay in maners. The necessitie of studentes may thus be supplyed of their owne, and they not forced by accepting of exhibition at some handes to admit some bondage vnder hand. Restraint will ridde needelesse number: sufficient liuinges will maintaine, and make the nedefull number sufficiently well learned. I neede not staie any longer here. For methinke all those good studentes ioyne with me in this fourme of the vniuersitie, whom want, and barenes of liuing will not suffer to tarie long enough there, and better it were for our countrie to haue some smaller meane well trayned, and sufficiently prouided, then a loose number, and an vnlearned multitude. And there were two questions more worthy the resolution, then all *Iohannes Picus* the erle of *Mirandula* his nine hundred propounded at *Rome*: the one whether it were agreable to the nature of learning, being liberall in condition to be *elemosinarie* in maintenaunce: the other whether it were for a common weale to haue the conceit bound to respectes, bycause of priuate exhibition, which ought to direct simply, without respect, sauing to the state alone. For sure where learning growes vp by props, it leaseth her propertie: where the stocke of it selfe will beare vp the bowes, there it must be best, if choice be made leader, and fit wittes bestowed on bookes. My three forraine pointes for the furtheraunce of learning be, *choice* for wittes, *time* for furniture, *maintenaunce* for direction: what shalbe peculiar to the partie, himselfe must tender, as therein being detter to *God*, and his countrie. *Diligence* to apply his wit, *continuaunce* to store his time, *discretion* to set furth his maintenaunce, are required at his handes.

The fourth meane for readers.

4. For *readers* of yeares, of sufficiencie, of continuance, methinke I durst enter into some combat that it were beyonde all crie profitable, and necessarie, to haue whom to follow, and of whom to learne how to direct our studies, for *yeares* auncient fathers: for *sufficiencie* most able to enstruct: for *continuance* cunning to discerne persons, and circumstaunces: for *aduise* skillfull to rule rash heades, which runne on to fast, being armed with some priuate opinion of their owne petie learning. What was *Plato* to the *Academikes*? *Aristotle* to the *Peripatetikes*? *Xeno* to the *Stoiks*? *Epicure* to the *Epicurians*? *Aristippus* to the *Anicerian* and *Cyrenaike*? and other such fathers to the famulies of their professions, but *readers*? It is a meruell to thinke on, how longe those fellowes continued in their profession as *Diogenes*

Laertius doth note. It should seeme that *Plato* taught aboue fiftie yeares, reckening the time that he left *Speusippus* his deputie during his trauell into *Ægypt* and that way: whereby both himselfe proued an excellent maister, and his hearers proued most excellent scholers. They that haue bene acquainted with cunning *readers* any where will subscribe to this I know.

Priuate studie tied to one booke led by one braine: not alway the best (as what counsellour is commonly worse to ones selfe, then himselfe?) so proceeding as the first impression leads, be it what it can be, cannot compare for iudiciall learning with the benefit of hearing one, nay of repeating to one vpon interrogatories after reading, to trie his iudgement, his keeping, and remembrance: which one hath red, and digested all the best bookes, or at the least all the best bookes in that kinde, whereof he maketh profession: which hath a iudgement settled and resolute by the helpe of all those good braines: which hath dealte with thousandes of the pregnantest wittes, whom experience hath taught stay, whom the common weale by sufferance commendes as sufficient. He that is not acquainted with such an excellent reader or teacher (for both the names import one thing) and that with repetition, but pleaseth himselfe with his owne priuate studie, as he taketh more paines vndoutedly, so getteth he lesse gaine I dare assure him, hauing in one lecture the benefit of his *readers* vniuersall studie, and that so fitted to his hand, as he may streight way vse it, without further thinking on: wheras when he hath beaten his owne braines priuatly about a litle, for want of time to digest, being to forward to put foorth, he vttereth that which he must either amend vpon better aduice, or quite reuoke when he findes he is ouer shot. Wherfore such *readers*, or rather such *nurses* to studie must needes be maintained with great allowance, to make their heauen there, where ye meane to vse them. Whose seruice, for the benefit that comes from them will saue their whole hier in very bookes, which the student shall not so much neede, when his *reader* is his librarie: neither must they be soules, as we tearme them, though of great reading, neither is it enough to haue read much, but they must be of great gouernment withall, which are to bring vp such a frie of gouerners. And therefore that great sufficiencie doth still call for great recompence to be tyed to a stake for it all ones life time.

That this wish is most profitable to the vniuersitie, and hurthfull no not to any particular.

But now I pray you by this wish of mine be the vniuersities in common sence any whit endammaged? if they were, so the harme were but some litle, and the good exceeding great, the dammage might be consumed by the greatnes of the good. I finde not any harme offered them, they lease no landes studentes be not put to pensions, they that be thought fit, finde better and fuller maintenaunce, better meane is made to proue learned, by such excellent *readers*, which the cunninger they be, the more affable they be, and thereby the fitter to satisfie any studentes dout in that which they professe. And where yong men may staie vntill they be singular, and haue good meanes to make them singular, is not the thing to be wished, and he that wisheth it, not to be thought to wish the *vniuersitie* harme, where it is vniuersally holpen? If this transposing of houses to this vse were commaunded by authoritie, and by some helpe of wealthy patrones for the common good sake, were happily accomplished, the *vniuersitie* should lease nothing, though they breake vp for a time, and the studentes gaue place, to masons, and carpenters, nay though the whole reuenew of all the colledges were for that time bestowed vpon the alteration. And yet all that trouble should not neede, if the first were first begune, and so particularly in order, neither should any student now well placed complaine of the chaunge if he would set himselfe to any certaine profession. This is but my conceit which the effect will confirme, and wise considerations will finde, that it carieth a good ground: besides that it is all ready in verie neare possibilitie, without any great charge, and with verie great good, as also certainetie, and greatnes of annuitie would streight way raise vp *readers*, and afterward continew them. How good, and how easie a thing this were, the attempt by so many particular *readers* would shew, which being themselues excellently well learned in those argumentes, that I do appoint to colledges, and professing them in conuenient houses of their owne, would vndoutedly drawe as many into their priuate hostelles, as there be now studentes in publicke colledges. All this my wish offereth greater difficulty, in the maner, how to worke it: then dout of profit, in the thing, if we had it. Howbeit harder thinges haue bene easily accomplished, but any more profitable was neuer compassed: neither doth it repent me to wish that, which I would reioyce to see. If the hindring lie in cost, it is somwhat, and yet but small, considering what is ready: if in good will: that is all, and yet but ill, considering what it hindereth. For no learning is so well got, where her helping meanes be seuered, as where all be vnited, which those colledges would cause: a thing neither of nouelty, as of an old ground and elswhere practised: neither iniuriouse, to any offering profit to all. I do finde my selfe so armed in the point, as if there were any hope in the thing to be effected, I could answeare any obiection of difficultie, which might arise against it, either from without the *vniuersitie*, or from within, eitther for any communitie, or for any priuate, that it would be best for all, neither any breach of good now well laied, nor any hindraunce to any, which findes himselfe at ease, as the present is now appointed. But will ye haue euerie one rise through all these degrees of learning, ear he become a professour? yea surely I. but who moueth the question? either he that cannot iudge, who is therefore to be pardoned: or he that would be doing, who is therefore to be blamed: or he that doth not way it, which would be desired to do: or he whom neede hasteneth, whose case is to be pitied. And yet of all these foure, only he, that desireth to shew him selfe ripe in his owne, though raw in other mens opinion, will contrarie the conclusion: for ignoraunce, will yeeld vpon better instruction: iust consideration, wil relent after waing: good wittes oppressed with want, and yet waing the truth, will wish for more wealth to tarie their full time, and the cariage of their cunning: but the hastie heades, to whom any delaie is present death, which will be doing, eare they can do well, but in their owne conceites they will stand against it, and scrape all defences, though while they do scrape, they descrie them selues to be extreme ignorant. For if sufficiencie be the onely meane to perfit the professour, and to profit the publike, insufficiencie ouerthrowes both. And as he that meaneth to turne before, may lymit his ascent: so he that will be perfit in the end and last profession ought at the least to haue the contemplatiue knowledge of all that goeth before, though he practise but at pleasure. The generall gaine thereby is this, that while the studentes youth is wedded to honest, and learned meditation, the heat of that stirring age is cooled which might harme in publicke, and set all on fire: ripe iudgement is got, to stay, not to stirre: and all ambitiouse passions meruellously daunted through resolutenes of iudgement. It is no reason, where see ye the like? but it is a great reason, the like is worth seeing, and who so comes neare, is still better liked, then he that dowteth of it. The want of triall, is some shift for a time, but the triall that hath bene, may lead vs to the like, and procure good allowance. And sure till the yong professours be made to tarie longer, and studie sounder, neither shall learning haue credit, nor our countrie be but sicke. It is not my complaint, though I ioyne with the complainantes. If ye meane to take learning before you, you will neuer moue the question. It is not he that hath, and knoweth, which moueth the question, but he that knoweth not and should. What should a *diuine* do with the *mathematikes*? why was *Moses* trained in all the *Ægyptians* learning? Nay in one reason for all, why will ye condemne in *diuinitie*, or execute in *lawe*, the sciences which ye know not, but finde the name condemned? and I pray you with what warrant? what if that be not the name? or what if the thing be not such? a condemnation without euidence where the iudge presumeth, and knoweth not the skill, which he saith is naught. The *Physician* should haue all, and if he haue not, he is most to be blamed, bycause the parentes of his profession durst not professe without them, and make them vnder meanes. To be short I wish they had them, which mislike that they haue not, and giue ignorance the raigne. For if they had them, we should heare no speach, but praise and proufe, admiration and honour.

But to turne to my byace againe which was the mother, and matter to my wish, this colledge for teachers, might prooue an excellent nurserie for good schoolemaisters, and vpon good testimonie being knowne to so many before, which would vpon their owne knowledge assure him, whom they would send abroad. In the meane time till this come to passe, the best that we can haue, is best worthy the hauing, and if we prouide well for good teachers, that prouision will prouide vs good teachers.

The admission of teachers.

There remaineth now one consideration in the admitting not of these, whom I admit without any exception, for all sufficiencie in religion, in learning, in discretion, in behauiour: but of such as we daily vse, and must vse, till circumstances be bettered, which are in compasse of many exceptions. The admitter or chuser considering what the place requireth, must exact that cunning, which the place calleth for: the partie himselfe must bring testimonie of his owne behauiour, if he be altogither vnknowen: and the admission would be lymited to such a schoole in such a degree of learning, as he is found to be fit for. For many vpon admission and licence to teach in generall, ouerreach to farre, and marre to much, being vnsufficient at randon, though seruing well for certaine by way of restraint. Thus much for the trainer, which I know will better my patterne if preferment better him: with whom I shall haue occasion to deale againe in my grammer schoole: where I will note vnto him what my opinion is in the particularities of teaching.

CHAPTER 42.

How long the childe is to continue in the elementarie ear he passe to the toungues, and grammer. The incurable infirmities which posting hast worketh in the whole course of studie. How necessarie a thing sufficient time is for a scholer.

HASTIE preasing onward is the greatest enemie, which any thing can haue whose best is to ripe at leasure. For if ripenes be the vertue, before it is greene, after it is rotten: and yet the excesse is the lesse harme: bycause it may ioyne, and be compounded with the vertue, and be called rotten ripe: and at the least be cast away, without any more losse, then of the thing it selfe, as it appeareth in frutes. The defect to plucke before ripenes, breedes ill in the partie which tasteth therof, and causeth the thing after a bite or two to be cast away to: vnlesse it be in longing wymen, whose distemperate delite vpon a cause not common, doth giue vs to iudge, that too timely taking, is but for some disordered humours. This plucking before ripenes in my position tendeth to this ende. I haue appointed in my elementarie traine, *reading, writing, drawing, singing, playing*: now if either all these be vnperfitly gotten, where all be attempted, or some, where some: when the childe is remoued to the grammer schoole, what an error is committed? The thinges being not perfit, to serue the consequence, either die quite if they be not seuearly called on: or come forward with paine, where the furtherance is in feare. How many small infantes haue we set to *grammer*, which can scarecely reade? how many to learne *latin*, which neuer wrate letter? And yet though some litle one could doe much better then all his fellowes, it were no harme for him to be captaine a good while in his *elementarie* schoole, rather then to be a meane souldier in a captaine schoole. The displeasoures be beyond all proportion pernicious, beyond all multitude many, which this posting pulles after it. And if moning could amend them, I would not onely mone them, that they be so many, but also mourne for them, that they be so helpeles. It is a world to see the weakenes of children, and the fondnes of friendes in that behalfe. It is to much, that may be vnderstood, where so much is said: the fault is generall, and the onely cause, which both makes children loth to learne, and the maisters seeme to be tormenters in their teaching. For the maister hasting on to the effect of his profession, and the scholer drawing backe, as not able to beare the burden: there riseth a conflict in the maister, with passion, if it conquere him: against passion if he conquere it. If the maister be verie sharp witted in deliuering, and the boy slowheaded in receiuing, then the passion will lightly conquer. Which it cannot doe, where wisedome and consideration in the maister be armed aforehand with pacience, or where experience, and wearines of extremitie haue wrought a calmenes. And as in the maister passion breedes heat, so in the childe infirmitie breedes feare, and so much the more, if he finde his maister somwhat to fierce. Whereupon neither the one nor the other can do much good at all, and all through this hastie imperfection being the matter of heat in the one, and of feare in the other. Whereof if the boy were not in daunger how peart would he be, and what a pleasure would the maister take in such a perfit perteling? but when the childe is so weake, as both he himselfe feeles it in his learning, and the maister findes it in his teaching, tell the parent so he will not beleeue it. So blynde is affection in the parent which cannot see: and in stoore of teachers, he shall finde some which will vndertake, and condemne the misliker. Whereby chaunge feedes his humour for the time, and repentance his follie long after, when the default proues vncurable, and the first maister is admitted among the prophetes. Such a thing it is to preuent illes in time, and when warning is giuen not to mocke the intelligence, nor to blame the watchman.

If the imperfections which come more of haste then of ignoraunce from the Elementary schoole would take vp their *Inne* there, and raunge no further, the moane were not so much, bycause there were some meane to redresse: but now as one billow driueth on an other: so hast beginning there makes the other successions in learning trowle on too too headlong. Be young children set to soone to their *Grammer* onely? be none sent to the *Vniuersitie*, which when they come thence from yeares after, might well with good gaine returne to the *Grammer* schoole againe? I will not saye that they were not ready when they went, but peraduenture they were not ready, and forgat that they were so. Do not some good honest wittes in the middest of their studie finde the festering of haste, and wishe though in vaine that they had bene more aduised in their passage? and if they recouer that which they misse and wish for, do they not finde the learned conclusion trew: that such thinges be extreme painful to setled memories, which were very pleasaunt passages to the youngest boyes? He that beginnes his *Grammer* in any language, when he is a *Graduate*, may perhaps wish for some way without *Grammer*, and couet a *Compendium*. The *Vniuersities* can best iudge of the infirmities in our *Grammer* schooles, when they finde the want in those yonglinges, whom they haue from vs, but not sent by vs: we our selues see them, but we cannot salue them. Priuate affection ouerrules all reason: straungenesse betwene the parent and maister cuttes of conference in the remouing: and in some places multitude of schooles marres the whole market: where store is the sore, and oportunitie to alter an allurement to the worse. So that by degrees the *Elementarie* feebleth the *Grammarian*: and the *Grammarian* transporteth his weaknesse from his schoolemaister to his *Vniuersitie tutour*. Such a matter it is to stay hast at the first, which distempereth till the last. I would not haue the *Vniuersities*, but to thinke freindly of me, bycause though I finde fault, I seeke it not: neither blase I it with discredit to them, but wish it healed with the profit of my countrey, as I well know the most, and best of them there do.

Doth not want of sufficient time (I meane not for taking degrees, bycause that time may be complete from the proceeders first ariuall into the *Vniuersitie*) but for want of age and yeares: and therwithall for the want of that, which yeares do bring, oftimes send abroad youthes, whose degrees deserue place, but their depth deserues none? That prentice is to hastely out of his yeares, which being at one and twentie free from his maister, is eare foure and twentie free from his thrift both reft of goodnesse, and left goodlesse. If men abroad had not a sensible iudgement in yeares, that young ware cannot be but greene, how sprooting faire so euer it doth shew: youth might deceiue them with titles, as it deceiues it selfe with opinions. *Yeares* without *stuffe* maye beguile before *triall*: *yeares* with *stuffe* will abide the *stampe*: *Stuffe* without *yeares* is wounderous for a while, but it is subiecte to quicke withering, and to fade of wonder. Neither *stuffe* nor *yeares*, is extreme pitifull, and the very ground of my complaint, bycause neither few yeares can prouide great *stuffe*, yea to the best witte: nor many yeares to any witte, without great studie, which is a death there, where the defecte is great. How fortuneth it then, that either freindes be so foolish, or studentes so vnstayed, to haste so with so much waste? The causes be: *impacience*, which can abide no tarying, where a restlesse conceit is full frawght: *libertie*, to liue as he listeth, bycause he listeth not to liue as he should: *brauerie*, to seeme to be some body, and to cary a countenaunce: *hope* of preferment, to desire dignities before abilitie to discharge. In the meane while: the *common weale* becomes priuate: the *generall* weapeth, while the *particular* winneth: and yet the winning is no soundnesse, but shew. What notable men haue dealt with, and against the forestaulling of sound time in professions? Among many if onely *Viues* the learned *Spaniard*, were called to be witnesse, he would craue pardon for his owne person, as not able to come for the goute, but he would substitute for his deputie his whole twentie bookes of disciplines, wherin he entreateth, how they come to spoile, and how they may be recouered. Lacke of time not onely in his opinion, but also in whose not? bringes lacke of learning, which is a sore lacke, where it ought not to be lacking. The cankar that consumeth all, and causeth all this euill is haste, an *vnaduised, rashe, hedlong counsellour*, and then most pernicious when it hath either some apparence in reason that the child is ripe: or the hartning of some maister, which either is disposed to follow where he seeth replying past cure: or that cannot discern colours, bycause he is that in his degree, which the childe is in his: both vnripe: the one to teach, the other to remoue.

But what if hope of exhibition make an Vniuersitie man straine? and either perswade abilitie, or promise to supplie, where abilitie wantes? Nay what if exhibitours of some litle, seeke recompence to soone, and halfe force some poore scholer to toile with imperfection?

When the vnripe boye findeth any such meane to go to the Vniuersitie, the maister shall neuer know, till he be booted, if he do know then: for feare of stopping his iourney by contrarie counsell: that is by reason to stay him, which runnes to his owne harme.

Time of it selfe, as it is the noblest circunstance wherwith we haue to deale: so it hath a bredth in it selfe capeable of to much, to litle, and enough.

To much *time* is seldome found fault with iustly, though some time pretended, bycause it is seldome taryed for in this kinde wherwith I deale.

To litle *time* is that wheron I complaine, and so much the more harmefull, bycause hast to attaine vnto the desired ende makes it seeme no fault till the blow be giuen.

Time enough is that meane which perfiteth all, the *Elementarie* in his kinde, the *Grammarian* in his, the *Graduate* in his, and so profiteth the *common weale* by perfiting all: the *prerogatiue* to thought: the *mother* to truth: the *tuchestone* to ripenesse: the *enemy* to errour: mans only stay, and helpe to aduice.

For the Grammarians *time*, though it be not within this argument, as many other thinges which the affinitie drew in, yet thus much may I say. That his perfitnesse hath a pitche, and his yeares yeilde his good, as it shall appeare in his owne place, whose time must needes be limited, bycause he is so placed after the *Elementarie,* and before the *Uniuersitie,* as the well appointing of his *time* shall disapoint neither of them. For the *times,* and yeares of studie before degrees in the Vniuersitie, *Plato* himselfe in his exquisite *republike* cannot, nor doth not appoint them better then they be there already, if the *Grammar,* and *Elementarie* haste marred not, and made them that come to soone seeke also to proceede to soone, yet euen so fulfilling statutes, which appoint the continuing yeares, though smallie for their benefit, which are not appointed in yeares, and lesse then not appointed in substaunce. The distances betwene degrees orderly employed, and the midle learninges being caryed before them, as it is imported by their stiles: might worke in the most very reasonable knowledge, for methode and ground in habite, though not for particulars, which be alwayes endlesse, still without art, though most within experience, for their most needfull number. Now if that helpe of readers, which I wished for, were put in execution, me thinke, the world should see, a marueilous number of excellent professours in euery degree. I am to long in talking of to litle: but the times hanging one vpon another haue led me thus onward: wherfore it is now time for me to determine that time, which I do take to be enough for the *Elementarie*. When the child can read so readily, and roundly, as the length of his lesson shal nothing trouble him for his reading: when he can write so faire and so fast, as no kinde of exercise shalbe tedious vnto him for the writing: when his penne or pencill shall delite him with bragge: when his *Musicke* both for voice, and hand is so farre forward, as a litle voluntarie will both maintaine, and encrease it: all which thinges the second maister must haue an eye vnto: then hath the *Elementarie* had time enough. If the parent account not of all, yet perfitnesse in his choice must be his cheife account. The childes ordinarie exercises, will continue his writing, and reading, himselfe will alwaye be drawing, bycause it deliteth his eye, and busieth not his braine. But for *Musicke,* the maister and the parentes delite must further it. For that in those yeares, children be Musicall rather for other then for them selues. Once in, this is a certaine ground, and most infallible, that in tarying long, and perfiting well, there is no losse of time, specially seeing those qualities euen alone, be a pretie furniture of houshold if they be well gotten. The hasting on to fast to see the frute too soone, when circunstances perswade tarying, is to winne an houre in the morning, and to lease the day after. Thus much concerning the *Elementarie* time, determinable not by yeares, but by sufficiencie. If yeares could be limittes to knowledge, as they be very good leaders, the rule were more certaine: but where witte goeth not by yeares, nor learning without, sufficiencie is the surest bounder, to set out, wherin enough is. Howbeit in the *Elementarie,* and so forth I will limit the time somwhat nearer, with all the considerations, both for varietie of the matters which are to be learned, and the men which are to teach, and such thinges as seeme not so proper to be set downe here.

CHAPTER 43.

How to cut of most inconueniences wherwith schooles and scholers, maisters and parentes be in our schooling now most troubled. Wherof there be two meeanes, vniformitie in teaching and publishing of schoole orders. That vniformitie in teaching hath for companions dispatch is learning, and sparing of expenses. Of the abbridging of the number of bookes. Of curtesie and correction. Of schoole faultes. Of friendlinesse betwene parentes and maisters.

A GREAT learned man[73] in our dayes thought so much of the troublesome and toilsome life, which we teachers lead, as he wrate a pretie booke of the miseries of maisters. We are to thanke him for his good will: but when any kinde of life be it high, be it low, is not troubled with his proportion to our portion, we will yeild to misery. Our life is very painfull in deede, and what if beyond comparison painfull? Much a do we haue, and what if none more? Yet sure many as much, though they deale not with so many, and moe more miserable, bycause they better not so many. But I will neither rip vp those thinges, which seeme most restlesse in vs, though the argument offer spreding: neither will I medle with any other trade, no lesse troublesome then teaching, by comparing to seeme to lessen: bycause comparisons in miseries be vncomfortable to both, though some ease to either. To what purpose should I shew, why the maister blames this, the parent that, the child nothing more then the rod, though he will not but deserue it? Such a disease we haue to repine at the paine, and not to waye the offence, which deserueth the paine. Why beat ye him sayeth one? Why offendeth he sayeth none? so harde a thing it is to finde defense for right, so easie a thing it is to finde qualifying for wrong. Therefore to omit these vnpleasant rippinges, I will deale with the remedies how to cut of the most of those, which he calles miseries, I terme *inconueniences*, wherwith the trade of teaching at this day seemeth to haue a great conflict. Which counsell though it be first laid for the youngest scholers, yet may it well be translated further, and beseeme both the biggest, and best, in any learned course.

These remedies I take to be two: 1. The one *vniformitie* in *teaching*, which draweth after it, *dispatch* in *learning*, and *sparing* of *expenses* about to great a number of bookes.

2. The other is *publike schoole lawes*, set downe, and seen, which bring with them for companions *agreement* of parentes and teachers, *continuance* of scholers, *conference to amend*, *comfort* to freindes, and *commoditie* to the common countrey.

[73] P. Melancthon.

Vniformitie in teaching.

For *vniformitie* in *teaching* how many gaules that will heale, wherwith schooles be now greiued, it will then best appeare, when it shalbe shewed, what good it will worke, and how necessarie a thing it is, to haue all schooles reduced vnto it. That there is to much variety in teaching, and therfore to much ill teaching (bycause in the midst of many bypathes, there is but one right waye) he were senseles, that sees not: if he either haue taught, or haue bene taught himselfe. Which whence it springeth, diuersities of iudgement bewraie, that men haue gotten by better or worse training vp in youth: by lesse or more trauell in studie: by longer or shorter continuance at their booke: by liking or misliking some trade in teaching: by accommodating themselues to the parentes choice: and many wayes moe, which either brede varietie, or else be bred by varietie. But of all varieties there is none vayner, then when ignoraunce sweares that that is an *aphorisme,* the contrarie wherof sound knowledge hath set downe for a sure *oracle*. Now in this confusion of varieties what hinderance hath *youth*? what discredite receiue *schooles*? what inequalities be the *Vniuersities* molested with? what toile is it to *Tutours*? how small riddaunce to *readers*? when diuersities of groundworke do hinder their building, and the scholers weakenesse discrieth his maister? And yet oftimes the weake maister bringes vp a strong scholer, by some accident not ordinarie, and the cunninger man by some ordinarie let makes small shew of his great labour. Do not the learners also themselues commonly when they come to yeares and misse that commoditie, which ther maisters could not giue them, being very weake themselues, then blame their fortune and feele the want of foresight? For if varietie had bene wipte awaye by vniformitie, euen the weakest maister might haue done very well if he had had but a meane head to follow direction being set downe to his hand.

This pointe is so plaine as many of the best learned, and of the best teachers also oftimes complaine of it, and wish the redresse, though they still draw backe, and spare their owne pains for any thing they publish: perhaps not hauing the oportunitie and leasure which so great an enterprise craueth: perhaps being induced by hope that some other will start vp, and publish the amendment. Whereby all the youth of this whole Realme shall seeme to haue bene brought vp in one schoole, and vnder one maister, both for the matter and manner of traine, though they differ in their owne inuention which is priuate and seuerall to euery one by nature, though generall and one to euery one by art. Which thing must needes turne to the profit of the *learner,* whose *straying* shalbe straited, that he cannot go amisse: to the ease of the *teacher* whose *labour* shalbe lightened, by the easinesse of his curraunt: to the honour of the *countrey,* which thereby shall haue great store of sufficient stuffe: and the immortall *renown* of that carefull *Prince* which procured such a good. Which benefit say I must proceede from some *vniforme* kinde of teaching set downe by authoritie, that one waye to supplie all wantes, and no one to disdaine, where obedience is enioyned. And wheras *difference* in iudgement worketh *varietie*: *consent* in knowledge will plant *vniformitie*. Which consent, as it must be enforced by authoritie, so must it proceede from some likenesse of abilitie in teachers, namely in that thing wherof they are teachers: though both in executing the same, and for some other qualities they may differ much.

Now the onely waye to worke this likenesse or rather samenesse in abilitie, where otherwise the oddes is so odde, were to set downe in some certain plat, the best that may seeme to be, if that which is best in deede may not be had, as why not? both what and how to teach, with all the particular circunstances, so farre forth as they ordinarily do fall within common compasse, and may best be seeme the best ordered schooles, which both the meane teacher may wel attaine vnto, and the cunning maister may rest content with, and so they both in that pointe proue equall, while the meaner mounting vpword with fethers made for him, and the cunninger comming downward at the shew of the lure, they both meete in the middle waye, and flying forward like freindes, pay their price with their pastime, and mend their faire with their praye, no dishonour offered him, whom mo qualities do commend: and a great helpe to him that cannot swimme without. In whom diligence borne vp, will worke no lesse wonder, nay may fortune more, then greater learning in the other, whom either ouer weyning may make insolent, or loytering negligent. And sure as I may be deceiued herein, so haue I some reason very fauourable to my seeming, that it were more fitting for the common profit, to prouide a certaine direction to helpe the meane teacher, which will continue in the trade without either any or very late changing of his course, and so a long time do much good, then to leaue it at random to the libertie of the more learned, who commonly vse teaching, but to shift with for a time, and be but pilgrimes in the profession, still minding to remoue to some other kinde of life either of more ease, which allureth soone, or of more gaine, which enforceth sore. So that in the meane time the scholers cannot profit much, while the maisters deale like straungers, which entending one day to returne to their countrey, as nature calleth homeward, though profit bid tary, cannot haue that zealous care, which the naturall countrieman, and continuall trauellour of nature hath, and of duetie sheweth. And though conscience cause some odde honest man to worke well, and discharge his duetie in that rowling residence: yet neither be priuiledges generall, nor lawes leuelled after some few, and that foolish fellow was fretished for cold, which followed the fond *swallow*, that flew out to timely, and to farre before her fellowes. An order must be generall to the liking of the better, who should alwaye wishe it, and the leading of the weaker, who shall alway neede it.

If when this order for matter and manner of teaching shalbe set downe, the executor proue negligent, and prolong the effect, or else quite defeat it, by ill handling of that, which was well ment, the surueiors and patrones of schooles, must ouerlooke such teachers, of themselues if they can, if not they may call for the assistaunce of *learning*, which for cunning can, and of curtesie will seeke to further such a thing. Our preceptes be generall, the particular must perfourme, and amend his owne accident. I haue but sleightly noted the surface of *vniformitie* in teaching, and the disioynting of skill by misordered varietie, and yet who is so blinde as he may not thereby discerne, that the one strips away the euilles, which the other bringes in, and thereby cuttes of many encumbraunces from schooles?

Dispatch in learning.

Now *vniformitie* in *teaching* once obtained, doth not *dispatch* in *learning* incontinently follow? which consisteth in choice of the best and fittest authours at the first, and continuaunce in the same: in the best exercises and most proper to the childes ascent in learning: and generally in the maisters orderly proceeding, and methode in teaching: whereby the child shall not learne any thing, which he must or ought to forget, vpon his maisters better aduise: nor leaue any needefull thing vnlearned till his maister grow to better aduise. The maister himselfe shall not neede to chaunge his course, as he chaungeth his skill, now coursing on to fast by to much rashnes: now retiring to late by to louse repentaunce: finally neither the maister nor the scholer shall busie themselues to long about a litle, and neuer the better, nor hast to fast on, and neuer a whit the further. The best course being hit on at the first, as appointment may procure it, one thing helpeth an other forward naturally, without forcing: that which is first taught maketh way for that which must follow next, and continuall vse will let nothing be forgot, which is once well got, and the rising vp by degrees in learning will succede in proportion, with out losse of time or let of labour, either by lingring to long, or by posting to fast, which cannot now possibly be brought about, while thinges be left to the teachers discretion, whereof, as the most be not alway the best, so euen the verie best cannot alway hit those thinges, which in deede are best, while the *customarie education* is helde for a sanctuarie: *alteration* to the better is esteemed an heresie: *allowance* is measured by priuate liking: *vnthankefulnes* is made harbour to desert: and the very *bookes* which we vse be not appropriate to our vse. I touch no mo stoppes then may easily be remoued, if *authoritie* take the matter in hand. Priuate lettes must haue priuate lessons, and personall circumstance shall haue rowme to pleade in, at an other time.

These enormities then shew them selues, when children do chaunge both schooles and maisters: where alteration hindereth beyond all crie, the new maister either thinking it some discredit to himselfe to beginne where the old left, or misliking the choice which the former hath made, or in deede by dispraysing him to seeke to grace himselfe: or the order of his schoole not admitting the succession, as in deede they be all diuerse. Sometimes the boy being vngrounded, by his maisters ignorance if he could not, by his negligence if he did not the thing which he could, will not bende to be bettered, but must keepe the same countenaunce which he himselfe conceiueth of himselfe. And this commonly falles out so, when the parentes be peuish, and thinke their childe disgraced if he be once set backward (for so the tearme is) whereas in verie deede he is bidde but to looke backe, to see that which he neuer saw, and ought to haue seene verie substantially. Which disorder proceeding from the parentes ouerruleth vs all, causing great weakenes, and much mismatching in the fourmes of our schooles: so that we either cannot, or may not finde fault euen to amend it, whereas the order being one, and planted by authoritie, though the childe vse to chaunge often, yet his profiting is soone perceiued: and the parentes also wilbe well contented, when they suspect no partialitie by priuate passion, and see indifferencie in publicke prouision. Such be the frutes which *varietie* bringes foorth, *perillous* in great affaires, still gathering strength by traine in those petie principles: wheras to the contrarie *vniformitie* is full of contentment. Nothing continueth one in our schooles but the common grammar set furth by authoritie, which confirmeth mine opinion both by pollicie in the first setting out, and by profit in the long continuing, wherein we all agree perforce as in a case of higher countenaunce, and already ruled. Which booke whether it may stand still with some amendement, or of necessitie must be cast some other way, for better method, it shall then be seene when comparisons come in season, that the alteration may shew, whether there were cause to chaunge, or some iniurie offered to chaunge without cause. For both that booke, and all the like, which serue for direction and method must be fashioned to the matter which they seeme to direct by rule and precept, being not of themselues, but made to serue others. This we haue by it, that *vniformitie* out of al controuersie is best, but whether it selfe be best, that is yet in controuersie.

Sparing of expenses.

For *sparing* of *expenses*, the second commoditie which *vniformitie* bringes with her, this is my opinion: while it is left to the teachers libertie to make his owne choice, both for the booke which he will teach and the order how, betweene the varietie of iudgementes, and inequalitie of learning in teachers, which by order must be made one, by consent neuer will, the parentes purses are pretily pulled, and poore men verie sore pinched both with chaunge of bookes, the maister oft repealing his former choice: and also with number, while euery booke is commended to the buyer, which either maketh a faire shew to be profitable: or otherwise is sollicited to the sale, as in our dayes necessitie must sell, where such an ouerflush of bookes growes chargeable to the printer. For the old periode is returned, that *Iuuenall* found in his time, learned and vnlearned must needes write, he is marde that comes lag. Nay ordinarily some few leaues be occupied in the best chosen, and biggest booke, besides the oft leasing and much spoiling of them sachels and all, to their gaines it may be said that sell them, though to the parentes losse that buy them, and those of the meaner sort, whose children maintaine schooles most, and swarme thickest in all places and professions, which thing might be farre better vsed, if the best onely were bought, and with the losse of his bookes the childe lost no more. All which inconueniences may easily be remeadied, and with small adoe. For whatsoeuer is needeful to be vsed in schooles, may be verie well comprised in a small compasse, and haue all his helpes with him being gathered into some one pretie volume compounded of the marrow of many: neither will the charge be great, the ware being small, and our profession is not to perfit, but to enter. Neither yet hereby is any iniurie done to good writers, whose bookes may verie well tarie for the ripenes of the reader, and that place which is dew to them, in the ordinarie ascent of learning and studie, being no intruders into rowmes to meane for them, and content to take that place whereunto they are marshalled by their value, and degree: to their praise which made them, when the student can iudge: to the studentes profit, when he can vnderstand: and the fast retaining of them, when order maintanes memorie.

In our *grammer* schooles we professe the toungues nay rather the entraunce of toungues. Euerie profession that is penned in any toungue ministreth to her student those wordes that be proper to her owne subiecte. Which wordes be then best gotten when they follow the matter, as they will do most willingly in the peculiar studie of the same profession. If a *grammarian* therefore be entred to *write, speake,* and *vnderstande* pretily in some well chosen argument best to follow for aptnes ech way, though he neither know all, nor most wordes in any toungue, which is reserued to further studie: yet our schooles be discharged of their dewtie, in doing but so much. They that assigne *grammer* maisters wherein to trauell, appoint them *histories,* and *poetes,* though they make some choice of men, and some distinction of matter in regard of vertuous maners and purenes of stile. In our schooles what time will serue vs to runne ouer all these? nay to deale but with some few of them throughly? how then? Is not some litle well pickt, and printed alone the praise of our profession and the parentes ease? And be not the maine bookes to be consigned ouer to the right place in their owne calling? Some vaines be rapt, and will needes proue *poetes,* leaue them the art of *poetrie,* and the whole bookes and argumentes of *poetes*. Some will commend to memorie, and posteritie such actes and monumentes, as be worthy the remembrance: Let them haue the rules, whereby the penning of *histories* is directed to write thereby with order: and the matter of *histories* to furnish out their stile. If men of more studie and greater learning haue leysure and list to reade, they may vse *histories* for pleasure, as being but an after meates studie: neither tyring the braine, nor tediouse any way: as they be not generally to build on for iudgement: bycause ignorance of their circumstances make some difficultie in applying, and great daunger in prouing. They may also runne ouer *poetes,* when they are disposed to laugh, and to behold what brauery *enthousiasme* inspireth. For when the *poetes* write sadly and soberly, without counterfeating though they write in verse, yet they be no *poetes* in that kinde of their writing: but where they couer a truth with a fabulous veele, and resemble with alteration. We are therefore to cull out some of the best, and fittest for our introductorie, and to send away the rest to their owne place, in the peculiar professions, and that not in *poetes* and *histories* alone, but also in all other bookes whatsoeuer, which be at this day admitted into our schooles. The *poetes* wordes be verie good, and most significant, as it appeareth by *Platoes* whole penning, whose eloquence is thought fit for sainctes, if any heauenly creature had a longing to speake *greeke*. And in the latin they haue the same grace, in his iudgement, which best vnderstoode what wordes were best, as being himselfe the best, and eloquentest oratour, speaking of them in that booke,[74] wherein he both sheweth his eloquence most, and vseth the personages of the most eloquent *oratours,* to deliuer his minde. The quantitie of *syllabes* is to be learned of them, to auoide mistiming, as the wise writer *Horace* pointeth the poet therfore first to frame the tender mouth of the yong learner.

Moreouer some verie excellent places most eloquently, and forcibly penned for the polishing of good manners, and inducement vnto vertue may be pickt out of some of them, and none more then *Horace*. We may therefore either vse them, with that choice: or helpe the pointe our selues if we thinke it good, and can pen a verse that may deserue remembraunce. Suche an helpe did *Apollinarius* offer vnto his time, as *Sozomenus,* and *Socrates* the scholer, report in their ecclesiasticall histories. For *Iulian* the renegate spiting at the great learning of *Basil, Gregorie, Apollinarie,*

[74] De oratore.

and many moe which liued in that time, which time was such a breeder of learned men, as in *Christian* matters and *religion* we reade none like, by decree excluded the *christian* mens Children from the vse of prophane learning wherin the christian diuines were so cunning as they stopt both his, and his fauorites mouthes with their owne learning, they passed them all so farre. Then *Apollinarius* conueighed into verses of all sortes, after the imitation of all the best prophane poetes diuine and holy argumentes gathered out of scripture whereby he met with *Iulians* edict, and furnished out his owne profession, with matter and argument of their owne. Now in misliking of profane arguments some such helpe may be had and appropriate to our youth. But there must be heede taken, that we plant not any poeticall furie in the childes habit. For that rapt inclination is to ranging of it selfe, though it be not helpt forward, where it is, and would not in any case be forced where it is not. For other writers, *number* and *choice* of wordes, *smoothnes* and *proprietie* of composition with the *honestie* of the argument must be most regarded. *Quintilianes* rule is very true and the verie best, and alway to be obserued, in chusing of writers for children to learne, to picke out such as will feede the wit with fairest stuffe, and fine the toungue with neatest speach. So that neither slight, and vnproper matters, though eloquentlie set foorth, neither weightie and wise being rudely deliuered be to be offered to children, but where the honestie and familiaritie of the argument is honored and apparelled with the finesse and fitnes of speach. Which thing if it be lookt vnto in planting *vniformitie,* and pointing out fit bookes, besides many and infinite commodities which will grow thereby to the whole realme, assuredly the multitude of many needelesse volumes, will be diminished and cut of. So that *vniformitie* in schooling may seeme very profitable seeing it will supplant so great defectes, as the likelyhood giues, and plant the redresse, which in nature it importeth: besides that which the common weale doth gaine by acquainting yong wittes euen from their cradeles, both to embrace and apply orderly *vniformes,* which in thinges subiect to sense is delitefull to behold: in comprehensions of the minde is comfortable to thinke on: in executions and effectes is the staie whereon we stand, and the steddiest recourse to correct errors by. I am led by these reasons and many the like, to thinke that either nothing in deede, or very litle in shew, can iustly be alleaged to the contrary but that such an order must needes be verie profitable, to giue schooles a purgation to voide them of some great inconueniences: as I take the thing also to be verie compassable, if authoritie shall like of it, without which an opinion is but shewed, and dieth without effect.

I entend my selfe by the grace of God to bestow some paines therein, if I may perceaue any hope to encourage my trauell. If any other will deale I am ready to staie, and behold his successe: if none other will, then must I be borne with, which in so necessarie a case do offer to my countrie all my duetifull seruice. Wherein if any vpon some repining humor shall seeme to stomacke me, bycause being one perhaps meaner then he is himselfe, I do thus boldly auaunce my doinges to the stage, and view of my countrie: yet still he step foorth and shew vs his cunning he hath no wrong offred him, if another do speake while he wilbe silent. And whosoeuer shall deale in generall argumentes, must be content to put vp those generall pinches, which repining people do vse then most, when they are best vsed, and esteeme it some benefit, when doing well he heareth ill: and thinke that he hath gotten a great victorie if he please the best, and profit the most, as he may profit all and yet displease many: either through *ignorance* bycause they cannot discerne: or through *willfulnes* being wedded to preiudice: or ells through *disdaine* bycause it spiteth some, to see other aboue spite. A disease proper to basest dispositions, and of meanest desert, to pinch the heele where they pricke at the head.

But such as meane to do well, how souer their power perfourme, so the height of their argument ouertop not their power to farre, and discouer great want of discretion in meddling with a matter to much surmounting their abilitie, they may comfort and encourage themselues with that meaning, if their doing do answere it in any resonable proportion, and thinke it a thing, (as it is in deede) naturally, and daily accompanying all potentates either in person, or propertie, and therefore no disgrace to any meaner creature to wrastle with repyning and sowre spirites euen verie then, when they worke them most good, which are readyest to repine. If the doinges be massiue they will beare a knocke: if they be but slender, and will streight way bruse, beware the warranting. As in this my labour I dare warrant nothing, but the warines of good will, which euen ill wil shall see: if it haue any sight to see that is right, as commonly that way it is starke blinde, and so much the more incurablely, bycause the blindnes comes either of vnwillingnes to see, or of an infected sight, that will misconsture and depraue the obiect. I craue the gentle and friendly construction of such as be learned, or that loue learning, and yet I neede not craue it, bycause learning that is sound in deede and needes no bolstering, and all her louers and fauorers, be verie liberall of friendly construction, and nothing partiall to speake the best, euen where it is not craued. I must pray, if prayer will procure it, the gentle and curteouse toleration of such, as shall mislike. For as I will not willingly do that, which may deserue misliking: so if I once know wherein, I will satisfie thoroughly. And therefore in one word, I must pray my louing countriemen, and friendly readers, this to thinke of me, that either I shall hit, as my hope is, and then they shall enioy it: or if I misse, I will amend, and my selfe shall not repent it.

Schoole orders publicke.

2. The second remedie to helpe schoole *inconueniences* was to set downe the schoole *ordinaunces* betwene the maister, and his scholers in a publicke place, where they may easily be seene and red: and to leaue as litle vncertaine or vntoucht, which the parent ought to know, and whereupon misliking may arise, as is possible. For if at the first entry the parent condiscend, to those orders, which he seeth, so that he cannot afterward plead eitheir ignorance, or disallowing, he is not to take offence, if his childe be forced vnto them when he will not follow, according to that fourme, which he himselfe did confirme by his owne consent. And yet when all is done the glosse will wring the text. Wherefore the *maner* of teaching, the ascent in fourmes, the *times* of admission, the *preuention* to haue fourmes equall, the *bookes* for learning, and all those thinges, which be incident vnto that *vniformitie*, wherof I spake, being already knowen to be ratified by authoritie, as I trust it shalbe: or if not, yet the same order in the same degrees being set downe, which the maister priuately according to his owne skill entendes to kepe: it shalbe very good to take away matter of iarre betwene the parentes and the maister, in

the same table publickly to be seene, and shewed to the parentes, when they bring their child first to schoole, besides all that, which I haue generally touched to set downe also in plaine and flat termes, 1. what *houres* he will kepe, bycause there is great consideration in that, what to haue fixed and perpetuall, and wherein to giue place to particular occasions, as there be very many, why all children cannot kepe all *houres*, though the schoole *houres* must still be certaine: and discretion must be the determiner. 2. Againe what *occasions* he will vse to let them go to play, which be now very many, and very needefull, while ordinarie exercises be not as ordinarily admitted, as ordinarie schooling, is ordinarily allowed: 3. and such other thinges as the schoole shall seeme necessarily to require. For a certaintie resolueth, and preuentes douting.

Of curtesie and correction.

But he must cheifly touch what *punishment* he will vse, and how much, for euery kinde of fault that shall seeme punishable by the *rod*. For the *rod* may no more be spared in schooles, then the *sworde* may in the *Princes* hand. By the *rod* I meane *correction*, and *awe*: if that sceptre be thought to fearfull for boyes, which our time deuised not, but receiued it from auncientie, I will not striue with any man for it, so he leaue vs some meane which in a multitude may worke obedience. For the priuate, what soeuer parentes say, my ladie *birchely* will be a gest at home, or else parentes shall not haue their willes. And if in men great misses deserue and receiue great punishment, sure children may not escape in some qualitie of punishment, which in quantitie of vnhappinesse will match some men. And if parentes were as carefull to examine the causes of beating, as they are nothing curious to be offended without cause for beating, themselues might gaine a great deale more to their childrens good: and their children lease nothing, by their parentes assurance. But commonly in such cases rashnesse hath her recompence, the errour being then spied, when the harme is incurable, and repentance without redresse. Terme it as ye list, beate not you saye for learning but for lewdnesse. Sure to beate him for learning which is willing enough to learne, when his witte will not serue, were more then frantike: and vnder the name of not learning to hide and shrowd all faultes and offenses, were more then foolish: and what would that childe be without beating, which with it can hardly be reclaimed? in whom onely lewdnesse is the let, and capacitie is at will? The ende of our schooles is learning: if it faile by negligence, punish negligence: if by other voluntarie default, punish the default. Spare learning: so that still the refuge must be to the maisters discretion: both for manners, and for learning, whom I would wish to set downe as much in certaintie as he can, at the beginning, and to leaue as litle as he may to the childes report, who will alway leane and sway to much to his owne side, and beare away the bell, euen against the best maister, cheifly if his mother be either his counsellour, or his attourney: or the father vnconstant, and without iudgement.

The maister therfore must haue in his table a *catalogue* of schoole faultes, beginning at the commandementes, for *swearing*, for *disobedience*, for *lying*, for *false* witnesse, for picking, and so thorough out: then to the meaner heresies, *trewantry, absence, tardies,* and so forth. Such a thing *Xenophon*[75] seemes to meane in rekening

[75] 1. παιδί.

vp the faultes, which the *Persian* vsed to punish, though he limit not the penaltie, what, nor how much. Which in all these I wish our maister to set downe with the number of stripes also, immutable though not many. Wherin the maister is to take good heed, that the fault may be confessed, if it may be, without force, and the boye conuicted by verdit of his fellowes, and that very euidently. For otherwise children will wrangle amaine, and affection at home hath credulitie beyond crye, which makes the boy dare, what reason dare not. If any of their fellowes be appointed monitours, (as such helpes of Lieutenauncie must be had, where the maister cannot alwaye be present himselfe) and take them napping, they wil pretend spite, or some priuate displeasure in most manifest knauerie. And if ye correcte, as your Lieutenant must haue credit, if you meane to keepe state, that must go home to proue beating without cause. If the maister differre execution, that delaie will enstruct them to deuise some starting hole, and that also if it be not heard in schoole wilbe heard at home.

To tell tales out of schoole, is now as commonly vsed to the worst, as in the old world it was high treason to do it at all. There be as many prety *stratagemes* and deuises, which boyes will vse to saue themselues, and as pleasaunt to heare as any *apopthegme* in either *Plutarch*, *Ælianus*, or *Erasmus*. The maister therefore must be very circumspecte, and leaue no shew, or countenaunce of impunitie deserued, where desert biddes pay. It were some losse of time in learning, to spend any in beating, if it did not seeme a gaine that soundeth towardes good, and seekes amendement of manners. It is passing hard, to reclaime a boye, in whom long impunitie hath graffed a carelesse securitie, or rather some deepe insolencie: and yet freindes will haue it so, and beating may not be for discouraging the boye, though repentaunce be in rearward. It is also not good after any correction to let children grate somwhat to long of their late greife, for feare of to greate stomaking, onlesse the parentes be wise and stedfast, with whom if a cunning, and a discrete maister ioyne, that childe is most fortunate which hath such parentes, and that scholer most happie which hath light on such a maister. "But certainly it is most true, let plausibilitie in speach vse all her excusing and blanching colours that she can, that the round maister, which can vse the rod discretely, though he displease some, which thinke all punishment vndiscrete, if it tuch their owne, doth perfourme his duetie best, and still shall bring vp the best scholers: As no maister of any stuffe shall do but well, where the parentes like that at home, which the maister doth at schoole: and if they do mislike any thing, will rather impart their greife and displeasure with the maister priuately, to amend it, then moane their child openly, to marre that way more then they shall make any way. The same faultes must be faultes at home, which be faultes at schoole, and receiue the like reward in both the places, to worke the childes good by both meanes, correction as the cause shall offer, commendacion as neede shall require."

They that write most for gentlenesse in traine reserue place for the rod, and we that vse the terme of seueritie recommend curtesie to the maisters discretion. Here is the oddes: they will seeme to be curteous in termes, and yet the force of the matter makes them confesse the neede of the rod: we vse sharp termes, and yet yeilde to curtesie more, then euen the verie patrones of curtesie do, for all their curifauour.

Wherin we haue more reason to harp on the harder stringe for the trueth of the matter, then they to touch but the softer, so to please the person: seeing they conspire with vs in the last conclusion, that both correction and curtesie be referred to discretion. Curtesie goeth before, and ought to guide the discourse, when reason is obeyed which is very seldome: but the corruptnesse in nature, the penalties in lawe, courage to enflame, desire to entice, and so many euilles assailing one good do enforce me to build my discourse vpon feare, and leaue curtesie to consideration: as the bare one reason of reason obeyed, a thing still wished, but seldome wel willed, doth cause some curteous conceit, not much acquainted with the kinde of gouernment, vpon some plausible liking, to make curtesie the outside, and keepe canuase for the lyning: but euer still for the last staffe to make discretion the refuge. Wherin we agree, though I priuately chide him, and saye why dissemble ye? Vnder hand he aunswereth me, I lend the world some wordes, but I will witnesse with you, I do not speake against discrete correction, but against hastinesse, and crueltie. Sir I know none, that will either set correction or curtesie at to much libertie, but with distinction, vpon whom they be both to be exercised: neither yet any, that will praise cruelty: and all those, that write of this argument, whether Philosophers or others allow of punishment, though they differ in the kinde.

And it is said in the best common weale,[76] not that no punishment is to be vsed, but that such an excellent naturall witte, as is made out of the finest mould would not be enforced, bycause in deede it needes not: neither will I offer feare, where I finde such a one: neither but in such a common weale shall I finde such a one. And yet in our corrupt states we light sometime vpon one, that were worthy to be a dweller in a farre better. And I will rather venture vpon the note of a sharp maister to make a boye learne that, which may afterward do him seruice, yea though he be vnwilling for the time, and very negligent: then that he shall lacke the thing, which maye do him seruice, when age commeth on, bycause I would not make him learne, for the vaine shadow of a curteous maister. It is slauish sayeth *Socrates* to be bet. It is slauish then to deserue beating sayeth the same *Socrates*. If *Socrates* his free nature be not found, sure *Socrates* his slauish courage must be cudgelled, euen by *Socrates* his owne confession. For neither is punishment denied for slaues, neither curtesie for free natures. This by the waye, neither *Socrates* nor *Plato* be so directly carefull in that place, for a good maister in this kinde, as the place required, though they point the learner. And in deed where they had *Censores* to ouersee the generall traine, both for one age and other, there needed no great precept this waye. If parentes might not do this, neither children attempt that, then were maisters disburdened: If all thinges were set in stay by publike prouision, priuate care were then mightily discharged. But *Socrates* findes a good scholer which in naturall relation inferreth a good maister. And yet *Philippe* of *Macedonie*, had a thousand considerations in his person, moe then that he was *Alexanders* father, and it is not enough to name the man, onelesse ye do note the cause why with all, and in what respect ye name him. A wise maister, which must be a speciall caueat in prouision, wil helpe all, either by preuenting that faultes be

[76] 7 De rep. Plato.

not committed, or by well vsing, when soeuer they fall out, and without exception must haue both correction and curtesie, committed vnto him beyond any appeal. *Xenophon*[77] maketh *Cyrus* be beaten of his maister, euen where he makes him the paterne of the best Prince, as *Tullie* sayeth[78] and mindes not the trueth of the storie, but the perfitnesse of his deuise, being him selfe very milde as it appeareth still in his *iourney* from *Assyria* after the death of *Cyrus* the younger.[79] For a *soule* there could not be one lesse *seruile* then he, which was pictured out beyond exception: for *impunitie*, there could not be more hope, then in a Prince enheritour, and that is more, set forth for a *paterne* to Princes. And yet this Princes child in the absolutenesse of deuise, was beaten by his deuise, which could not deuise any good traine exempt from beating beinge yet the second ornament of *Socrates* his schoole.

The case was thus, and a matter of the *Persian* learning. A long boye had a short coate, and a short boye had a long one: The long boye tooke awaye the short boyes coate, and gaue him his: both were fit: But yet there arose a question about it. *Cyrus* was made iudge, as iustice was the *Persian* grammer. He gaue sentence, that either should haue that which fitted him. His maister bette him for his sentence: bycause the question was not of fitnesse, but of right, wherein eche should haue his owne. His not learning, and errour by ignorance, was the fault, wherfore he was punished. And who soeuer shall marke the thing well, shall finde, that not learning, where there is witte to learne, buildeth vpon *idlenesse*, vnwilling to take paines, vpon *presumption* that he shall carie it awaye free, and in the ende, vpon *contempt* of them, from whom he learned to contemne, where he should haue reuerenced. Slight considerations make no artificiall anatomies, and therfore wil smart, bycause they spie not the subtilities of creeping diseases. It is easie for negligence in scholers, to pretend crueltie in maisters, where fauour beyond rime, lendes credit beyond reason. But in such choice of maisters where crueltie maye easily be auoided, nay in such helpe by Magistrate, where it may be suppressed: and in such wealth of parentes which may change where they like not, if I should here a young gentleman say he was driuen from schoole, he should not driue me from mine opinion, but that there was follie in the parentes, and he had his will to much followed, if his parentes had the training of him, or that his gardian gaue to much to his owne gaine, and to litle to his wardes good, if he were not himselfe some hard head besides, and set light by learning, as a bootie but for beggers. For gentlenesse and curtesie towarde children, I do thinke it more needefull then beating, and euer to be wished, bycause it implyeth a good nature in the child, which is any parentes comfort, any maisters delite. And is the *nurse* to liberall wittes, the maisters *encouragement*, the childes *ease*, the parentes *contentment*, the *bannishment* of bondage, the *triumph* ouer torture, and an *allurement* to many good attemptes in all kinde of schooles.

But where be these wittes, which will not deserue, and that very much? and where much deseruing is, who is so shamles as to deny correction, which by example doth good, and helpes not the partie offender alone. Giue me meane dispositions to deserue, they shall neuer complaine of much beating: but of none I dare

[77] 1. παιδ.

[78] Ad Quintum Frat.

[79] *Ανάβασις.*

not say, bycause insolent rechelessenes will grow on in the very best, and best giuen natures, where impunitie profers pardon, eare the fault be committed. My selfe haue had thousandes vnder my hand, whom I neuer bet, neither they euer much needed: but if the rod had not bene in sight, and assured them of punishment if they had swarued to much, they would haue deserued: And yet I found that I had done better in the next to the best, to haue vsed more correction, and lesse curtesie, after carelessenesse had goten head. Wherfore I must needes say, that in any multitude the rod must needes rule: and in the least paucitie it must be seene, how soeuer it sound. Neither needeth a good boye to be afraid, seeing his fellow offender beaten, any more then an honest man, though he stand by the gallowes, at the execution of a fellon. This point for punishment must the maister set downe roundly, and so as he meaneth in deede to deale, bycause the pretence is generally, not so much for beating, as for to sore beating, which being in sight, the conclusion is soone made, and he that will preuent that sore, may see that set downe, which is thought sufficient. Whervnto if the parent submit himselfe in consent, and his childe in obedience the bargain is thorough, if not there is no harme done.

If the schoole rest vpon the maister alone, thus must he do if he meane to do well, and to continue freindship where he meanes to do good. If it be some free foundacion, the founders must ioyne with the maister, if they meane that the frute of their cost shalbe commodious to their cuntrey. Leaue nothing to had I wist where ye may aunswere ye wist it. When any extraordinary fault breaketh out, as *Solon* said of parricide, that he thought there was none such in nature, conference with the parent, and euident proofe before punishment, will satisfie all parties. And euer the maister must haue a fatherly affection, euen to the vnhappyest boye, and thinke the schoole to be a place of amendment, and therfore subiect to misses.

The maistres yeares and alonenesse.

For the maisters yeares, I leaue that to the admitters, as I do his alonenesse. Sufficiency of liuing wil make marriage most fit, where affection to their owne, worketh fatherlynesse to others: and insufficiencie of liuing will make a sole man remoue sooner, bycause his cariage is small. Most yeares should be most fit to gouerne, both for constantnesse to be an ancker for leuitie to ride at, which is naturally in youth: and for discretion and learning, which yeares should bring with them. But bycause there be errours I leaue this to discretion. The admitters to schooles haue a great charge, and ought to proue as curious as the very best Godfathers, whose charge yet is farre greater, then the account of it is made, among common persons. These thinges do I take to be very necessarie meanes, to helpe many displeasures wherwith schooling is anoyed, and to plant pleasure in their place. And yet when all is done the poore teacher must be subiect to as much, as the sunne is, to shine ouer all, and yet see much more then he can amend: as the diuine is, which for all his preaching, cannot haue his auditorie perfit: as the Prince is, who neither for reward nor penalty can haue generall obedience. The teachers life is painfull, and therfore would be pityed: it is euidently profitable, and therfore would be cherished: it wrastles with vnthankfullnesse aboue all measure, and therefore would be comforted, with all encouragement. One displeased parent will do more harme vpon a head, if he take a pyrre at some toy, neuer conferring with any, but with his owne cholere: then a thousand of the thankfullest will euer do good, though it be neuer so well deserued. Such small recompence hath so great paines, the very acquaintance dying when the childe departes, though with confessed deserte, and manifest profit: Such extreme dealing will furie enforce, where there is no fault, but that conceit surmiseth, vnwilling to examine the truth of the cause, and lother to reclame, as vnwilling to be seene so ouershot by affection. This very point wherby parentes hurte themselues in deede, and hinder their owne, though they discourage teachers, would be looked vnto by some publike ordinaunce, that both the maisters might be driuen to do well, if the fault rest in them: and the parentes to deale well, if the blame rest there: considering the publike is harmed, where the priuate is vncharmed, to ende it in meter as my president is.

But in the beginning of this argument I did protest against *Philip Melanchthons* miseries, and therefore I will go no further, seeing what calling is it, which hath not his cumbat against such discurtesies? The prouerbe were vntrue, if man should not be as well a wolfe to man, as he is tearmed a God and did not more harme, in vnkyndenesse, then good in curtesie: so maruelosly fraught with ill and good both, as *Plinie,* cannot iudge whether nature be to a man, a better mother, or a bitterer stepdame. But patience must comfort where extremitie discourageth: and a resolute minde is a rempare to it selfe, vpon whom as *Horace* saith, though the whole world should fall, it might well crush him perforce, but not quash him for feare.

CHAPTER 44.

That conference betwene those which haue interest in children: Certainetie of direction in places where children vse most: and Constancie in well keeping that, which is certainely appointed, be the most profitable circumstances both for vertuous manering and cunning schooling.

OF all the meanes which pollicie and consideration haue deuised to further the good training vp of children, either to haue them well learned, or vertueously manered, I see none conparable to these three pointes: *conference* betwene those persons, which haue interest in children, to see them well brought vp: *certainetie* in those thinges, wherein children are to trauell, for their good bringing vp: *constancie* in perfourming that, which by *conference* betweene the persons is set *certaine* in the thinges: that there be either no change at all after a sound limitation: or at least verie litle, saue where discretion in execution, is to yeald vnto circumstaunce. Therfore I entend to vtter some part of mine opinion concerning these three things, *conference* to breede the best: *certainetie* to plant the best: *constancie* to continue the best: and first of *conference*. Which I find to be of foure cooplementes: *parentes* and *neighbours*: *teachers* and *neighbours*: *parentes* and *teachers*: *teachers* and *teachers*: whereof euerie one offereth much matter for the furthering of both learning and good maners in children. Vnder the name of *neighbours* I comprehend all forraine persons, whom either commendable dewtie by countrie lawe: or honest care of common curtesie doth giue charge vnto, to helpe the bettering of children, and to fraie them from euill.

Conference betwene parentes and neighbours.

1. Now if parentes in pointes of counsell vse to conferre with such, they may learne by some others experience: how to deale in their owne. And as this point is naturally prouided to assist infirmitie, which craues helpe of others, where it standes in dout: so there is a naturall iniunction wherby all men are charged to bestow their good and faithfull counsell, where it is required, doing thereby great good to the parties, and no harme to themselues, vnlesse it be to be rekened a harme, to gaine the opinion of wisedom, the estimation of honestie, and the note of humanitie, and a well giuen disposition. This consideration resteth most in the partie mouer, which is to receiue aduise, when himselfe shall require it. The next is an euident signe of an excellent inclination, which of it selfe will doe good, euen bycause the thing is good, though he be not conferred with. For if such persons will conferre with parentes, when they spy any thing that is not well in their

children is it not honorable in them to deale so honestly? is it not wisdome in parentes to constrew it most friendly? is it not happie for those children which haue such carefull forraine helpers abroad, such considerate naturall hearers at home? A simple meaning in both the parties, the *neighbour* to tell friendly, the *parent* to take kindely, and to excute wisely will do maruelous much good. And what is this else but to loue thy neighbour as thy selfe, when thou mindest his childe good, as thou doest thine owne? And what is it else but to thinke of thy neighbour, as thou wouldest be thought on thy selfe, when thou beleeuest him in thine, as thou wouldest be beleeued in his? A true president of naturall *humanitie*, a religious patterne of honest *neighbourhoode*, which in no other thing can declare more good will, in no other thing can do one more good, then in respect to his children, whether ye consider the childrens persons, or the thing which is wished them. For in deede what be children in respect of their persons? be they not the effectes of Gods perfourmaunce in blessing? of his commaundement in encrease? be they not the assurance of a state which shall continew by succession, and not dy in one brood? be they not the parentes naturall purtracte? their comfort in hope, their care in prouision? for whom they get all, for whom they feare nought? And can he which desireth the good of this so great a blessing from heauen, so great a staie for the countrie, so great a comfort to parentes, deuise how to pleasure them more in any other thing? for to wish children to be honest, vertuous, and well learned, is to wish that to proue perfitly good, which standeth in a mammering, to proue good or bad. And can this so great a good wish but proceede from a passing honest disposition, and most worthy the embrasing? Nay most happy is that state, where youth hath such a staie, in such libertie as it is, not to helpe vnlesse one list. Hereupon I conclude that *conference* betwene *parentes* and others, whether by way of asking counsell, or by aduertisemente to check faultes, is very profitable for the weale of the litle ones.

Conference betwene teachers and neighbours.

2. This *conference* may fall betwene the *neighbour* and the *teacher*. Wherein the *teacher* must be verie warie bycause he hath to deale with the informer for credit: with his scholer for amendment: with the parent for liking. When the parent dealeth with his owne childe, either of his owne knowledge, or by credited report, his doome is death or life, the childe hath no appeale, but either must amend, or feele the like smart. At the *teachers* dealing, vpon any aduertisement, there may and wilbe taken many pretie exceptions. Why did you beleeue? why should he medle? why dealt you in this sort? And whatsoeuer quarell miscontentment can deuise, being incensed with furie: or some extreme heat, as angrie nature is an eager monster. And in deede some ouerthwart conceit may moue the complainant, whatsoeuer the pretence be. Againe some wise man, may light vpon so conuenient a maister, as he may proue a better meane to redresse, then the parent will be, in whom blinde nature will neither see the childes fault, nor the friendes faith. But how soeuer it be, the maister must be warie, where his commission is not absolute. But in the wise handling of this ciuill *conference* the childe shall gaine much towardes his well doing, when wheresoeuer he shall be, or whatsoeuer he shall do, he shall both finde it true, and feele it so, that either his parent or his maister, or

both together see him, if any other bodie see him.

Conference betwene parentes and teachers.

3. The next *conference* is betweene *parentes* and *maisters,* whereof though I haue saide much, yet can I neuer say to much, the point is so needefull: bycause their friendly and faithfull communicating workes perpetuall obedience in the childe, contempt of euill, and desire to do well: seeing both they trauell to make one good. There is nothing so great an enemie to this so great a good as credulitie is in parentes, not able to withstand the childes eloquence, when shed of teares, and some childish passion do plead against punishment for assured misdemeanour. But though for the time such parentes seeme to wynne, bycause they haue their will: yet in the conclusion, they want their will, when they wish it were not so. Before change either of place, to proceede onward to further learning: or of maisters when the old is misliked, and a new sought for, then this *conference* is a meruelous helpe. For in change of place, it growndes vpon knowledge, and growes by aduice: in change of maisters, it is mistresse to warines not to lease by the change. For can the new maister vnderstand and iudge of the childes fault in so small a time, as the old maister may amend it if he be conferred with? You are offended with the former maister, haue ye conferred with him? haue ye opened vnto him your owne griefe, your childes defect, his owne default? are ye resolued that the fault is in the maister? may not your sonne forge? or may he not halt, to procure alteration vpon some priuate peuishnes? *Cyrus* as *Zenophon* writeth[80] surprised the king of *Armenia* being tributarie to the *Medians* but minding to reuolt, when the *Assyrians* armie should enter into *Media*. And yet though he found him in manifest blame, he left him his state, as the best steward for the *Medians* vse, considering the partie pardoned is bound by defect, he that shall be chosen, will thanke his owne merit, not the chusers munificence. Such consideration had *Cyrus*, and such *conference* with him, whom he knew to be a foe, before he surprised him, and yet found the frute of his considerate *conference* and his determination vpon his *conference*, to be exceding good and gainefull for himselfe after, and his friendes for the time. A number of ills be auoided, and a number of goodes obtained by this same *conference* betwene *parentes* and *maisters*. If the *maister* be wise and aduisedly chosen though he chaunce to misse, he knowes to amend: if he neither be such a one, nor so considerately chosen, yet *conference* will discouer him, and shew hope her listes, and what she may trust to. But not to dwel any longer in this point, wherein elsewhere I haue not bene parciall, I must needes say thus much of it at once for all, that no one meane either publike or priuate makes so much for the good bringing vp of children, as this *conference* doth.

Conference betwene teachers.

4. The last *conference* I appoint to be betwene those of the same professions, whereby the generall traine is generally furthered. For whersoeuer any subiect is to be dealt in by many, is not the dealers *conference* the meane to perfit dealing? and to haue that subiect absolutely well done, which it selfe is subiect to so many doers? Is either the patient any worse if the *Physitians* conferre, or their facultie

[80] παιδ. 3.

baser by their being togither? is not the case still clearer, where there is *conference* in law? is not the church the purer were *conference* is in proufe? and doth not the contrarie in all do much harme in all? And do ye thinke *that* conference among teachers would not do much good in the traine? or is the thing either for moment so meane, or for number so naked, as it may not seeme worthy to be considered vpon? Or can there any one, or but some few, be he or they neuer so cunning, discerne so exactly, as a number can in common *conference*? do not common companies which professe no learning, both allow it, and proue it, and finde it to be profitable? where it is vsed among teachers for the common good, it profiteth generally by sending abroad some common direction. In places where many schooles be within small compasse, it is very needefull to worke present good, and to helpe one another, where all may haue enough to bestow their labour on.

But this *conference*, and that not in *teachers* alone must be builded vpon the *honest care* of the *publike good*, without *respect* of *priuate gaine*: without *sting* of *emulation*: without *gaule* of *disdaine*: which be and haue bene great enemies to conference: great hinderers to good schooling: nay extreame miners in cases aboue schooling, and yet for the footing of that, which must after proue fairest, good schooling is no small onset. I neede not to rip vp the position to them, that be learned, which know what a mischiefe the misse of *conference* is, where it ought to be of force, and is shouldered out by distempered fantsie. He that can iudge, knoweth the force of this argument, which followeth: "where many illes seeke to chooke one good, which themselues were displaced, if that good tooke place: that good must needes be a great one, and worthy the wishing, that it may procure passage." Of *conference* I must needes say this, that it is the cognisance of humanitie, and that of the best humanitie, being vsed for the best causes that concerne humanitie, and all humaine societie. I dare enter no deeper in this so great a good: but certainely in matters of learning there would be more *conference*, euen of verie conscience. And if that honest desire might bring downe great hart, the honorable effect would bring vp great good, in all trades beyond crie, in our traine beyond credit. In matters of engrosing, and *monopoleis*, in matters of forestauling and intercepting there is dealing by *conference* among the dealers, which we all crie out of, bycause it makes vs crie, in our purses. And yet we are slow to trie that in the good, which proues so strong in the ill, and was first pointed for good. I vse no authorities to proue in these cases, where reason her selfe is in place, and standeth not in neede of alleaging of names, bycause she may well spare her owne retinew, where her hoste himselfe doth tender his owne seruice.

Certaintie.

2. The next point after *conference* is the chiefe and best offspring of all wise *conferences*, *certainetie* in direction, which in all thinges commendes it selfe, but in bringing vp of children it doth surpasse commendation, both for their manners and their learning. This same so much praised *certainetie* concerneth the limiting of thinges, what to do and what to learne, how to do and how to learne, where, when, and so furth to do that, which fineth the behauiour, and to learne that which aduanceth knowledge. For children being of themselues meere ignorant must haue *certainetie* to direct them: and trainers being not dailie to deuise, are at once to set

downe certaine, both what themselues will require at the childrens hand for the generall order: and what the children must looke for at their handes for generall perfourmance. This *certainetie* must specially be set sure, and no lesse soundly kept, in *schooles* for *learning*, in priuate *houses* for *behauiour*, in *churches* for *religion*, bycause those three places, be the greatest aboades, that children haue.

Certainetie in schooles.

1. Concerning *certainetie* in schoole pointes, and the benefit thereof, I haue delt verie largely in the last title: so that I shall not neede to vse any more spreading in that point, sauing onely that I do continue in the same opinion: as the thing it selfe continueth in it selfe most assurance of best successe, when the childe knoweth his *certainetie* in all limitable circumstances, whether he be at schoole himselfe to prouide that must be done: or if he be not there, yet to know in abscence, what is done there of course. So that where ignorance of orders cannot be pretended, there good orders must needes be obserued, which ordenarily bringe foorth a well ordered effect. The best and most heauenly thinges be both most certaine, and most constantly certaine, and the wisest men the certainest to builde on, in the middest of our vncertaineties. So that *certainetie* must needes be a great leuell, which procureth such liking in those thinges where it lighteth. In *schooling* it assureth the parentes, what is promised there, and how like to be perfourmed, by sight of the method and orders set downe: it directeth the children as by a troden path, how to come thither, as their iourney lieth: it disburdeneth the maisters heade, when that is in writing, which he was in waying, and when experience by oft trying hath made the habit able to march on of it selfe without any renewing: whereunto mutabilitie is euerie day endaungered.

Certainetie in priuate houses.

2. The second point of *certainetie* entereth into families and priuate *houses*, which in part I then touched, when I wished the parentes so to deale at *home*, as there might be a *conformitie* betwene *schoole* and *home*. This point will preuent two great inconueniences euen at the first, besides the generale sequele of good discipline at home. For neither shall schooles haue cause to complaine of priuate corruption from home, that it infecteth them, when nothing is at home done or seene, but that which is seemely: neither shall the schooles lightly send any misdemeanour home, when the childe is assured to be sharpely chekt, for his ill doing, if it appeare within doares. This is that point which all writers that deale with the *œconomie* of householdes, and pollicie of states do so much respect, bycause the fine blossomes of well trained families, do assure vs of the swetest flowres in training vp of states, for that the buddes of priuate discipline be the beauties of pollicie. I shall not neede to say, what a good state that familie is in, where all things be most certainely set, and most constantly kept, which do belong to the good example of the *heades*, the good following of the *feete*, the good discipline of the whole *house*. Though some not so resolute wittes, or gredier humours will neither harken to this rule, neither keepe it in their owne, bycause the distemperature is both blinde, and deafe, where the minde is distempered, and violently giuen ouer either to extreame desire of gaine, or to some other infirmitie which cannot stoup to

staid order: yet those *families* which keepe it, finde the profitablenesse of it. There children so well ordered by *certaineties* at *home*: when to rise: when to go to bed: when and how to pray euening and morning: when and how to visit their parentes ear they goe to bed, after they rise, ear they go abroad, when they returne home, at tables about meat, at meeting in dutie with officious and decent speches of course, well framed, and deulie called for, cannot but proue verie orderly and good. He that in his infancie is thus brought vp, will make his owne proufe his fairest president, and what housholde knoweth not this is extreame farre of from any good president. Obedience towardes the prince and lawes is assuredly grounded, when priuate houses be so well ordered: small preaching will serue there, where priuate training settes thinges so forward. Being therefore so great a good, it is much to be thought on, and more to be called for.

Certaintie in Churches.

3. Now can *certaintie* being so great a bewtifier both to publik *schooles*, and priuate houses, be but very necessary to enter the Church with children vpon *holydaies*? to haue all the young ones of the Parish, by order of the Parish set in some one place of the Church? with some good ouer looking, that they be all there, and none suffred to raunge abroad about the streates, vpon any pretence? that they may be in eye of parentes and parishioners? that they may be attentiue to the Diuine seruice, and be time learne to reuerence that, wherby they must after liue? I do but set downe the consideration, which they will execute, who shall allow of it, and deuise it best, vpon sight of the circunstance. How other men will thinke herof I know not, but sure methinke, both publikly and priuately, that *certaintie* in *direction* where it may be well compassed, is a merueilous profitable kinde of regiment, and best beseeming children, about whose bettering my trauell is employed. In the very executing it sheweth present pleasure, and afterward many singular profites: and is in very deede the right meane to direct in *vncertainties*, as a stayed yearde to measure flexible stuff. *Bladders* and *bullrushes* helpe *swimming*: the *nurses* hand the *infantes going*: the *teachers line* the *scholers writing*, the *Musicians tune*, his *learners timing*: what to do? by following *certaintie* at first to direct *libertie* at last. And he that is acquainted with *certaintie* of *discipline* in his young yeares will thinke himselfe in exile, if he finde it not in age, and by plaine comparisons, will reclaime misorders, which he likes not, to such orders as he sees not. Who so markes and moanes the varietie in *schooling*, the disorder in *families*, the dissolutenesse in *Church*, will thinke I saye somwhat.

Constancie.

3. The third part of my diuision was *constancie*. For what auaileth it to *conferre* about the best, and to set it in *certaine*, where *mutabilitie* of mindes vpon euery infirmitie either of iudgement, or other circunstance, is seeking to retire, and to leaue that rouling, which was so well rewled. In this point of *constancie* there be but two considerations to be had, the one of knowledge in the thing, the other of discretion in the vse. For he that is resolued in the goodnesse and pith of the thing, will neuer reuolt, but like a valiant general building vpon his owne knowledge, is certaine to conquere, what difficultie so euer would seeme to dasle his eyes, or

to dash his conceit. It is weake *ignorance* that yeildes still, as being neuer well setled: it is *pusillanimitie* that faintes still, not belieuing where he sees not. Assured *knowledge* will resemble the great *Emperour* of all, which is still the same and neuer changeth, which set a lawe, that yet remaines in force euen from the first, among all his best and most obedient thinges. The *sunnes* course is *certaine*, and *constantly* kept. The *moone* hath her mouing without *alteration*, and that so *certaine*, as how many yeares be their eclypses foretold? A good thing such as wise *conference* is most like to bring forth, would be *certainly* knowen, and being so knowen would be *constantly* kept. The fairest *bud* will bring forth no frute, if it fall in the prime, but being well fostered by seasonable weather, it will surely proue well. The greatest thinges haue a feeble footing, though their perfitnesse be strong, but if their meane be not *constant*, that first feeblenesse will neuer recouer that last strength. I medle not with change of states, nor yet with any braunches, whose particular change, quite altereth the surface, of any best setled state, but with the training of children, and the change therin: which being once certaine would in no case be altered before the state it selfe vpon some generall change do command alteration, whervnto all our schooling must be still applyed, to plant that in young ones, which must please in old ones. As now our teaching consisteth in toungues, if some other thing one daye seeme fitter for the state, that fitter must be fitted, and fetcht in with procession. But yet in changes this rule would be kept, to alter by degrees, and not to rush downe at once. Howbeit the nature of men is such, as they will sooner gather a number of illes at once to corrupt: then pare any one ill by litle and litle with minde to amend.

Concerning *discretion*: there is a circunstance to be obserued in thinges, which is committed alwaye to the executours person, and hath respect to his iudgement, which I call no change, bycause in the first setting downe that was also setled, as a most certaine point to rule accidentarie *vncertainties*, which be no changes, bycause they were foreseene. Such a supplie hath iustice in positiue lawes by equitie in consideration, as a good chauncellour to soften to hard constructions. That is one reason why the *monarchie* is helde for the best kinde of gouernment, bycause the rigour and seueritie of lawe, is qualified by the princesse mercie, without breche of lawe, which left that prerogatiue to the princesse person. The conspiracie which *Brutus* his owne children made against their father for the returne of *Tarquinius* euen that cruell Prince, leanes vpon this ground, as *Dionysius* of *Halicarnassus*, *Liuie*, and others do note. So that *discretion* to alter vpon cause in some vncertaine circunstance, nay to alter circunstance vpon some certaine cause, is no enemie to *certaintie*. When thinges are growen to extremities then change proues needefull to reduce againe to the principle. For at the first planting, euery thing is either perfitest, as in the matter of creation: or the best ground for perfitnesse to build on, as in truth of religion: though posteritie for a time vpon cause may encrease, but to much putting to burdeneth to much, and in the ende procures most violent shaking of, both in religious and politike vsurpations.

But this argument is to high for a schoole position, wherefore I will knit vp in few wordes: that as *conference* is most needefull, so *certaintie* is most sure, and *constancie* the best keeper: that it is no change, which *discretion* vseth in doing but her duetie: but that altereth the maine. Which in matters engraffed in generall conceites would worke alteration by slow degrees, if foresight might rule: but in extremities of palpable abuse it hurleth downe headlong, yea though he smart for the time whom the change doth most helpe. But in our schoole pointes the case falleth lighter, where whatsoeuer matter shalbe offered to the first education, *conference* will helpe it, *certaintie* will staye it, *constancie* will assure it. Thus much concerning the generall positions wherin if I haue either not handled, or not sufficiently handled any particular point, it is reserued to the particular treatise hereafter, where it will be bestowed a great deale better, considering the present execution must follow the particular.

CHAPTER 45.

The peroration, wherin the summe of the whole booke is recapitulated and proofes vsed, that this enterprise was first to be begon by Positions, and that these be the most proper to this purpose. A request concerning the well taking of that which is so well ment.

THVS bold haue I bene, with you (my good and curteous countriemen) and troubled your time with a number of wordes of what force I know not, to what ende I know. For my ende is, to shew mine opinion how the great varietie in teaching, which is now generally vsed, maye be reduced to some vniformnesse, and the cause why I haue vsed so long a preface, as this whole booke, is, for that such as deale in the like arguments, do likewise determine before, what they thinke concerning such generall accidentes, which are to be rid out of the waye at once, and not alwaye to be left running about to trouble the house, when more important matters shall come to handling. Wherin I haue vttered my conceit, liking well of that which we haue, though oftimes I wishe for that which we haue not, as much better in mine opinion, then that which we haue, and so much the rather to be wished, bycause the way to winne it is of it selfe so plaine and ready. I haue vttered my sentence for these pointes thus, wherin if my cunning haue deceiued me, my good will must warrant me: and I haue vttered it in plaine wordes, which kinde of vtterance in this teaching kinde, as it is best to be vnderstood, so it letteth euery one see, that if I haue missed, they may wel moane me, which meaning all so much good haue vnhappily missed in so good a purpose. Vpon the stearnesse of resolute and reasonable perswasions, I might haue set downe my Positions aphorismelike, and left both the commenting, and the commending of them to triall and time: but neither deserue I so much credit, as that my bare word may stand for a warrant: neither thought I it good with precisenesse to aliene, where I might winne with discourse. Whervpon I haue writen in euery one of those argumentes enough I thinke for any reader, whom reason will content: to much I feare for so euident a matter, as these Positions be, not assailable, I suppose, by any substantiall contradiction. For I haue grounded them vpon reading, and some reasonable experience: I haue applied them to the vse, and custome of my countrey, no where enforcing her to any forreine, or straunge deuise. Moreouer I haue conferred them with common sense wherin long teaching hath not left me quite senselesse. And besides these, some reason doth lead me very probable to my selfe, in mine owne collection, what to others I know not, to whom I haue deliuered it, but I must rest vpon their iudgement. Hereof I am certaine that my countrey is already very well acquainted with them, bycause I did but marke where vpon particular neede, she her selfe hath made her owne choice, and by embrasing much to satisfie her owne vse, hath recommended the residue vnto my care, to be brought by direction vnder some fourme of statarie discipline. Now then can I but thinke that my countreymen will ioyne with me in consent, with whom my countrey doth communicate such fauour? Seeing her fauour is for their furtheraunce, and my labour is to bring them to that, which she doth most allow.

The examining of all the contentes of this booke.

And what conclusion haue I set downe wherin they maye not very well agree with me, either for the first impression which set me on worke, or for the proofe, which confirmeth the impression? My first meaning was to procure a generall good, so farre as my abilitie would reach, I do not saye that such a conceit, deserueth no discourtesie for the very motion, how soeuer the effect do aunswere in rate: but this I may well thinke, that my countreymen ought of common courtesie to countenaunce an affection so well quallified, till the euent either shrine it with praise, or shoulder it with repulse. I do not herein take vpon me dictatorlike to pronounce peremptorily, but in waye of counsell, as one of that robe, to shew that, which long teaching hath taught me to saye, by reading somwhat, and obseruing more. And I must pray my good countrymen so to construe my meaning, for being these many yeares by some my freindes prouoked to publish something, and neuer hitherto daring to venture vpon the print, I might seeme to haue let the raine of all modesty runne to lowse, if at my first onset I should seeme like a *Cæsar* to offerre to make lawes. Howbeit in very deede my yeares growing downward, and some mine obseruations seeming to some folkes to craue some vtteraunce, vpon shew to do some good: I thought rather to hasard my selfe in hope of some mens fauour, then to burie my conceit with most mens wonder. But before I do passe to mine Elementarie, which I meane to publish next after this booke, I must for mine owne contentation examine what I haue done in this, to see whether I haue hit right, or writen any thing that may call repentaunce. 1. Was I not to cut this course, and to begin at Positions? 2. And are not these the cheife and onely groundes in this argument? 3. And in speking of these haue I in any point passed beyond my best beseeming? 1. For the first. Whether I ought to begin at Positions, or no, that is not in doubte now I hope, bycause I made that pointe very plaine in the beginning of my booke: but whether I haue done well to dwell so long in them, that maye seeme to deserue some excuse, if I mislike it my selfe: or els some cause, to satisfie other.

If I had had to do with either *Romain*, or *Grecian*, in their owne language, where these thinges be familiarly knowen, I would not haue taryed in them any long while, but dealing with my countrymen in my countrey toungue, in an argument not so familiar to my countrey, and yet desiring to become familiar vnto her: I thought it good rather to saye more then enough, to leaue some chippinges: then by saying to litle, to cause a new cruste, where none should be: and to referre the rest of my suppressed meaning to my learneddest reader, to whose vse as I needed not to write, so in deede I do not, though I wish him well, and pray the like againe. They that frame happy men, absolute oratours, perfit wisedome, paragonne Princes, faultelesse states, as they haue their subiect at commaundement, which they breede in the commentarie of their owne braines: so their circunstances being without errour, where their maine is without match, neede very few wordes, as being in daunger of very few faultes. But I deale with a subiect, which is subiect to all vncertainties: with circunstances, which are chekt with many obiections, lying open, to much disturbance, cauilled at by euery occasion: where one sillie errour, is of strength enough, to ouerthrow a mans whole labour. I thought it good therefore to declare at large, what my meaning was, to satisfie therby euen the meanest vnderstandinges, that waye to procure mine opinion the freer passage, when it should passe by none, which vnderstood it not. I could not but begin with them, bycause herafter I shall haue so many occasions to make mention of them, to directe the traine by them, to referre my selfe vnto them, which if they had not bene handled here, they might and would haue troubled me there. Besides this, I would gladly (if I could obtaine so much at their handes) that all my countrymen did thinke, as I do in these same pointes, that by their consent my good speede might go on, with the readier and rounder currant, so that I cannot conceiue, but that I was both to begin my treatise at Positions, as the primitiue in such discourses, and to dwell long in them, to satisfie my most readers.

2. Now whether these be the cheife groundes in preparatiue to that, which I entend to deale in, I thinke there is none, but may very easily iudge. For what is it whervnto my trauell to come hath promised her endeuour? to helpe children to be well taught for learning: to tell their maisters, how to exercise them for health: to aide the common course of studie in what I can for the common good. And what accidentes belong vnto such an argument, if these which I haue quoated out do not? Must there not be a time to begin, to continue, to ende the course of schoole learning? Then time must needes come in consideration. Must there not be somthing, wherin this time must be bestowed, both to haue the minde learned, and the body healthfull? Then the matter of traine, and the kinde of exercises could not haue bene passed ouer. Must there not be some vpon whom these thinges are to be imployed in these times, of both the sexes, and of all degrees? Then the generall schooling of all young ones, and the particular training of young maidens, and bringing vp of young gentlemen must needes haue their handling. Could these thinges be done with out conuenient place? cunning teachers? and good schoole orders? I thinke no. And therefore I picked these out, as the onely circunstances, that were proper to mine argument, and that were to be handled eare I entred my argument, if I had neuer seene any writer before vse the same choice.

3. But how haue I delt in them. For the time to begin I haue measured it by strenght of body and minde that may well awaye with the trauell in learning without emparing of the good of either parte. For the continuing time in euery degree of studie, I haue limited it by sufficiencie and perfitnesse of habit, before the student remoue. For the ending time, the bounder of it is abilitie to serue the common countrey, and the priuate student in euery particular calling. In this distinction and sorting of time, I thinke I haue so dealt, as no reason will gainsaye me. 2. For pointing so many thinges to be learned in the Elementarie schoole, as I do it vpon good warrant, so is no man iniuried by it, and euery man may be helpt by it. For

though neither all men deale with all, nor all men can obtaine all, it is no reason but that those which will and may, shall know what is best to get: and that those which neither will nor can, yet maye see, what they maye and ought to get, if circunstances serue. For the traine is to be framed after the height, which freedome in circunstance maye well attaine vnto. A poore mans purse will not stretch so farre: must abilitie therfore be to much restrained? Some mans time will not dispense with all: must therfore the libertie of leasure be forced to the fetter? Some parente makes light of that, which some other esteemeth greatly: must he therefore be disapointed of his liking, which alloweth to serue his humour, which misliketh? Some maime in some circunstance may be some particular let: must therefore parciality in not pointing the best proue the generall losse.

The best being set downe, without euident dispaire to come by it, or manifest noueltie to disgrace it, why should it not be sought for by them, which are willing to haue it, and know the meanes how? It is no noueltie for some to towre aboue the clowdes though other in the same flight do but flutter about the ground, and yet with commendation. For where the whole is good, and partible by degrees, euerie ascent hath his praise, though the prerogatiue be his that mounteth highest. And therefore my plat is to satisfie those which will medle with the most, and yet so left at libertie, as it may serue euen them, which seeke but for the least. 3. For the choice of wittes and restraint of number, not to pesture learning with to great a multitude, no wisedome will blame me. 4. For the helpe and health of body, that the doinges of the soule may be both strong and long, to ioine ordinarie exercise in forme of traine, who so shall mislike, I will match him with melancholie, with fleame, with reumes, with catarres, and all needelesse residences, to see how they will musle him. The limitation of certaineties in maisters for their securitie, and parentes for their assurance, if it be well wayed; is worth the wishing. 5. For the places and personall circumstances, who so will cauill, neither deserues such a place to be trained in, nor such a maister to be trained by, nor such parentes to prouide him such a traine. 6. For the good bringing vp of yong gentlemen, he that taketh no care, is more then a foole considering their place and seruice in our countrie: and so of all the rest. 7. But did any man thinke that I would not mention my dealing in trayning vp of yong maidens, whether that be to be admitted in such sort as I haue appointed it? That is such a bulwarke for me, as who so shall seeme to pinche me for dealing liberally with them, had neede to arme himselfe against them. For they will translate the crime, and becomming parties themselues discharge me from daunger for vsing them so curteously. Is that point in suspition of any noueltie or fantasticallnes to haue wymen learned? Then is *nature* fantasticall for giuing them abilitie to learne: *custome* for putting them to it: *pollicie* for placing them where to vse it: in all ages in all degrees, in all countries, both at home and abroad. Innouation it is not, for I reade it, I see it, I finde it, it is not my deuise. I put the case, that it were one of my wishes, that wymen might learne, if they did not. Assuredly the proufe that wee see, the profit that we feele, the comfort that we haue, the care that we haue not, the happines we enioy, the mishap we auoide, the religion we liue by and like, the superstition we fly from and hate, the clemencie we finde, the cruelitie we feare, by the meere benefit of our learned princesse, whom God hath so rarely endewed and endowed, giue me leaue to wish that sexe most successe in learning, and her maiesties person all successe in liuing: all the residew, all the best, and her highnes alone all aboue the best: as wish can aspire, where nothing else can come. In generall I do not remember any thing, that I haue dealt in, but it may be very well digested by any stomake, if it be not to farre distempered.

My wishes perhaps may seeme sometimes to be nouelties. Nouelties perhappes, as all amendementes be to the thing that needeth redresse, but not fantasticall, as hauing their seat in the cloudes. If no man did euer wish, then were I alone. If my wish were vnpossible though it made shew of very great profit, impossibilitie in deede, would desire profit in wish to be content with repulse: but where the thing is both profitable, and possible to, why should not profitable possibilitie haue rowme, if wishing may procure it? I wish commodious situation and rowmh in places for learning and exercise. Our countrie hath it not echwhere, nay scant any where as yet. Euen by wishing that it had, I graunt that it hath not: but I would not haue wished it, if the meane had bene hard: and the motion naturally goeth before the effect. I wish that the colledges in the vniuersities were deuided by professions: I wish graue and learned readers: I wish repetition to the same readers, yea euen for the best graduate, that is yet an hearer. I wish neither heresie nor harme, ne yet any thing, but that may very well be wrought, and deserues endlesse wishing till it be brought to an ende. I wish restraint to stop ouerflush, and such other things whereto I dare stand, and assuredly beleeue, that I wish my countrie very great good, as I hope many wilbe partakers with me in wish, to be partakers of the good. But some wil say what neede you to medle with so much, or so high matters your selfe creeping so low? Syr, I did professe in the beginning vnder ech title to deale in the generall argument, for all my professing the elementarie example. And by the way I do thinke, that I may deserue some more equitie in construction, bycause I do entend to my great paines to helpe my wish forward, and to trauell for the helping, and healthing of all studentes. Wherfore I conclude thus, that seeing my dealing in those positions was occasioned of so good a ground, and hath so passed through them, as I hope it may abide the tuch. I must craue of my good and curteouse countriemen to laie vp allouance in hope, and misliking in pardon, till the euent dischardge both, and make me bound to all, and some benefited by me.

FINIS.

APPENDIX.

RICHARD MULCASTER.[81]

The birthplace of Richard Mulcaster seems to have been the old border tower of Brackenhill Castle, on the river Line. The exact date of his birth is uncertain, but it was probably 1530 or 1531. The Mulcasters had for centuries been an important family on the Border. Among the old Exchequer Records in the Tower is a letter from Sir Robert de Clifford, King's Captain of the counties of Cumberland, Westmorland, and Lancashire, to the Treasurer and Barons of the Exchequer, desiring them to excuse Sir William Molcastre, Sir Thomas de Felton, Robert de Molcastre, and Richard de Molcastre from appearing in the Court of Exchequer according to their summons, by reason of their attendance on him in defence of the Marches; dated at Lochmaben Castle, 4th July, 1299. The Sir William Mulcaster here spoken of was for five years in succession High Sheriff of Cumberland, and was much engaged in the war with Scotland. An old pedigree of the Mulcasters drawn up in Queen Elizabeth's time says that Sir William Mulcaster in the reign of "Edward Longshanks entayled his landes at Torpenham, Bolton, Bolton-Yetten, and Blennerhasset on his eldest son, Robert Mulcaster, whom he marryed to Eufemia, sister to Raphe Nevil, Erle of Westmerland, and Erle Marshal of England. He entayled his landes at Brackenhill and Solport on his second sonne, Richard Mulcaster." The elder branch, however, did not thrive. In the next generation "Sir Robert Mulcaster became ane Unthrift, and for smale summes of present money in hand did alien his landes in parcels to his Unkel the Erle of Westmerland, who knowing the title to be weake by reson of the entayle did straytway selle the said landes. Sir Robert presently after the sayle died." But the Richard Mulcasters have flourished on and on through the centuries, and these particulars were communicated to me by the last Richard Mulcaster, who lived to see this reprint of his ancestor's book.

In the fifteen hundreds, St. Bees was a noted place for instruction, and Bishop

[81] Almost all we know of Mulcaster is given in "Gentleman's Magazine" for 1800——*i.e.*, vol. lxx, part i, pp. 419-421, 511, 512; and part ii, pp. 600 and 604. The writer, "E. H.," is always said to be Henry Ellis. Besides this we have H. B. Wilson's "History of Merchant Taylors' School." It is a pity these writers do not always refer us to their authorities. I have had much kind assistance from Rev. J. H. Lupton, the author of "Life of Colet," &c. I much regret that the late Rev. Richard Mulcaster, of Anglesea House, Paignton, did not live to see the use I have made of materials collected by him for an article on his ancestor, which materials he was good enough to place in my hands.

Grindal and Archbishop Sandys were brought up there. But the Mulcaster of the first half of the century sent his sons Richard and James to be "frappit" by the mighty Udal at Eton. The *vates sacer* of Udal is Tusser, without whose help he could hardly have been remembered. As it is, his name inevitably calls up the lines— —

> "From Paul's I went, To Eton sent,
> To learn straightways The Latin phrase,
> When fifty-three Stripes given to me,
> At once I had,
> For fault but small, Or none at all;
> It came to pass, That beat I was,
> See, Udall, see! The mercy of thee
> To me poor lad."

(*From Tusser's Metrical Autobiography, printed with his "Points of Husbandry,"* 1573.)

In 1548 (according to A. Wood) Richard Mulcaster gained his election from Eton to King's, Cambridge; but for reasons unknown he did not take a Cambridge degree, but migrated to Oxford, where in 1555 he was elected Student of Christ Church, and the year following was "licensed to proceed in Arts." Here he became distinguished by his knowledge of Eastern literature, and "that great English Rabbi, Hugh Broughton," a contemporary, speaks of him as one of the best Hebrew scholars of the age. But the University had been preyed upon by "Reformers," and many students had to beg for their living. So Mulcaster went to London and became a schoolmaster in 1558. Three years later the Merchant Taylors' Company opened their new school at Lawrence Pountney Hill (between "Caning," now Cannon, Street and the River), and made Mulcaster their first Master.

Thus we find Mulcaster's reign at Merchant Taylors' began three years before the birth of Shakespeare, Mulcaster himself being about thirty years old. But his monarchy was by no means absolute, and he was not always happy in his relations with the Company. The Merchants probably thought of him as one of their servants, and he, as "by ancient parentage and linnial discent an Esquier borne" (so he describes himself in his wife's epitaph), thought himself a better man than they. Certainly many of his successors, though unable to lay stress on their parentage, would have grumbled at the terms imposed upon him.

The instructions to the Master are in many ways interesting. He was told that he was to teach the children not only good literature, but also good manners; he was to resign his post whenever ordered to do so by the Governors, but might not depart without giving the Governors a year's notice; and he was never to be absent from the school more than twenty working days in the year. The number of boys is limited to 250, and these are to be taught by the High Master and two or three Ushers. "The children shall come to the school in the morning at 7 of the clock both winter and summer, and tarry there until 11, and return again at 1 of the clock, and depart at 5." "Let not the school master, head usher, nor the under ushers, nor any of them, permit nor license their scholars to have remedy nor leave to play except only once a week when there falleth no holiday. And these remedies to be had upon no other day but only upon Tuesdays in the afternoon or Thursdays in the forenoon. Nor let the scholars use no cock-fighting, tennis-play, nor riding about of victoring [*sic*] nor disputing abroad, which is but foolish babbling and loss of time." ("History of Merchant Taylors' School," by H. B. Wilson, 1812, i, 17.)

The Company agreed to pay to Mulcaster £40——*i.e.*, £10 each for the High Master and the ushers; but Mr. Hills, the Master of the Company, undertook to double Mulcaster's £10 out of his own purse. Some years afterwards Mr. Hills had heavy expenses with one of his children, and was obliged to discontinue his grant to Mulcaster; which led to a serious disagreement. But there seem to have been "difficulties" about other matters as well. In the very middle of his twenty-six years' mastership (26th November, 1574) we find the following significant entry in the Minutes of the Court:——"Mr. Richard Moncaster convented at this Courte to be admonished of suche his contempt of the good orders made for the government of the Grammar Schole founded by the Worshipful company in St Lawrence Pountney's parisshe where he is now Scholemaister; And also of suche his injurious and quarrellinge Speache as he used to the Visitors of the said Schole at the last callinge thereof, refused to here his fformer doings in that behalf recyted, willinge the said Mr. Warden and assistants to procede against him angrily or otherwise as they listed, so as he mighte have a copie of their decree." (H. B. Wilson's "Hist, of M. T. Sch.," p. 56.) However, the "Esquier borne" found it prudent to yield. In the following month (14th Dec., 1574) it is recorded that Mr. Richard Muncaster confessed before the Court that he had spoken "merely of choller," and promised obedience for the future. Four years later he was in high favour with the Company, for at the Court holden 29th April, 1579, an order was passed by which the Company undertook, in consideration of Mulcaster's "painful services for near 20 years," to provide for his wife if she survived him. But this was the only recognition his "painful services" received. After Hills's grant of £10 a year had ceased, Mulcaster applied to the Company for a larger salary than he had received from them; but this very reasonable request was refused. Mulcaster then urged that he had been giving additional stipend to the senior Usher, and he made a claim for the amount he had lost by the stoppage of Hills's subsidy. In reply to this the Court voted that he "might seeke his remedie." He then petitioned humbly, but without avail, and in high dudgeon he resigned his post in 1586, either quoting or inventing the expression, *Servus fidelis perpetuus asinus*.[82] In the appointment of his successor (Wilkinson) he had no influence, and the dispute between Mulcaster and the Company was carried on, the Company making a counter claim against him for £50, and offering to waive this claim only on receiving from Mulcaster a receipt in full. The quarrel was never made up, and years afterwards when Mulcaster had left St. Paul's he applied to the Merchant Taylors' Company for a gratuity and was refused.

So at about the age of fifty-five, Mulcaster found himself out of office. Five years before this he had published his "Positions" (1581), and the year after, the "First Part of the Elementarie." Why the Second Part never appeared we cannot tell. Perhaps in this country publishing books about education was then, as now,

[82] Mr. Lupton has pointed out to me a passage in Bishop Pilkington's "Works" (Parker Soc.), p. 447: "The servant, he will write on the wall *Fidelis servus, perpetuus asinus*."

an expensive occupation, and Mulcaster having lost half his income could publish no longer.[83]

Ten years later he became High Master of St. Paul's School. In 1598 Elizabeth made him Rector of Stanford Rivers, in Essex, but as he was High Master of St. Paul's for twelve years, he must have been non-resident at his living till 1608. Then at all events he took up his abode at Stanford Rivers, where his wife died in 1609. It seems strange that Mulcaster should have remained at the head of a great school till he was about seventy-seven years old, but there is no reasonable doubt of it; and that he lived to a great age is proved by his wife's epitaph in which he records that they had been married fifty years. He himself died in 1611, only five years before Shakespeare, who was his junior by more than thirty years.[84]

Though Mulcaster himself has been well-nigh forgotten, he had relations, friendly or otherwise, with some of his contemporaries who are in no danger of being forgotten——Queen Elizabeth, Shakespeare, Sir Philip Sydney, and Edmund Spenser.

[83] In the "Gentleman's Magazine," vol. lxx, p. 603, we read of a second edition of the "Positions" published in 1587, in 4to. W. C. Hazlitt ("Handbook," p. 404, ed. 1867) says the "Positions" was reprinted in 1587 and 1591.

[84] Our information is very scanty. H. B. Wilson, the historian of Merchant Taylors' School, a very painstaking writer, says that Mulcaster was "Surmaster of St. Paul's, 1586; Vicar of Cranbrook, in Kent, 1st April, 1590; Prebendary of Sarum, 29th April, 1594; Rector of Stanford Rivers, in Essex, 1598; died 15th April, 1611." Did Mulcaster go first as "Surmaster" to St. Paul's? Knight, in his "Life of Colet," says Mulcaster "came in upper master in 1596," which is consistent with his being "surmaster" previously. But after his reign of twenty-six years at Merchant Taylors' he would not be likely to accept any mastership where he would be a subordinate. Mr. Lupton tells me that in Gardiner's "Registers of St. Paul's School," Richard Smith is put down as "surmaster" from 1586 to 1599, when he was pensioned, "being fallen into decay of his eyesight and impotency;" but a note speaks of these dates as probable, not certain. From Fuller we should suppose that Mulcaster left St. Paul's before he was seventy-seven years old; but it seems certain that he was "high-master" till 1608. He must therefore have been for some years non-resident, either in his school or in his parish. Fuller inaccurately puts him down as a *Westmorland* worthy; but as Fuller got information from hearers of Mulcaster the following passage is valuable:——"In the morning he (Mulcaster) would exactly and plainly construe and parse the lessons to his scholars; which done, he slept his hour (custom made him critical to apportion it) in his desk in the school; but woe be to the scholar that slept the while! Awaking, he heard them accurately; and Atropos might be persuaded to pity as soon as he to pardon where he found just fault. The prayers of cockering mothers prevailed with him as much as the requests of indulgent fathers, rather increasing than mitigating his severity on their offending child. In a word he was *plagosus Orbilius*, though it may truly be said (and safely for one out of his school) that others have taught as much learning with fewer lashes. Yet his sharpness was the better endured because unpartial, and many excellent scholars were bred under him; whereof Bishop Andrews was the most remarkable. Then quitting that place (St. Paul's School) he was presented to the rich parsonage of Stanford Rivers, in Essex. I have heard from those who have heard him preach, that his sermons were not excellent; which to me seems no wonder, partly because there is a different discipline in teaching Children and Men; partly because such who make divinity (not the choice of their youth but) the refuge of their age seldom attain to eminency therein." (Fuller's "Worthies," edited by John Nichols (2 vols., 1811), vol. ii, p. 431.)

Elizabeth, as we have seen, gave Mulcaster a living. This was not till near the end of her reign, but he seems to have been long in her favour. This book, the "Positions," was dedicated to her, and the tone of the letter in which Mulcaster addresses his Sovereign is not that of a stranger, but rather of an old acquaintance, who is sure of a friendly reception. In the fifteen hundreds a very common entertainment was the performance of plays by boys. In the Queen's book of household expenses we find: "18th Mch. 1573-4. To Mr. Richard Mouncaster for 2 plays presented before her on Candlemas-day, and Shrove Tuesday last, 20 marks: and further for his charges 20 marks." Again: "11th Mch. 1575-6. To Richard Mouncaster for presenting a play before her on Shrove Sunday last, 10 pounds." This performance seems to have been continued for many years. In the *Liber Famelicus* of Sir James Whitelocke (Camden Society's Publications, No. LXX), Sir James tells of his bringing up at Merchant Taylors'. He was born in 1570 and was elected from the School to be a probationer of St. John's College, Oxford, in June, 1588. He says: "I was brought up at School under Mr. Mulcaster in the famous school of the Merchant Taylors in London, where I continued until I was well instructed in the Hebrew, Greek, and Latin tongues. His care was also to increase my skill in music, in which I was brought up by daily exercise in it, as in singing and playing upon instruments: and yearly he presented some plays to the Court, in which his scholars were [the] only actors, and I one among them; and by that means [he] taught them good behaviour and audacity" (p. 12).

It has been suggested to me by Mr. Lupton that Shakespeare may have had Mulcaster in his mind when he put Holofernes the schoolmaster in *Love's Labour's Lost*. There was, as we know, rivalry between Shakespeare and the boy actors, and when Armado says (Act V, sc. 2), "I protest the schoolmaster is exceeding fantastical; too too vain, too too vain," he uses a common expression of Mulcaster's.

That Shakespeare had a contempt for the schoolmasters or "pedants" of his time is tolerably clear, and he must have seen in Mulcaster a typical schoolmaster and also a rival of his in producing court entertainments. Holofernes is both a "pedant" and a court entertainer, but in other respects he does not answer to Mulcaster, for he is a parish schoolmaster and teaches both boys and girls. However, as Mulcaster was a favourite at court, Shakespeare, if really thinking of him, may have had reasons for not making the resemblance too striking.

In *Hamlet* (Act II, sc. 2) there is a very remarkable dialogue which shows the rivalry that then (*i.e.*, about 1603) existed between "the tragedians of the City" and "the boys." There is, too, a very beautiful epitaph by Ben Jonson on a boy who had become famous for playing the part of an old man. Mulcaster no doubt had had a great share in keeping the playing of boy actors in fashion; but he probably had nothing to do with "the children of Powles" whose acting was stopped by edict from about 1589 to 1600, and then started again with increased popularity (see J. P. Collier, "Annals of the Stage," edition of 1879, vol. i, pp. 271 ff), or with "the children of the Revels" who acted at Blackfriars Theatre, and are probably the "aiery of children" talked of by Rosenkrantz.

To return to Elizabeth, it seems that Mulcaster took part in preparing the pageant at Kenilworth in 1575. I have not read the accounts by George Gascoigne and

Robert Laneham or Langham to which Collier refers ("Annals of Stage," i, 225), but the late Mr. Mulcaster gives some Latin verses preserved by Gascoigne which were, as he says, "devised by Master R. Muncaster." The "Middlesex Minstrel" also recited King "Ryence's challenge to King Arthur." Of this Bishop Percy says: "It was sung before Queen Elizabeth at the grand entertainment at Kenelworth Castle in 1575, and was probably composed for that occasion" (Percy's "Relics," Wheatley's edition, 1877, vol. iii, p. 24). If so, it may have been Mulcaster's as well as the Latin verses, though for my part I doubt his writing so simply.

On Elizabeth's death in 1603, Mulcaster published "Nænia consolans in mortem Serenissimæ Reginæ Elizabethæ," in which he seems quite consoled by the accession of James.

Mulcaster was a correspondent of Sir Philip Sydney's, and he wrote to him in Latin. This was against his own principles, for perhaps his best chance of being remembered rests in his vigorous protest against the use of Latin, and his advice to his learned countrymen to write in their own language (*cfr.* Masson's Life of Milton).

Perhaps Mulcaster's enthusiasm for English may have influenced one of his pupils who lived to write imperishable verse in it. The late Mr. Mulcaster, in his MS. notice of his ancestor, surmised that Spenser may have been a "Merchant Taylor" and therefore have come under Mulcaster. The guess was a happy one. Dean Church, in his volume on Spenser ("English Men of Letters"), tells us how the account books of the executors of a bountiful citizen, Robert Nowell, have been preserved, and that at his funeral in 1568 two yards of cloth were given to selected scholars of the great London Schools. The names of these scholars are recorded, and at the head of the Merchant Taylors' list stands Edmund Spenser.

It is very remarkable that a schoolmaster noted for his classical attainments should before the last decade of the fifteen hundreds have urged the literary use of the mother tongue. It is remarkable, too, that this man was the master of Edmund Spenser. In these and some other respects Mulcaster seems to have been more memorable than Ascham. Yet Ascham is known by all, and Mulcaster is unknown, not only by ordinary Englishmen, but even, as it would seem, by scholars like Mr. George Saintsbury, the author of a book on Elizabethan Literature. In Professor Arber's invaluable work for the bibliography of our old books, his "Transcript of the Registers of the Company of Stationers of London, 1554-1640," we find in vol. ii, p. 178*b*, the following curious entry:— —"Thomas Chare *sub manu Episcopi Londinii.* Sexto die Marcii [1581] Receaved of him for his license to printe *positions whereupon the trayning up of children and so consequentlie the wholle course of learninge ys grounded* . . . xvj*d*. Provyded alwaies that yf this booke conteine any thinge prejudiciall or hurtfull to the booke of maister ASKHAM that was printed by master Daie called the Scholemayster, That then this lycense shal be voyd." But Ascham's widow needed no protection from the Bishop of London. His posthumous book did for the English language what Mulcaster tried to do in vain: it showed how English might be used for clear and even graceful expression. Mulcaster thought that the English language had then reached its highest point. In his very curious and interesting allegory of the progress of language ("Elementarie," pp. 66 ff.) he says that Art selects the best age of a language to draw rules from, such as the age of Demosthenes in Greece, and of Tully in Rome. "Such a period in the English tongue," he continues, "I take to be in our days for both the pen and the speech." And this language, then at its best, was, he thought, shown at its best in his own writings. After enumerating its excellencies he says, "I need no example in any of these, whereof mine own penning is a general pattern." This tempts one to exclaim with Armado, "I protest the schoolmaster is exceeding fantastical; too too vain, too too vain" (*Love's Labour's Lost*, Act V, sc. 2), and posterity has most emphatically rejected the offered pattern. Dean Church describes the writers of that time as "usually clumsy and awkward, sometimes grotesque, often affected, always hopelessly wanting in the finish, breadth, moderation, and order which alone can give permanence to writing," ("Spenser," p. 3). Some of these epithets certainly hit Mulcaster hard. I have spent much time on what he calls his "so careful, I will not say so curious writing" ("Elementarie," p. 253), and I perfectly agree with him when he says, "Even some of reasonable study can hardly understand the couching of my sentence and the depth of my conceit" (*ib.*, p. 235). This, no doubt, explains to us why Mulcaster has been long forgotten.

But if he had taken less pains with his "style," Mulcaster would have been recognised as a master of his subject. A right conception of education could not be formed by the worshippers of "learning;" and the false ideal set up at the Renascence has had a disastrous effect on European education ever since. But Mulcaster, scholar though he was, was not in bondage to scholarship. With him education was not instruction in the classics. How few schoolmasters have asked the question, "Why is it not good to have every part of the body and every power of the soul to be fined to his best?" ("Positions," p. 25.) The following passage from the "Elementarie" (p. 22) shows how much he had risen above the ideal of the learned:— —"The end of education and train is to help nature unto her perfection, which is, when all her abilities be perfected in their habit. . . . Consideration and Judgment must wisely mark whereunto Nature is either evidently given or secretly affectionate, and must frame education consonant thereto." And having shown this admirable conception of the end to be attained, he sets to work to consider what are the powers that need training. "We have," he says, "a perceiving by outward sense, to feel, to see, to smell, to taste all sensible things; which qualities of the outward being received in by the *common sense*, and examined by *fancy*, are delivered to *remembrance* and afterward prove our great and only grounds unto further knowledge" ("Elementarie," p. 28). Here we see him feeling after the foundation of a science of education. He goes still further when in the "Positions" (p. 19-20) he tells us of the natural inclinations in the soul, and of the three things which we shall find "peering out of the little young souls," viz.: Wit to take, Memory to keep, and Discretion to discern.

Michelet ("Nos Fils," p. 170) with justice gives credit to Montaigne for avoiding the great blunder of his time, and basing his scheme of education, not on what was to be learned, but on the nature of the learner, *"non l'objet, le savoir, mais le sujet, c'est l'homme."* This was indeed a wonderful step in advance, a step which placed Montaigne before most schoolmasters of that time, perhaps of any succeeding time. But in Mulcaster we have a schoolmaster who in Montaigne's own day seems to have shown similar wisdom. Perhaps admirable results might have followed had Mulcaster's mode of expression only been somewhat less "curious."

Looking to human nature as a whole, Montaigne and Mulcaster saw that "it was not a mind, it was not a body that we have to educate, but a man, and we cannot divide him." A writer of the present day who is supposed to be in the van of modern thinkers has given us his notion of "Education as a Science." In some respects the conception of the Elizabethan writer seems to me more complete and truly scientific. Mulcaster thinks that the educator should care both for mind and body, and adapt his "train" to each of them. The treatment of the body recommended in the "Positions" will surprise some Continental authors, who seem to think that physical education had hardly been considered before the appearance of Locke's "Thoughts."

There are several other points where Mulcaster seems to me to show remarkable wisdom. He does not approve of a very early start in the learned languages, and is specially strong against the "hastening on" of a "sharp young wit;" so that one of the earliest English writers on education warns us against some of the latest English practices (see "Positions," pp. 14, 23-24; also "Elementarie," xi, pp. 52 ff).

Another of our head-masters, whose teaching now, alas! comes to us also recommended by the proverb, *Optimi consiliarii mortui*, Edward Thring, has testified to the difficulty and to the importance of instructing the younger classes properly. Mulcaster is so strong on this point that instead of handing over the younger boys in a crowd to the least experienced and worst paid master, as the custom still is, he would have the forms smaller at the bottom than at the top of the school, and would have the best and best paid teacher for them ("Positions," pp. 182 ff.)

His wisdom appears, too, in his curriculum for the young. What a blessing for them could he have arranged their studies all over Europe instead of his contemporary, Sturm! He would have taught them to read and write their own language, to draw, to sing, and to play some musical instrument, and he maintains that if instead of beginning with Latin the child were put through a preliminary course in these five things, he would learn "the tongue" sooner and do more between 12 and 16 than from 7 to 17 the other way ("Elementarie," chap. xi). So school instruction in drawing and singing was recommended by this old schoolmaster more than 300 years ago. I take up the New England "Journal of Education," dated 2nd February, 1888, and I find a well-known writer, Col. T. W. Higginson, telling us: "I can remember when the introduction of singing, and later of drawing, into our public schools was regarded as a finical whim, suitable for girls' schools only. *Emollit mores*, each of these practices is found to help school discipline and refine the taste, so that the whole tone of school life is elevated." Thus we are at length adopting Mulcaster's proposals, and quoting in their favour what Ovid said 2,000 years ago.

It is interesting, by the way, to observe that the unfortunate "three R's" had not been invented in Mulcaster's time, and his "Elementarie," with its five studies, ignores arithmetic.

The five studies are intended for those who are to be put to learning, and those only; but we see that Mulcaster would have had *every one* taught to read and write ("Positions," p. 113).

We have seen that we are at length introducing drawing and singing, as Mulcaster advised. In one particular he is still in advance of us. He would have at the University a college for training teachers. "Is the framing of young minds," he asks, "and the training of their bodies so mean a point of cunning? Be schoolmasters in this realm such a paucity as they are not even in good sadness to be soundly thought on?. . . He that will not allow of this careful provision for such a seminary of masters is most unworthy either to have had a good master himself or hereafter to have a good one for his." ("Positions" p. 193.)

In another respect Mulcaster showed much good sense, and though perhaps not in advance of his own generation he was far before the generations of the two succeeding centuries. I was at a private meeting connected with the founding of Girton College, when, I remember, the late Professor Brewer denied that girls in the Elizabethan age were better educated than in the days that followed. Joseph Payne, who was also present, expressed a strong opinion that they *were*. If he had had his copy of the "Positions" with him (his collection of rare books on education included this work) he might have proved his point by apposite quotation. This was twenty years ago. Much has been done for girls' education since then; and in one respect at least the Victorians have advanced beyond the Elizabethans, for no English writer can now say with Mulcaster, "I set not young maidens to public grammar schools, a thing not used in my country; I send them not to the universities, having no precedent thereof in my country." ("Positions," p. 135.)

I have now, I think, said enough so show that at least for the history of education Mulcaster's books are of great interest and value. Travellers are always ready to run any risks in exploring the source of great rivers. When we consider how many millions of the human race using English as their mother tongue receive instruction in school, it might seem worth while to spend some little time and trouble in tracing back the history of that instruction, and seeing what it was in its earliest days. Such knowledge as is now obtainable must be derived from a few books, among which Mulcaster's are almost the first, both in time and in importance. I know of nothing earlier except Elyot's "Governor" and Ascham's "Schoolmaster." The next English work on education known to me is W. Kemp's "The Education of Children" in 1588, which probably furthered his wish that the good town of Plymouth might "bring forth some young imps and buds of learning;" but this is in every way a small book. The next important book is John Brinsly's "Ludus Literarius; or, the Grammar School," and this was not published till 1612.

The first edition of the "Positions" was dedicated to Queen Elizabeth. This, which is as far as I have seen the second, I should dedicate to no contemporary, not even to the Queen herself; but to the coming New Zealander. The prescient eye of Macaulay sees that Mulcaster's scheme of instruction will by that time have been adopted, and our intelligent descendant will be able to draw. I hope he will know of the old book in which drawing in schools was first recommended. He will, I feel certain, take a deep interest in the most important discovery of his age, the new science of education, and gratitude for this science will make him think kindly of those quaint old writers, standing almost together, "foreshortened in the tract of time," who in the days of Elizabeth and Victoria made the first crude suggestions and surmises towards it.

16th February, 1888. R. H. Q.

Printed by Libri Plureos GmbH in Hamburg,
Germany